AGING

and

OLD AGE

Richard A. Posner

AGING

and

OLD AGE

THE UNIVERSITY OF CHICAGO PRESS

CHICAGO AND LONDON

Richard A. Posner is Chief Judge of the U.S. Court of
Appeals for the Seventh Circuit and senior lecturer at the
University of Chicago Law School. His many publica-
tions include *Cardozo: A Study in Reputation,* from the
University of Chicago Press; *Sex and Reason;* and *Over-
coming Law.*

The University of Chicago Press, Chicago 60637
The University of Chicago Press, Ltd., London
© 1995 by The University of Chicago
All rights reserved. Published 1995
Printed in the United States of America
04 03 02 01 00 99 98 97 96 95   1 2 3 4 5
ISBN: 0-226-67566-1 (cloth)

Library of Congress Cataloging-in-Publication Data

Posner, Richard A.
    Aging and old age / Richard A. Posner.
        p.   cm.
    Includes bibliographical references and index.
    1. Aged—Social conditions.   2. Aged—Legal
status, laws, etc.
    3. Aging—Economic aspects.   4. Old age—Eco-
nomic aspects.
    5. Gerontology.   I. Title.
    HQ1061.P67   1995
    305.26—dc20   95-16462
                                              CIP

Contents

Introduction

Old age, and aging more generally, raise a host of fascinating issues made extraordinarily timely by the rapidly growing number and percentage of elderly people in our society. This book is written in the conviction that the economics of nonmarket behavior can enable fresh insights into a number of issues related to aging to which economists have given little or no attention. Examples include geronticide (euthanasia of old people), age discrimination in employment, judicial retirement, creativity and leadership as functions of age, voter turnout and jury participation by elderly people, negligent and criminal behavior by them, the allocation of resources to the prevention and treatment of geriatric illness, the characteristic attitudes and habits of the elderly, their changing social status, and the political economy of public policies relating to the elderly. I hope to show, in fact, that economics can provide a unifying perspective in which to view the whole range of social problems concerning the elderly.

My analysis is both positive and normative. That is, it is concerned both with advancing the understanding of aging and old age and with evaluating, or, more modestly, creating a framework for evaluating, public policies related to age. And it is interdisciplinary. I mine disciplines ranging from evolutionary biology and cognitive psychology to philosophy and literature for insights into aging and old age. The idea that our young and old selves are different persons—an idea philosophical rather than economic in character—and selection bias, a statistical concept, play especially prominent roles in my analysis, as does Aristotelian psychology. But economics wields the baton of my multidisciplinary orchestra. The basic hypothesis of the book is that economics can do a better job of explaining the behavior and attitudes associated with aging, and of solving the policy problems that aging presents, than biology, psychology, sociology, philosophy, or any other single field of natural or social science.

I have written with several audiences in mind. One is the multidisciplinary gerontological community; for it, the main surprise will be the pervasive relevance of economics to gerontology. A second audience consists of economists interested in nonmarket behavior, or, more broadly, in the application of economic theory to subjects lying outside the traditional boundaries of economics. To this group, the surprise will be the amount of work bearing directly or indirectly on subjects that are or ought to be of interest to economists that has been done by the mostly noneconomist scholars of the gerontological community. A third audience consists of those lawyers, judges, philosophers, bioethicists, social scientists, and other professionals and scholars who are interested in specific topics in or overlapping the study of aging and old age, such as pension regulation, euthanasia, subsidies for health care, compulsory retirement, mental competence, favoritism and discrimination on grounds of age, and intergenerational equity. All of these matters arise in legal cases. Lawyers and judges are often surprised to discover that matters which swim into their view in cases have been studied extensively by nonlegal disciplines. There may even be a few people interested simply in their own aging who will find things of value in the book.

I have tried to make the book intelligible to these different audiences. I use few formal models, and they are very simple and fully explained and, even so, can be skipped by the mathless reader without serious loss of understanding. No previous acquaintance with economics is assumed, or is necessary to follow any of the analysis.

Despite my professional affiliation, this is not primarily a book about the laws related to the aged. But I do discuss a number of legal applications, ranging from age discrimination and pension laws through criminal sentencing and tort liability to judicial-retirement policies. And my choice of subject was decisively influenced by my experience as a federal judge. The Age Discrimination in Employment Act (ADEA) and the Employee Retirement Income Security Act (ERISA) have generated many cases in my court. And the occupation of being a federal judge, an occupation whose incumbents have never been subject to—whom Article III of the Constitution appears to forbid subjecting to—a mandatory retirement age, is the preeminent Nestorian profession. Many federal judges work full time, or nearly so, well into their eighties (Justice Holmes did not retire until he was

90, and there have been other nonagenerian judges as well), and octogenarians have written some of the most important judicial opinions in our history. Concerns that judges are too old have been voiced from time to time, most famously in defense of Franklin Roosevelt's "Court-packing plan" (1937), which would have authorized the appointment of an additional Supreme Court Justice for every Justice who refused to retire or resign upon reaching the age of 70, until the Court had fifteen members. The threat to judicial independence posed by this proposal was so manifest that, ever since, there has been little discussion of the problem of elderly judges, even though it is well known within professional circles that some federal judges, including Supreme Court Justices, have continued to sit long after their judicial performance became severely compromised by age-related disabilities.

Federal judges take for granted the existence of the federal laws regulating pensions and retirement and forbidding as "discrimination" certain forms of differential treatment of the aged, and they also take for granted their own peculiar tenure provisions. Judges are very good at taking things for granted. The structure of adjudication fosters a reactive, even a passive, attitude toward both the doctrinal content and the institutional form of the judge's work. The umpireal role is inherently rather passive. Someone else stages the contest, and contest succeeds contest at a dizzying rate (especially for an appellate judge, who may hear two or three hundred different cases every year) and in random sequence. The judge, for whom judging is in any event likely to be, in this country as in England, a second career, comes in late to the play and leaves early, without ever being invited behind the scenes. I have no quarrel with the basic structure of appellate adjudication. But one of its consequences is that judges tend not to be well informed about the background of the cases they adjudicate or the institutional structure they inhabit. This is especially true with regard to a feature like old age that carries a heavy emotional charge yet is not a familiar and well-digested field of study the major findings of which are readily accessible to persons who are not experts in it. As in my book *Sex and Reason* (1992), so here, one of my goals in tackling the subject is simply to inform myself and my fellow judges about a pervasive, emotional, but little understood phenomenon (or cluster of phenomena) that provides a backdrop to and the subject matter of several important areas of modern law, and that in the case of old age is also a salient characteristic of an influential group of law's makers and appliers. It is not so taboo a subject as sex, but considerable reticence, embarrassment, and denial surrounds the public discussion of many aspects of it, notably the aspects emphasized in this book. I have tried to draw back the veil. To this end, although most of my analysis is of a theoretical or, less grandly, a speculative cast, I have tried to back it up with data wherever possible. There is no shortage of data on old age.

In writing about aging from an economic standpoint, I am not writing on a clean theoretical slate, as was virtually the case when I took an economic approach to sex in *Sex and Reason*. The economic literature on old age is vast and technically sophisticated.[1] But it is focused on retirement issues, such as the determinants of the age of retirement and the financing (whether through private or public pensions) of consumption during retirement. It largely ignores the psychological and even the physical aspects of aging, although, as we shall see, both aspects can be given an economic interpretation.

Not all economists who write about aging are preoccupied with retirement. Arthur Diamond has written on scientific creativity, and on scientists' receptiveness to new theories, as functions of age; I discuss his work in chapter 7. And Isaac Ehrlich and Hiroyuki Chuma have written about the efforts of elderly people to extend their life (see chapter 5). There are other exceptions.[2] But they are few. As a result, while the economic literature is illuminating on such questions as whether the savings and consumption decisions of the old are influenced by a bequest motive and what effect social security has on the participation of middle-aged and elderly persons in the labor force and on the savings rate of the society as a whole, a variety of other questions have largely been ignored. Among the ones I try to answer are, Why are old people less willing to take financial and other risks than young people? Do organizations age in ways parallel to how persons age? Docs "blind" refereeing of articles submitted to scholarly journals

1. That literature is well reviewed in Michael D. Hurd, "Research on the Elderly: Economic Status, Retirement, and Consumption and Saving," 28 *Journal of Economic Literature* 565 (1990). For an earlier literature review, see Robert Clark, Juanita Kreps, and Joseph Spengler, "Economics of Aging: A Survey," 16 *Journal of Economic Literature* 919 (1978). For an excellent nontechnical overview, see Victor R. Fuchs, *How We Live,* ch. 7 (1983).

2. Of which the most curious may be Ray C. Fair, "How Fast Do Old Men Slow Down?" 76 *Review of Economics and Statistics* 103 (1994), a statistical study of men's track-and-field and road-racing events. There is no economic model. The distinguished author believes that his finding that in a number of racing events a man of 85 is only 49 percent slower than he was at 55 may have policy relevance; specifically, may indicate "that societies have been too pessimistic about losses from aging for individuals who stay healthy and fit." Id. at 117. I do not understand the significance of his finding for policy. But I am sure that Professor Fair will be interested to learn, if he does not know already, that the U.S. Tennis Association has a tournament for players 85 years and older. Dan Shaughnessy, "Seniors Serve as Inspiration," *Boston Globe,* Sept. 7, 1994, p. 57. Asked to identify the "single common denominator" that explains what "allows these gentlemen to compete at this game after all these decades," an 87-year-old player replied sensibly, "The common denominator is that we're still alive." Id. at 59.

discriminate unwarrantedly against older scholars? Why don't old people have high crime rates, since the expected cost of imprisonment is truncated by their diminished life expectancy? (Stated differently, what is the significance of "last-period" analysis for the behavior of the old?) Are old people victims of "ageism"? Do they, on the contrary, have too much power? Why do old people vote more than young people, and why is the gap greater in congressional than in presidential elections? Since children cannot vote, should elderly people be deprived of the vote in order to maintain a proper balance between the interests of young and old people? Why do people so often postpone the making of a will until death is imminent? Should there be a mandatory retirement age for judges? Relatedly, how could one possibly *measure* the effect of age on judicial productivity? Why are old people admired in some societies and despised, even killed, in others? Why do black people tend (as we shall see they do) to respect the old more than white people do? Is the life of an older person less valuable in some meaningful sense of "value" than that of a younger one? Why does creativity peak at different ages in different fields? Do old people really tend to be more verbose than young ones and if so why? Why do so many sick old people nevertheless cling to life? Should we make it easier for them to die? Should publicly funded medical research seek to equalize the longevity of American men and women? Should it concentrate less on diseases that kill elderly people and more on conditions such as blindness and deafness that reduce the quality of elderly lives? What is the effect of trying to stamp out age discrimination on the distribution of lifetime wealth across persons— and should an old person even be considered the same person that he or she was when young? Is saving for one's old age morally different from saving in order to leave bequests to one's children or grandchildren? Many of these may not sound like economic questions, but that is because most people (including many economists) have too narrow a conception of economics.

The economic concepts that I shall use to power and direct my analysis are familiar. They are drawn from established fields of economics such as the economics of information, the economics of health, the economics of law, and the economics of human capital, although some I apply outside of their usual domain (for example, by treating an individual's young self and his old self as distinct rational actors) or with a new twist. The book's principal novelty as a contribution to economics is its attempt to shift the emphasis in the economics of aging and old age from the financial, or market, aspects of the subject to the nonfinancial, nonmarket aspects. But the shift in emphasis can, I argue, furnish new insights even into well-studied issues concerning retirement.

Consistent with a commitment to genuine multidisciplinarity, I got the idea of applying the economics of information to aging not from any economic literature but from a passage in Aristotle's treatise on rhetoric. He is discussing how to argue to young and old respectively and he says that this depends on their outlooks on life, which are different. He lists many differences but my eye was particularly caught by the following: The "lives [of the young] are mainly spent not in memory but in expectation; for expectation refers to the future, memory to the past, and youth has a long future before it and a short past behind it: on the first day of one's life one has nothing at all to remember, and can only look forward." The old, in contrast, "live by memory rather than by hope; for what is left to them of life is but little as compared with the long past; and hope is of the future, memory of the past."[3] If we equate memory to knowledge and hope/expectation to imagination,[4] and if we think of knowledge and imagination (roughly what psychologists call "crystallized" and "fluid" intelligence) as the two principal components of reason, the balance shifts with age. Translated into economic terms, this shift will play a major role in my analysis, whereas most of the previous economic work on aging has abstracted from the cognitive, emotional, ethical, and other differences between young and old. Almost the only difference recognized by that work is the difference in proximity to the end of life, because death truncates the payback period for investments in human capital. We shall see that this need not always be the case—that from an economic standpoint the period over which an individual maximizes his utility need not end with his death—and, more important, that it is not the only significant difference between young and old. The cognitive change identified by Aristotle is also important, as is the well-documented decline in mental and physical capabilities that is a correlate of aging and that, moreover, interacts with the change noted by Aristotle.

It would be only a slight exaggeration to say that most economists who write about the life cycle implicitly deny aging in the sense of a decline or other change in relevant capacities. Their implicit conception of the function that relates the capacity to produce or consume to age is a horizontal line that drops abruptly to zero at death or retirement. Yet nothing in the theory of human capital, a theory central to the economics of aging, re-

---

3. Aristotle, *Rhetoric*, bk. 2, ch. 12, in *The Complete Works of Aristotle*, vol. 2, pp. 2213, 2214 (Jonathan Barnes, ed., 1984) (W. Rhys Roberts, trans.). The page and column references to the Greek text are 1389a and 1390a.
4. The word that Roberts translates first as expectation and then as hope is the same—ἐλπίσ—and it has both meanings.

quires that the physical and cognitive changes associated with aging be ignored. Human capital (earning capacity, with "earnings" broadly defined to include nonpecuniary as well as pecuniary returns) includes innate capacities—such as mathematical or musical aptitude, quick reflexes, and physical strength—as well as acquired ones, and even the acquired need not always be the product of training. The innate capacities are subject to biological decay, while the acquired ones include, as Aristotle recognized, knowledge (which is also subject to decay) gained simply through living and working, that is, through experience, which is correlated with age, as well as knowledge acquired in schools and in training programs. One reason the innate capacities in particular have been slighted in the economic research on aging is that economists have tended to cut off their study of the life cycle at retirement, which normally precedes the steepest decline in capacity. Yet the decline begins earlier, sometimes much earlier. A related point is that retirement itself, when it is viewed functionally, may occur long before the standard retirement age of 65 (standard, though of course not uniform, since Bismarck's social welfare legislation). Economists have taken little interest in deviations from the standard life cycle.

As the point about functional versus nominal retirement suggests, although my focus is on *old* age this is a less confining category than one might think. The federal age discrimination law defines the protected class to include all employees 40 years of age or older. Many cases under the law concern early retirement, that is, retirement before the employer's regular retirement age. Aging, moreover, is ordinarily a protracted and continuous, rather than a discrete, process. In some fields, such as professional athletics, you may be "old" at 30; and in some intellectual fields as well, such as theoretical physics and computer software design, the career peak comes at an early age. The age grading of occupations or activities (that is, the assigning of roles on the basis of chronological age), an important feature of primitive societies, is not limited to old people. Indeed, the study of old age is inseparable from that of the entire life cycle. That is why the title of this book includes "aging" as well as "old age," although the latter is my primary concern. Some topics of particular significance for old people, such as the punishment of recidivists, euthanasia, the measure of damages for loss of the nonpecuniary utility of life, and the optimal allocation of medical resources, have application to young people as well. Similarly, the analysis of judicial performance at advanced ages has implications for understanding the judicial process generally, while the pattern of litigation under the age discrimination law casts light on the determinants of plaintiffs' success in litigation generally. So the book in places spills over its banks, while in other places it does not reach them, so vast is the subject of old age and the literature that deals with its various facets.

A thumbnail sketch of the book's organization may help in orienting the reader. The first four chapters set the stage. Chapter 1 presents the essential biological data concerning old age, which have tended to be overlooked or sugarcoated in the social scientific literature. The data show that there really is such a thing as "normal aging"—people *age;* they do not just become more prone to illness and accident—and I show that the denial of this fact can actually create an exaggerated view of the disabilities of the elderly. One of the questions examined in the chapter is whether there is a genetic program for old age. The answer—"no"—plays, paradoxically, a role in subsequent chapters in explaining *in genetic terms* certain features of the experience of old age.

Chapter 2 is longer, but also sunnier. It presents additional background data—demographic, historical, and economic, rather than biological—concerning human aging and old age. It also offers a preliminary assessment of the widespread popular and scholarly concern that the nation is becoming ominously gerontified. I argue that although the population is indeed aging, this is not the disaster that alarmists descry and decry. They have exaggerated the costs of an aging population and ignored the benefits—which is not to deny that there are costs, and that they are growing.

The next two chapters lay the principal theoretical foundations for my analysis by developing a series of economic models of aging. Chapter 3 begins with the application of the conventional human-capital model of the life cycle to old age. But soon I am expanding the model in several directions, for example by considering the bearing of posthumous utility (not limited to the utility derived from making bequests) and of what I call "relational" human capital, which includes friendship and other personal, including business, relationships. Chapter 4 rings further changes on the conventional model by assuming that, among other things, the passage from youth to old age entails cognitive changes in the form of the shifting balance between imagination and knowledge that I have already mentioned; that the speed at which subjective time passes also changes (it speeds up); and that physical and mental abilities decline with age. The decline is gradual for most people until extreme old age, but can, I argue with the aid of the concept of "excess capability," be modeled as if there were an inflection point at age 65 for many activities. I also emphasize boredom, viewed as the obverse of habit, as an economically analyzable factor in the decision to retire. And I introduce and defend the proposition, which plays a big role in the book, that the difference between one's young and one's old self may be so profound that the two selves are more fruitfully viewed as two persons rather than as one. Chapters 3 and 4 thus attempt to redeem my promise to present an approach to the economics of aging that takes aging seriously.

Chapters 5 through 9, constituting part 2 of the book, extend the approach. In chapter 5, I use the approach to generate the "economic psychology" of old age. The term is meant to suggest the possibility of deriving psychological traits from economic theory rather than, as is generally done in economics, treating such traits as exogenous. I argue, for example, that old people are (on average—always an important qualification in dealing with large and amorphous social aggregates such as "the elderly") worse listeners and less considerate speakers than young people. The old invest less in the creation of human capital and therefore have less to gain from receiving inputs of information from other people. And because they transact less, they have less incentive to conceal egocentrism and to engage in cooperative rather than self-aggrandizing conversation and also less to gain from concealing traits that would reduce opportunities for advantageous transactions.[5]

Chapter 6 proposes solutions to a number of puzzles concerning the behavior of the elderly with regard to driving and automobile accidents, crime, suicide, sex, residential patterns, bequests, voting and jury service, and (once again) retirement—such puzzles as the conjunction of very low crime and criminal-victimization rates with high accident rates and very high suicide rates and the conjunction of high voter turnout with low juror turnout. The effort is to demonstrate to any doubters, first, that "old age" really is a meaningful category for analysis, by identifying a distinctive set of age-related behaviors, and second that economics can play its usual useful role of making sense out of seemingly arbitrary variations in social behavior.

Chapter 7 explores the relation between age and creativity or achievement. I emphasize the importance to the age profile of different activities of distinguishing between lived experience and practical wisdom, on the one hand, and book learning and abstract reasoning, on the other. I also try to explain the difference between "creative" occupations and leadership, as well as the cluster of age-related changes in the character as distinct from

---

5. Cf. M. F. K. Fisher, *Sister Age* 234 (1964): "I have formed a strong theory that there is no such thing as 'turning into' a Nasty Old Man or Old Witch. I believe that such people, and of course they are legion, were born nasty and witch-like, and that by the time they were about five years old they had hidden their rotten bitchiness and lived fairly decent lives until they no longer had to conform to rules of social behavior, and could revert to their original horrid natures."

quality of creative work that has led to the suggestion that there is an "old-age style" or "later-life style" in the arts. Chapter 8 extends the analysis of elderly achievement to judicial output, with special attention to appellate judges. I use citation analysis to generate empirical evidence that judges do in fact tend to retain their capabilities to advanced ages, though not without measurable impairment. I explain the gradualness with which judicial productivity declines with age by reference to the importance of judicial experience and of writing skills (which decline with age less than most other cognitive skills do) to the successful performance of judicial, especially appellate, tasks, but also by reference to the humble but recurrent factor of selection bias. Between them, chapters 7 and 8 furnish a number of clues to the wide variance in rates of aging across different activities.

Chapter 9 examines the even wider differences in the social status of the aged in different societies, differences that run the gamut from compulsory geronticide to ancestor worship. I lay particular stress on premodern societies (where the variance is greatest)—trying to explain why the elderly have a very high status in some of these societies and a very low one in others—and on the transition to modernity. I also discuss the practice of age grading and the question whether there might be fruitful analogies and interactions (I think there are some of both) between the aging of individuals and the aging of firms, nations, and other institutions.

Parts 1 and 2 attempt to develop an economic theory of aging that will have enough explanatory and predictive power to deserve being taken seriously not only as a source of knowledge but also as a guide to reflection on the many normative issues, both ethical and legal, that the phenomenon of aging presents. Part 3 examines the normative issues directly. These can be divided into macroeconomic and microeconomic issues. The former is encapsulated by the "rip-off" question. Are the old ripping off the young? If so, by how much, and how can it be controlled? The "rip-off" question is analyzed in chapter 11, though the foundations for the analysis are laid, and the answer prefigured, in chapter 2.

The second class of normative issues, the microeconomic, involves particular markets or activities. Chapter 10 is illustrative. It is about euthanasia ("geronticide" when the persons "euthanized" are elderly). I argue that legalizing physician-assisted suicide might lower rather than, as critics and supporters alike believe, raise the suicide rate. I review a number of other objections to the practice as well, such as that it will result in physicians' rushing infirm patients to their deaths, and conclude (with an assist from the political theory of John Stuart Mill) that physician-assisted suicide should be decriminalized in cases of terminal illness and profound physical impairment. But I argue against allowing one's younger self to kill one's older self by committing to die upon the occurrence in the future of a specified condition, such as advanced senility.

Chapter 11 takes up a number of other ethically charged issues involving public policy toward the elderly. These are compulsory and subsidized pensions, the subsidization of health care for the aged, the allocation of medical research between diseases of old men and diseases of old women, and the question whether democracy gives too much power to old people, especially compared to children. I argue, again counterintuitively, that women might be made better off by a reallocation of medical research from the diseases of elderly women to the diseases of elderly men and that elderly people may have the right amount of voting power after all, when their role as "representatives" of the future elderly selves of the currently young and middle-aged is recognized. In this chapter philosophical questions are prominent, including the recurrent question whether and for what purposes the young and old phases of an individual's life should be considered different stages of a single self, on the one hand, or different selves, on the other. I point out that the tension between young and old selves complicates the problem of financing the medical and home-care costs of the elderly, costs that will grow as the number of elderly grows, and quite possibly faster. But I conclude that there is no firm basis for believing that elderly people either have obtained, or will obtain as their numbers increase, excessive transfer payments from the young and the middle-aged.

Chapters 12 and 13 apply the positive and normative analysis developed in the earlier chapters to a variety of legal issues. These include issues raised by the federal law regulating private pensions (ERISA), by tort, criminal, and property cases involving the elderly, and by the continued imprisonment of young criminals, under sentence of life in prison, when they become old. My principal emphasis, however—it is the subject of chapter 13, the longest chapter in the book—is upon age discrimination, including the issue of mandatory retirement at fixed ages. I examine the rationale for the Age Discrimination in Employment Act and the Act's probable efficacy, expense, and allocative and distributive effects; and this leads me also to consider the pros and cons of mandatory retirement, which the Act has now largely abolished. My conclusion is that the Act is largely ineffectual, and to the extent effective is probably perverse in its effects on the distribution of income and causes harm to elderly workers. It exemplifies the fact, which is often overlooked, that "social" as well as "economic" regulation may disserve any plausible conception of the public interest once the actual presuppositions and consequences of the regulation are understood—and may even disserve its ostensible beneficiaries.

The scope of the book is broad, both as to subject and as to method, and thus bucks the trend (which I believe however to be on the whole a healthy one) toward ever greater specialization in scholarly research. It proposes a new way of looking at an old (no pun intended) and variegated subject, and the specific answers that it offers to specific questions should be viewed as suggestive rather than definitive. Yet despite this disclaimer of dogmatic certitude, the book will definitely not please everyone. It will displease not only those who are offended by the application of rational-choice theory to "noneconomic" phenomena, but also the Chicken Littles of this world, who are clamorous about the fell consequences (as they see them) of the rapid aging of the population, and the professional advocates for the elderly, who exaggerate the plight of their constituency. Although I do not join Cicero in considering old age the happiest part of a wise person's life, and although I do not think that we have or are likely to get an optimal set of public policies toward aging, neither do I think that the continued aging of the population in the United States portends a national disaster, requiring drastic measures such as abolishing social security or even scaling it back greatly. The costs of an aging population have been exaggerated and the benefits largely ignored. In this instance at least, as I hope the reader will be persuaded, the facts of the matter are less alarming than the fears about it.

In researching and writing this book, I have incurred immense debts. Benjamin Aller, Mark Fisher, Scott Gaille, Richard Hynes, Wesley Kelman, Steven Neidhart, Andrew Trask, Clinton Uhlir, John Wright, and Douglas Y'Barbo rendered invaluable research assistance. Christopher Hill furnished helpful research leads, and Edward Laumann, George Priest, Steven Schlesinger, and Tom Smith provided me with valuable data. For generous and exceedingly helpful comments on earlier drafts of one or more chapters I am indebted to Michael Aronson, Ian Ayres, Gary Becker, Wayne Booth, Margaret Brinig, Christine Cassel, Arthur Diamond, John Donohue, Larry Downes, Ronald Dworkin, Frank Easterbrook, Jon Elster, Richard Epstein, Robert Ferguson, David Friedman, Victor Fuchs, David Greenwald, John Griffiths, Christine Jolls, William Landes, John Langbein, Edward Lazear, Lawrence Lessig, Martha Nussbaum, Jay Olshansky, Tomas Philipson, Charlene Posner, Eric Posner, Mark Ramseyer, Eric Rasmusen, George Rutherglen, Cass Sunstein, John Tryneski, and Carolyn Weaver. These readers not only caught many mistakes but also opened up new vistas of inquiry for me. My greatest debt of all is to Gary Becker, not only for his helpful comments on the manuscript but also for a series of stimulating discussions of its subject matter and for his foundational research on the economics of human capital upon which this book builds.

Earlier versions of several chapters provided the text for the 1994 Tanner Lectures on Human Values at Yale University. I tried out other parts of my argument at lectures or talks at the University of Virginia School of Law, the Economic and Social Research Institute of Ireland, the City Front Forum of the University of Chicago, the Law and Economics Workshop of Harvard Law School, and an annual meeting of the American Law and Economics Association. I thank the members of the audiences on all these occasions for their many stimulating comments.

Since one of the points I emphasize is that the values and perspective of elderly people may differ greatly from those of young and middle-aged people, I should disclose that I wrote this book at the age of 55.

Part One

*Aging and Old Age
as Social, Biological,
and Economic Phenomena*

1

What Is Aging, and Why?

The Process of Aging

As we get older, we "age." Or do we? Some gerontologists believe that the expression "normal aging" is an oxymoron; that "aging" does not denote a process at all, but merely describes a medley of unhappy outcomes. As we get older we are more susceptible to most diseases,[1] so maybe all it means to "age" is to become increasingly afflicted by one or, more commonly, several diseases until finally we are overpowered. On this construal the only difference between an old person and a young one is that the former is likelier to be sicker. If he happens not to be sicker, then he will be identical to a young person.

One can acknowledge the fuzzy edges of the concept of "disease"[2] without finding this conception of aging remotely persuasive. For one (little) thing, it ignores Aristotle's point—the changing balance over the life cycle between imagination and knowledge, a change that cannot be described, without great semantic violence, as a form of illness. For another, the idea that "aging" denotes merely an increasing frequency of disease ignores forms of physical and mental change that, while aptly characterized as marking a decline in capability, are again not aptly described

1. Dramatically so, beyond a point: of *healthy* 60-year-old men, only 30 percent can be expected to be alive and healthy at 80. E. Jeffrey Metter et al., "How Comparable Are Healthy 60- and 80-Year-Old Men?" 47 *Journal of Gerontology* M73, M75 (1992). But medical science is continuously improving these odds.

2. As famously illustrated by debates in psychiatry and law over whether homosexuality is a "disease," and whether having a psychopathic or sociopathic personality is a disease.

as diseases. Most professional athletes in most sports, even if they escape significant injury, are "old" by their late twenties or early thirties, but they are not sick. Their muscles and nervous systems are not diseased in any useful sense of the word. It is simply that their reflexes and running speed have slowed slightly but critically.[3] There are physiological causes of this slowing, of course, and they could if one wanted be called "disease" factors. But the "disease" of diminished athletic capabilities in one's twenties and thirties (or menopause in a woman's forties or fifties) is sufficiently different in the most socially relevant respects from such conditions as cancer, coronary artery disease, stroke, and diabetes to warrant—to demand—being called by a different name.[4]

Aging is most usefully viewed as a process one element of which is an inexorable decline across a broad range of bodily (including both physical and mental) capabilities: call this "bodily decline."[5] Other elements of aging, or that are correlated with it—the nonsomatic elements, examined more closely in subsequent chapters—include the increasing proximity of death as we get older, which affects the balance between imagination and knowledge as intellectual resources and the incentive to invest in human capital; the effect of habit on adaptability to changed circumstances; the accrual of experience in working at specific jobs, as distinct from the accrual of general life experience that Aristotle associated with aging; and boredom as a consequence of long years of working at the same job. These are age-correlated changes, but they are not explicitly somatic and not all of them are declines.

3. Richard Schulz and Christine Curnow, "Peak Performance and Age among Superathletes: Track and Field, Swimming, Baseball, Tennis, and Golf," 43 *Journal of Gerontology* P113 (1988). Mental performance, at least on pen-and-paper tests—an important qualification, as we shall see—also begins to diminish perceptibly at early ages; in one study (from which unhealthy persons were excluded), most of the decline occurred by ages 35 to 44. Kurt A. Moehle and Charles J. Long, "Models of Aging and Neuropsychological Test Performance Decline with Aging," 44 *Journal of Gerontology* P176, P177 (1989) (tab. 1).

4. For evidence that good physical health has only limited efficacy in retarding the characteristic memory loss from aging, see Douglas H. Powell (in collaboration with Dean K. Whitla), *Profiles in Cognitive Aging,* ch. 5 (1994); Wojtek J. Chodzko-Zajko et al., "The Influence of Physical Fitness on Automatic and Effortful Memory Changes in Aging," 35 *International Journal of Aging and Human Development* 265 (1992).

5. More precisely, though not necessarily more accurately, aging can be defined as "those series of cumulative, universal, progressive, intrinsic, and deleterious functional and structural changes that usually begin to manifest themselves at reproductive maturity and eventually culminate in death." Robert Arking, *Biology of Aging: Observations and Principles* 9 (1991). Unless, of course, death occurs earlier for reasons unrelated to aging. For a comprehensive treatise on the biology of aging (both human and animal), see Caleb E. Finch, *Longevity, Senescence, and the Genome* (1990).

The physical side of bodily decline (using "physical" narrowly, in the sense in which it is contrasted with "mental") involves diminution in such areas as athletic and related motor capabilities, reflexes, and muscle tone; physical strength, energy, and stamina; acuity of vision, hearing, and other senses; fertility and potency; scalp hair, hair color, and the smoothness of skin; the efficiency of the immune system; height and the percentage of weight accounted for by muscle. The mental side of the declivity includes loss of memory (especially short-term memory), diminution in reckless physical courage and in sexual desire, diminished willingness to take financial risks, impairment of puzzle- and problem-solving ability, and reduced willingness to adopt new ideas or reexamine one's old ideas. Some of the psychological changes may not be entirely somatic—we shall see that unwillingness to reexamine one's old ideas has a counterpart in the behavior of business firms, which do not age in a physical sense—but all have, I believe, a somatic component. Mind and emotions, at least in a scientific perspective, are dependent on bodily states; and the same, or at least the same kind of, cytological and other physiological changes that produce the symptoms of physical decline likewise produce those of mental decline.[6]

Although the process of aging can usefully be distinguished from the age-related increase in susceptibility to specific diseases, that increase is a reality which must not be ignored. Aging would have significance for issues such as the financing of medical care even if there were no normal aging process but just an enhanced susceptibility to disease.

Resistance to the fact that there is such a thing as normal aging has become common in our culture of heightened sensitivity. To some, age stereotyping is every bit as vicious as racial stereotyping. The concern is that if everybody is believed to age, this might be thought to imply that every old person is less competent intellectually than an otherwise similar young person. That would indeed be false. Two distributions can have different means but still overlap considerably. That is certainly the case in comparing the capabilities of young and old people; and for two reasons—that

6. For evidence and analysis of age-related physical and mental decline, see, for example, id., ch. 5; Powell, note 4 above, at 69 (fig. 4.1); *Handbook of Mental Health and Aging,* chs. 6–13 (James E. Birren et al., eds., 2d ed. 1992); Timothy A. Salthouse, *Theoretical Perspectives on Cognitive Aging* (1991), esp. ch. 7; *Handbook of the Psychology of Aging,* pt. 3 (James E. Birren and K. Warner Schaie, eds., 3d ed. 1990); Nathan W. Shock et al., *Normal Human Aging: The Baltimore Longitudinal Study of Aging,* ch. 6 (1984); James L. Fozard et al., "Age Differences and Changes in Reaction Time: The Baltimore Longitudinal Study of Aging," 49 *Journal of Gerontology* P179 (1994); Kathryn A. Bayles and Alfred W. Kaszniak, *Communication and Cognition in Normal Aging and Dementia,* ch. 5 (1987); Michaela Morgan et al., "Age-Related Motor Slowness: Simply Strategic?" 49 *Journal of Gerontology* M133 (1994).

people age at different rates, and that people start to age from different levels of capability. A 75-year-old who had outstanding capabilities when he was 30, and has aged slowly, not only may be immensely more capable than a 75-year-old who was mediocre at 30 and has aged rapidly; he may also—and this is what bothers people who complain about "ageism"—be more capable than a mediocre 30-year-old.

But that there is increasing variability[7] within age cohorts and overlap between persons in different age cohorts does not refute the existence of normal aging; it assumes it. Even cognitive as distinct from purely physical aging—gradual until about the age of 65 and accelerating from then till death—is normal and, pending scientific breakthroughs at present unforeseen, inevitable for all of us.[8] Further evidence is that good physical and even mental health appears not to retard cognitive aging significantly,[9] as one would expect it to do if such aging were simply a by-product of illness. Nor does such aging appear to be, to a significant extent, an artifact of age-cohort effects due to changes over time in environmental conditions such as poverty and lack of education, or of sampling bias, or of disuse because of lack of intellectual challenge or stimulation ("use it or lose it").[10] Far from being "ageist," moreover, a refusal to acknowledge normal, and in particular normal cognitive, aging can create exaggerated doubts about the competence of old people, doubts that the conception of normal aging can allay. If cognitive decline is *not* a normal aspect of aging, but rather is always a symptom of disease, the implication is that the vast majority of old people are afflicted with senile dementia. Almost all elderly people experience a cognitive decline the symptoms of which are difficult to distinguish from the earliest manifestations of dementia; yet in most the condition does not progress to dementia.[11] It is possible, given the steep age gradient of dementia (of which more presently), that anyone who lived long enough would become demented; but most people die before then.

7. Emphasized in Powell, note 4 above, esp. at pp. 12–14 and fig. 1.3; see also Dorothy Field, K. Warner Schaie, and E. Victor Leino, "Continuity in Intellectual Functioning: The Role of Self-Reported Health," 3 *Psychology and Aging* 385, 390 (1988). Increased variability is virtually inevitable as a matter simply of mathematics. Imagine two groups that start off with a capability of 100 and 50 respectively, and the members of each group age at different rates. After many years, slow agers in the group that started at 100 will have a capability near 100, say 90, while fast agers in the group that started at 50 will have a very low capability, say 10; so the spread between the best and worst of the two groups will have widened with age.

8. See Powell, note 4 above, ch. 4, for a careful review; Salthouse, note 6 above.

9. See note 4 above.

10. See Salthouse, note 6 above, chs. 3 and 4.

11. Cf. Rajendra Jutagir, "Psychological Aspects of Aging: When Does Memory Loss Signal Dementia?" 49 *Geriatrics* 45 (1994).

To avoid confusing normal cognitive aging with dementia requires distinguishing carefully among the following terms: (1) Alzheimer's disease, or, as it nowadays is often called, SDAT (Senile Dementia of the Alzheimer's Type), (2) dementia, (3) senile dementia, and (4) normal age-related cognitive decline. Alzheimer's disease, though commonly used by lay people as a synonym for senile dementia, is actually a specific type of rapidly progressive dementia that produces distinctive changes in the brain tissues and that, though more common after age 65, can strike at earlier, sometimes much earlier, ages; sufferers from Down's syndrome are often hit by Alzheimer's disease in their teens. So renaming Alzheimer's disease "Senile Dementia of the Alzheimer's Type" has been a source of confusion; indeed originally the term Alzheimer's disease was limited to *presenile* dementia.[12] Some students of the disease continue to distinguish between Alzheimer's (presenile) and SDAT (senile), although they appear to be a single disease which merely hits people at different ages, like many cancers.

Dementia is the most general term for disabling mental deterioration, and thus embraces a variety of specific disease states; and senile dementia denotes dementia in old people. SDAT appears to account for a majority of cases of senile dementia, perhaps as many as 80 percent, the rest being due to such diseases or conditions as stroke, alcohol abuse, Parkinson's disease, Vitamin B-12 deficiency, and hydrocephalus. For my purposes the differences between SDAT and senile dementia are unimportant. I shall use "SDAT," "Alzheimer's," and "senile dementia" interchangeably.

The number of old people afflicted with senile dementia is not known with precision but has been responsibly estimated at 11.3 percent of the entire 65-and-over population.[13] The percentage rises rapidly with age. In the 65 through 74 group, it is only 3.9 percent; it rises to 16.4 percent for persons 75 through 84 and to 47.6 percent for those 85 and older.[14] Thus, while almost all old people suffer from some cognitive decline, especially in fluid intelligence, which peaks earlier than crystallized,[15] only a minority suffers from dementia, though it is a substantial minority.

12. Denis A. Evans et al., "Estimated Prevalence of Alzheimer's Disease in the United States," 68 *Milbank Quarterly* 267 (1990).

13. Id. at 273. See also James C. Anthony and Ahmed Aboraya, "The Epidemiology of Selected Mental Disorders in Later Life," in *Handbook of Mental Health and Aging,* note 6 above, at 27, 33.

14. Evans et al., note 12 above, at 274.

15. See Jutagir, note 11 above, at 46; Paul B. Baltes, Jacqui Smith, and Ursula M. Staudinger, "Wisdom and Successful Aging," 39 *Nebraska Symposium on Aging* 123, 139–143 (1992); and recall the discussion of these terms in the Introduction.

We must be careful in interpreting these numbers. They do not differentiate between the mild early symptoms of dementia and the severe late ones, and a further complication is that mild dementia does not always progress to the severely demented state that is characteristic of SDAT. (This intermediate state between normal age-related cognitive decline and progressive dementia is called "Mild Cognitive Impairment," or MCI.) If attention is limited to cases of severe rather than merely mild or moderate cognitive impairment, the prevalence in the three age groups is said to fall to 0.3 percent, 5.6 percent, and 19.6 percent, respectively.[16] But these may be underestimates. The population sample on which they are based excluded institutionalized persons, among whom the prevalence of severe cognitive impairment is higher.[17] Even taken at face value, the figures show a very steep age gradient,[18] implying that a continued rapid increase in the size of the very oldest age group will cause an even more rapid increase in the percentage of severely demented people in the elderly population.

To summarize the discussion thus far, age brings with it (1) increased susceptibility to a number of diseases, (2) somatic changes that are a consequence of normal aging, and (3) nonsomatic changes that are a consequence of the same process. Somatic changes are of two kinds, (a) physical and (b) mental. Nonsomatic changes are of three kinds: (a) the increasing proximity of death (a purely "external" change, a change in the person's environment rather than in himself), which is the emphasis in the literature of human capital; (b) the increased ratio of knowledge to imagination in the cognitive balance—Aristotle's point; and (c) changes due to time spent working (experience and its baleful obverses, inflexibility, boredom, and sometimes burnout) and therefore merely correlated with aging.

Not only are these changes correlated with each other, all being related

16. Evans et al., note 12 above, at 281. See also Fred Plum, "Dementia," in *Encyclopedia of Neuroscience,* vol. 1, p. 309 (George Adelman, ed., 1987).

17. In a study from which institutionalized persons were *not* excluded, the percentages of persons suffering from severe cognitive impairment from all causes in the three age groups was 2.9, 6.8, and 15.8 percent, respectively. Anthony and Aboraya, note 13 above, at 35.

18. One study found that only 1 percent of the 65–70 population has severe dementia, while 43 percent of the 95-and-over population has it. Again both figures are underestimates because persons having severe dementia but not institutionalized were excluded from the numerator, so the percentages are of institutionalized demented persons in the entire (institutionalized and non-institutionalized) elderly population. C. G. Gottfries, "Senile Dementia of the Alzheimer's Type: Clinical Genetic, Pathogenetic, and Treatment Aspects," in *Human Development and the Life Course: Multidisciplinary Perspectives* 31, 34 (Aage B. Sørensen, Franz E. Weinert, and Lonnie R. Sherrod, eds., 1986). For other estimates of the prevalence of senile dementia of various severities, see Powell, note 4 above, at 140, 144–145 (tabs. 7.2, 7.4–7.5).

to age; some interact. Of particular significance for later chapters is the interaction between the decline of fluid intelligence and the knowledge shift identified by Aristotle. The combined effect is a pronounced age-related shift from abstract to concrete reasoning,[19] or in terms of another useful Aristotelian dichotomy, from exact (logical or scientific) to practical reasoning.[20] This immediately helps us understand why, for example, adjudication is a more geriatric profession than theoretical physics.

We should keep in mind that not all physical and mental changes correlated with age are seriously negative and that some are even positive, depending on circumstances. The "redistribution" of hair from the scalp to the body, the wrinkling of the skin, and the thickening of nose and ears have only cosmetic significance, though that is, of course, important to many people. The pluses include escape from the diseases of the young and slowing in the rate of growth of cancer cells. And there are changes that are pluses for some people (perhaps for society as a whole), though not for others, such as the reduction in sexual drive, anger, and aggressiveness that accompanies diminished production of testosterone. Some middle-aged and even elderly people are better-looking than they were when young.

The symptoms of old age do not all appear at the same time or progress at the same rate. Despite my reference to "inexorable" decline, symptoms of aging sometimes appear suddenly, as with the onset of presbyopia in one's forties, or of tinnitus, or of pattern baldness, and may plateau rather than continue to grow worse. The rate of decline differs not only across capabilities, but also, as I have pointed out, across persons,[21] making the classification of people in age groups an inescapably arbitrary method of identifying the elderly. No one escapes the aging process, however, so that even a "healthy" old person will be less capable along a variety of physical and mental dimensions than an otherwise identical young person—though the qualification "otherwise identical" is crucial. The percentage of unhealthy old persons is much greater than that of unhealthy young persons, since age-related changes such as the diminished efficiency of the immune system increase susceptibility to illness. The probability of death doubles every eight years or so after a person reaches 30.[22] The incidence of serious

19. For evidence, see Salthouse, note 6 above, at 276–277; Steven W. Cornelius, "Aging and Everyday Cognitive Abilities," in *Aging and Cognition: Knowledge Organization and Utilization* 411 (Thomas M. Hess, ed., 1990).

20. See Richard A. Posner, *The Problems of Jurisprudence* 71–73 (1990), and references there.

21. For a dramatic example, see Arking, note 5 above, at 56–59 and fig. 3–8.

22. Id. at 42–43 and fig. 2–17.

illnesses, especially of degenerative (as distinct from infectious) illnesses such as cancer, stroke, and heart diseases, also rises at an increasing rate with age.

Anyone who doubts that there are palpable, substantial, systematic, universal, measurable, demoralizing, and in the present state of biological and medical knowledge inevitable declines in physical and mental functioning even for the "normal" or "healthy" aged in this the world's most medically pampered society—anyone who believes that these age-related "declines" are a product of mass delusion or of vicious, irrational prejudice—is out of touch with reality.[23] But there is scope for rational debate over when decline sets in, how steep it is, how much variance there is among persons within particular age groups, and the degree to which the cognitive effects of aging may, up to a point anyway, be offset by experience of life, including work experience, and by compensatory strategies such as being more careful or taking more time to plan or accomplish tasks.[24] The *rate* of aging, moreover, mental and especially physical, can be, and is being, retarded by improvements in diet, by increased exercise, and by advances in medical technology.[25] We cannot eliminate old age, but we can postpone it; we *have* postponed it. We are much less likely to think of a healthy 60-year-old or even 70-year-old as being "old" than we were thirty years ago. So while there are more "old" people alive today than ever before, there are fewer than the shift in the age distribution might be thought to imply.

And there is a danger of exaggerating the economic and social significance of the characteristic age-related declines in physical and mental performance. Declines in mental functioning tend to be measured by pen-

23. For some striking evidence of age-related decline, see James N. Schubert, "Age and Active-Passive Leadership Style," 82 *American Political Science Review* 763 (1988); for a comprehensive review of the evidence, see Powell, note 4 above, ch. 4; and see the other references in note 6. This is not just a conspiracy of the young and the middle-aged against the old; some of the most vivid, eloquent, and arresting depictions of that decline come from elderly people themselves. Notable examples are Simone de Beauvoir, *Old Age* (1972), esp. ch. 7, and B. F. Skinner, "Intellectual Self-Management in Old Age," 38 *American Psychologist* 239 (1983).

24. See, for example, K. Warner Schaie and Sherry L. Willis, "Adult Personality and Psychomotor Performance: Cross-Sectional and Longitudinal Analysis," 46 *Journal of Gerontology* P275 (1991); Neil Charness and Elizabeth A. Bosman, "Expertise and Aging: Life in the Lab," in *Aging and Cognition: Knowledge Organization and Utilization,* note 19 above, at 343; James E. Birren, Anita M. Woods, and M. Virtrue Williams, "Behavioral Slowing with Age: Causes, Organization, and Consequences," in *Aging in the 1980s: Psychological Issues* 293, 302–303 (Leonard W. Poon, ed., 1980); Daniel Goleman, "Mental Decline in Aging Need Not Be Inevitable," *New York Times* (national ed.), April 26, 1994, p. B5.

25. See, for example, John W. Rowe and Robert L. Kahn, "Human Aging: Usual and Successful," 237 *Science* 143 (1987); Baltes, Smith, and Staudinger, note 15 above, at 133–134.

and-paper tests and other laboratory-type experimental procedures that exaggerate the decline in *useful* capabilities over the life span.[26] A related but more fundamental point, which I explore in chapter 4, is that the physical and mental capabilities of the young are often in excess of the economic and social demands placed upon them, so that up to a point—the point at which the excess has been aged away—the aging process may not cause a socially relevant diminution in capabilities. Another source of an exaggerated impression of the effects of aging is failure to grasp a point that I shall make in chapter 5—that elderly people rationally substitute time (which is cheap for them) for other inputs into activity and as a result move and speak more slowly, more hesitantly, than they are physically and mentally capable of doing.

In view of the large preponderance of women in the elderly population, an important question is whether aging affects men and women differently. If so, old men and old women would be on average more different from each other than young men and young women even after correction for transient features of the social environment, for example the fact that today's old women had less education relative to men than today's young women. This issue has been studied extensively, and as yet inconclusively. But it appears that, if there are sex differences in the rate or character of aging, they are small.[27] There are, of course, more elderly women than elderly men. But it appears that, in a comparison of survivors, men and women of the same age are not at different points in the process of aging—do not differ in "agedness"—though they do differ, on average, in their proximity to death.

Aging and Evolution

We have not yet considered *why* the body (and hence mind) ages. The best explanation is genetic.[28] Maintenance of an animal's body, like mainte-

26. Paul Verhaeghen, Alfons Marcoen, and Luc Goossens, "Facts and Fiction about Memory Aging: A Quantitative Integration of Research Findings," 48 *Journal of Gerontology* P157 (1993). For particularly (I think excessively) far-reaching criticisms of the evidence for age-related decline in mental ability, see Gisela Labouvie-Vief, "Individual Time, Social Time, and Intellectual Aging," in *Age and Life Course Transitions: An Interdisciplinary Perspective* 151 (Tamara K. Hareven and Kathleen J. Adams, eds., 1982).

27. Powell, note 4 above, ch. 6. Elderly women tend, however, to be somewhat more frail than men of the same age. Margaret J. Penning and Laurel A. Strain, "Gender Differences in Disability, Assistance, and Subjective Well-Being in Later Life," 49 *Journal of Gerontology* S202 (1994).

28. Thomas B. L. Kirkwood, "Comparative Life Spans of Species: Why Do Species Have the Life Spans They Do?" 55 *American Journal of Clinical Nutrition* 1191S (1992). Evolutionary

nance of an automobile, is costly. The more resources that are devoted to maintenance, the fewer that are available for the evolutionarily critical attribute of reproduction; a highly complex animal built to live a *really* long time would require a very long, and hence to parents very costly, period of gestation and infant development. So fewer of these built-to-last animals would be produced. If accidental destruction of such an animal, which maintenance would not prevent, was a significant risk, the added longevity might not offset (whether through the provision by this exceptionally long-lived animal of additional protection to its descendants, or by its having a longer reproductive life) the reproductive cost to its parents. Less complex animals, such as the turtle, that are at reduced risk of accidental destruction tend to be long-lived because the costs of "designing" the animal for long life are lower.[29] But if reproductive fitness is sacrificed to durability unnecessarily, because the durability does not translate into commensurate survival, the parents of the more durable creature will have fewer descendants than their less durable competitors and their line will eventually become extinct.

This analysis, which is supported by evidence that animals age, mentally as well as physically, much as human beings do,[30] explains why we wear out and die, and more specifically why the death rate increases rapidly after our prime reproductive period. But it does not provide much insight into the psychology or behavior of old people. For, as our sketch of the genetic theory of aging will have prepared us to see, it is unlikely that there is a genetic program for extended human survival, although this depends on how extended. It is relatively easy to see why in the evolutionary era— the prehistoric era in which, through the operation of natural selection, human beings evolved to approximately their present biological state—it

---

theories of aging are summarized briefly in Steven M. Albert and Maria G. Cattell, *Old Age in Global Perspective: Cross-Cultural and Cross-National Views* 27–29 (1994); S. Jay Olshansky, Bruce A. Carnes, and Christine Cassel, "The Aging of the Human Species," *Scientific American,* April 1993, pp. 46, 49–50; and Arking, note 5 above, at 83–88. For a fuller summary, see Bruce A. Carnes and S. Jay Olshansky, "Evolutionary Perspectives on Human Senescence," 19 *Population and Development Review* 793 (1994), and for an extended treatment, see Michael R. Rose, *Evolutionary Biology of Aging* (1991).

29. J. Whitfield Gibbons, "Life in the Slow Lane: Lugging a Shell Around Has Its Rewards, as Turtles Have Known for Millions of Years," *Natural History,* 1993, no. 2, p. 32. This is a serious article, despite the childish title.

30. See, for example, Diana S. Woodruff-Pak, "Mammalian Models of Learning, Memory, and Aging," in *Handbook of the Psychology of Aging,* note 6 above, at 234; National Research Council, *Mammalian Models for Research on Aging* 307 (1981). "A failing memory and an inability to remember new names and faces have their counterpart at the animal level." P. L. Broadhurst, *The Science of Animal Behaviour* 110 (1963).

might have been adaptive for men to live for several years beyond their prime, or women to live several years after menopause terminated their reproductive capacity. The older man could still reproduce, and his accumulated knowledge (particularly valuable in a preliterate culture) might compensate for physical decline in enabling him to furnish valuable protective services to his children and grandchildren.[31] The older woman could better protect her younger children, who would not yet be fully grown, as well as assist in the care of her grandchildren.[32] If these older (not elderly by our standards) people were valuable to their younger relatives during the evolutionary era, and hence valued by them—otherwise the older people would not have had good prospects for survival—this may explain why most people even today, even in the United States, feel some respect and protectiveness for older people, or at least for their own elderly relatives; these feelings may be instinctual.

The idea that nonreproducing relatives can promote inclusive fitness (the number of copies of their genes in their descendants), and therefore that there may be a genetic program for their survival and for their protection by their other relatives, is no longer a novelty. It is, for example, the key to the genetic theory of homosexuality.[33] Equation 1.1 formalizes the idea.[34] The optimal life expectancy of individual i at a particular age (L_i) is shown as a function of i's remaining reproductive potential (p_i) and of k's remaining reproductive potential (p_k), where k is some relative (kin) of i, discounted by a measure of the closeness of the kinship (r_k) and by the

31. David Gutmann, *Reclaimed Powers: Toward a New Psychology of Men and Women in Later Life* 216 (1987).

32. Jane B. Lancaster and Barbara J. King, "An Evolutionary Perspective on Menopause," in *In Her Prime: New Views of Middle-Aged Women* 7 (Virginia Kerns and Judith K. Brown, eds., 2d ed. 1992); Peter J. Mayer, "Evolutionary Advantages of the Menopause," 10 *Human Ecology* 477 (1982). Gutmann, note 31 above, at 163–173, 232, stresses the executive role of the postmenopausal woman in the extended family characteristic of early families. Another way to make the general point is that menopause is a form of birth control, which by reducing the number of a woman's children increases the probability that at least some will survive. Cf. Sarah Blaffer Hrdy, "Fitness Tradeoffs in the History and Evolution of Delegated Mothering with Special Reference to Wet-Nursing, Abandonment, and Infanticide," 13 *Ethology and Sociobiology* 409 (1992).

33. For which there is growing evidence, reviewed in my book *Overcoming Law*, ch. 26 (1995). Particularly striking is the evidence of much greater concordance for homosexuality between identical than between fraternal twins, the former having a closer genetic relationship but presumably no greater environmental similarity than the latter, since twins generally have the same home environment regardless of whether they are identical or fraternal.

34. See Denys de Catanzaro, "Evolutionary Pressures and Limitations to Self-Preservation," in *Sociobiology and Psychology: Ideas, Issues and Applications* 311, 317–318 (Charles Crawford, Martin Smith, and Dennis Krebs, eds., 1987).

benefits that i's continued existence confers on k (b_k), all summed over all of i's kin. So:

$$L_i = p_i + \Sigma \ (b_k r_k p_k).\tag{1.1}$$

The equation shows that a reduction in an individual's personal reproductive fitness, say because of menopause, can be offset by an increase in the reproductive fitness of kin whom the individual assists.

Although evolutionary theory may explain the survival of persons to middle age, there probably were very few *old* people in the human evolutionary era. People lived in hunter-gatherer societies. Life in such societies is physically challenging, because, among other reasons, it is nomadic— people move around a lot. There is little surplus food with which to maintain people who are not directly productive (see chapter 9) and little surplus energy for carrying helpless old people from camp to camp. Only 8 percent of Yanomama Indians, a primitive South American tribe, survive to the age of 65, compared to 85 percent of modern Americans.[35] In true neolithic cultures, as little as 2 percent of the population may have survived to the age of 50.[36] With few people surviving to old age, there could not have been much natural selection among old people having different qualities— a process that would result eventually in the accentuation of those qualities that enabled a person to have more descendants—because there could not have been much variance. We know there were plenty of young women in the evolutionary era, just as today, so it is plausible to imagine that selection took place in favor of those having qualities—such as fertility and affection for children and attractiveness (and being attracted) to males likely to be good protectors of children—that would tend to increase the number of their descendants. But with so few old people for selection to work on, a comparable process is not easily envisaged for them.[37] The social and material progress of mankind has brought about a stage of life that the genes have not choreographed.

Of course there is an element of circularity in arguing that the fittest

---

35. Albert and Cattell, note 28 above, at 31 (tab. 2.1).

36. Gy. Acsádi and J. Nemeskéri, *History of Human Life Span and Mortality* 188 (1970) (tab. 58). See generally William Petersen, "A Demographer's View of Prehistoric Demography," 16 *Current Anthropology* 227, 232–234 (1975); Gottfried Kurth, "Comment," id. at 239. For a higher estimate, see Nancy Howell, "Toward a Uniformitarian Theory of Human Paleodemography," in *The Demographic Evolution of Human Populations* 25, 35, 38 (R. H. Ward and K. M. Weiss, eds., 1976). These statistics are of course potentially misleading, since if the vast majority of persons die in infancy or childhood, a large fraction of adults might be elderly people even though the probability (at birth) of survival to old age was very low.

37. As emphasized in Carnes and Olshansky, note 28 above, at 801–802.

elderly were not selected for because not enough people survived to what we would regard as old age to enable natural selection to work on them. If old age conferred a substantial benefit on one's descendants, perhaps by enabling the transmission to them of valuable information that would increase their reproductive fitness, we might expect more old people to survive, even if the "design" of their bodies that enabled such survival sacrificed some reproductive fitness to their greater durability. But the informational value of older people to society may not grow much after they are middle-aged; and it may be that only a tiny fraction of each age cohort need survive even to middle age in order to pass on to the succeeding cohort essential information about food, predators, and social structure.[38] If so, there would be little evolutionary value to "engineering" human beings to survive into old age, and there would be an inevitable cost in diminished reproductive fitness.

The underlying point is that our genetic endowment, including our biological "clock," is adaptive to a different environment from that of today. Recall my earlier point about excess capability. If life was physically and perhaps even mentally more challenging in the hunter-gatherer era than it is in the modern era,[39] the young may have become programmed with physical and mental capabilities that are not required for most activities of modern life, while the old with their diminished capabilities may nevertheless be capable of coping in the modern era to a degree impossible in a hunter-gatherer society. The less that is demanded of human beings, the more likely they are to be able to meet the demand despite diminished capacity. Aging is not an accident of evolution, but survival to old age may be.

This discussion illustrates how evolutionary biology can cast light on social issues relating to old age even if survival to old age lacks survivorship properties in a Darwinian sense: even if, like birth-control pills and sperm banks, old age as we understand it did not exist in the environment from which we derive our genetic legacy. We shall consider in subsequent chapters, particularly chapter 5, other examples of the paradoxical fruitfulness of genetics in explaining the genetically unprogrammed stage of life that we call old age.

38. This assumes, but plausibly, that members of the older generation cannot feasibly confine the transmission of their knowledge to their own descendants.

39. There is more *scope* for a variety of mental abilities in the modern world; but constant alertness, concentration, and quickness are not conditions of survival, as they may well have been in the conditions of extreme hardship and precariousness that characterized human life in the evolutionary period.

If natural selection implies that we are "designed" for limited durability, the conquest of old age by medicine may seem a quixotic endeavor,
and the proper focus of geriatric research the alleviation of the disabilities
of old age. Biologists who accept the genetic account of aging that I have
been sketching do tend to believe that we simply are not programmed by
our genes for indefinite life.[40] They may be right. There may be a biological
limit to the number of times human cells can divide and thus replace themselves as they wear out. But if so, the limit is not known and, in any event,
may, for all one can know today, be extendable indefinitely by the medical
science of the future.[41] Just more effective control of known risk factors
that are controllable with existing techniques would increase life expectancy substantially.[42] Consistent with this suggestion, recent data from
Sweden confirm the likelihood that life expectancy will continue increasing even in populations where it already is very long.[43] Even without major
research breakthroughs, it is entirely possible that a life expectancy at birth
of 85 years is achievable.[44] That would imply a large expansion in what is
already a very large elderly population.

40. See, for example, Carnes and Olshansky, note 28 above, at 802–804. For a good account
of the debate over whether there is a biological limit to the human life span, see Marcia Barinaga,
"How Long Is the Human Life-Span?" 254 *Science* 936 (1991).

41. For good discussions, see Samuel H. Preston, "Demographic Change in the United
States, 1970–2050," in *Demography and Retirement: The Twenty-First Century* 20, 30–37
(Anna M. Rappaport and Sylvester J. Schieber, eds., 1993); Kenneth M. Weiss, "The Biology of
Aging and the Quality of Later Life," in *Aging 2000: Our Health Care Destiny*, vol. 1: *Biomedical
Issues* 29 (Charles M. Gaitz and T. Samorajski, eds., 1985).

42. Kenneth G. Manton, Eric Stallard, and Burton H. Singer, "Methods for Projecting the
Future Size and Health Status of the U.S. Elderly Population," in *Studies in the Economics of
Aging* 41 (David A. Wise, ed., 1994).

43. James M. Vaupel and Hans Lundström, "Longer Life Expectancy? Evidence from Sweden of Reductions in Mortality Rates at Advanced Ages," in id. at 79.

44. S. Jay Olshansky, Bruce A. Carnes, and Christine Cassel, "In Search of Methuselah:
Estimating the Upper Limits to Human Longevity," 250 *Science* 634 (1990).

2

Old Age Past, Present, and Future

My aim in this chapter is to introduce the reader to the basic demographic and economic facts concerning elderly people. Many of these facts are used in later chapters and could have been introduced for the first time in those chapters. But it may help the nonspecialist reader's orientation, and the specialist's maintenance of perspective, to have them set out in a coherent narrative at the outset. The first part of this chapter is historical and, in a limited way, comparative. The second and third parts focus on the current and future United States. I argue that the aging of the population, once its economic and not merely its financial aspects are understood and the loose use of terms like "dependency ratio" corrected, should not be considered a disaster, although it certainly is not an occasion for complacency.

The History of Old Age

Old people are found in all societies, but in very different proportions. (The threshold of old age also differs across societies.) I alluded to Nestor, the old man of the Homeric epics, in the Introduction. It is often supposed that old people must have a special value in a preliterate society such as that depicted in the Homeric epics—and an African motto declares, "When an old man dies, a library burns." [1] But we shall see in chapter 9 that the reality is more complex than this. The social status of the old has varied bewilderingly across different cultures and eras, and even within them. If Nestor

1. Georges Minois, *History of Old Age: From Antiquity to the Renaissance* 9 (1989).

cuts a great figure in the *Iliad,* Odysseus's father, Laertes, cuts no figure in the *Odyssey;* for that matter old Priam doesn't cut a very impressive figure in the *Iliad.*

We do not know a great deal about the age profile even of Western populations much before the nineteenth century. Estimates such as that 10 to 15 percent of the citizen population of Sparta was 60 or older[2] are highly tentative, to say the least.[3] They are also misleading if one is trying to get a sense of life expectancy, because a low birth rate or a high rate of death of young men in battle or young women in childbirth can result in a high percentage of a very small population being old even if people deteriorate with age so rapidly that few of those spared death in childhood or early adulthood survive to old age. Historically, falling birth rates have been more important than increased longevity in raising the average age of a nation's population.

Coming to more recent times, we know that there were plenty of old people in medieval Europe, that they were mostly men because so many women died giving birth, and that many old men found a refuge in monastic and priestly vocations, where the age-related decline in performance as a warrior was not disqualifying.[4] We also know that ours is not the first epoch in Western history to experience a rapid aging of the population. The fraction of old people in the population soared in the fourteenth and fifteenth centuries, because the Black Death tended to spare the old.[5] The increase spurred communal living for the elderly—the nursing home and retirement community are not new ideas—and the concept of retirement emerged as a way of coping with a felt surplus of old people.[6] There have been retired people as long as there has been recorded history, and probably longer. But the idea of stopping work before forced by ill health or decrepitude to do so—the idea of retirement as a distinct, more or less universal phase of the life cycle—is relatively recent.

2. Ephraim David, *Old Age in Sparta* 9–13 (1991).

3. Tim G. Parkin, *Demography and Roman Society* (1992), an exemplary study, declines to endorse *any* estimates of the elderly population of ancient Rome. For a useful compendium of estimates spanning the fourteenth through eighteenth centuries, see Herbert C. Covey, "The Definitions of the Beginning of Old Age in History," 34 *International Journal of Aging and Human Development* 325, 332 (1992).

4. Minois, note 1 above, at 179–183.

5. Id. at 210–217. In fifteenth-century Tuscany, about 15 percent of the population was over 60 (compared to 23 percent in the United States today), with males in the majority. Id. at 213.

6. Id. at 211, 246. A sudden decline in the young population would, it is true, be expected to increase the demand for older workers, but given their limited working capacity the ratio of dependent old to productive young might still increase on balance.

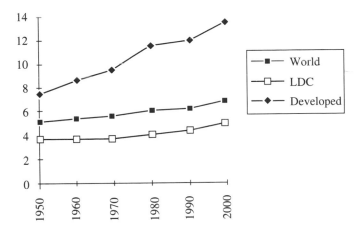

Figure 2.1 Percentage of population 65 or older

After the era of the plague ended, the percentage of old people fell. In eighteenth-century America, it appears that no more than 2 percent of the population was 65 years old or over. As late as 1851, only 4.7 percent of English people were 65 or older and only 0.65 percent 80 or older. The corresponding figures for the United States were 3 percent (1870) and 0.37 percent. The difference between the American and the English figures probably reflects the large number of young immigrants in the United States rather than a greater mortality of old people here.[7] Over the entire period 1551 to 1901, the over-60 population of England oscillated between 5 and 10 percent.[8]

As recently as 1950, the percentage of people 65 and older in the wealthy nations had not yet reached 8 percent (figure 2.1).[9] Since then, rising real income (a causal factor in longevity), better health care, and a falling birth rate have raised the percentage substantially. Between 1950

7. The statistics are from U.S. Bureau of the Census, *Seventh Census of the United States: 1850* xlii (1850); U.S. Bureau of the Census, *Historical Statistics of the United States: Colonial Times to 1970* 15 (1976); David Hackett Fischer, *Growing Old in America* 222 (1977) (tab. 1); B. R. Mitchell, *British Historical Statistics* 15–16 (1988); Mitchell, *European Historical Statistics 1750–1970* 37 (1976); Nathan Keyfitz and Wilhelm Flieger, *World Population: An Analysis of Vital Data* 312, 479 (1968).

8. E. A. Wrigley and R. S. Schofield, *The Population History of England 1541–1871: A Reconstruction* 216 (1981) (fig. 7.4).

9. The data used to construct figure 2.1 and figure 2.2, as well as tables 2.1 and 2.2, are from United Nations, Department of International Economic and Social Affairs, *The Sex and Age Distribution of Population: The 1990 Revision of the United States Global Population Estimates and Projections* (Population Study No. 122, 1991).

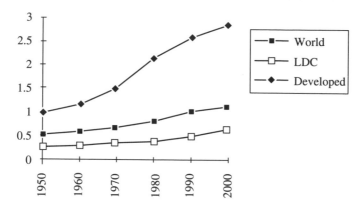

Figure 2.2 Percentage of population 80 or older

and 1990, the percentage of the population in the developed world that was 65 years old or older rose from less than 8 percent to more than 12 percent. It is expected to be almost 14 percent by the year 2000.

The corresponding growth in the percentage of the population that is 80 years or older, depicted in figure 2.2, has been even more dramatic— from 1 percent to 2.6 percent. By the year 2000, it is expected to be almost 3 percent. The contrast with the less-developed ("Third-World") countries is striking. There the percentages of old and very old are not much higher today than they were in Western Europe and North America in 1850.

Tables 2.1 and 2.2 present data for the United States, and for several other countries selected for comparison. The percentage of the U.S. population that is 65 or older grew from 8.1 percent in 1950 to 12.6 percent in 1990 and is projected to reach 12.8 percent by the end of the century. Although high historically and compared with countries like Nigeria, these figures are generally lower than the corresponding figures for Western European countries and Japan, countries that have both lower rates of immigration and lower birth rates than the United States. The disparity is less marked with regard to the percentage of the population that is 80 or older, perhaps because of heavy expenditures on health care for aged Americans.

The tables contain forecasts of the elderly population in the next century because they are part of the data set from which the tables were constructed, but such forecasts should be taken with a large grain of salt; they may easily be overtaken by continuing rapid advances in medical science. Another point to bear in mind about gerontological statistics is that they are unreliable for the very old—persons 90 and older and especially

Table 2.1 Percentage of Population 65 or Older

Country/Area	1950	1960	1970	1980	1990	2000	2010	2020
Canada	7.7	7.5	7.9	9.5	11.4	12.7	14.4	18.8
France	11.4	11.6	12.9	14.0	13.8	15.4	15.7	19.3
Germany (FRG)	9.4	10.8	13.2	15.5	15.4	17.0	20.4	22.2
Japan	4.9	5.7	7.1	9.0	11.7	15.9	19.6	23.7
Nigeria	2.4	2.3	2.4	2.5	2.5	2.6	2.8	3.2
Sweden	10.3	12.0	13.7	16.3	18.1	17.1	18.8	21.8
United Kingdom	10.7	11.7	12.9	15.1	15.4	15.2	15.7	18.2
United States	8.1	9.2	9.8	11.3	12.6	12.8	13.6	17.5
World	5.1	5.3	5.4	5.9	6.2	6.8	7.3	8.7
Less-developed	3.8	3.8	3.8	4.0	4.5	5.0	5.6	7.0
More-developed	7.6	8.5	9.6	11.5	12.1	13.7	14.8	17.4

Table 2.2 Percentage of Population 80 or Older

Country/Area	1950	1960	1970	1980	1990	2000	2010	2020
Canada	1.1	1.2	1.4	1.8	2.3	3.0	3.7	4.1
France	1.7	2.0	2.3	3.1	3.5	3.3	3.8	3.9
Germany (FRG)	1.0	1.5	1.9	2.7	3.7	3.6	4.6	5.9
Japan	0.5	0.7	0.9	1.4	2.2	3.0	4.3	6.0
Nigeria	0.2	0.2	0.2	0.2	0.2	0.3	0.3	0.4
Sweden	1.5	1.9	2.3	3.2	4.3	4.8	5.0	5.2
United Kingdom	1.5	1.9	2.2	2.8	3.4	3.6	4.0	4.2
United States	1.1	1.4	1.8	2.3	2.8	3.3	3.8	3.9
World	0.5	0.6	0.7	0.8	1.0	1.1	1.3	1.5
Less-developed	0.3	0.3	0.4	0.4	0.5	0.6	0.8	1.0
More-developed	1.0	1.2	1.5	2.1	2.6	2.8	3.5	4.1

100 and older—because some very old people exaggerate their age. There is still prestige to being a nonagenarian and especially a centenarian. There may be fewer than half as many centenarians in the United States as the official estimate of 50,000.[10]

10. Bert Kestenbaum, "A Description of the Extreme Aged Population Based on Improved Medicare Enrollment Data," 29 *Demography* 565 (1992), esp. p. 573. For a rich compendium and analysis of statistics concerning the aging of the American population, see Jacob S. Siegel, *A Generation of Change: A Profile of America's Older Population*, ch. 1 (1993).

Anxiety over Gerontification

Two major concerns have been voiced about the rapidly growing number
of elderly people in wealthy countries like the United States. The first is the
heavy medical expense of older people. Although as yet there appears to
be no correlation, after other causes are corrected for, between the average
age of a nation's population and the nation's per capita expenditures on
health care,[11] the combination of increasing medical costs due primarily to
advances in medical technology with a rapid increase in the number of
elderly people portends a significant increase in aggregate medical expenditures unless the demands for health care of younger people are to be
scanted. Already persons 65 and older, though less than 13 percent of the
population, account for more than a third of all expenditures on health care
in the United States.[12] And this ignores the cost, as yet largely nonmonetary
because borne by family members in the form of personal services rather
than cash outlays, of the home care that many elderly people require. As
we shall see in chapter 11, this cost is real—it is not just a matter of children's bounteous and unstinting desire to care for their aged parents.

The second concern is that the increase in nonworking life expectancy
associated with the growing fraction of elderly people implies a decline in
the ratio of productive to consuming years over the life cycle, and that the
elderly will use their political muscle to force the productive young to support the consuming old. The decline in the ratio of producing to consuming
years over the life cycle is not an inevitable concomitant of increasing longevity. The ratio depends among other things on the age of retirement,
which might increase proportionately to increases in longevity. But this has
not happened. On the contrary, the average age of retirement has been declining at the same time that life expectancy has been rising. Figure 2.3
compares, for the period 1950 to 2000, the average life expectancy of men
with their average retirement age.[13] In 1950, male life expectancy was actually below the average age of retirement, while by 1990 it exceeded the

11. Thomas E. Getzen, "Population Aging and the Growth of Health Expenditures," 47
Journal of Gerontology S98 (1992).

12. Daniel R. Waldo et al., "Health Expenditures by Age Group, 1977 and 1987," *Health
Care Financing Review,* Summer 1989, p. 111; U.S. Senate Special Committee on Aging et al.,
Aging America: Trends and Projections 133 (1991 ed.). All statistics in the rest of this chapter are
for the United States.

13. The sources for figure 2.3 are Cynthia Taeuber, *Sixty-Five Plus in America* 25 (U.S.
Bureau of the Census, Current Population Reports, Special Study P23–178 RV, revised May 1993)
(tab. 3-1); Murray Gendell and Jacob S. Siegel, "Trends in Retirement Age by Sex, 1950–2005,"
Monthly Labor Review, July 1992, pp. 22, 27 (1992) (tab. 4); U.S. Senate Special Committee on
Aging et al., *Aging America: Trends and Projections* 25 (1987–1988 ed.).

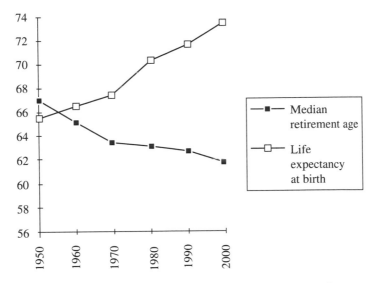

Figure 2.3 Median retirement age and life expectancy at birth, U.S. males

average age of retirement by almost a decade. A comparable graph for women would show a greater life expectancy (as we shall see shortly) and a higher age of retirement, but the difference between the two figures would be approximately the same as shown in figure 2.3 for the men.

Life expectancy at birth is only a crude guide to the age distribution of the adult population, because it is sensitive to changes in infant and child mortality. But infant and child mortality has been low for many years, so confining attention to adult life expectancy, as in figure 2.4,[14] does not alter the picture presented by the previous figure. The trend depicted in figure 2.4 is, incidentally, one of long standing. In 1840, only 50 percent of 20-year-old Americans could expect to survive to 65 and 38.8 percent to 70. By 1910, these figures had risen to 69.3 percent and 59.5 percent respectively.[15]

Given biological constraints on longevity, one would expect efforts at increasing it to encounter sharply diminishing returns. Yet, on the contrary, as shown in figure 2.5, which plots the rate of change in adult life expectancy, the annual rate of increase has itself been increasing throughout most

14. The sources for figures 2.4 and 2.5 are "U.S. Longevity at a Standstill," in Metropolitan Life Insurance Company, *Statistical Bulletin,* July-Sept. 1992, pp. 2, 8; and Life Tables from the 1950, 1970, and 1990 editions of U.S. Bureau of the Census, *Statistical Abstract of the United States.* A pattern similar to that in figure 2.4 is generated by data on life expectancy at age 50. See, for example, Peter Laslett, "The Emergence of the Third Age," 7 *Ageing and Society* 133, 144 (1987) (tab. 2).

15. Fischer, note 7 above, at 225 (tab. 4).

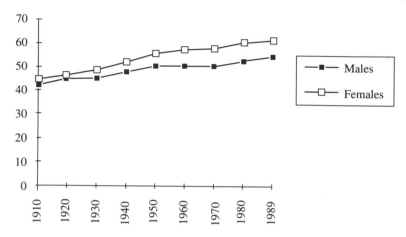

Figure 2.4 Remaining life expectancy at age 20 for white Americans, 1910–1989

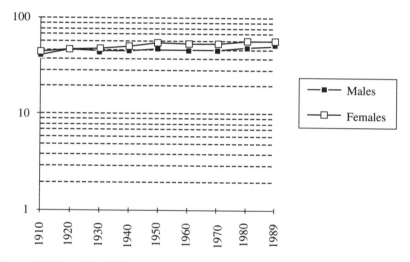

Figure 2.5 Remaining life expectancy at age 20 for white Americans, 1910–1989. Log scale

of the century. It is no surprise, therefore, that, as shown in figure 2.6,[16] the percentages of the population that are old and very old have accelerated markedly in recent decades, helped by a declining birth rate. We saw in chapter 1 that there is no firm reason to believe that increases in life expec-

16. The sources for figure 2.6 are U.S. Bureau of the Census, *Historical Statistics of the United States: Colonial Times to 1970,* note 7 above, at 15, and U.S. Senate Special Committee on Aging et al., note 12 above, at 7 (tab. 1-2).

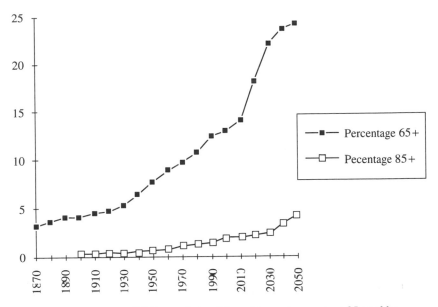

Figure 2.6 Percentage of U.S. population 65 or older and percentage 85 or older, 1870–2050

tancy have reached or are about to reach some "natural" limit, although it is possible that a life expectancy much above 85 years at birth for the population as a whole cannot be attained without major research breakthroughs.

The increase in longevity has not been equal for both sexes. Throughout the twentieth century female longevity has been increasing substantially faster than male (see figure 2.4) and the result is a considerable imbalance between the number of elderly men and the number of elderly women. In 1989 there were only 39 percent as many men as women among Americans 85 and older, meaning that women outnumbered men by better than 5 to 2 in this age group, while in the entire population 65 and above women outnumbered men 3 to 2.[17]

The growth in the number of older people has been paralleled by a decline in the labor-force participation of this group because of the trend to earlier retirement. The combination of these trends has caused the "old-age dependency ratio," when defined mechanically as the ratio of the number of people 65 or older to the number of people 20 to 64 years old, to rise from .173 in 1960 to .209 in 1990. The Social Security Administration and the Bureau of the Census predict a further increase in the ratio to between

17. Id. at 17 (chart 1-9). See also Leonard A. Sagan, *The Health of Nations: True Causes of Sickness and Well-Being* 22 (1987) (fig. 1.3).

.392 and .416 in 2050.[18] Such futuristic demographic forecasting is unreliable; and the very term "dependency ratio" is misleading because it assumes that all persons 65 and older are retired and therefore in a sense dependent—though possibly only on their own accumulated wealth—and that all persons 20 through 64 are working. Both assumptions are false. Defined functionally, as the ratio of nonworkers to workers, the dependency ratio has fallen—and steeply—since the mid-1960s, mainly because of the greatly increased participation of women in the labor force. The ratio is expected to rise after about 2005, but not to return to the level of the mid-1960s.[19] Even redefined, the old-age dependency ratio is misleading because "dependency" on one's own previous earnings, reflecting a personal decision to reallocate consumption from earlier to later years of life, is a different kettle of fish, ethically and economically, from dependency on the current generation of workers.

This is not to deny, of course, that the dependency ratio is influenced by patterns of retirement. Voluntary retirement was much less common in the United States before social security than it has become since.[20] In 1840, 70 percent of white American males over 65 were employed, and presumably most of the others were physically incapable of working. Thirty years later, 64 percent of American men aged 60 or over were employed, and sixty years after that the percentage was actually a shade higher. With the enactment of the Social Security Act in 1935, the labor-force participation rate of elderly Americans started to plunge, and by 1980 it had fallen to 32 percent.[21] In 1950, as shown in table 2.3,[22] 83 percent of American men aged 60 to 64 and a remarkable 21 percent of those 75 and older were employed, compared to 90 percent of men 55 to 59. By 1990, when

18. Samuel H. Preston, "Demographic Change in the United States, 1970–2050," in *Demography and Retirement: The Twenty-First Century* 19, 23 (Anna M. Rappaport and Sylvester J. Schieber, eds., 1993).

19. Stephen H. Sandell, "Prospects for Older Workers: The Demographic and Economic Context," in *The Problem Isn't Age: Work and Older Americans* 3, 5 (Stephen H. Sandell, ed., 1987) (fig. 1.1).

20. Gordon F. Streib, "Discussion," in *Issues in Contemporary Retirement* 27 (Rita Ricardo-Campbell and Edward P. Lazear, eds., 1988). But it was more common than generally believed. See chapter 9.

21. The sources of these statistics are William Graebner, *A History of Retirement: The Meaning and Function of an American Institution, 1885–1978* 12 (1980); Roger L. Ransom and Richard Sutch, "The Decline of Retirement in the Years before Social Security: U.S. Retirement Patterns, 1870–1940," in *Issues in Contemporary Retirement,* note 20 above, at 1, 13 (fig. 1.6); Carole Haber and Brian Gratton, *Old Age and the Search for Security: An American Social History* 104–110 (1994).

22. The source of the data in table 2.3 is Gendell and Siegel, note 13 above, at 25 (tab. 2). The figures for the 1990s are projections—and may not be accurate, as we shall see.

Table 2.3 Labor-Force Participation Rates for Persons Aged 45 to 49 through 75 Years or Older, by Sex, for Selected Years 1950–2000

	45–49	50–54	55–59	60–64	65–69	70–74	75 and over
Men							
1950	96.5	95.0	89.9	83.4	63.9	43.2	21.3
1960	96.9	94.7	91.6	81.1	46.8	31.6	17.5
1970	95.3	93.0	89.5	75.0	41.6	25.2	12.0
1980	93.2	89.2	81.7	60.8	28.5	17.9	8.8
1990	92.3	88.8	79.8	55.5	26.0	15.4	7.1
2000	91.8	89.0	79.2	54.2	27.3	15.6	7.3
Women							
1950	39.9	35.7	29.7	23.8	15.5	7.9	3.2
1960	50.7	48.7	42.2	31.4	17.6	9.5	4.4
1970	55.0	53.8	49.0	36.1	17.3	9.1	3.4
1980	62.1	57.8	48.5	33.2	15.1	7.5	2.5
1990	74.8	66.9	55.3	35.5	17.0	8.2	2.7
2000	82.7	74.8	61.9	39.5	19.7	8.5	2.7

80 percent of men 55 to 59 were employed, the employment rate of the 60–64-year-olds had fallen to 56 percent and that of the 75-and-over group to 7 percent. Of course, these declines were not because elderly people were becoming ever less capable of working, but because they could afford to retire voluntarily.

Among women, the declining retirement age has been offset by a growing rate of participation in the labor force,[23] except among women 75 and older—but they represent a cohort with a history of very limited labor-force participation. We shall see that when the sexes are combined, postretirement employment factored in, and comparison made with the recent rather than remote past, it appears that the labor-force participation rate of older people is actually growing rather than continuing to decline.

Even a continued decline in the labor-force participation of the elderly would have relatively little social or economic significance, and perhaps no significance for government policy, if average annual income in retirement were falling as the length of retirement increased. The old would be consuming no more in the aggregate, but merely spreading their consumption over a longer period. Retirement incomes and spending have, however, been ris-

23. See also Amanda Bennett, "More and More Women Are Staying on the Job Later in Life Than Men," *Wall Street Journal,* Sept. 1, 1994, p. B1.

ing, not falling, relative to incomes from work. Between 1957 and 1990 the median incomes of persons aged 65 or older more than doubled, greatly outpacing the growth in the median income of the population as a whole[24]—and this without regard to the value of Medicare. With these and other adjustments, it appears that the elderly are at least as well off as the nonelderly and quite possibly better off[25]—and that they may have caught up with the nonelderly as early as 1973.[26] "Few of the elderly are millionaires, but most are wealthy—and becoming wealthier—at least compared with younger households."[27] By 1991, only 12.4 percent of persons 65 or older were below the poverty line, compared to 14.2 percent of all ages.[28] And all this is without imputing any value to leisure, which retired people have more of than working people, or (the same point) without imputing any cost to work.

These statistics are somewhat misleading, however. Income and longevity are positively correlated, which means that some people survive to old age because they are prosperous, rather than being prosperous because society is generous to elderly people. Nevertheless, there is little doubt that elderly people have improved their relative economic position, which means that they would account for a growing fraction of total consumption even if people were not living longer or retiring earlier. But they are, implying a possibly dramatic shift in the relative income shares of productive and nonproductive adults, especially when medical expenditures are counted as a form of consumption. This shift, viewed in economic rather than purely financial terms (for economics is concerned with the allocation of resources rather than with balance sheets and income statements as such), is only partly offset by the increase in the number of working women. When women join the labor force, they substitute market for nonmarket work. Nonmarket work has value. The net addition to the social product is there-

24. Taeuber, note 13 above, at 4–7 and n. 104. More dramatic still, between 1970 and 1984 the median real income of elderly (that is, over 65) households rose by 35 percent, compared to only 1 percent for households of persons aged 25 to 64. Alan J. Auerbach and Laurence J. Kotlikoff, "The Impact of the Demographic Transition on Capital Formation," in *Demography and Retirement: The Twenty-First Century,* note 18 above, at 163, 174.

25. Michael D. Hurd, "Research on the Elderly: Economic Status, Retirement, and Consumption and Saving," 28 *Journal of Economic Literature* 565, 576–578 (1990); John R. Wolfe, *The Coming Health Crisis: Who Will Pay for Care for the Aged in the Twenty-First Century?* 10 (1993).

26. See Sheldon Danziger et al., "Income Transfers and the Economic Status of the Elderly," in *Economic Transfers in the United States* 239, 264 (Marilyn Moon, ed., 1984).

27. John C. Weicher, "Wealth and Poverty among the Elderly," in *The Care of Tomorrow's Elderly* 11, 24 (Marion Ein Lewin and Sean Sullivan, eds., 1989); see also Pamela B. Hitschler, "Spending by Older Consumers: 1980 and 1990 Compared," 116 *Monthly Labor Review,* May 1993, p. 3.

28. *Social Security Bulletin: Annual Statistics Supplement 1993* 148 (tab. 3.E2).

fore less than the increase in market income, although the latter increase is the relevant one if we are considering the impact of retirement on public finance, which is the usual focus of discussions of the dependency ratio.

Restoring Perspective

Before becoming too alarmed by statistical indicators of incipient, if not galloping, gerontification, the reader should ponder the following points:

1. The "real" dependency ratio, as I have already pointed out, depends not only on the fraction of the population that is old, but also on the fraction of children and of nonworking adults, since these classes are dependent too. The growth in the number of working women has reduced the number of nonworking adults and, through a negative effect on the birth rate (the opportunity costs of having children are higher for women who have good career opportunities in the job market), the number of children. Properly measured, the dependency ratio in the United States is actually falling. It is expected to rise again in the next century, but we should not be too troubled by that prospect. As a nation uniquely attractive to immigrants—most of whom are young adults—and still relatively uncrowded, the United States could by liberalizing its immigration laws lower the dependency ratio pretty much at will. Even when that possibility is put to one side (for many readers of this book will not agree that the United States is "still relatively uncrowded"), the financial implications of the continued aging of the population are less ominous than popularly believed. Expenditures on the old will grow, but not dramatically relative to increases in per capita income, and will be offset in part by falling education expenditures as a result of the decline in the number of children.[29]

Now it is true that this rosy forecast depends on the unrealistic assumption that health-care costs will not increase in real (that is, inflation-adjusted) terms. But it is a legitimate assumption to employ in studying the effect of changes in the age distribution of the population on the economy, because the *interactive* effect of rising health costs with an increasing fraction of elderly people (whose per capita health costs are above average) is relatively small. Health costs have been rising so much faster than the upward shift in the age distribution of the population that this shift is only a minor factor in the so-called "crisis" in costs of health care.[30] It may be no factor at all. As is well known and regularly deplored, medical expenditures

---

29. Michael D. Hurd, "Comment," in *Studies in the Economics of Aging* 33 (David A. Wise, ed., 1994).

30. Id. at 36–37.

are heavily concentrated in the last stages of life (the year, month, and week before death) (see chapter 5). Suppose that *all* a person's medical costs were incurred in the last year of life—an exaggeration, of course, but an illuminating one. Then an increase in the average life span would *reduce* the average cost of medical care, by spreading the total cost per person (assumed to be constant) over more years.[31]

Even if the rosy forecast proves false, this should be known far enough in advance to make it politically feasible to reduce the level of transfers to the (future) aged, as we shall see in chapter 11. But as we shall also see there, this is not a complete answer with respect to the costs of health care and of home care. However much benefits are cut, our society is not going to allow elderly people to be abandoned. It will defray the costs of their medical care and basic life needs by hook or by crook; only the identity of the payors will change as a consequence of cutting the benefits provided by programs designed specifically for the elderly, such as Medicare and social security. If the advance of medical science and technology continues to add years of life without an offsetting reduction in illness and infirmity, the aggregate cost of medical and home care for the elderly will rise even if the unit costs of these services relative to the unit costs of other goods and services do not.

2. Average retirement ages are misleading proxies for cessation of employment, because many workers—in fact an estimated 25 percent—take up other jobs, either part time or full time (mostly the former), after retiring from their career jobs.[32] A falling average age of retirement is therefore consistent with a stable or even increasing rate of labor participation by older persons. In fact, contrary to the implications of table 2.3, the labor-force participation rate of persons 65 and older has increased, though only slightly, since 1985 (figure 2.7).[33] The term "retirement" is ill specified.

3. Old people are much less likely to commit crimes, a major source of both private and social costs in this country, than young people. The old do have higher automobile accident rates than the young, but this is an artifact of how such rates are computed. As we shall see in chapter 6, the actual contribution of elderly drivers to accidental injuries is small and the private value of their driving is large.

31. See Wolfe, note 25 above, at 27.

32. Daniel A. Myers, "Work after Cessation of Career Job," 46 *Journal of Gerontology* S93, S100 (1991); Dean W. Morse, Anna B. Dutka, and Susan H. Gray, *Life after Early Retirement: The Experiences of Lower-Level Workers,* ch. 3 (1983). See also Erdman B. Palmore et al., *Retirement: Causes and Consequences,* ch. 7 (1985).

33. The data in figure 2.7 are from various issues of *Employment and Earnings,* published by the Bureau of Labor Statistics of the Department of Labor.

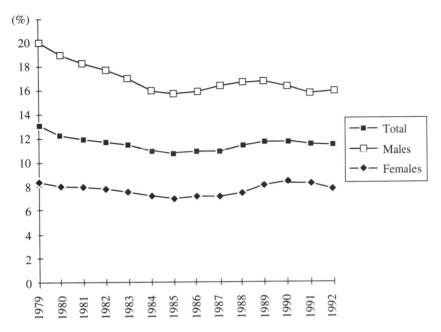

Figure 2.7 Labor-force participation for U.S. population age 65 and over, by sex

4. Household production, and other forms of nonmarket production such as volunteer services, are an important source of a nation's wealth when "wealth" is considered in real and not merely pecuniary terms. Retirement causes people to increase their nonmarket production, because the opportunity cost of that production the income they would be earning in market production were they not retired—is now lower. The increase in nonmarket production (excluding leisure, discussed next) does not come close to fully offsetting the decline in their production for the market, but there is a partial offset.[34]

5. Even the increased "production" of leisure (or, equivalently, consumption of leisure activities) by old people is, to an economist, a source of genuine wealth, at least for those old people who could get jobs in the

34. A. Regula Herzog et al., "Age Differences in Productive Activities," 44 *Journal of Gerontology* S129 (1989); Phillip B. Levine and Olivia S. Mitchell, "Expected Changes in the Workforce and Implications for Labor Markets," in *Demography and Retirement: The Twenty-First Century,* note 18 above, at 73, 77–78. Martha S. Hill, "Patterns of Time Use," in *Time, Goods, and Well-Being* 133, 151–153 (F. Thomas Juster and Frank P. Stafford, eds., 1985) (fig. 7.5), documents the shift in the allocation of time by the elderly from market production to personal care (sleeping, washing, and so forth), leisure, household production, and organizational activity (political, religious, charitable, and so forth).

market but who derive greater utility from leisure activity, or inactivity, in retirement. Indeed, for people who obtain a net utility from continuing to live,[35] whether because they enjoy life or dread death, increased longevity is a source of utility, and so in an economic sense of welfare or wealth, even if the increased longevity must be paid for in higher costs of medical care and in a lower production of market goods and services.

6. Leisure, moreover, is usually regarded as a superior good, in the sense that more of it is bought as people's incomes rise; at least this seems a plausible explanation for the long secular decline in hours of work.[36] A shift in time from working to leisure is a symptom not that the value of a nation's output is declining, but that it is growing.

7. Increases in nonworking life expectancy must be distinguished from increases in *disabled* life expectancy. One can imagine a system of health care that increased the life expectancy of retired people without making them healthier, with the result that the percentage of retired people who were immobilized, debilitated, demented, demoralized, or in pain would rise because they were living longer. But the same wave of medical technology (preventive as well as curative) that has increased adult life expectancy has reduced the prevalence of disability and hence dependency among the old, for example through better treatment of hip fractures, degenerative joints, osteoporosis, circulatory diseases, cataracts and other visual disorders, and diabetes.[37] In addition, the average education and income of old people have been rising—and both education and income are positively correlated with health in old age.[38]

---

35. Which is not, as one might suppose, every living person, because of the cost of suicide— of which more in chapter 10.

36. The reason for the hedge ("at least this seems") is that an increase in the wage rate increases the opportunity cost of leisure, and this substitution effect may dominate the income effect. For evidence that the income effect dominates, producing a backward-bending supply curve of labor as a function of wages, see, for example, B. K. Atrostic, "The Demand for Leisure and Nonpecuniary Job Characteristics," 72 *American Economic Review* 428, 435 (1982) (tab. 3); John D. Owen, "The Demand for Leisure," 79 *Journal of Political Economy* 56, 69 (1971).

37. Kenneth G. Manton, Larry S. Corder, and Eric Stallard, "Estimates of Change in Chronic Disability and Institutional Incidence and Prevalence Rates in the U.S. Elderly Population from the 1982, 1984, and 1989 National Long Term Care Survey," 48 *Journal of Gerontology* S153 (1993). This study determined disability by evaluating the subjects' ability to perform basic activities of daily living, such as dressing oneself and going to the bathroom, and instrumental activities of daily living, such as preparing meals. Another careful study, however, found only modest reductions in disability. Eileen M. Crimmins and Dominique G. Ingegneri, "Trends in Health among the American Population," in *Demography and Retirement: The Twenty-First Century,* note 18 above, at 225, 237–238.

38. See next chapter, text and reference at note 22; also J. Paul Leigh and James F. Fries, "Education, Gender, and the Compression of Mortality," 39 *International Journal of Aging and*

But we must not push these points too hard. For example, it would be a mistake to conclude from the positive correlation between income and health that subsidizing pension income is not a net transfer to the old because it is bound to be offset by reduced health-care transfer payments to them. The subsidization of pensions also increases longevity (because there is a positive correlation between income and longevity and not just between income and health), and hence increases the demand for health care. And medical advances that reduce disability in the short run can increase it in the long run. Breaking a hip used to be the death warrant for many elderly people. Now the hip is repaired and the patient lives to an age when he or she is quite likely to be disabled by something else. As in this example, so generally, the increase in the number of old people has outpaced the reduction in the fraction disabled, so that the *number* of disabled has risen, though not as fast as the number of elderly. By 1991, 4.2 percent of the population 65 and over were in nursing homes (17.5 percent of those 85 and older),[39] while another 15 percent to 30 percent had disabilities serious enough to require some assistance.[40] These percentages will grow. At present, the costs of home care and nursing-home care, which are considerable, are not being covered by Medicare but are being borne by the elderly themselves and their families,[41] except that the Medicaid program defrays the cost of nursing-home care for the indigent aged.

8. Yet it remains unclear how large the *net* transfer of wealth from young to old in our society is. To the extent that elderly people are altruistic toward young members of their families and affluent, they will compensate the young in bequests, gifts, or other forms of transfer payment for the forced transfers (mainly brought about by social security, including Medicare) from young to old that have so increased the incomes of elderly households; at the same time, the young, including the altruistic young,

---

Human Development 233 (1994); Marti G. Parker, Mats Thorslund, and Olle Lundberg, "Physical Function and Social Class among Swedish Oldest Old," 49 *Journal of Gerontology* S196 (1994).

39. Al Sirrocco, "Nursing Homes and Board and Care Homes: Data from the 1991 National Health Provider Inventory," *Advance Data* No. 244, Feb. 23, 1994, p. 4 (National Center for Health Statistics) (tabs. 8, 9).

40. The lower figure is computed from U.S. Senate Special Committee on Aging et al., note 12 above, at 144, and is for the period 1985–1986. The higher figure is based on an estimate that "about one-third of the population over 65 needs some kind of assistance." Roxanne Jamshidi et al., "Aging in America: Limits to Life Span and Elderly Care Options," 2 *Population Research and Policy Review* 169, 173 (1992). If only about 4 percent of the elderly are in nursing homes, the one-third estimate implies that 29 percent of the elderly population require some assistance short of institutionalization (29 + 4 = 33).

41. Id. at 173.

will reduce their voluntary transfers to the old.[42] Private decisions often offset the impact of government programs; that is one reason why so many government programs are ineffective. Even nonaltruistic persons, moreover, are compelled by taxation to defray the cost of educating the young, and this gives them a moral claim to support by the young when the latter reach working age and the taxpayers of their parents' generation who supported them reach retirement age.

The widespread belief that the elderly constitute a selfish voting bloc which is distorting the optimal functioning of democratic government is exaggerated; subsequent chapters will explain why. Concern that the increase in the average age of the population will slow down the rate of technological progress also is exaggerated, as we shall see. The fact, moreover, that elderly people are a stabilizing force in politics and culture may be a net plus from the standpoint of social welfare.

Governmentally compelled transfers from young to old differ from other forced redistributions in the further respect that while men do not become women (with the debatable exception of a handful of transsexuals) or whites become blacks, most young people become old people, so in a sense they are transferring money to themselves. But not too much weight should be placed on this point. Some people do not survive to old age. And people are not indifferent about the allocation of consumption across the various stages of their life. One's young and one's old self can even be viewed as separate persons (as discussed in chapter 4). The actual transfers, moreover, are generally from today's young to today's old rather than from today's young to their own future selves. These transfers may actually reduce the probability of generous transfers to today's young when they are old by increasing the federal government's budget deficit and reducing the rate of economic growth. And they may engender resentment of, and political opposition to, future transfers to the old. The age cohort that is young today may be a net loser over its life span.

9. Retirement ages may not continue to fall; may in fact rise. The determinants of the retirement age are complex, as we shall see in subsequent chapters, but they clearly include the number of younger workers and the generosity of private pension plans and of social security retirement benefits. Changes already legislated in the social security program have reduced the expected value of retirement income,[43] while the coming decline in the number of young workers as the baby-boom generation ages will increase

42. See, for example, Gary S. Becker, *A Treatise on the Family* 275–276 (enlarged ed. 1991), and references cited there.

43. Levine and Mitchell, note 34 above, at 92–94.

the cost to employers of replacing older with younger workers.[44] Since retirement benefits are reduced when retirement is taken early,[45] retirement will occur later the longer the worker expects to live, because he will enjoy the higher retirement income from retiring later for a longer time.[46] So increased life expectancy can be expected (other things being equal) to raise the average retirement age.

10. To the extent that retirement is correlative with old age, it is important to understand that "old age," like "poverty," is a relative term. Different societies have dated the onset of old age at different ages, ranging from 30 to 70.[47] The earlier dates are mostly found, as one would expect, in societies in which life expectancy is very short and the means for correcting the characteristic physical problems of middle age (such as presbyopia) limited or nonexistent. The steady increase in adult life expectancy, and continued improvements in medicine, can be expected to result in an upward adjustment in the perceived onset of old age, causing the percentage of the old to fall. We must not suppose that the term "old age" denotes a natural kind or that 65 or even 80 will forever be thought the onset of it.

This is the most important point of all. Every day it becomes clearer that millions of Americans, mainly but not only of the upper middle class, have been shifted by a combination of nutrition, exercise, and medical technology from the ranks of the old to the ranks of the middle-aged. Forty years ago, most 60-year-olds and all 70-year-olds were thought, by themselves and others, "old." Today a great many people retain a reasonable simulacrum of "youth" (more precisely of middle age) until their late seventies. People do not like to be old. The shift of millions of people from old to not-old has been a massive source of utility to the persons shifted and to their families. Of course, the shift has costs. One is the cost in medical care of keeping young. Another is the added burden of elder care on young and middle-aged adults, for along with a shift from old to not-old has come a shift from dead to old. Some of those shifted from old to not-old find themselves "paying" for their good fortune by having to care for a sick old parent who but for nutrition, exercise, or medical technology would be dead—not to mention having to pay heavy taxes to support social

44. Id.

45. For example, one can begin drawing social security retirement benefits at age 62, but the benefits are only 80 percent of what they would be if one waited to 65. A similar pattern ("backloading") characterizes most pension plans. See chapter 12.

46. John R. Wolfe, "Perceived Longevity and Early Retirement," 65 *Review of Economics and Statistics* 544 (1983).

47. Covey, note 3 above. We shall see in chapter 5 that Aristotle fixed the onset of old age for men at 50.

security and Medicare, plus other programs that help older people. The costs are emotional and psychological, as well as time and taxes. But of that we hardly need reminders. We are acutely conscious of the costs of the aging of the American population and tend to overlook the benefits. One benefit of shifting people from the ranks of the elderly infirm to the middle aged is to postpone the average date of retirement, which is strongly correlated with health.[48]

Although the picture is decidedly a complex one, full of uncertainty, my research has persuaded me that both the net fiscal and the net full costs, both current and future, of the aging of the American population have been exaggerated. If true, this is very important, because efforts to solve the "problem" of the shifting age distribution of the population are bound to deflect resources from what may be more serious social problems.

Why there should be widespread exaggeration of the "problem" is unclear. One possibility is that people have difficulty adjusting their thinking about aging to the fact that if they are to live longer, with a larger fraction of their life spent in retirement, and if they are to incur substantial medical costs to achieve this additional longevity and to maintain their health in their newly extended old age, they will have to sacrifice some of their standard of living during their working lives, whether by working longer or harder, saving a larger fraction of their income for their medical and other consumption needs in retirement, or paying higher taxes.

I do not counsel complacency about the phenomenon of aging or about the issues of public policy that it presents. The comforting thought that the problem of an aging population can be solved if people are brought to realize that they are going to have to spread their income over more years may founder, as we shall see, on the fact that the young self asked to set aside more money for his old age may not fully internalize the welfare of his old self. But understanding the phenomenon of old age, and the issues of social policy that it raises, is not assisted by an attitude of dread, born of popular misconceptions about the social and demographic consequences of the dramatic upward shift in the age distribution. I am not a Pollyanna. I dread old age as much as the next person. I suggest merely that it may be a more serious personal problem than it is a social, an economic, or a political one.

48. See, for example, Herbert S. Parnes and David G. Sommers, "Shunning Retirement: Work Experience of Men in Their Seventies and Early Eighties," 49 *Journal of Gerontology* S117, S123 (1994).

3

A Human-Capital Model of Aging

The Simplest Life-Cycle Model

The basic model that economists have used to advance the understanding of aging comes from what has grown to be an imposing theoretical and empirical literature on human capital.[1] That model will be the starting point—but only the starting point—for my investigation of the economics of aging. For those readers who are not familiar with the model, I offer a brief summary. Then I suggest ways of enriching the model to make it more serviceable for theorizing about aging and old age. The process of enrichment is continued in the next chapter, by the end of which we shall have an economic model flexible enough to handle a variety of psychological and behavioral phenomena that conventional human-capital economics cannot explain.

A number of important phenomena, however, including differences in earnings among individuals and also over the life span of a single individual, *can* be explained by reference to differences in investment in human capital. Economists use the term in the sense, strictly analogous to physical capital, of an asset that yields earnings over time rather than immediately. The earnings can be pecuniary or nonpecuniary, although the former are usually emphasized. Formal education and on-the-job training are examples of activities that create human capital.

---

1. See Gary S. Becker, *Human Capital: A Theoretical and Empirical Analysis, with Special Reference to Education* (3d ed. 1993), and for a capsule summary Becker, *A Treatise on the Family* 26–27 (enlarged ed. 1991).

Much investment in human capital is indirect. For example, even when formal education is "free," the individual pays for it in forgone earnings during the period when he is in school and therefore not in the job market. He may pay for on-the-job training, too, by receiving a lower wage than he would if his employer were not investing in training him. He will not have to pay for it if it is the kind of on-the-job "training" that consists simply of experience—of learning by doing.[2] Such human capital is acquired without cost. And even an employee who acquires human capital that is costly to produce may not have to pay for it. Much of the human capital that on-the-job training creates, unlike that created by formal education, is usable only in the particular employer's employ ("specific human capital"). The employee will be reluctant to pay for such training because, if the capital it creates is specific, he cannot use the threat to quit his current job and take his human capital elsewhere to extract a higher wage. At the same time, the employer will be more willing to pay for such training than he would be in the case of general human capital, precisely because the employee cannot easily (through quitting or threatening to quit) appropriate the specific human capital that the training would create. Employers are highly reluctant to invest in the creation of general human capital because they have no assurance of recouping their investment. This is one reason why much of that capital is created in formal educational institutions rather than in the workplace.

A rational person, whether employer or employee, would not incur the costs, direct or indirect, of creating or acquiring human capital unless they were offset by higher productivity or, in the case of the employee, by higher earnings. Earnings must therefore contain a component that is implicitly a repayment (with interest) of the earner's investment in human capital. The greater the individual's investment in human capital, the greater must be the present value of his anticipated earnings in order for him to recover the investment with interest commensurate with what he could have obtained in an alternative form of comparably risky investment. Heavy investing by a present or future worker in his human capital (as by undergoing protracted training in a graduate or professional school) thus creates a steep age-earnings profile. Earnings are low or even negative during the investment period and therefore have to be high during the recoupment period in order to make the investment worthwhile.

2. See Kenneth J. Arrow, "The Economic Implications of Learning by Doing," 29 *Review of Economic Studies* 155 (1962); Becker, *Human Capital,* note 1 above, at 67–68. He will not have to pay much, at any rate; to the extent that he works longer hours in order to obtain valuable experience, he gives up leisure, and the value of that leisure is a cost of obtaining the experience.

Like physical capital, human capital depreciates. This is due not only to a literal wearing out, as by memory loss or diminished dexterity—factors not emphasized in most human-capital analysis—but also to a changing work environment, which reduces the value of particular knowledge or skills. It might seem that if people did not die, age, or retire, they would replace their human capital as it depreciated, and so the portion of their earnings that represented the recovery of their investment in human capital would be unchanged. Not quite. If their income rose with age because of their greater experience, so would the cost of any new investment in human capital, insofar as the making of such an investment required them to take time away from work (as by going back to school); the lost income would be a cost of the schooling, just like tuition. Even so, if people were eternal there would be no pronounced age peaks in earnings. Instead, earnings would level off at the point at which the last dollar's worth of investment in human capital produced a dollar of additional earnings. Since people do die, and before that retire, and have at least a general idea of when they will retire, they would eventually cease reinvesting in their human capital even if the cost of investing were invariant to age. If the minimum payback period for some investment in human capital is twenty years, a rational person will not make the investment if he expects to be working for only ten more years. So even if people did not age in the sense of becoming less adapted to working or to learning new skills (but did die, at predictable ages not much greater than at present), and even if because they did not age and had a constant income they could invest in human capital at the same cost at any point in the life cycle, we would not expect an 80-year-old to enroll in medical school.

If because of the age-related increase in the cost of investing in human capital or the age-related decrease in the expected return, or both, the rate of investment in new human capital eventually declines with age below the rate of depreciation of the worker's existing human capital, there will be net depreciation. This will impart a downward thrust to the component of earnings that represents repayment of human capital and thus to total earnings. This effect may be masked by economy-wide productivity gains, which lift earnings generally.[3] But that qualification is not germane to my concerns here and if it is ignored, along with a point that I shall discuss— the backloading of wages for incentive reasons—then the age-earnings

---

3. Not completely masked, however, because the gains in hourly wage rates tend to be offset by a decline with age in the number of hours worked. See Gilbert R. Ghez and Gary S. Becker, *The Allocation of Time and Goods over the Life Cycle* 85 (1975) (fig. 3.1).

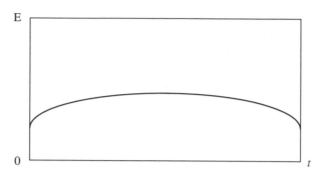

Figure 3.1 The age-earnings profile

profile (more precisely, at this stage of the analysis, the time-worked/earnings profile) will have an inverted U shape, as in figure 3.1.

Earnings (E) are plotted on the vertical axis and years worked (time, t) on the horizontal. A simple model of their relation is

$$E(t) = a + b_1 t - b_2 t^2, \tag{3.1}$$

where $E(t)$ is annual earnings as a function of time (years worked from first job to retirement), a is an earnings component that is independent of investment in human capital and is assumed to be constant over time, b_1 represents an annual increase in earnings brought about by investments in human capital, and $-b_2$ represents an annual reduction in earnings caused by net depreciation of the individual's stock of human capital. The peak year of earnings (t^*) is found by differentiating $E(t)$ with respect to t and setting the result equal to zero (satisfaction of the other conditions for a maximum can be assumed). This procedure yields

$$t^* = \frac{b_1}{2b_2}, \tag{3.2}$$

implying that an individual reaches his peak year of earnings later the more his earnings are raised by investments in human capital (b_1) and the smaller the effect of age in reducing his earnings by causing him to invest less in replacing human capital as it depreciates (b_2).[4]

Although for simplicity I have been assuming that it is the individual himself who pays for the investment in human capital, the analysis is the

---

4. If, as is common in human-capital models, the dependent variable in equation 3.1 is expressed as the natural logarithm of earnings, then b_1 and b_2 become percentages, the first representing the rate of return to human capital and the second the depreciation rate of human capital. This refinement is not necessary for my purposes.

same if the employer pays. Death or retirement will truncate the employer's return from the investment in his employee, and so the prospect of the employee's death or retirement will eventually cause the employer to stop reinvesting in the employee's human capital to replace losses from depreciation.

If age-related disinvestment in human capital caused an actual fall in earnings, rather than a leveling off or a slowing down in the rate of increase, a point would be reached where the employee would have little or no monetary incentive to remain employed; and this would then explain retirement. As noted earlier, however, secular increases in wage levels, driven by secular gains in productivity, counteract the effect on earnings of unreplaced losses in human capital, so that employees often do not reach their earnings peak until their last year of employment. (There may be additional reasons for such a late peak, as we shall see.) If the employee has been saving a part of his income against such time as he may be unable to work or not want to work, his anticipated income from savings will be rising as his income from work is leveling off, and, depending on the cost of and anticipated income from continued working, he may decide that he is better off retiring. The cost of continued working may be high because the effects of aging may compel the worker to exert increasing effort in order to be able to meet the requirements of the job, and the anticipated income from his continued working may be low for the same reason as well as because of diminished incentive to continue investing in his human capital. Notice, moreover, that while disinvestment in human capital influences the age of retirement, it is also influenced by it, since the anticipated age of retirement fixes a horizon beyond which the firm cannot expect any return on its investment in its employee's human capital.

The longevity of Americans can be expected to continue to rise, and we should consider the probable effects on the formation of human capital. Two offsetting (not necessarily perfectly offsetting) effects can be conjectured. One is a rise in the amount of investment in human capital, a rise due to the longer potential payback period. The other is a fall in the amount of that investment if the aging of the population increases the demand for caretaking of elderly people, because such caretaking is a low-skilled job.[5] The second effect assumes that increased longevity will result in an increased number of helpless old people. This is a plausible assumption, as we saw in the preceding chapter, and is reason for concern. But there is no

---

5. David Owen Meltzer, "Mortality Decline, the Demographic Transition, and Economic Growth" 47, 75–77 (Ph.D. diss., University of Chicago Dept. of Economics, Dec. 1992).

basis for some of the most alarmist predictions about the consequences of future increases in longevity. An example is Leon Kass's prediction that if average life expectancy were extended by 10 or 20 years there would be disastrous social consequences *even if the additional years involved no aging.*[6] Kass believes that either the cost of supporting the lengthier retirements implied by this extension would be crushing, or, if retirement ages were raised in order to alleviate that cost, the young would be frustrated by the absence of promotional opportunities since old people would not be making way for them. These concerns make no sense on Kass's assumption that the additional years of life would be added to the individual's prime. Retirement would be later because productivity would decline more slowly with age. The resulting decline in the dependency ratio (see chapter 2) would increase national output, creating new jobs for the young. Midlife career changes would become more common because the return to midlife investments in new human capital would be greater,[7] and some of the midlife career switchers would find themselves working for younger people in their new jobs. Boredom (of which more in the next chapter) would be an additional inducement to these career changes; and with these changes there would no longer be a reason to expect retirement ages to be as low as they are today, and there would be no blockage of the advancement of the young. It would not even be clear that there were more old people. People would be living longer, but more of their years would be prime rather than elderly.

Aging as a change in the individual, a process to which I have begun to allude, is not a part of the simplest life-cycle model employed in the human-capital literature. In that model, the only difference among persons of different ages is their proximity to death. Most economic analyses adopt this model of aging, abstracting from such things as age-related declines in flexibility, imagination, strength, or other potentially job-related capabilities. Gary Becker, for example, refers to such changes as "life-cycle effects" that his model does *not* incorporate.[8] Jacob Mincer, in another important study of human capital, does attempt to measure the pure effect of aging on earnings. He finds that the effect is much smaller than that of experience, but notes some negative effect of age after 50.[9] He does not

6. Leon R. Kass, *Toward a More Natural Science: Biology and Human Affairs* 302–305 (1985).

7. Cf. Yoram Weiss, "Learning by Doing and Occupational Specialization," 3 *Journal of Economic Theory* 189 (1971).

8. Becker, *Human Capital,* note 1 above, at 86–87, 92.

9. Jacob Mincer, *Schooling, Experience, and Earnings* 80 (1974).

consider the possibility, discussed below, that some of the older worker's wage is an incentive payment to discourage shirking (or to reward the worker for not having shirked in the past) and hence overstates his current productivity. Neither Becker nor Mincer is interested in elderly or retired persons, or in occupations such as professional athletics or theoretical physics in which significant aging effects are felt long before normal retirement age.

One way to distinguish empirically between aging effects and proximity-to-death effects would be to compare, with respect to choice of occupation, investment, education, leisure activities, and other activities, elderly people on the one hand with young or middle-aged people who have truncated life expectancies but are in apparent good health, on the other. For example, a person newly infected with the AIDS virus (HIV) has roughly the same life expectancy as a 65-year-old[10] and is unlikely to have, as yet, significant symptoms. The conventional human-capital model implies that, after correction for differences in income and for other differences between such persons and elderly persons who have the same life expectancy (a big difference is that the former will not have pension entitlements to fall back upon), the behavior of the two groups will be similar. It does appear to be similar, so far as investing in human capital is concerned; the truncation of the payback period causes disinvestment.[11] And there is a high suicide rate among HIV-infected persons (even before they have reached the point in the progression of the disease at which they are classified as persons with AIDS),[12] just as there is, as we shall see in chapter 6, among elderly persons. In other respects, however, young people who have curtailed life expectancies similar to those of the elderly but are as yet relatively asymptomatic do not manifest the characteristic attitudes and behaviors discussed in this book, such as increased employment of crystallized relative to fluid intelligence, "inconsiderate" communication, penny-pinching, an increased propensity to vote, decreased creativity, and "behavioral slowing."

10. And likewise a criminal defendant who has just been sentenced to death. The interval between sentence and execution has been running about 10 years. The average interval between becoming infected with HIV and the onset of AIDS is also about 10 years, and death usually follows within two years. See generally Tomas J. Philipson and Richard A. Posner, *Private Choices and Public Health: The AIDS Epidemic in an Economic Perspective* (1993).

11. Cf. John G. Bartlett and Ann K. Finkbeiner, *The Guide to Living with HIV Infection* 17, 264 (1991).

12. Cesar A. Alfonso et al., "Seropositivity as a Major Risk Factor for Suicide in the General Hospital," 35 *Psychomatics* 368 (1994); James R. Rundell et al., "Risk Factors for Suicide Attempts in a Human Immunodeficiency Virus Screening Program," 33 *Psychomatics* 24 (1992).

A more complicated model is necessary to do justice to the problems specific to aging than one that treats it just as a matter of proximity to death or retirement. The following sections add some of the essential complications. Others are added in the next chapter, where the useful though unrealistic simplifying assumption (maintained in the remainder of this chapter, as in the human-capital literature on aging generally) that the individual does not experience *physical* changes over his life span is finally dropped.

Posthumous Utility and the Last-Period Problem

Contrary to what I have been assuming so far, death need not cut off the recovery of an investment in human capital. In the usual case, it is true, the investment generates the funds necessary to recoup it with appropriate interest by increasing the worker's productivity, and that productivity plunges to zero if he dies. But some investments become embodied in forms that survive death. Suppose an old man writes a book that he does not expect to be published until after he dies. The time he takes away from other activities in order to equip himself to write the book—which might require his doing research in a field new to him, or assembling notes and diary fragments if he is planning to write an autobiography—is an investment, and it may not be recouped until long after his death. Yet even if he cannot capitalize the expected royalties by selling the copyright in the book to a publisher for a lump sum—and how much more good would the lump sum do him if he is going to die soon?—the investment in writing it may still be a profitable one from his standpoint. If he is altruistic toward members of his family, he will derive present utility from the prospective increase in their utility when they receive royalties after his death. Or if the prospect of posthumous fame is a source of present utility to him, that prospect may compensate him for the investment. And—a point combining the altruistic and selfish dimensions of posthumous utility—the book may be designed to enhance or even restore the author's reputation for probity or other virtues, his "good name." The prospect of improving his reputation may be a source of direct present utility to the author and also of indirect, altruistic utility to him because reputation is a family asset as well as an individual asset.

Although I have cast my discussion of posthumous utility in terms of investments in human capital, it is relevant to other costly activities undertaken near the end of the life cycle. A person may, out of altruistic concern for family or comrades, or selfish concern for his own reputation, or desire for posthumous fame or glory, sacrifice his life.

The general problem of which the effects of death's imminence on incentives are an example has been discussed in economics under the name of the "last-period" problem. People keep promises, obey the law, avoid shirking, and do other good things, economists assume, because the prospective gains from doing them exceed the prospective losses. But what if they have no prospects, because they are about to die, or, more realistically, their prospects are truncated because of the proximity of death or of some other mode of exit (retirement, switching jobs, switching countries—whatever) from the relevant arena of rewards and punishments? One possible market response is the backloading of compensation. If an employee has an entitlement to a generous pension that he will lose if he is found guilty of malfeasance, he will have an incentive to behave himself even if he is in the last period of his employment and criminal punishment for his malfeasance is not a realistic prospect.[13] And likewise if he is paid currently more than his marginal product, so that if he is fired he will not be able to get another job that would pay as much.[14] He may be paid very well simply because the firm has invested heavily in his specific human capital, which by definition he cannot carry away with him if he goes to another job. His marginal product will be high because he has so much human capital, and his employer can therefore afford to pay him well—and has an inducement to do so in order to prevent him from quitting, which would wipe out the firm's investment in his human capital.

An individual's concern, altruistic or selfish, with the posthumous consequences of current behavior is another possible solution to the last-period problem. The concern may be so intense that there is no last period. That is the case for people who are convinced that there is an afterlife in which good people are rewarded and bad ones punished. The phenomenon of the atheist's death-bed conversion is thus readily understandable: afterlife benefits and costs are now so imminent that however radically they are discounted whether for futurity or uncertainty they are likely to dominate benefits and costs in this life, which are severely truncated by imminent

13. Gary S. Becker and George J. Stigler, "Law Enforcement, Malfeasance, and Compensation of Enforcers," 3 *Journal of Legal Studies* 1, 6–13 (1974). The pension is funded by the worker's accepting a lower wage. In effect, he posts a bond, which he pays for by accepting the reduction in wage and which he forfeits if he misbehaves and is fired.

14. The drop in wage would thus be the penalty for his malfeasance. Edward P. Lazear, "Why Is There Mandatory Retirement?" 87 *Journal of Political Economy* 1261 (1979); Lazear, "Agency, Earnings Profiles, Productivity, and Hours Restrictions," 71 *American Economic Review* 606 (1981). Empirical support for the Becker-Stigler and Lazear "bonding wage models" is found in Laurence J. Kotlikoff, "The Relationship of Productivity to Age," in *Issues in Contemporary Retirement* 100 (Rita Ricardo-Campbell and Edward P. Lazear, eds., 1988).

death. (This point is related to Pascal's famous wager.) Believers in an afterlife who sacrifice current consumption to improve their afterlife prospects in effect reallocate consumption from the present to a posthumous future. The pyramids of the Pharaohs attest to people's willingness to make very large such reallocations.

The phenomenon is not limited to religious believers. One does not have to believe in an afterlife to be concerned with one's fame or reputation after death, or with the welfare of one's family after one's death, or just with leaving behind some worthwhile trace of one's presence in the world.[15] Indeed, the nonbeliever may be more concerned with these things than the believer, for whom worldly success, including fame as well as money, and even happiness, may seem trivial goods.

This analysis suggest an economic reason (everyone knows the emotional reason) why many people postpone making a will until death is imminent: until then the expected benefits to the intended recipients of a bequest may be sufficiently remote to have little weight in the intending donor's utility function. The analysis also helps show why it is superficial to urge heavy taxation of bequests on the ground that the recipients of bequests have not earned them. At least if the bequest was intended, rather than being an accident of the donor's having died before he managed to spend all his money, the tax, to the extent anticipated by him, is on him as well as on the heirs because by reducing his posthumous or vicarious consumption it reduces his present utility.

The last-period problem and the suggested solutions for it have two implications for the timing of retirement and for the balance between consumption and savings in retirement. First, the more altruistic a person is, the later he will retire, since by working longer he can accumulate more wealth to transfer to his family either during his life or, through bequests, at his death.[16] Second, when he does retire, he will save more and consume less from his retirement income, the more altruistic he is. Since most altruism is familial, we would expect that as between two otherwise similar retired people, the one with more children would save a larger percentage of his retirement income. Efforts to test this hypothesis have had some success but not enough to command a consensus among economists.[17]

15. For an interesting discussion, see Ryan J. Hulbert and Willy Lens, "Time and Self-Identity in Later Life," 27 *International Journal of Aging and Human Development* 293 (1988).

16. The choice between inter vivos (life) gifts and bequests (death gifts) will depend on whether donor or donee is the more efficient saver, which is likely to be influenced by tax considerations.

17. Michael D. Hurd, "Research on the Elderly: Economic Status, Retirement, and Consumption and Saving," 28 *Journal of Economic Literature* 565, 617–629 (1990).

The fact that people die with any bequeathable wealth at all, rather than holding all their wealth in the form of annuities, might seem to provide decisive evidence of the existence and importance of a bequest motive, and hence of altruism in old people. But there are purely selfish reasons for wanting to have liquid wealth, for example to meet extraordinary demands or to be able to hedge against inflation. Although in principle an annuity can be indexed against inflation and made borrowable against for emergency needs, this requires complex contracts which a person planning for his retirement may not fully understand or trust. A further complication is that annuitization of part of the retiree's wealth is not, as it might appear to be, inconsistent with his wanting to leave a bequest. Because of uncertainty as to when one's benefactor will die, heirs have difficulty allocating consumption over their life cycle. This uncertainty can be eliminated by the testator's buying an annuity that will give him whatever level of income he desires for his life with no residue at death, while giving the rest of his wealth to his heirs.[18]

The last-period problem may seem particularly acute in cases in which a person works until he dies, as is true with respect to many American judges. Yet we shall see in chapter 8 that, paradoxically, the last-period problem disappears when one is speaking of *literally* the last period.

Relational Human Capital

The concept of human capital is not limited to investment in skills of a technical, impersonal nature (such as proficiency in operating a forklift or analyzing a balance sheet) or even skills that are used in market activities. This is fortunate in terms of the subject of this book because the principal activities of elderly people are not market activities. Personal relationships, such as marriage, relations with children and other relatives, and friendship, require investments in time and effort in order to yield maximum returns. Courtship and the early days of a friendship are examples of periods during which individuals are incurring time and other costs to build relationship-specific human capital, though often reaping immediate benefits as well.[19] It might seem to follow that since the returns from invest-

18. Laurence J. Kotlikoff, John B. Shoven, and Avia Spivak, "Annuity Markets, Savings, and the Capital Stock," in *Issues in Pension Economics* 211 (Zvi Bodie, John B. Shoven, and David A. Wise, eds., 1987).

19. The principal costs often are forgone other relationships: the more time spent in courting one person, the less time there is for other courtships. Many long courtships end in marriage for no better reason than that the parties have run out of the time and contacts necessary to explore the other opportunities afforded by the "marriage market."

ments are truncated for older people, the elderly would marry and form friendships at a lower rate than young people even if there were no other pertinent differences between old and young. Old people would then be more lonely than young, because spouses and friends would be more difficult to replace as they died. But this ignores the lower opportunity costs of time for old people, at least when they are retired, as most are. Since retirement involves an abrupt change from full-time work to no work, the fall in the opportunity costs of time for elderly people will be experienced as a vertical shift from one horizontal cost distribution to another.[20] This shift, in conjunction with the age-related diminution in the expected returns from new friendships, should produce a decline in the formation of new friendships as retirement approaches, a rise right after retirement, and then a further decline until death.

This is shown in figure 3.2. Retirement is assumed to take place at age 70. Before retirement, the benefits (b) and costs (c) (both measured in units of utility, U) of forming a new friendship, as functions of age (a), cross at age 60. No new friendships are formed after that until retirement, but formation continues from then until age 75, when the continued decline (due to the decline in the number of years over which a return can be enjoyed) in the benefits from new friendships again crosses the cost curve, which was lowered by retirement. The benefits are likely to decline especially steeply when the new friendship is with a contemporary, because the death of either friend will terminate the friendship. And most friendships in the United States, of elderly as of other people, are between contemporaries,[21] for especially in a dynamic society members of the same age cohort tend

20. In one study, women who "during most of their lives . . . had been tied to the local community by their children, husbands, or jobs" were found to have expanded their network of friends when old age freed them from the time demands of their previous responsibilities. Rebecca G. Adams, "Patterns of Network Change: A Longitudinal Study of Friendships of Elderly Women," 27 *Gerontologist* 222, 226 (1987). See also Sarah H. Matthews, "Friendships in Old Age: Biography and Circumstance," in *Later Life: The Social Psychology of Aging* 233, 251 (Victor W. Marshall, ed., 1986).

21. Lois M. Tamir, *Communication and the Aging Process: Interaction throughout the Life Cycle* 128–129 (1979); Arlie Russell Hochschild, *The Unexpected Community* 27–30 (1973); Beth Hess, "Friendship," in *Aging and Society*, vol. 3: *A Sociology of Age Stratification* 357 (Matilda White Riley, ed., 1972); Vivian Wood and Joan F. Robertson, "Friendship and Kinship Interaction: Differential Effect on the Morale of the Elderly," 40 *Journal of Marriage and the Family* 367, 372 (1978). (This is an example of "age grading," discussed in chapter 9.) Of course, the older the sample, the younger the average age of the friends will be (as in Rebecca Gay Adams, "Friendship and Its Role in the Lives of Elderly Women" 39, 45 [Ph.D. diss., University of Chicago Dept. of Sociology, Aug. 1983]), since the upper tail of the age distribution is truncated by death: if a centenarian has friends, they are unlikely to be other centenarians, because the class is so small.

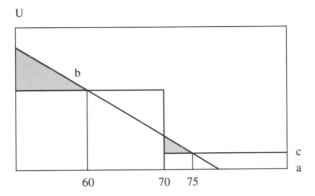

Figure 3.2 Formation of new friendships in old age

to have more shared values and experiences than members of different cohorts.

Loneliness can be expected to accelerate in extreme old age. The loss of friends will be increasing rapidly at the same time that the net utility from forming new friendships is declining. The latter decline might conceivably be tempered, even reversed, by the fact that, since new friendships are a substitute for old ones, the demand for the former should increase as the supply of the latter decreases because of death. But an offsetting factor would be the declining supply of new friends in the aging person's own age cohort, from which most new friends would be expected to come.

Empirical testing of these hypotheses is complicated by the fact that people who survive to old age are not a random sample of their age cohort. They are apt to be healthier than average, of course, but also more intelligent, better educated, and more affluent, since health, income, education, and intelligence are all positively correlated.[22] Hence an 80-year-old and a 70-year-old may differ less from each other than the difference in their ages might seem to imply. If, for example, more intelligent people are apt to be less gregarious than less intelligent ones, the average very old person may be less lonely in old age than the average younger old person, even if the former has fewer friends, simply because intelligent people, who do not have as many friends, on average live longer.[23]

I said earlier that friendships between members of different age cohorts

22. See, for example, Isaac Ehrlich and Hiroyuki Chuma, "A Model of the Demand for Longevity and the Value of Life Extension," 98 *Journal of Political Economy* 761, 774–775 (1990).

23. Cf. Ethel Shanas, "The Psychology of Health," in Ethel Shanas et al., *Old People in Three Industrial Societies* 49, 67 (1968).

tend to be rare. This might seem surprising. An old person will have learned a lot from living through the different stages of the life cycle, and his accumulation of knowledge and insight would, one might think, constitute a valuable source of useful information to a young person. The old person has low opportunity costs of time and therefore plenty of time for friendship with the young. Moreover—we might call this the "reverse last-period" phenomenon—the old person is likely to be a disinterested (not uninterested) friend. He has little to gain from refusing to share his wisdom with the young; keeping it to himself can do him little good now that he is no longer actively transacting. The infrequency of friendship between members of different age cohorts thus suggests that the wisdom of the old probably has little value to the young. I believe that this is true, but that it is true not because the cumulative life experience of the elderly is not genuine wisdom but rather because it is not effectively communicable. To the extent that the experience of an earlier generation can be as it were codified, it can be communicated to the young through books or other impersonal means. To the extent that it is uncodifiable, it often cannot be communicated at all, no matter how intimate the relationship; it depends on lived, not read-about, experience. I return to this important distinction in later chapters, especially chapter 7.

The concept of relational human capital that I have been discussing is similar to the concept of "social [human] capital" introduced by the sociologist James Coleman.[24] Although Coleman stresses the role of such capital in education and I have been discussing it in regard to one's circle of friends, it is also important in the workplace. Salesmen, lawyers, accountants, editors at publishing houses, politicians, lobbyists, investment counselors, travel agents, and a host of other purveyors of services build up networks of personal contacts during their careers. These networks are sources of information, referrals, recommendations, and, when the relations among the members of the network are ones of trust, repeat business. Thus, like other forms of human capital, these networks, and the "good reputation" that they both create and signify (for it is difficult to build or maintain a network if one acquires a bad reputation as someone to transact with), enable the individual to increase his earnings.[25] It might seem that,

24. James S. Coleman, "Social Capital in the Creation of Human Capital," 94 *American Journal of Sociology* S95 (1988). Similar points can be found in the economic literature on the costs of transactions. See, for example, Yoram Ben-Porath, "The F-Connection: Families, Friends, and Firms and the Organization of Exchange," 6 *Population and Development Review* 1, 4–12 (1980).

25. See Curtis 1000, Inc. v. Suess, 24 F.3d 941, 947 (7th Cir. 1994), for an illustration.

unlike the case of other forms of human capital, there would be little or no depreciation with age of this "network" capital. Indeed, one might expect it to grow automatically, continuously, monotonically, and largely cost-lessly, like experience, and yet be less likely than experience to generate boredom because of diminishing returns (and because learning by doing is in a sense a product of repetition) or to degenerate into mindless habit. In fact, depreciation will be rapid when the members of one's network begin to retire. Even before then, normal job turnover will cause members of one's network to drop out, and replacing them may entail travel and other effortful activity that becomes more costly with age. The benefit of rebuilding one's network will decline, moreover, as one approaches retirement even if the members of one's network are not retiring, since the payback period from networking as from other investments in human capital will be truncated. Nevertheless, we should expect a slower age-related decline from peak performance in activities in which network human capital is important than in activities in which it is unimportant.

To summarize, although even the simplest human-capital model of behavior over the life cycle has great explanatory and predictive power—and is a powerful antidote to alarmist predictions about the consequences of continued increases in longevity—it requires supplementation in order to yield the maximum of insight into the behavior of elderly persons. Such phenomena as striving to complete a book even though death is imminent, deathbed conversion, bequest behavior, the postponing of the making of one's will until death is imminent, and the formation of new friendships in old age are not illuminated by the simple human-capital model. But they can be explained in economic terms once the model is enriched by bringing in the possibility of posthumous utility and disutility, the last-period and "reverse last-period" concepts, and the concept of relational human capital. I have also emphasized, as I shall be doing throughout the book, the importance of selection or retention bias in deflecting us from a true understanding of aging. The elderly are not a random draw from their age cohort.

4

An Economic Model of Aging
with Change Assumed

I come now to the most important respects in which the standard life-cycle model used by economists must be modified for the study of aging and old age. For thus far I have said only a little about aging as a process in which a person changes. In the standard model, as I have emphasized, aging is implicitly nothing more than movement toward a fixed horizon. This is an important aspect of aging but leaves out the fact that people change as they approach the horizon; their location on the time line changes, but not only their location. Recognition that human capital depreciates and must therefore be renewed if it is not to decline may seem to imply something akin to the wear and tear that machinery and other forms of physical capital undergo. If so, this would mean, contradicting my description of the standard model, that the standard model does assume age-related change in the individual worker. But, as I noted briefly in chapter 3, depreciation need not imply change in the depreciating good. Just as a product may have to be written off purely because of a change in consumer tastes or in the price of a substitute, so the skills and know-how employed in doing a job may obsolesce purely because of changes in the equipment with which the worker works or in other complements to labor, unrelated to any change in the worker's capabilities. For example, since law changes as old statutes are repealed and new ones enacted, and as old cases are overruled or superseded by new ones, a law professor, to maintain his productivity as a teacher, must—at any age—invest some time in relearning his fields.[1]

1. On the depreciation of legal-knowledge capital, see William M. Landes and Richard A.

And even if there is, as there usually is, human wear and tear—say, forgetfulness or "rustiness" about rarely used but important procedures (for cxample in an emergency)—requiring periodic retraining, as with airline pilots, this "rusting" phenomenon need not be age-related. If a 25-year-old and a 60-year-old require the identical refresher courses every six months to keep up some vital but seldom-used job skill, their investment in human capital is no more age-related than the requirement of an oil change every six months is a function of the aging of an automobile. And rising income may make the cost of investing in human capital rise with age, while the approach to retirement will reduce the payback period for any such investment and hence the incentive to invest for long-term improvement or maintenance of productivity (not my six-month example). These things, too, are independent of any age-related decline. Yet we saw in the first chapter that it is not just myth that people undergo inexorable and cumulatively momentous changes, both somatic and nonsomatic, as they age. These changes are so important that room must be found for them in an economic model of employment and retirement.

The Knowledge Shift, Discount Rates, and the Age-Decline Curve

Two kinds of thinking, and their relation to aging. Among the non-somatic changes associated with aging, the balance between memory and imagination, or between experience and analysis, or between retrospect and prospect, between thinking back and thinking forward, as sources of knowledge[2] for coping with the vocational and other challenges of life, shifts with age in favor of the former term in each pair. The shift is neutral in the sense that whether it enhances or reduces performance depends on the character of the activity in which the individual is engaged. If the relation of experience to imagination were merely additive, the accrual of experience with age could only enhance performance unless, as I have yet to consider, age brings about a deterioration in imaginative power. I am assuming, with Aristotle, that the relation is one of substitution, that experience displaces imagination. This implies that imaginative power does in

---

Posner, "Legal Precedent: A Theoretical and Empirical Analysis," 19 *Journal of Law and Economics* 249 (1976).

2. I am thinking of "knowledge" mainly in the sense of knowing how to do things, rather than in the sense of abstract knowledge. But the relevant know-how includes knowledge of how to do abstract things, like solving complex equations.

fact deteriorate with age, although Aristotle himself, as we shall see in the next chapter, apparently did not notice this implication.

In the somatic category, consisting of the complex of changes both physical and mental that result from bodily changes that are correlated with age, we can classify under the heading of "decline" any change that reduces a person's capability, at a given level of effort, of engaging in productive (not necessarily market) activities. As with the knowledge shift, some somatic changes may enhance rather than reduce capability in some activities, for example by boiling away some of the hormone-driven emotional intensities of young people that can interfere with the performance of certain tasks.

An important interaction between somatic change and the knowledge shift concerns the distinction between fluid and crystallized intelligence. As we glimpsed in the Introduction, the first relates to problem-solving abilities, the second to one's basic, ingrained knowledge base—one's competences in such things as language skills (including reading and writing), face recognition, autobiographical history, maxims of conduct ("common sense"), and spatial orientation.[3] There is a parallel between fluid intelligence and imagination, on the one hand, and between crystallized intelligence and experience, on the other. I do not mean "imagination" in the sense of creativity, but in the more mundane sense of making a model or abstract representation of a problem so that it can be solved by a theoretical procedure. Imagination in its simplest arithmetical form is illustrated by determining the number of persons in a movie theater at a specified time by subtracting the number of persons who have left the theater since it opened for business that morning from the number of persons who have entered, as distinct from going into the theater and counting the persons there. When a young person performs a task, he is likely to rely more heavily, relative to an older person, on his modeling abilities than on lessons learned from experience, as he would be doing if he picked a solution from a range of solutions that he had used previously in similar situations;[4]

3. See, for example, D. B. Bromley, *Behavioural Gerontology: Central Issues in the Psychology of Ageing* 194–195 (1990); Eugene A. Lovelace, "Cognitive Aging: A Summary Overview," in *Aging and Cognition: Mental Processes, Self-Awareness and Interventions* 407 (Eugene A. Lovelace, ed., 1990); Donald H. Kausler, "Automaticity of Encoding and Episodic Memory Processes," in id. at 29; Anderson D. Smith et al., "Age Differences in Memory for Concrete and Abstract Pictures," 45 *Journal of Gerontology* P205 (1990); Paul B. Baltes, Jacqui Smith, and Ursula M. Staudinger, "Wisdom and Successful Aging," 39 *Nebraska Symposium on Motivation* 123, 128–131 (1992).

4. For evidence of substitutability (obviously not total) of accumulated knowledge for speed in processing information, see Timothy A. Salthouse, "Speed and Knowledge as Determinants of

he has less experience than an older person to draw on. If, as psychologists believe with considerable evidence, fluid intelligence declines with age much faster than crystallized intelligence does, the effect is to accentuate what I am calling the knowledge shift. Older people will rely on experience relative to imagination more than younger people do not only because they have more experience to draw on but also because they are less adept at solving problems through the exercise of what I am calling imagination.

If the knowledge accumulated by an older person is transferable to a younger one at low cost, the combination of the knowledge shift with the decline (even if quite gradual) of fluid intelligence may decisively favor the young. Suppose an older person has spent years developing some algorithm that, once discovered, can be learned in a few hours. Then a young person may be able to acquire an important part of the older person's knowledge base at negligible cost, so that the only difference between the two will be that the young person is quicker at using the algorithm to solve new problems. It does no more good for old people to have knowledge that is available to the young at low cost because embodied in books than for them to have knowledge that they cannot transmit to the young at all because it is the inarticulable embodiment of lived experience. In either case, the old cannot appropriate the benefits of their knowledge by "selling" it to the young.

Young people learn faster than old, in part because they have better memories; this is an aspect of the age profile of fluid intelligence. The disparity in rate of learning is particularly marked in language acquisition. So we would expect (other things being equal, which they often will not be) that the average age of immigrants to countries in which a different language from that of the immigrant's homeland is spoken would be lower than that of immigrants to countries in which the same language is spoken.[5] We expect immigrants to be young because if they anticipate a higher income in the new country than in their homeland they can maximize the difference by immigrating at the earliest possible time.[6] But that is a point

---

Adult Age Differences in Verbal Tasks," 48 *Journal of Gerontology* P29 (1993); Neil Charness and Elizabeth A. Bosman, "Expertise and Aging: Life in the Lab," in *Aging and Cognition: Knowledge Organization and Utilization* 343 (Thomas M. Hess, ed., 1990).

5. The positive effect on earnings of fluency in the language of the country of destination of the immigrant appears to be very great. See references in Robert J. LaLonde and Robert H. Topel, "Economic Impact of International Migration and the Economic Performance of Migrants" 75– 82 (Working Paper No. 96, Center for the Study of the Economy and the State, University of Chicago, Aug. 1994).

6. Gary S. Becker, *Human Capital: A Theoretical and Empirical Analysis, with Special Reference to Education* 87 and n. 32 (3d ed. 1993). I am speaking, as is common in economics, of

independent of the decline caused by aging, which I wish to stress, here the decline in fluid intelligence.

Young people are generally considered more flexible than old, old more rigid than young; and the preceding discussion helps explain why. Abstract reasoning is more flexible than casuistic or other experience-based reasoning because it is the very nature of abstraction to be applicable to a wide variety of particulars. So quite apart from better recent memory, though that is also a property of the young, the costs of learning new things are lower to young than to old people. There is an argument, broadly Aristotelian, that one can move from particular to particular, using reasoning by analogy, without the interposition of a syllogism or other abstract model. If the argument were sound, it might imply that the old were as flexible thinkers as the young, only using different tools. But the argument probably is unsound, as we shall see in the next chapter.

Limitations on entry into a line of endeavor, such as the limitations imposed by mandatory apprenticeships in guilds or professions, are in part limitations on generational competition. We can begin to see why the current generation might want to impose such limitations on the upcoming generation.

Subjective time and the discount rate. Some somatic changes, though neutral, can have important consequences for behavior. Most people report that as they get older, time seems to go by faster.[7] The young are looking forward and, being generally optimistic (see next chapter), are looking forward with hope. They are therefore impatient; and we know that a watched pot does not boil. The old are pessimistic, and therefore are not watching. A related point is that a person's life tends, as he ages, to become more

---

central tendencies rather than of every case. Elderly people often immigrate to be near their children; and some immigrants do not intend to learn the language of their new country but instead to reside in a community in which everyone speaks their native language.

7. When one is old, "time passes quickly, as if he [the old man] were gathering speed while coasting downhill. The year from 79 to 80 is like a week when he was a boy." Quoted in *The Art of Growing Older: Writers on Living and Aging* 50 (Wayne Booth, ed., 1992). See also Simone de Beauvoir, *Old Age* 373–376 (1972); Leonard W. Doob, *Patterning of Time* 234–244 (1971). For empirical evidence, see David Licht et al., "Mediators of Estimates of Brief Time Intervals in Elderly Domiciled Males," 21 *International Journal of Aging and Human Development* 211 (1985) (finding that as people age, they increasingly underestimate time intervals—an indication that subjective units of time contract with age); Michael A. Wallach and Leonard R. Green, "On Age and the Subjective Speed of Time," in *Middle Age and Aging: A Reader in Social Psychology* 481 (Bernice L. Neugarten, ed., 1968); and studies cited in Johannes J. F. Schroots and James E. Birren, "Concepts of Time and Aging in Science," in *Handbook of the Psychology of Aging* 45, 49 (James E. Birren and K. Warner Schaie, eds., 3d ed. 1990).

routinized, habit-driven, and freer from novelty than when he was young—
these are all aspects of the knowledge shift—and so there is less to notice,
to arrest attention, and thus to interrupt the flow of subjective time.[8]

The effect of the acceleration of "time's wingèd chariot" is to bring
the future closer to the present. This suggests that the discount rate (the rate
at which a future value or cost is equated to a present one) declines over
the life cycle. There is both evidence that it does and an evolutionary explanation.[9] We know from equation 1.1 that as people age, and their reproductive potential therefore decreases, they can increase their inclusive fitness (in effect, maximize their genes in future generations) by measures
that increase the future consumption, and hence reproductive potential, of
their children or more remote descendants at the expense of their own current consumption. Of course, few people (and no animals) consciously endeavor to increase their inclusive fitness. But during the era in which human
beings were evolving rapidly, people who carried genes that promoted inclusive fitness became a larger and larger proportion of the population, and
they bequeathed their genes to their modern descendants. So we can expect
people to become more future-regarding as they age and their reproductive
potential declines. But only up to a point, since as I emphasized in the first
chapter there does not appear to be a genetic program for the behavior of
people past middle age.

There is another reason to expect elderly people to have, on average,
lower discount rates than the young. People who have low discount rates
will invest more in their long-term health[10] and will therefore be disproportionately represented among persons who survive into old age. Notice
that this explanation of the lower discount rates of older people, unlike the
first, assumes no age-related change in anyone's discount rate. Discount
rates are assumed constant over the life cycle but persons who happen to
have the higher rates will tend over time to be selected out, so that the
average discount rate will fall. (The importance of selection bias in explaining the behavior of elderly people is a recurrent theme of this book.)

The lower the discount rate, other things being equal, the higher the
savings rate will be. People who have a high discount rate want to consume

8. Cf. Joseph E. McGrath and Janice R. Kelly, *Time and Human Interaction: Toward a
Social Psychology of Time* 75 (1986).

9. On both points, see the references and discussion in Alan R. Rogers, "Evolution of Time
Preference by Natural Selection," 84 *American Economic Review* 460, 477 (1994).

10. For evidence, see Victor R. Fuchs, "Time Preference and Health: An Exploratory
Study," in *Economic Aspects of Health* 93 (Victor R. Fuchs, ed., 1982); Isaac Ehrlich and Hiroyuki
Chuma, "A Model of the Demand for Longevity and the Value of Life Extension," 98 *Journal of
Political Economy* 761, 774 (1990).

now, while those with a low discount rate are more concerned with protecting their future consumption. We might expect discount rates to rise steeply near the anticipated end of one's life, as there is then not much future left to save for. But this is just the last-period problem in another guise. The stronger the bequest motive, the less likely are the discount rates of very old people to rise.

Capability and decline. We must take a closer look at decline caused by aging. I am mainly interested in the effects of normal aging, rather than of disease. Disease is, however, positively correlated with age. Strenuous, dirty, or dangerous occupations tend to take a heavy toll of workers' health and fitness, inducing (or compelling) retirement at earlier ages than from light, safe work.[11] We say of certain jobs that they "age" the worker, but it would be more precise to say that age and the conditions of employment are cofactors in workers' health and hence in their occupational longevity. Decline of visual acuity is a normal concomitant of age even for persons spared glaucoma, cataracts, macular degeneration, and other common diseases, which like most diseases are more common in older people. But under the name of "presbyopia," it is equally well described as the consequence of a degenerative eye disease. The healthy old are rarely in as good physical or mental shape as the healthy young, but with this caveat it is the declining work-performance capabilities of the healthy old that interest me.

Assume for the sake of simplicity that a worker's output is a product purely of his innate capability and of his effort, neither influenced by acquired human capital (which I wish to ignore). This assumption will enable us to focus first on capability viewed as a function of age. This function has an inverted U shape. An infant has no capability for work, and neither does a person disabled by extreme old age, which for simplicity of exposition I shall peg at 80. Capability rises for a number of years but, since I am abstracting from acquired human capital and focusing on somatic change, peaks quite early—for many, perhaps most, types of work, probably in the teens. Assume for the sake of simplicity that the capability required to perform the job is a constant, implying realistically that very young and very

11. See, for example, Martin Neil Baily, "Aging and the Ability to Work: Policy Issues and Recent Trends," in *Work, Health, and Income among the Elderly* 59 (Gary Burtless, ed., 1987); Gary Burtless, "Occupational Effects on the Health and Work Capacity of Older Men," in id. at 103; Monroe Berkowitz, "Functioning Ability and Job Performance as Workers Age," in Berkowitz et al., *The Older Worker* 87 (1988).

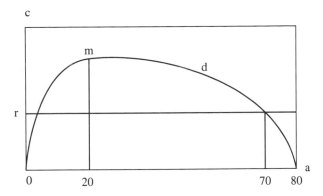

Figure 4.1 Actual and required capability as a function of age

old people will alike be incapable of performing it. We can then relate actual and required capability as in figure 4.1.[12]

Capability (*c*), on the vertical axis, is plotted against age (*a*), on the horizontal, describing an inverted U that peaks (*m*) at age 20, when *c* = *m*, and declines to zero at age 80. The horizontal line labeled *r*, for required capability, cuts the curve of actual capability at two points (though so modest are the abilities required for the imaginary job pictured in the diagram that even a young child can perform it). We are interested in the segment of the curve to the right of its peak, the segment I have labeled *d* (for decline), which can be represented as

$$d = m - k(a),\qquad(4.1)$$

where $k(a)$ relates changes in capability to age. Capability falls below the requirements of the job when $r > d$, or equivalently when $r - m + k(a) > 0$. This point will be reached sooner the more demanding the requirements for the job, the more modest the worker's capability at his peak age, and the greater the decline in his capability as a function of increasing age.

This is not to say that the worker will quit or be fired as soon as he reaches the age at which the requirements of his job just exceed his capability for performing it, even if he is paid a wage just equal to the marginal value of his output—and we saw in chapter 3 that he may be paid much

12. Cf. Joseph J. Spengler, "Introductory Comment: Work Requirements and Work Capacity," in Juanita M. Kreps, *Lifetime Allocation of Work and Income: Essays in the Economics of Aging* 3, 6–7 (1971).

more by the time he is nearing retirement. Output is a function of effort as well as of capability. Up to a point, therefore, a decline in capability can be made up by an increase in effort. But such an increase imposes additional nonpecuniary cost on the worker, and the cost increases with age, since beyond some point aging diminishes the capacity for effort, as well as skill. This point implies that, independent of conventional human-capital considerations, the aging worker will reach a point at which either his marginal product is zero, or the cost of work to him in effort exceeds the wage and other benefits from working relative to the benefits (primarily leisure and pension) of retirement[13] or of switching to lighter work.[14] When I say "output," I mean implicitly output per hour or other unit of time, in other words productivity. So the fact that by working more slowly the aging worker might be able to produce a year's output in two years would not show that he was capable of meeting his employer's work requirements.

Notice that even though the curve that describes age-related decline falls gradually (perhaps, up to a point, imperceptibly, if either experience or relational human capital is important in the particular job), its intersection with the curve of required capability creates a discontinuity. To the left of the intersection, decline is irrelevant; to the right, the worker no longer has value to the firm. This discontinuity is not the whole story of the relation between work and age, but it can help us understand the possible rationality of the discontinuity involved in being employed full time one day and no time the next day and every succeeding day.

Another point to be noted is the difference between m and r—that is, between peak capability and required capability. As I pointed out in the first chapter, human beings evolved in a challenging environment. The work environment of today is for most Americans considerably less challenging. A clerk behind the counter of a shop need use only a small fraction of his endowment of physical and mental capabilities to perform his job to the boss's satisfaction.[15] So even though those capabilities—acute vision

13. Evidence of this is the strong negative effect of age on labor-force participation by the elderly, after correction for education, health, pension entitlements, and other factors influencing such participation. Giora Hanoch and Marjorie Honig, "Retirement, Wages, and Labor Supply of the Elderly," 1 *Journal of Labor Economics* 131 (1983).

14. Thomas N. Chirikos and Gilbert Nestel, "Occupational Differences in the Ability of Men to Delay Retirement," 26 *Journal of Human Resources* 1, 23 (1991); Roger L. Ransom and Richard Sutch, "The Labor of Older Americans: Retirement of Men On and Off the Job, 1870–1937," 46 *Journal of Economic History* 1, 19 (1986).

15. See, with respect to memory, Paul Verhaeghen, Alfons Marcoen, and Luc Goossens, "Facts and Fiction about Memory Aging: A Quantitative Integration of Research Findings," 48 *Journal of Gerontology* P157 (1993), and with respect to sight, William Kosnik et al., "Visual Changes in Daily Life throughout Adulthood," 43 *Journal of Gerontology* P63 (1988). This is not

and hearing, facility at memorization, computational speed, fleetness of foot, and the rest—tend to erode over the course of a career,[16] and even if there are no offsetting gains from experience or maturity and no accrual of valuable social human capital, it may be many years before the clerk's ability to do his job declines to a point at which he either cannot do it at all or cannot do it without a costly (to him) increment of effort. Until that point is reached, he may be able to compensate for diminution in occupationally relevant capabilities with small increases in effort.

These observations suggest that aging per se need not reduce occupationally relevant capacity, and may thus help explain why most studies do not find age-related declines in productivity.[17] An additional explanatory factor, one much stressed in the "optimistic" literature about older workers, is that they are less likely either to quit or to soldier on the job than younger workers. There is a good economic reason. Unlike younger workers, they have built up a lot of firm-specific human capital for which they are being compensated in their present wage, and it would be wiped out if they quit. This makes them more vulnerable, and hence more loyal, though the downside from the employer's standpoint is that it may also make them more susceptible to the blandishments of unions. Because of their greater vulnerability to discharge, whether justifiable or opportunistic, older work-

---

to deny that there are better and worse clerks, only that the capabilities that decline steeply with age (such as visual acuity) are not important to the performance of their jobs.

16. See, for example, Sara J. Czaja and Joseph Sharit, "Age Differences in the Performance of Computer-Based Work," 8 *Psychology and Aging* 59 (1993).

17. See, for example, Bruce J. Avolio, David A. Waldman, and Michael A. McDaniel, "Age and Work Performance in Nonmanagerial Jobs: The Effects of Experience and Occupational Type," 33 *Academy of Management Journal* 407 (1990); Seymour Giniger, Angelo Dispenzieri, and Joseph Eisenberg, "Age, Experience, and Performance on Speed and Skill Jobs in an Applied Setting," 68 *Journal of Applied Psychology* 469 (1983); Jack Levin and William C. Levin, *Ageism: Prejudice and Discrimination against the Elderly* 80–81 (1980); William McNaught and Michael C. Barth, "Are Older Workers 'Good Buys'?—A Case Study of Days Inns of America," *Sloan Management Review,* Spring 1992, p. 53; and see generally Robert Clark, Juanita Kreps, and Joseph Spengler, "Economics of Aging: A Survey," 16 *Journal of Economic Literature* 919, 927–929 (1978). All such studies, as noted in the text below, suffer from selection bias.

Some studies do find age-related declines in productivity. Two studies of a Fortune 500 firm find significant declines in productivity in all of the classes of worker studied (male and female office workers, salesmen, saleswomen, and male managers), beginning in their forties. These studies are summarized in Laurence J. Kotlikoff, "The Relationship of Productivity to Age," in *Issues in Contemporary Retirement* 100 (Rita Ricardo-Campbell and Edward P. Lazear, eds., 1988). See also the earlier studies of factory and clerical workers summarized in Mary Jablonski, Larry Rosenblum, and Kent Kunze, "Productivity, Age, and Labor Composition Changes in the U.S.," *Monthly Labor Review,* Sept. 1988, pp. 34–35; Mildred Doering, Susan R. Rhodes, and Michael Schuster, *The Aging Worker: Research and Recommendations* 37, 62–63, 86–88 (1983); Czaja and Sharit, note 16 above. For an excellent review of the literature, see Berkowitz, note 11 above.

ers have more to gain from job security and a rigid seniority system than younger workers do.[18]

Although the aging worker may be less likely to quit, he is more likely to retire or to become disabled through illness. And part of his vulnerability and hence loyalty may come from the fact that because of the decline of his fluid intelligence it may be very difficult for him to learn a new job—and this may hamper him in his present employment as well, if the employer's job requirements are changing, and may therefore make him all the more vulnerable. So the loyalty of the older worker is not just a pure plus, but also an effort to offset a minus. And this point completely to one side, the studies that find that, on balance, older workers are just as productive as younger ones have, for two related reasons, a strictly limited significance for the evaluation of age-related decline. The first reason is selection bias. Employers will tend to weed out unproductive older workers. The ones who remain will be productive but their productivity will overstate that of their age group. Second, since most elderly workers are retired, studies of age-related declines in productivity tend in fact to compare middle-aged with young employees, rather than old with middle-aged or young employees, and it would be question-begging to extrapolate the findings in these studies to the old.

The more a job calls for the exercise of physical or mental abilities that are strongly age-related, such as physical strength and agility, or physical or mental dexterity, the earlier the age at which the average worker will be incapable of performing up to his employer's expectations. So (to anticipate chapter 9) we would not expect old people to command a great deal of reverence or respect in a society such as ours. Although work is becoming less dirty, dangerous, and strenuous with the shift in employment from manufacturing to services, mass education enables the transfer at low cost of much of the painfully accumulated experience of the old to the young. And rapid social and technological change causes rapid depreciation of

18. See Richard B. Freeman and James L. Medoff, *What Do Unions Do?* ch. 8 (1984); Barry T. Hirsch and John T. Addison, *The Economic Analysis of Unions: New Approaches and Evidence* 58, 178 (1986); A. van de Berg and W. Groot, "Union Membership in the Netherlands: A Cross-Sectional Analysis," 17 *Empirical Economics* 537, 552 (1992) (tab. 2). In 1993, only 6.8 percent of American workers 16 to 24 years of age were represented by unions, and only 14.9 percent of those 25 to 34. The corresponding figures for workers 45 to 54 and 55 to 64 are 25.7 percent and 23 percent respectively. (For workers 65 and over the figure falls to 10 percent, but few of these workers are in unionized occupations.) Bureau of Labor Statistics, *Employment and Earnings,* Jan. 4, 1994, p. 248 (tab. 57). When other factors are corrected for, however, the effect of age on support for union representation is seen to be weak and equivocal, perhaps because of a tendency of unionism to flatten age-earnings profiles. Hirsch and Addison, above, at 58.

human capital, which the old may lack the incentive to replace or, given the decline in fluid intelligence, the ability to replace at reasonable cost. This leaves unexplained how the old have in recent decades managed to increase their share of the nation's wealth relative to the young, but the answer may lie in interactions between characteristics of the elderly and of the democratic process that are examined in later chapters.

The shorter the distance between the worker's peak capability and the lesser capability, assumed constant for all ages, actually required for the job, the earlier (holding the rate of age-related decline constant) the age at which the worker will no longer be capable of doing the job. Occupations that draw their members from the upper tail of the distribution of physical or mental qualities that peak early illustrate this point, ranging from professional athletics to particle physics. Physically strenuous occupations other than professional athletics and a few military specialties do not draw from the upper tail yet may require a capability close to the worker's peak, which implies early retirement too. Most studies, it is true, find that the minimum capabilities required for performing most jobs in the modern American economy do not begin to deteriorate measurably until about age 60 (and often later),[19] although productivity may decline earlier. But most jobs are not all jobs. And the converse of the point in the first chapter about the tendency of pen-and-pencil tests ("psychometric" tests, in the jargon of psychology) to measure unneeded capabilities is that they may miss subtle but occupationally relevant declines in application, focus, flexibility, or effort.

A further reason to doubt that all or even most workers are coasting comfortably well above the requirements of their job even if age has eroded their capabilities to a significant extent is that promotions and demotions can be and are used to narrow the gap between actual and required capability. Employers use promotions to move abler workers into more demanding jobs—jobs with more exacting requirements (r), hence requirements closer to the worker's peak-age capability (m). We might expect that as age-related decline lowered the worker's m, the process of promotion would be reversed and the worker demoted to jobs with progressively lower r's. The effect in terms of figure 4.1 would be to impart an inverted U shape to r between its intersections (cutting from below and then from above) with the curve describing the worker's changing capability over his life span.

19. See, for example, K. Warner Schaie, "The Seattle Longitudinal Study: A 21-Year Exploration of Psychometric Intelligence in Adulthood," in *Longitudinal Studies of Adult Psychological Development* 64, 127–128 (K. Warner Schaie, ed., 1983).

For reasons that are not well understood, at least by economists, and that precede and appear to exist quite independently of the Age Discrimination in Employment Act or the minimum-wage law, demotions are rarely used as a means of adjustment to declining capabilities; they are considered demeaning. The result is to hold r constant after the worker has passed his peak, thus accelerating retirement. The worker would rather lose some income by retiring earlier than suffer the humiliation of a demotion.

The Retirement Decision

Assume for the sake of simplicity that the worker must decide whether to retire at age 65 or at age 70. Economic analysis says retire now (at $t = 1$) if the expected utility (U) of retiring now exceeds that of continuing to work and retiring later $(t > 1)$. That is, retire now if one's retirement income, suitably discounted to present value, will exceed the sum of one's working income, net of the costs of work, and of the retirement income to which one will be entitled if one retires later, with these income figures suitably discounted too. Consider a highly simplified model. A person considering retiring is assumed to know with certainty that he will live to the age of 80, and his choice is between 5 more years of working followed by 10 of retirement, or 15 years of retirement beginning now. If he postpones retirement, he has utility from two different streams of benefits. One consists of an annual pecuniary income for 5 years from work (at wage I_p) plus annual nonpecuniary income (during the same period) from work of I_o. I_o will be a negative number if the person incurs net disutility (as a result of danger, fatigue, boredom, the strain of commuting, diminished leisure, unpleasant superiors, or whatever) from work rather than deriving net positive utility from it as a result of the prestige, excitement, socializing, or other psychic goods that it yields. The other stream of benefits from postponing retirement begins in the sixth year and consists of annual pension income (some fraction, $1/\alpha$, of working income) plus nonpecuniary income from the substitution of leisure for work (I_l). Both streams must be discounted to present value at some interest rate (i) and then compared with the present value of pension and leisure income if the person retires now. The worker's annual pension income will normally be smaller if he retires sooner rather than later. So β, the denominator of the fraction of working income that will be received as pension income when retirement is taken sooner, will exceed α; $I_p/\beta < I_p/\alpha$.

Putting these points together and employing the summation sign, Σ, since we are adding up annual streams of costs and benefits, we have the following formula: retire now only if the present value of retirement now exceeds the present value of retirement later, or in symbols only if

$$\sum_{t=1}^{t=15} U \frac{(I_p / \beta + I_l)}{(1 + i)^t} \geq \sum_{t=1}^{t=5} U \frac{(I_p + I_o)}{(1 + i)^t} + \sum_{t=6}^{t=15} U \frac{(I_p + I_l)}{(1 + i)^t}. \quad (4.2)$$

The strictly financial factors in the model which influence the choice whether to retire early, such as the structure of the pension entitlement and the ratio of pension to working income, are the subject of a vast literature,[20] and are touched on in subsequent chapters. Other points need to be considered as well, however:

1. The higher the worker's discount rate, the likelier is retirement at the earliest opportunity. Even if, as my model assumes, by working another year one can earn a higher pension, the cost in hassle, fatigue, forgone leisure, and other costs of work will be incurred in that year, while the benefit (the higher pension) will be spread out over a more distant future, one's remaining life and perhaps that of one's spouse as well, depending on the terms of the pension contract. The higher one's discount rate, the smaller will be the present value of future benefits. So workers who have low wages may retire earlier than well-paid workers simply because low earnings and high discount rates are positively correlated; persons with high discount rates invest less in their human capital (the returns on which are postponed) and so have lower earnings.

2. Retirement will tend to be later for people who derive net nonpecuniary utility rather than disutility from working (I_o in inequality 4.2).[21] The sources of worry about the elimination of mandatory retirement for professors (see chapter 13) are that a large fraction of a professor's compensation

20. For a good introduction, see Joseph F. Quinn, Richard V. Burkhauser, and Daniel A. Myers, *Passing the Torch: The Influence of Economic Incentives on Work and Retirement* 85–87, 199 (1990). On the economics of retirement generally, see the useful summary by Edward P. Lazear, "Retirement from the Labor Force," in *Handbook of Labor Economics,* vol. 1, p. 305 (Orley Ashenfelter and Richard Layard, eds., 1986).

21. For evidence, see Randall K. Filer and Peter A. Petri, "A Job-Characteristics Theory of Retirement," 70 *Review of Economics and Statistics* 123 (1988); Chirikos and Nestel, note 14 above; Chirikos and Nestel, "Occupation, Impaired Health, and the Functional Capacity of Men to Continue Working," 11 *Research on Aging* 174, 192, 197–198 (1989); cf. Herbert S. Parnes and David G. Summers, "Shunning Retirement: Work Experience of Men in Their Seventies and Early Eighties," 49 *Journal of Gerontology* S117, S123 (1994); Martin D. Hanlon, "Age and Commitment to Work," 8 *Research on Aging* 289 (1986). F. Thomas Juster, "Preferences for Work and Leisure," in *Time, Goods, and Well-Being* 333 (F. Thomas Juster and Frank P. Stafford, eds., 1985), presents convincing evidence that many jobs yield a high level of intrinsic satisfaction. See also Nan L. Maxwell, "The Retirement Experience: Psychological and Financial Linkages to the Labor Market," 66 *Social Science Quarterly* 22, 30–31 (1985).

is nonpecuniary, and some of it would be lost by retirement, and that the cost of working as a professor is low even at advanced ages. The combined effect is to make I_o strongly positive. At the opposite extreme, we expect retirement to be early, other things being equal (often they are not), from jobs that are dirty, dangerous, unhealthful, strenuous, or stressful. Since blacks are disproportionately represented in such jobs, they can be expected to retire earlier on average than whites do (after other differences are corrected for) and to be happier in retirement than whites.[22] A complicating factor, however, is that job satisfaction and retirement satisfaction are positively correlated. The reason is that persons in the managerial and professional classes are more likely to have social skills, hobbies, and income that enable them to get the maximum benefit out of the increased leisure that retirement gives them.[23]

The concept of excess capability is pertinent to the issue of the disutility of work. Consider the simple case in which at all ages to the left of the intersection of r and d in figure 4.1, the nonpecuniary utility of work (prestige, sociability, etc.) just equals the disutility (stress, effort, etc.), so that $I_o = 0$. Consider now what happens when the individual ages beyond that point. In order not to fall below the minimum requirements of the job, he will have to increase his effort, and the cost to him of working will rise. I_o will turn negative and retirement will therefore become a more attractive choice. The general point is that aging will create pressure to retire if, as is plausible, it reduces productivity in working more than it reduces productivity in leisure.

A neglected pair of factors in economic analysis of the cost of work, though distinct from the also neglected factor of somatic aging, are boredom and "burnout." They are not identical. Burnout is a reaction to stress. There is evidence that it actually is more common among younger than

22. For evidence that blacks do tend to retire earlier than whites, at least when retirement is functionally conceived to include early retirements due to disability, see Rose C. Gibson, "Reconceptualizing Retirement for Black Americans," 27 *Gerontologist* 691 (1990), and E. Percil Stanford et al., "Early Retirement and Functional Impairment from a Multi-Ethnic Perspective," 13 *Research on Aging* 5, 18 (1991). For evidence that they enjoy retirement more, see Rose C. Gibson, "Aging in Black America: The Effects of an Aging Society," in *Aging in Cross-Cultural Perspective: Africa and the Americas* 105, 119, 121 (Enid Gort, ed., 1988). An additional point, omitted in my very simple model, is that retirement will tend to be later, the longer the worker expects to live, because the effect on total retirement income of working longer, and thus qualifying for higher retirement benefits, will be greater. Blacks have a significantly shorter life expectancy than whites and therefore have less to lose by earlier retirement that will reduce their annual retirement benefits.

23. See C. T. Whelan and B. J. Whelan, "The Transition to Retirement" (Economic and Social Research Institute of Ireland, Paper No. 138, July 1988).

among older workers.[24] But selection bias may be at work here. Workers who are especially susceptible to stress will be selected out of stressful jobs early; those who remain may *eventually* experience burnout because of the cumulative character of stress.[25] Boredom in the sense relevant to my analysis should also be distinguished from the kind of restlessness, also more common among the young (and intelligent), that comes from doing "boring" work.[26] My concern is with career boredom, the boredom people often feel when they are doing the same thing year after year with no prospect of change. This boredom resembles, though it is not identical to, the burnout that is caused by the accumulation of stress over a long period of years.

As long as by gaining experience or otherwise increasing his human capital in a nonstressful job the worker is doing different things, boredom or burnout is unlikely even if the worker remains in the "same" job or line of work for many years. But at some point after the worker has reached a plateau in his career and his work becomes repetitive, boredom may begin to grip him; and burnout as well, if it is a stressful job like being a policeman, or a teacher in a public school in a rough neighborhood. Boredom and burnout are sources of nonpecuniary costs of work that although time-related are not age-related except insofar as the length of time that one has been in a job is positively correlated with age. The distinction between time-related and age-related effects will become important when, in subsequent chapters, we consider the productivity of very old federal judges, and also the prospects for raising the average retirement age. To anticipate a bit, because judges in Anglo-American legal systems tend to be appointed at relatively advanced ages and remain in office well into old age, they illustrate a class of workers in which the effects of time on the job and the effects of age should be separable. Boredom implies that within occupations, other things being equal, workers who entered the occupation earlier are likely to retire at a younger age, or, equivalently, that the probability of retirement at a given age is higher the longer the worker has been in the occupation.

Boredom illustrates a time-dependent cost in which time and cost are positively related, while habit illustrates a time-dependent cost *and* benefit

24. Cynthia L. Cordes and Thomas M. Dougherty, "A Review and an Integration of Research on Job Burnout," 18 *Academy of Management Review* 621, 633 (1993).

25. For evidence, see George J. Schunk and Harold T. Osterud, "Duration of Pediatric and Internal Medicine Practice in Oregon," 83 *Pediatrics* 428 (1989).

26. See Amos Drory, "Individual Differences in Boredom Proneness and Task Effectiveness at Work," 35 *Personnel Psychology* 141, 146 (1982).

in which cost is negatively related to time and benefit positively related to it.[27] Not only is it cheaper to brush one's teeth after brushing has become habitual, but to stop brushing (maybe in response to convincing evidence that it was actually bad for one's teeth) would make one uncomfortable. Breaking a habit, like breaking an addiction (an extreme example of habit), causes withdrawal symptoms, though in the case of a mere habit they usually are slight and fleeting. Working can be habit-forming. But with the approach of old age the "habit" becomes a very expensive one, both in greater effort and (assuming that age and time on the job are highly correlated) in boredom. Habit-formation is one way in which "learning by doing" works; tasks are performed more quickly and with less effort when they become habitual. But the other side of the coin is that habitual activity can become boring. So not only can learning by doing soon encounter steeply diminishing returns (the peak of the learning curve may be quickly reached); the returns can turn negative when habitual work becomes drudge work.

Another significance of habit for the economics of old age is that the work routines, methods, and practices of the older worker, having become habitual, would be difficult for him to change even if there were no age-related decline in fluid intelligence. Habit thus provides an additional reason for expecting old workers to be less flexible, less adaptable to changed circumstances, less likely to learn "new tricks," than younger ones.

3. The fact that at some point a person is likely to find himself retired is no more surprising than that infants are not employed. The very young and the very old have a negative marginal product of work; marginal product and income are generally positively correlated; and the lower a person's income from work, the more likely he is to choose leisure or have it chosen for him. A more interesting question is why so many people go from full-time work to retirement overnight, rather than reducing their work continuously. Not all do. Partial retirement is common.[28] An example discussed in subsequent chapters is the tapered retirement offered federal judges on attractive terms ("senior status"). Norway and Sweden have government programs in which workers approaching (Sweden) or just past (Norway) the normal retirement age can receive a partial pension in return for work-

27. Gary S. Becker, "Habits, Addictions, and Traditions," 45 *Kyklos* 327, 336 (1992); Marcel Boyer, "Rational Demand and Expenditures Pattern under Habit Formation," 31 *Journal of Economic Theory* 27 (1983).

28. Christopher J. Ruhm, "Bridge Jobs and Partial Retirement," 8 *Journal of Labor Economics* 482, 490–493 (1990).

ing fewer hours.[29] Still, "sudden" retirement is very common. The suddenness of the transition is understandable, however, if there are economies of scale to leisure[30] that offset any diminishing marginal utility of leisure, and if fringe benefits and other employer labor costs do not fall as fast as the fall in output from the employee's switching from full-time to part-time work. Imagine that each part-time worker required his own office, so that two part-time workers would cost the employer the expense of two offices whereas one full-time worker doing the work of the two part-timers would cost the expense of only one office. Since switching to part-time employment would therefore entail a reduction in the wage rate to compensate the employer for the higher office expense per worker, the employee's total income from work, being the product of the hourly wage and the number of hours worked, would fall faster than the reduction in working time.[31] At the same time, his nonpecuniary income from leisure would soar if he retired. Retirement would raise both the number of hours of leisure and, because of economies of scale in leisure, the utility of each leisure hour.

4. One might think that if most work does not produce nonpecuniary income comparable to that of leisure, the secular increase in pecuniary incomes must imply a falling average age of retirement because of diminishing marginal utility of income. Not necessarily. As I pointed out in chapter 2, higher wages[32] increase the opportunity cost of leisure at the same time that they reduce the marginal utility of pecuniary income. The first effect, the substitution effect, favors later retirement; the second effect, the income effect, favors earlier retirement. The drop in the retirement age in recent decades suggests that the income effect predominates, and there is independent evidence for this,[33] although other factors have been at work as well, as we shall see in subsequent chapters.

29. Helen Ginsburg, "Flexible and Partial Retirement for Norwegian and Swedish Workers," *Monthly Labor Review,* Oct. 1985, p. 33.

30. As argued in John D. Owen, *The Price of Leisure: An Economic Analysis of the Demand for Leisure Time* 72 (1969).

31. Robert L. Clark, Stephan F. Gohmann, and Daniel A. Sumner, "Wages and Hours of Work of Elderly Men," *Atlantic Economic Journal,* December 1984, p. 31, finds that for elderly men a 10 percent increase in the number of hours worked increases their average hourly wage rate by only 6 percent.

32. Contrary to popular belief, hourly wage rates have been rising since the 1960s. The trend has been obscured by the fact that standard methods of computing hourly wages, for example by dividing a weekly wage by 40, overlook a decline in the number of hours worked. F. Thomas Juster and Frank P. Stafford, "The Allocation of Time: Empirical Findings, Behavioral Models, and Problems of Measurement," 29 *Journal of Economic Literature* 471, 493–494 (1991).

33. Owen, note 30 above, at 121. See also references in chapter 2, note 36.

One Self or Multiple Selves?

The concept of multiple selves explained. When age-related changes in the individual, as distinct from changes in the location of an unchanging individual on the continuum between birth and death, are brought into the economic analysis of aging, one of the most elementary assumptions of conventional economic analysis becomes problematic. This is the assumption that a person is a single economic decision-maker throughout his lifetime. The idea that the individual can be modeled as a locus of competing selves (simultaneous or successive) is not new,[34] but it remains esoteric and is disregarded in most economic analysis. For example, economists who argue against awarding tort damages for nonpecuniary losses caused by severely disabling personal injuries because the utility of wealth is likely to be reduced in the disabled state[35]—as shown by the fact that people generally don't insure against such losses—are implicitly and uncritically adopting the standpoint of the pre-injured self, the one who makes the insurance decision. The injured self may want to spend heavily to offset so far as he is able the effects of the injury even though he has no hope of achieving the same utility that his pre-injured "predecessor" self enjoyed.[36]

The fact that the marginal utility of wealth is lower in the injured state—the fulcrum of the economic criticism of such damages awards—is

34. Illustrative discussions from different disciplines are Thomas C. Schelling, "Self-Command in Practice, in Policy, and in a Theory of Rational Choice," 74 *American Economic Review* 1, 6–10 (May 1984 Papers and Proceedings issue); Derek Parfit, *Reasons and Persons* (1984), esp. 305–306; Allen E. Buchanan and Dan W. Brock, *Deciding for Others: The Ethics of Surrogate Decision Making,* ch. 3 (1989); Elizabeth S. Scott, "Rational Decisionmaking about Marriage and Divorce," 76 *Virginia Law Review* 9, 59–62 (1990); George Ainslie, *Picoeconomics: The Strategic Interaction of Successive Motivational States within the Person* 29 (1992). The seminal economic paper is R. H. Strotz, "Myopia and Inconsistency in Dynamic Utility Maximization," 23 *Review of Economic Studies* 165, 173 (1955–1956). Analytically, the conflict between successive selves is similar to the conflict between generations with regard to the rate of saving (the higher the rate of saving, the more the current generation is conferring a benefit on future generations at the expense of the current one), the subject of a large literature in economics. See, for example, E. S. Phelps and R. A. Pollak, "On Second-Best National Saving and Game-Equilibrium Growth," 35 *Review of Economic Studies* 185 (1968). Debraj Ray, "Nonpaternalistic Intergenerational Altruism, 41 *Journal of Economic Theory* 112 (1987).

35. See, for example, David Friedman, "What Is 'Fair Compensation' for Death or Injury?" 2 *International Review of Law and Economics* 81 (1982); Paul H. Rubin and John E. Calfee, "Consequences of Damage Awards for Hedonic and Other Nonpecuniary Losses," 5 *Journal of Forensic Economics* 249, 251 (1992).

36. A similar argument is made (independently) in Steven P. Croley and Jon D. Hanson, "The Nonpecuniary Costs of Accidents: Pain-and-Suffering Damages in Tort Law" 42–44 (unpublished, Michigan Law School and Harvard Law School, Oct. 28, 1994).

irrelevant in a Paretian analysis if the occupants of the two states are deemed two persons rather than one, because one person is being made better off at the expense of the other.[37] But it is worse than irrelevant; it is wrong. The marginal utility of wealth is lower to the injured self only because his utility is being evaluated by the pre-injured self. It is the marginal utility of the future self *to the present self* that the present self is calculating. It is like saying that the value of an education to a child is what the child's parent is willing to pay for the child's education. Unless the present self is so altruistic toward the future self that it values the future self's consumption as highly as its own, it will place a lower value on the utility of the future self than the latter would. Total utility might therefore be reduced if the tort system were altered to reduce the amount of tort damages payable to a severely disabled person, even if the reduction in liability for such damages brought about no change in the number of disabling accidents. Liability insurance rates would fall, a result quite likely to be preferred by the able-bodied self, but at the expense of utility in the disabled state and hence to the detriment of the contingent disabled self.

Jon Elster has put the basic point well: "The absolute priority of the present is somewhat like my absolute priority over all other persons: I am I—while they are all 'out there.'"[38] Everyone knows that the farther in advance you invite an academic to attend a conference, the likelier he is to accept; yet when the date of the conference finally rolls around, he may bitterly regret his acceptance. Is he being irrational? I think not. Acceptance confers an immediate benefit, that of doing something that another person (who may be in a position to reciprocate) wants, or, equivalently, of avoiding disappointing another person. The cost is borne by a future self, and the farther in advance the invitation is tendered, the more tenuously connected to our present self will be the self who bears the cost. Granted, this is not the only possible explanation for "invitation regret." Others are that the long lead time is a signal of just how much the invitee's attendance is desired, and that it makes a plausible excuse (existing commitments of one kind or another) more difficult to concoct. Still, the multipleness of one's selves is one factor in the decision to accept an invitation that one knows one will regret later.

The principal applications of multiple-selves analysis have been to addiction, weakness of will, regret, self-deception, and, as we shall see in

---

37. The criticism remains valid in cases in which the tort victim is killed or is rendered permanently unconscious.

38. Jon Elster, *Ulysses and the Sirens: Studies in Rationality and Irrationality* 71 (1979).

chapter 10, voluntary euthanasia, rather than to old age.[39] This neglect is surprising. Aging brings about such large changes in the individual that there may well come a point at which it is more illuminating to think of two or more persons "time-sharing" the same identity than of one person having different preferences, let alone one person having the same preferences, over the entire life cycle. The tendency remarked by psychologists and some economists to give greater weight in making intertemporal choices to present pains and pleasures than seems rational[40] is entirely rational if the present self is seen as distinct from our future or contingent selves and naturally inclined to weight its own interests more heavily than those of these other persons,[41] albeit persons with whom it is linked by strong bonds of altruism based on continuity of identity. When elderly people are asked what they would do differently if they could relive their lives, their most emphatic answer is that they would get more education.[42] The costs of education (primarily forgone income from working) are concentrated in one's young years; the benefits are received over many years. So it is just the area in which one would expect the young self to underspend from the standpoint of the old self.

The normative use of the multiple-self concept attacked and defended. There are objections to the use of the concept of multiple selves, whether in the normative ("welfare economics") or in the positive analysis of old age. I begin with the normative. It can be argued that if young and old are different selves, so are the 20-year-old self and the 40-year-old self, or for that matter the 20-year-old self and the 21-year-old self, or the 65-year-old self and the 66-year-old self. We could end up with as many selves per person as there are years of life—or months of life, or perhaps hours of life. The concept of the person, in particular of the responsible person, would disappear. We would lose all purchase for arguing against becoming the wards of the state for the sake of our numerous future selves, for whom we cannot be trusted to make adequate provision.

39. I have found only two discussions, both very brief, of possible applications to aging. Daniel Wikler, "Ought the Young Make Health Care Decisions for Their Aged Selves?" 13 *Journal of Medicine and Philosophy* 57, 62–63 (1988); Michael Lockwood, "Identity Matters," in *Medicine and Moral Reasoning* 60, 64–65 (K. W. M. Fulford, Grant R. Gillett, and Janet Martin Soskice, eds., 1994).

40. See, for example, the essays in *Choice over Time* (George Loewenstein and Jon Elster, eds., 1992).

41. Cf. Ian Steedman and Ulrich Krause, "Goethe's *Faust,* Arrow's Possibility Theorem and the Individual Decision-Taker," in *The Multiple Self* 197, 204–207 (Jon Elster, ed., 1986).

42. Mary Kay DeGenova, "If You Had Your Life to Live Over Again: What Would You Do Differently?" 34 *International Journal of Aging and Human Development* 135 (1992).

This reductio ad absurdum points to real problems with using the concept of multiple selves to define the relation between the individual and the state. But there is a big difference of degree between, on the one hand, adjacent successive selves, so to speak, and on the other hand the young and old self separated by many intermediate successive selves, just as there is a big difference in degree, recognized in countless laws and social practices, between one's self as a child and one's self as an adult. Once when my mother was a vigorous woman of 65 or so she noticed a very frail old woman in a wheelchair and said to my wife, "If I ever become like that, shoot me." Two decades later she had become just like that but she did not express any desire to die; and while by that time she had become moderately demented she had not yet reached the stage at which it was no longer possible for an observer to know whether she wanted to live or die. I do not think that the change in her outlook was just a matter of her having exchanged outside for inside knowledge. Her younger self, had it been perched on a cloud, looking on, might well have found my mother's confinement to a wheelchair, and failing mental powers, an even worse fate than it had expected.[43] Aging changed my mother so much that she acquired a totally different outlook, becoming a stranger to her younger self.

Here is another way to see this point. Suppose you were convinced that senile people are happy, like children, or that very elderly but not senile people enjoy the garrulity, penny-pinching, and other characteristic but (to the nonelderly) negative characteristics of being old, discussed in the next chapter. In fact, amazing as it may seem to the young and the middle-aged, elderly people often *are* happier than nonelderly people, as we shall also see. Would knowing this make you more or less eager to survive to old age? I expect it would make you less eager, by amplifying the gulf in values and preferences between your current self and your contingent future elderly self.

For it is not a lack of information that drives a wedge between the young and the old self. If it were, then as the number of very old people, nursing homes, geriatric specialists, and so forth increased, as has been happening, young people would find the prospect of becoming old less depressing. They would understand better that most old people really do want to keep on living and do actually enjoy life as distinct from merely dreading death. No such change in the outlook of the young is discernible.

Some corroboration for this analysis is furnished by the monotonic decline with age in the percentage of Americans who believe that it is

---

43. I complete the story of my mother in chapter 11.

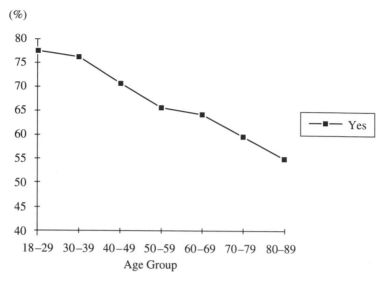

(%)

Figure 4.2 Is it proper to allow incurable patients to die?

proper to allow patients with an incurable disease to die, shown in figure 4.2.[44] Young people are much more likely to believe that it is proper, because they discount the utility of their future contingent diseased self.

Was the preference of my mother's younger self for not surviving into an infirm old age more authentic than the opposite preference of her older self? As a practical matter, of course, the younger self, controlling as it does the body, can impose many of its preferences on the older self, while the older self has no control over the younger. But I cannot find anything in economic theory that tells me whether this practical control should be elevated into a legal or moral right, entitling us for example to commit ourselves when young to die when we reach the age of 85 rather than be required to save for retirement. If my mother had been told what she would become, she would have been distressed at the prospect, just as I am distressed at the prospect, against which I cannot effectively contract (see chapter 10), of someday becoming senile. I am not saying that total utility is maximized by giving one's future selves "rights" against one's present self. I am saying that welfare economics does not provide an answer to the question whether future selves should be considered members of the com-

44. The data used in figure 4.2 are from the General Social Survey (GSS) conducted by the University of Chicago's National Opinion Research Center between 1988 and 1993. These and the other GSS data in this book were furnished to me by the Center through the good offices of Tom Smith.

munity whose utility is to be taken into account, along with the utility of the present self, by the community's legal and ethical rules.

This is a typical shortcoming of welfare economics. Even if welfare economics is thought to provide normative guidance in the form of a direction to government to try to maximize the total utility or total wealth of society, it cannot answer the question of what the boundaries of the society are. Should fetuses be included or not? What about the unborn generally? And therefore what about a person's future selves? I know of no other body of thought that offers a satisfactory answer to the question either. It is conventional enough to treat society as an aggregation of potential future persons as well as of those currently living—to suppose for example that we living Americans have some duty to hand on a habitable planet to our successors—although only that tiny subset of utilitarians that believes in maximizing total rather than average utility thinks we must weight the utility of potential future persons equally with that of us the living. But there one is speaking of future individuals, most of them strangers to us, rather than of our own successive selves, of whom we might be supposed adequate trustees—but perhaps not, if old and not old really do have different values, as in the example of my mother. And while it would be odd to weight the utility of the unborn equally with that of the living (something not done even by opponents of abortion),[45] most people would also think it odd to give no weight at all to the interests of future persons in making decisions about public expenditures on education or about the protection of the environment. If so, this could be thought to imply some duty to our future selves as well as to future individuals utterly distinct from ourselves; indeed the former might seem the clearer duty. But what exactly is the duty? The dilemma is that if the boundary of the community is drawn to include all contingent selves, as distinct from just current selves, it is too wide, while if it is drawn to exclude all but current selves, it is too narrow.

The concept of multiple selves will be resisted by those who believe that a proper human life is one lived in accordance with a rational plan of life,[46] implying continuous rather than punctuated selfhood.[47] Yet the integration of one's successive selves, all entitled to respect and consideration,

---

45. Richard A. Posner, *Sex and Reason* 280–281 (1992).

46. For the philosophical version, see John Rawls, *A Theory of Justice* 407–416 (1971). For the economic version, see Steven M. Goldman, "Consistent Plans," 47 *Review of Economic Studies* 533 (1980), and studies cited there.

47. "Rationality implies an impartial concern for all parts of our life." Rawls, note 46 above, at 293. "In the case of the individual, pure time preference is irrational: it means that he is not viewing all moments as equally parts of one life." Id. at 295.

seems as challenging and worthy a project for reflective human beings as drawing up and acting in conformity to a life plan for a single self. I grant that the question who is to do the integrating is a difficult one. The very question implies the existence of some master self, or even more obscurely of bargaining among the successive selves, perhaps behind some veil of ignorance. But the difficulties are merely concealed by ignoring the multiplicity of selves. The content of a rational life plan is a function of the age at which the plan is deemed to have been adopted. A plan that is impartial among the stages of life will be in effect the plan that integrates our successive selves.

We must be careful not to push the concept of multiple selves to the point of saying that an old person may not be punished for crimes he committed when young because they are different selves. The pragmatic reason is that such a policy would reduce the effect of the threat of punishment in deterring crime; and indeed one value of the concept of multiple selves lies in redirecting analysis from ideological battles over paternalism to pragmatic consideration of consequences. Similarly we ought not allow people to repudiate long-term contracts they made when they were young, for then most mortgages would be unenforceable, and the young would suffer. But if, therefore, old selves have duties, maybe they should have rights as well, which the state should protect, as through social security.

Yet, contrary to the example of social security, not all the implications of multiple-selves analysis are *dirigiste*. For example, the analysis highlights the arbitrariness, already noted in chapter 3, of taxing bequests heavily. A bequest reallocates consumption from one's present self to a vicarious future self, that of one's children or other heirs when one dies, and is thus no different in principle from saving for one's old age, a "bequest" by one's younger to one's older self. Some people are more altruistic toward their heirs than toward their own future selves; why should they be penalized by being taxed more heavily?

The utility of the concept of multiple selves in positive analysis. The concept of multiple selves has the methodological advantage of enlarging the domain of rational-choice analysis. This is important because rational behavior is easier to model, and to make empirically testable predictions concerning, than irrational behavior. Yet in tension with this point the most powerful objection to using the concept of multiple selves for positive analysis is precisely that it adds nothing useful to conventional economic analysis. In evaluating this objection, I find it helpful to draw an analogy to the concept of the firm. For many—until relatively recently for most—

purposes in economics it is quite adequate to treat the firm as if it were a single individual (a single "self") rather than as a collection of different individuals. This would be true for example if we wanted to predict the effect of an increase in the cigarette excise tax on the price and output of cigarettes. It would not be true if we wanted to predict the effect of a law altering the composition of the board of directors of corporations that manufacture cigarettes or placing a limit on executive salaries. To complicate analysis by departing from simple albeit unrealistic assumptions requires justification, however—for example, by showing that the more complicated analysis yields a richer set of empirically testable implications or has greater explanatory power. As the example of the firm shows, for some purposes the more complicated model *is* necessary. Let us consider whether the aging person is another example.

We might say, returning to my mother, that all she meant by her dramatic mode of expression was that she rationally forecast a very low, but not necessarily zero or negative, net utility from life in extreme old age. This would imply not that she wanted to make a legally enforceable suicide contract but that she intended to minimize her investment in longevity. She might also have intended to reduce her level of saving for old age, on the ground that (assuming no strong bequest motive) the utility of income received by her in extreme old age would be very low.[48] But this account is not complete. When my mother expressed dismay at the sight of the frail old lady in the wheelchair, she was not making a guess about the state of mind of that woman (a complete stranger), who in fact evinced no signs of being unhappy. My mother was evaluating the situation of the woman from the standpoint of my mother's current self.

A number of phenomena are illuminated by a model of the individual as a locus of successive selfish selves: the revulsion that we feel at the idea of enforcing against an unwilling person a contract to die if some future condition specified in the contract comes to pass, such as becoming senile (see chapter 10); the fact that discount rates of young and middle-aged persons are much higher than necessary to take account of the risk of death, and, what is closely related, the rather meager provision that most people make for their future and other contingent selves; the age-related decline in discount rates, which I mentioned earlier in this chapter; the different atti-

---

48. An important general point implied by this discussion is that increases in longevity need not result in increases in savings and may even result in higher discount rates, if because of the infirmities and disabilities of old age people anticipate a low level of utility from expenditures on consumption in old age.

tudes of old and young toward letting people with incurable diseases die (see figure 4.2); tort law's willingness to award substantial damages for the cutting off of a future elderly life (see chapter 12); even the tendency of elderly persons to pinch pennies (chapter 6). The first example, that of refusing to enforce a contract to die, may seem equivocal, as enforcement would be refused even if the change of mind occurred within hours or days of the signing of the contract. But all that this shows is that in some settings we are discouraged from killing even our immediate future selves.

Let me elaborate on the point about the discount (or interest) rate.[49] Even at a discount rate of only 2 percent, the present value of $1 to be received in 40 years is only 45 cents. Yet a 30-year-old has a much better than 45 percent chance of surviving to the age of 70—has in fact almost a 75 percent chance.[50] At a discount rate of 4 percent, the present value of $1 to be received in 40 years is only 21 cents. The "real" (that is, setting aside inflation) risk-free (other than the risk of mortality) interest rate demanded by the market is probably between 2 and 4 percent.[51] This implies that people are weighting their present consumption far more heavily than their future consumption (after adjusting for mortality), which is just what one expects if the present self and the future self are, in some meaningful sense, separate persons.

An alternative explanation, also consistent with the assumption of rationality, for some of these phenomena is that the costs of imagining future states of the world impede people in obtaining an accurate, vivid picture of future pleasures (and pains). Rational people, being able to invest "imagination capital" to reduce these costs, will, in order to maximize their utility, devote more resources to enhancing the presentness of pleasurable future states than that of painful ones.[52] A good example of a phenomenon explained by this approach, though not one the authors discuss, is the fact that people do not want to know the date on which they will die, even though

49. A discount rate and an interest rate are the same thing, the rate at which present and future costs or benefits are made equivalent. One speaks of a discount rate when one is interested in the present value of some future receipt or expenditure, and an interest rate when one is interested in the future amount into which a present investment or obligation will grow.

50. Computed from *Monthly Vital Statistics Report,* Sept. 28, 1993, p. 16 (tab. 6).

51. See, for example, L. T. Evans, S. P. Keef, and J. Okunev, "Modelling Real Interest Rates," 18 *Journal of Banking and Finance* 153, 157 (1994); Tong-sheng Sun, "Real and Nominal Interest Rates: A Discrete-Time Model and Its Continuous-Time Limit," 5 *Review of Financial Studies* 581, 605 (1992); T. Michael Kashner, "Present-Future Gratification Tradeoffs: Does Economics Validate Psychometric Studies?" 11 *Journal of Economic Psychology* 247, 263 (1990).

52. Gary S. Becker and Casey B. Mulligan, "On the Endogenous Determination of Time Preference" (unpublished, University of Chicago Dept. of Economics, July 20, 1994).

the knowledge would be immensely helpful in making a variety of decisions, such as how much to invest in one's human capital. Knowing the date of one's death would make one's death more vivid, more easily envisaged, creating, therefore, present disutility. In the imagination-capital model, just as in the multiple-selves model, "excessive" discounting of unpleasant future states, such as death or a bleak old age, is consistent with, even implied by, rationality.

It remains to be seen which approach will prove to be more useful in the positive analysis of old age (not the focus of the Becker-Mulligan paper). But at the very least the concept of multiple selves is a useful reminder of the limitations of expected-utility maximizing as a normative tool. It will play a role in part 3 of this book with respect to issues ranging from voluntary euthanasia of elderly persons to tort damages for the death of such persons. The normative use of the concept also has a positive dimension, as I have already suggested. It helps explain society's refusal to enforce every irrevocable commitment that people make and its efforts to discourage certain behaviors, such as drug addiction, that may seriously injure future selves.

One final qualification: I am not contending that a person's younger and older selves are, in fact, different persons. There is no fact of the matter,[53] just as there is no fact of the matter as to whether a firm is a single entity or a collection of individuals. The concept of multiple selves is a device for drawing attention to a problem with methods of analysis, economic and other, that assign decisive weight to the "individual's" preferences—for showing, for example, that economics, so often derided for taking too "atomistic" a view of human behavior, is sometimes not atomistic enough. For some purposes, such as evaluating a proposal to allow people to commit themselves to die upon the coming to pass of a specified future contingency, it is fruitful to think of the present self and the future self as two persons. For other purposes, however, such as evaluating a proposal to allow elderly people to repudiate obligations made when they were young, it is more fruitful to think of the present and the future self as one person. This dualism about selfhood is reflected in our language. Most of the time we treat the self as a unity from birth to death, but not infrequently we depart from the unitary model and say such things as, "I am not the man I

---

53. Or so I believe. For a powerful argument (not concerned with aging, however) that "persons" are (approximately) a natural kind, and not merely a social construct, see David Wiggins, *Sameness and Substance* 37 and ch. 6 (1980).

was," or "I am in two minds about the matter," or "X is a Jekyll and Hyde," or "I wasn't myself when I did that." [54] When we speak thus we are not, I contend, "merely" being metaphorical.

This chapter has covered a lot of ground, and a brief summary may be in order. The emphasis has been on the significance for the human-capital model of the life cycle of assuming, realistically and indeed unavoidably, that as people get older they change. The earliest change in adulthood is a shift in the balance between fluid intelligence (facility at abstract reasoning and at the acquisition of new skills and capacities) and crystallized intelligence (concrete reasoning based on one's established knowledge base) as the individual accrues experience and his fluid intelligence begins to decline. As a small example, this shift should lead, other things being equal, to an even younger average age of immigrants to countries in which the language is different from that of the immigrant's native land.

Later—and, as we shall see in subsequent chapters, at very different ages depending on the field of activity—the individual undergoes a more general decline in vocationally relevant capabilities, along with neutral but significant changes such as an acceleration of the rate at which time is felt to pass. This change, along with the pervasive factor of selection bias, may explain the empirical evidence that discount rates fall with age. Selection bias is also the key to explaining—and in fact explaining away—the studies that find no age-related decline in workers' performance. Workers no longer able to perform to their employers' expectations because of age are weeded out and so do not show up in such studies.

The significance of age-related decline for the age of retirement and for other job-related behaviors depends critically on the distance between peak age capability and the employer's required capability and on the rate of decline from the peak. Because of differences between "job" requirements in the period when human beings became adapted to their environment through the operation of natural selection, and job requirements in the very different environment of today, peak capabilities frequently exceed occupationally required capabilities. As a result of this phenomenon of "excess capability," a worker may be able to perform to his employer's satisfaction long after the worker has passed his peak, although the employer may use promotions, and less frequently demotions, to exploit the

---

54. "Was't Hamlet wrong'd Laertes? Never Hamlet. / If Hamlet from himself be ta'en away, / And when he's not himself does wrong Laertes, / Then Hamlet does it not." *Hamlet,* act V, sc. ii, ll. 229–232.

curve of the workers' capabilities more completely. Elite occupations are those in which the employer's required capability is close to the worker's peak, and in these occupations we expect much earlier retirement, de facto or de jure, than in other fields.

Although up to a point a worker can compensate for age-related decline by working harder, the added effort is a cost; and as the costs of work rise, retirement becomes more attractive. The nonpecuniary utilities as well as disutilities of work influence the age of retirement—so it tends to be earlier in dirty or dangerous jobs—as do the nonpecuniary utilities and disutilities of retirement itself, the worker's discount rate, and the income and substitution effects of rising wage rates. A neglected age-related source of nonpecuniary disutility of work is cumulative boredom, or, what is related but distinct, burnout due to cumulative stress. Like the acceleration in the rate at which subjective time passes, boredom and burnout as functions of time illustrate changes in the individual that while not aspects of decline can profoundly affect the behavior of aging persons. Finally, economies of scale in leisure, and the fixed component in employers' labor costs, help explain why retirement tends to be abrupt rather than tapered.

The change in the individual between youth and old age is so profound that it becomes plausible to imagine the individual's young and old selves as different persons, "time-sharing" the same body. The concept of multiple selves can be used to explain a number of phenomena, such as why discount rates tend to be much higher than necessary to take account of the risk of death, implying that the current self weights its utility much more heavily than that of a future self; why (a related point) many people make only meager provision for their old age; and why society refuses to enforce every irrevocable commitment that a person might want to make. The concept can also be used—though here great caution is necessary—to justify, nonpaternalistically, the conferral of certain rights on the future self against the selfishness of the current self.

Part Two

The Economic Theory
Elaborated and Applied

5

The Economic Psychology of the Old

Economists usually take values, preferences, and attitudes for granted and consider how, with them as givens, a rational actor, young or old, can maximize his utility by the choices that he makes of where to live, what occupation to follow, whom to marry, and so forth. I take a different tack here, and consider the extent to which the psychology of the old might fruitfully be modeled as a consequence rather than foundation of rational choice. I do not argue that old people always or even often make *conscious* choices as to whether, for example, to talk more and listen less than when they were young. I argue only that certain choices, conscious or unconscious, appear to be rational in the sense of utility maximizing, once the fundamental attributes of being old are understood. Many old people, of course, have serious mental problems which prevent rational choices, and my discussion excludes such people. Nor do I believe that all aspects of the psychology of the old can be given satisfactory economic explanations. Genetics, for example, will play a role in my attempt to explain that psychology.

The psychology of the old has received sustained, but on the whole rather pitiless, attention from the literary imagination,[1] although there are conspicuous exceptions, of which my personal favorites are the depiction

---

1. For anthologies and reviews of the literature on old age, see *The Oxford Book of Aging: Reflections on the Journey of Life* (Thomas R. Cole and Mary G. Winkler, eds., 1994); *The Art of Growing Older: Writers on Living and Aging* (Wayne Booth, ed., 1992); Simone de Beauvoir, *Old Age,* ch. 3 (1972); David H. Fowler, Lois Josephs Fowler, and Lois Lamdin, "Themes of Old Age in Preindustrial Western Literature," in *Old Age in Preindustrial Society* 19 (Peter D. Stearns, ed., 1982).

of the octogenarian Jolyon Forsyte in the first volume of John Galsworthy's *Forsyte Saga* and the depiction of the narrator's grandmother in *The Remembrance of Things Past*. On the pitiless side we recall from *As You Like It* man's "second childishness, and mere oblivion, / Sans teeth, sans eyes, sans taste, sans everything;" from *Much Ado about Nothing* the crack "When the age is in, the wit is out;" and from *Hamlet* the ridicule heaped on old age in the person of Polonius. We recall the senescent Lear—a magnificent ruin, but a ruin nevertheless—and, moving on from Shakespeare, the Struldbruggs of *Gulliver's Travels;* Keats's "few, sad, last grey hairs" shaken by palsy; T. S. Eliot's catalog of the gifts reserved to age, such as the "cold friction of expiring sense" and the "rending pain of reenactment / Of all that you have done, and been;" and Yeats's fulminations against old age ("this absurdity . . . this caricature, / Decrepit age that has been tied to me / As to a dog's tail").

The Eliot quotation is from "Little Gidding," the last of *Four Quartets,* a poem sequence that employs aging as a symbol of the temporal world, contrasted by Eliot, to its disadvantage, with the timeless world. In "East Coker," another of the poems in *Four Quartets,* we read: "Do not let me hear / Of the wisdom of old men, but rather of their folly, / Their fear of fear and frenzy, their fear of possession, / Of belonging to another, or to others, or to God." The Yeats quotation is from "The Tower," where he describes old age as "a kind of battered kettle at the heel" and as "the wreck of body, / Slow decay of blood, / Testy delirium / Or dull decrepitude, / Or what worse evil come— / The death of friends, or death / Of every brilliant eye / That made a catch in the breath." Yeats was 63 in 1928, when he wrote "The Tower."[2] In another great poem of this period, "Among School Children," also written when Yeats was in his early sixties, he called himself "a comfortable kind of old scarecrow," and asked rhetorically: "What youthful mother, a shape upon her lap / Honey of generation had betrayed . . . Would think her son, did she but see that shape / With sixty or more winters on its head, / A compensation for the pang of his birth, / Or the uncertainty of his setting forth?"

Even the defiant cry of Tennyson's aged Ulysses[3]—

2. But Eliot's early poem of old age, "Gerontion," published when he was in his early thirties, shows that you don't have to be old to write perceptively about old age

3. Faintly echoing Cicero, *De Senectute,* ch. X, § 32. Written when Cicero was 84, *De Senectute* (the full title is *Cato Maior de Senectute*) is one of the classics of upbeat writing on old age. Against Cicero we might set the following laconic summary by a distinguished modern classicist: "I have sought, but have not found, aspects of old age which compensate for its ills." Kenneth Dover, *Marginal Comment: A Memoir* 243 (1994).

> Old age hath yet his honour and his toil;
> Death closes all: but something ere the end,
> Some work of noble note may yet be done,
> Not unbecoming men that strove with Gods.
>
> . . . .
>
> Though much is taken, much abides; and though
> We are not now that strength which in old days
> Moved earth and heaven, that which we are, we are:
> One equal temper of heroic hearts,
> Made weak by time and fate, but strong in will
> To strive, to seek, to find, and not to yield

—has a certain weary and bleak tone, scant comfort to those of us who cannot say that we "strove with Gods." And, as a companion piece to "Ulysses," Tennyson wrote "Tithonus"—a poem about the man who, like the Cumaean Sibyl (Eliot's and Waugh's "handful of dust"), had the misfortune to receive the gift of immortality without an accompanying gift of eternal youth. In the epigraph of Eliot's great poem "The Waste Land," the Sibyl is asked what she wants. She answers, "I want to die."

Aristotle on Old Age

In the section of the *Rhetoric* from which I quoted in the Introduction, Aristotle has a remarkable description of "the character of elderly men— men who are past their prime."[4] Writing more than two millennia before the term "political correctness" entered the lexicon, he minces no words. His discussion is frankly stereotypical; as befits a treatise on rhetoric, which must point the reader to characteristic features of its subject, features that the speaker's audience will recognize, its focus is on central tendencies rather than on individual variations. It is not the complete truth about the old, but it is, I think, like the characteristic or if you will stereotypical literary depiction of old age, an important part of the truth. It is the part that tends nowadays to be suppressed because we live in an era of heightened sensitivity to any suggestion that any group defined by an unalterable char-

---

4. Aristotle, *Rhetoric*, bk. 2, ch. 12, in *The Complete Works of Aristotle*, vol. 2, pp. 2213–2215 (Jonathan Barnes, ed., 1984) (W. Rhys Roberts, trans.) (the page and column references to the Greek text are 1389a and 1390a). The Greek view of old age was not uniform, and Aristotle cannot be deemed its authoritative expositor. Its diversity is well brought out in Bessie Ellen Richardson, *Old Age among the Ancient Greeks: The Greek Portrayal of Old Age in Literature, Art, and Inscriptions* (1933).

acteristic such as race, sex, or age might be inferior to some other group, even if it is inferior only in its capacity for happiness.

Despite the prestige and enormous current interest in Aristotle, it may seem strange to use him as my authority on the psychology of aging, rather than modern psychologists. I shall be citing some modern psychological literature in this chapter, but I have been surprised by the relative paucity of studies on the effects of age on personality, character, and the emotions,[5] as distinct from the effects on reasoning ability and other strictly cognitive capacities. Remarkably, a number of the modern psychological studies of the effect of aging on personality find no significant effect.[6] The studies are not persuasive. They use categories such as "emotional stability," "information seeking" (in the broadest sense), and "friendliness" that do not correspond to areas in which age-related change is likely, such as openness to new ideas, caution, and pessimism.[7] Moreover, most of the studies are based on self-reporting by the participants,[8] and so the accuracy of the studies depends on the participants' having a high level of self-awareness. Aristotle's psychology of aging has not been superseded.

Aristotle tells us that because elderly men have lived a long time "they have often been taken in, and often made mistakes; and life on the whole is a bad business." As a result, "they are sure about nothing . . . They 'think,' but they never 'know.' " Experience has made them "cynical; that is, they tend to put the worse construction on everything," and distrustful. They are

5. For a review of the literature, see Nathan Kogan, "Personality and Aging," in *Handbook of the Psychology of Aging* 330 (James E. Birren and K. Warner Schaie, eds., 3d ed. 1990).

6. Dorothy Field, "Continuity and Change in Personality in Old Age—Evidence from Five Longitudinal Studies: Introduction to a Special Issue," 46 *Journal of Gerontology* P271 (1991). For illustrative such studies, see Paul T. Costa, Jr., Robert R. McCrae, and David Arenberg, "Recent Longitudinal Research on Personality and Aging," in Nathan W. Shock et al., *Normal Human Aging: The Baltimore Longitudinal Study of Aging* 171 (1984); Leonard M. Giambra, Cameron J. Camp, and Alicia Grodsky, "Curiosity and Stimulation Seeking across the Adult Life Span: Cross-Sectional and 6- and 8-Year Longitudinal Findings," 7 *Psychology and Aging* 150 (1992). For a contrary view, see Kogan, note 5 above, at 336.

7. One relevant category that Costa, McCrae, and Arenberg, note 6 above, do discuss is "masculinity"—and they find that it declines significantly with age. Id. at 191–192. Unfortunately the term is not defined; but presumably it encompasses the typical, or perhaps stereotypical, masculine traits, such as physical courage. (The study was limited to men.) For other evidence that personality changes with age when personality traits are carefully defined, see Joel Shanan, "Who and How: Some Unanswered Questions in Adult Development," 46 *Journal of Gerontology* P309, P313–P314 (1991).

8. One that is not is Dorothy Field and Roger E. Millsap, "Personality in Advanced Old Age: Continuity or Change?" 46 *Journal of Gerontology* P299 (1991). This study was based not on self-reporting but on personal interviews of a sample of aging persons, conducted 14 years apart by different interviewers, who reported their impressions. The use of different interviewers, while perhaps unavoidable, undermines the validity of the study.

also "small-minded, because they have been humbled by life: their desires are set upon nothing more exalted or unusual than what will help them to keep alive." This focus on keeping alive, together with bitter experience about how hard it is to get money and how easy it is to lose it, makes the elderly ungenerous and cowardly, "always anticipating danger." They are self-centered, too, guiding their lives too much by what is useful for them rather than by what is "noble"—by, that is, "what is good absolutely." Stated differently, "they guide their lives by reasoning more than by character; reasoning being directed to utility and character to excellence." "They are not shy, but shameless," feeling only "contempt for what people may think of them." "They lack confidence in the future; partly through experience—for most things go wrong, or anyhow turn out worse than one expects; and partly because of their cowardice." They are loquacious, "continually talking of the past, because they enjoy remembering it." "Their fits of anger are sudden but feeble." It is a mistake to suppose them "to have a self-controlled character; the fact is that their passions have slackened, and they are slaves to the love of gain." When they feel pity, they do so "out of weakness, imagining that anything that befalls anyone else might easily happen to them . . . Hence they are querulous, and not disposed to jesting or laughter." [9]

The aim of this chamber of horrors is not, however, to make us side with youth. Youth has many redeeming features (which age appears not to), but it is rich in its own foibles. Young people are hot-tempered and fickle, lack self-control, are preoccupied with honor and victory, are naively optimistic. "They look at the good side rather than the bad, not having yet witnessed many instances of wickedness. They trust others readily, because they have not yet often been cheated. They are sanguine . . . [because] they have as yet met with few disappointments." Their sanguine disposition makes them easily cheated, and together with their hot tempers makes them courageous: "the hot temper prevents fear, and the hopeful disposition creates confidence." And "they have exalted notions." "They think they know everything, and are always quite sure about it." [10]

We can see where this is leading: to a typically Aristotelian celebration of the mean, that is, of men in their prime:

> They have neither that excess of confidence which amounts to rashness, nor too much timidity, but the right amount of each. They neither trust everybody nor distrust everybody, but judge

9. Aristotle, note 4 above, at 2214–2215 (1389b–1390a in the Greek edition).
10. Id. at 2213–2214 (1389a–1389b).

people correctly. Their lives will be guided not by the sole consideration either of what is noble or of what is useful, but by both;
neither by parsimony nor by prodigality, but by what is fit and
proper . . . They will be brave as well as temperate, and temperate
as well as brave.[11]

Aristotle concludes by observing that "the body is in its prime from thirty
to thirty-five; the mind about forty-nine." [12]

The essential differences that Aristotle sees between young and old
are, first, that the young are optimistic and the old pessimistic;[13] the knowledge shift (that is, the changing balance between imagination and memory
as intellectual resources) involves an emotional and not merely a cognitive
change. Second, the old are more self-centered than the young.[14] They are
cowardly, putting their own safety above other goods; greedier than young
people; and "shameless"—they don't care whether people have a good
opinion of them.

What might explain these differences? (If nothing, we may be led to
wonder whether the description is adequate, or whether Aristotle isn't just
too preoccupied with finding means between undesirable extremes.)[15] Why
for example would the fact that the young rely more on imagination or
expectation in making judgments and the old more on experience or retro-
spection make the young optimistic and the old pessimistic?

11. Id. at 2215 (1390a–1390b).

12. Id. at 2215 (1390b). It is not known when Aristotle wrote the *Rhetoric*, but it has been
surmised that he worked on it between 340 and 335 B.C. (George A. Kennedy, "The Composition
of the *Rhetoric*," in Aristotle, *On Rhetoric: A Theory of Civic Discourse* 299, 301 [George A.
Kennedy, trans., 1990])—and he was 49 in 335.

13. For corroboration, see Carol D. Ryff, "Possible Selves in Adulthood and Old Age: A
Tale of Shifting Horizons," 6 *Psychology and Aging* 286, 293–294 (1991).

14. A longitudinal study of the vocabulary of a group of high-IQ lawyers (subjects of the
Terman Study of the Gifted) revealed during their seventies a shift in vocabulary from "the dyadic
activities of work and family to a slightly greater concern with soma and self—with one's own
functioning as an aging individual." Edwin Shneidman, "The Indian Summer of Life: A Prelimi-
nary Study of Septuagenarians," 44 *American Psychologist* 684, 692 (1989).

15. But we can at least acquit him of the charge of lacking sufficient empathy or inwardness
(not having been an old man when he wrote the *Rhetoric*) by recalling the elderly Montaigne's
assessment of old age, written from the inside: "We do not so much give up our vices as change
them, and in my opinion for the worse. Besides a foolish and tottering pride, a tedious garrulity,
prickly and unsociable moods, superstition, and an absurd preoccupation with money after we
have lost the use for it, I find in old age an increase of envy, injustice, and malice. It stamps more
wrinkles on our minds than on our faces, and seldom, or very rarely, does one find souls that do
not acquire, as they age, a sour and musty smell." "On Repentance," in Michel de Montaigne,
Essays 235, 250 (J. M. Cohen, trans., 1958). See also Beauvoir, note 1 above, pt. 2 (1972). For a
contrasting view, see Erik H. Erikson, Joan M. Erikson, and Helen Q. Kivnick, *Vital Involvement
in Old Age,* pt. 2 (1986).

The answer may lie in the fact that people are *naturally* optimistic. Charles Sanders Peirce argued that

> we seem to be so constituted that in the absence of any facts to go upon we are happy and self-satisfied; so that the effect of experience is continually to contract our hopes and aspirations. Yet a lifetime of the application of this corrective does not usually eradicate our sanguine disposition. Where hope is unchecked by any experience, it is likely that our optimism is extravagant. Logicality in regard to practical matters . . . is the most useful quality an animal can possess, and might, therefore, result from the operation of natural selection; but outside of these it is probably of more advantage to the animal to have his mind filled with pleasing and encouraging visions, independently of their truth; and thus, upon unpractical subjects, natural selection might occasion a fallacious tendency of thought.[16]

If Peirce is right that a limited tendency to view the world through rose-tinted glasses has survival characteristics and so is plausibly a part of our genetic endowment, we would expect the tendency to be blunted by experience, since experience would demonstrate that our youthful optimism was indeed excessive. Experience and age are positively correlated, so that the effect of experience in grinding down natural but exaggerated optimism would be to make the old more pessimistic than the young. The tendency would be furthered by the shifting balance between anticipated gains and anticipated losses as one ages; the older one is, the less likely is the future balance to be positive.[17] Pessimism in turn would imply a reluctance to take risks, financial or otherwise, because the old will have learned that it is silly to think oneself "lucky." This implies that in areas in which mistakes of

16. Charles S. Peirce, *Essays in the Philosophy of Science* 7–8 (Vincent Tomas, ed., 1957). To similar effect, see Lionel Tiger, *Optimism: The Biology of Hope* (1979), esp. p. 168; Martin E. P. Seligman, *Learned Optimism* 108 (1991); cf. Lauren B. Alloy and Lyn Y. Abramson, "Depressive Realism: Four Theoretical Perspectives," in *Cognitive Processes in Depression* 233, 256–257 (Lauren B. Alloy, ed., 1988). Seligman points out that the prevalence of depression suggests that a pessimistic outlook has survival qualities also: "there is clear evidence that nondepressed people distort reality in a self-serving direction and depressed people tend to see reality accurately." Seligman, above, at 111–115. See also Alloy and Abramson, above; Mark D. Evans and Steven D. Hollon, "Patterns of Personal and Causal Inference: Implications for the Cognitive Theory of Depression," in *Cognitive Processes in Depression,* above, at 344, 353–356. Nevertheless, far more people are nondepressed-optimistic than depressed-pessimistic. For example, "80 percent of American men think they are in the top half of social skills." Seligman, above, at 109.

17. Paul B. Baltes, Jacqui Smith, and Ursula M. Staudinger, "Wisdom and Successful Aging," 39 *Nebraska Symposium on Motivation* 123, 145–147 (1992).

optimism impose heavier social costs than mistakes of pessimism, responsibility should be entrusted to old rather than to young people.

A related point is that we can expect the old to be more "realistic" than the young,[18] more aware of human limitations and the operation of contingency, and therefore "wiser" in the sense that contrasts wisdom with brilliance.[19] Aristotle remarks elsewhere the widespread belief (which he endorses) that "a young man of practical wisdom cannot be found. The cause is that such wisdom is concerned not only with universals but with particulars, which become familiar from experience, but a young man has no experience, for it is length of time that gives experience."[20] The balance between abstract and concrete reasoning, or between exact and practical reason (the latter necessary in incompletely theorized domains of activity), shifts with age toward the second term in each pair. Wisdom and experience are not synonyms; one can be experienced without being wise. But perhaps one cannot be wise without experience. Experience is necessary not only to furnish the rich store of particulars needed for practical reasoning but also to wear away the foolish optimism of the inexperienced, the young. Hence the correlation between age and wisdom.

If wisdom grows with age, does anything decline? Put differently, can the wise do everything the brilliant young can and then some? The answer depends on something that is unclear in Aristotle's account—exactly what cognitive tools are used in practical as distinct from abstract reasoning. There is a tradition, which builds on Aristotle's brief discussion of reasoning by analogy[21] and is particularly strong in law,[22] that practical reason, especially when it takes the form of reasoning by analogy, enables the reasoner to move directly from particular to particular, without the interposition of a syllogism or other device of abstract reasoning. If so, maybe the weakening of fluid intelligence should not be expected to impair the ability of elderly people to apply their existing knowledge to new areas. But I think this is wrong, that an appeal to analogy is usually an appeal to a general law that the analogy instantiates, and that the analogy cannot be

18. See Ryff, note 13 above, at 292–293.

19. Baltes, Smith, and Staudinger, note 17 above, at 134–139; cf. Maria A. Taranto, "Facets of Wisdom: A Theoretical Synthesis," 29 *International Journal of Aging and Human Development* 1 (1989).

20. Aristotle, *Nicomachean Ethics,* bk. 6, ch. 8, in *The Complete Works of Aristotle,* note 4 above, vol. 2, p. 1803 (1142a). But it is men in their prime, rather than old men, whom Aristotle believes to have the practical wisdom denied the young.

21. See Aristotle, *Prior Analytics,* bk. 2, ch. 24, in *The Complete Works of Aristotle,* note 4 above, vol. 1, p. 110 (68b–69a).

22. For references and critique, see Richard A. Posner, *The Problems of Jurisprudence* 86–92 (1990).

used to justify the law. If, for example, a property lawyer, asked what should be the legal regime for natural gas, argues that it should be the same as the regime governing rabbits because both types of resource can move around "on their own," he is proposing a general rule applicable to all such resources, and the rule has to be defended as a sound general rule, which cannot be done by reference to analogies.[23] So I do not think that reasoning by analogy can bypass the fluid intelligence, enabling the old to reason as flexibly and imaginatively as the young. (I present some evidence on this point in chapter 7.)

I want to come back to the pessimism of the old. Since the old were once young, their pessimism entails disillusionment, including disillusionment about schemes for human betterment, for such schemes are usually founded on hope rather than on experience. The young may have read about the failure of such schemes but the old have lived the failure; and in many areas of human activity book learning is not an adequate substitute for lived experience (see chapter 7). Being pessimistic, disillusioned, and cynical, the old, however "wise," become preoccupied with their own survival and happiness, these being the only goods of certain goodness to them. From that obsession can spring avarice and shamelessness.

A puzzle in Aristotle's account is why people become more and more pessimistic with age, rather than remaining on a plateau of realism reached when they are in their prime. There is a possible economic explanation for at least one component of the pessimistic outlook of elderly people, the belief that things are getting worse—that they were better in the old days— that the country is "going to Hell in a handbasket." Over a period of decades, some aspects of the social environment get worse while others get better. It is rational that older people should be more conscious of the things that are getting worse than of the things that are getting better, and vice versa for young people. Many though not all improvements consist of novelties, as distinct from incremental improvements in cost or performance. The elderly, because of the age-related decline in fluid intelligence, have difficulty—incur large costs—in taking advantage of novelties. Thus, innovations in art, fashion, or styles of living are likely to be accepted much more readily by young than by old people;[24] the latter may even think the "innovations" retrograde. At the same time, young people have a less acute sense of what has been lost on the march to progress than old people do.

---

23. See id. at 89; also Richard A. Posner, *Overcoming Law*, ch. 24 (1995).

24. "As consumers, older adults have been shown to be among the last to adopt a product, service, or idea innovation." Mary C. Gilly and Valarie A. Zeithaml, "The Elderly Consumer and Adoption of Technologies," 12 *Journal of Consumer Research* 353 (1985), citing studies.

The old actually experienced the good things that are no more. The young can only read about them—and may not bother to do so, having other calls on their time. In sum, the costs of information about the costs of progress will be lower to the old than to the young, but the costs of information about the benefits of progress will be higher, though I admit an exception for cases in which the young take for granted improvements of which the old are acutely aware, such as air conditioning and the polio vaccine.

In this analysis, the distance between the location of young and of old on the continuum that runs between extreme optimism and extreme pessimism really is increasing in age. But it is doing so for economic reasons, albeit ones shaped by the physiological process of aging, which affects the costs and benefits of current and prospective experience relative to retrospective experience.

We can also give an economic twist to the idea that the old are more self-centered than the young, though we shall have to qualify the idea later. The key is the last-period concept, discussed in chapter 3. The social virtues, including fair dealing, trustworthiness, being a good listener, generosity, and forbearance or self-control, are oriented toward transacting and, what is closely related, toward the acquisition of new human capital that will enable the obtaining of even more valuable transactions in the future. Being "a good listener" illustrates both points. The good listener is polite, thus reducing the costs to other people of transacting with him, and by attending carefully to what other people say he increases his own stock of useful information. In addition, by limiting his own speaking the good listener reduces the risk that he will make "revealing" disclosures about himself that may repel potential transaction partners.[25] The closer the horizon of one's transactional activity is, the fewer will be the benefits from adhering to virtues that increase the expected value of transacting. We might thus expect the old to indulge in fewer regrets than the young, after correction for the fact that the old will have a larger stock of regretted actions. The utility of regret lies in reducing the likelihood of repeating what has turned out to be a mistaken action. The old have more experience, but also less to gain from learning from experience.

The Dread of Death

The most puzzling thing about the suggestion that old people are more self-centered than the young is the inordinate fear of death that Aristotle as-

---

25. On the instrumental value of privacy in the sense of secrecy, see the discussion in *Overcoming Law*, note 23 above, ch. 25.

cribes to old people. "They love life," he says, "all the more when their last day has come." [26] How can that be, when the old have many fewer years to lose by dying than the young and when those years may confer limited utility at best, because of poor health? The lower utility of the coming years, moreover, is expected ex ante rather than merely experienced ex post, and so should affect behavior; for remember that the old are pessimistic.

The lower discount rates of the old (see chapter 4) can be only a small part of the answer; likewise the greater excitability of the young. Death is more imminent for the old, and the probability within a given interval greater. Yet confront an old and a young person with the same probability of death, and the old person may be just as fearful as the young even though he has much less to lose from dying now.

Evolutionary biology may supply part of the explanation. All human beings of minimal mental competence fear death. This fear, which religious, political, and military leaders have devoted endless ingenious thought to overcoming, is instinctual, programmed. Its contribution to inclusive fitness (the survival of a person's genes over future generations) is obvious. A rational creature that has such a fear is more likely to survive long enough to maximize his reproductive potential than one who lacks it. It is true that the survival of the very old contributes little to inclusive fitness because they have little reproductive potential (none in the case of elderly women). It may actually reduce their inclusive fitness by putting them in competition with the younger members of their own families for scarce supplies of food and other resources. But if, as we saw in the Introduction, selection pressures have not produced a distinctive genetic program for the old, there is no reason to expect them to have lost the instinctual dread of death just because it has no survival value. (If it has a negative survival value, the genetic tendency to promote the reproductive fitness of one's offspring may come into play and alter the outlook of the old, as we shall see in chapter 9.) We can thus appreciate the biological sense of Claudio's observation that "The weariest and most loathed worldly life / That age, ache, penury, and imprisonment / Can lay on nature is a paradise / To what we fear of death." [27]

There is an economic as well as a biological reason why the old should dread, or should behave in conformity with the hypothesis that they dread, death as much as the young. The economic literature on damages in

26. Aristotle, note 4 above, at 2214 (1389b).
27. *Measure for Measure,* act III, sc. i, ll. 132–136.

wrongful-death cases points out that for a person who derives a positive utility from living and does not have a very powerful bequest motive, no amount of money will compensate him for giving up his life on the spot.[28] For he will derive little or no utility from the money. By the same token, again setting aside the case of negative utility of life or of a strong bequest motive, a person should be willing to expend all his resources, if necessary, on avoiding an immediate death. Those resources will have zero value to him if he dies immediately; they have no opportunity cost. When faced with the prospect of imminent death, therefore, a person will behave at all ages as if the value of his life were "infinite" to him, although what is really going on is that the cost to him of resources expended on avoiding death is zero. This behavior will actually be encountered more commonly among old people than among young ones because the old are more exposed to the risk of imminent death.

If dread of death has survival value, so presumably should happiness, since the more that people enjoy life the more effort they will expend on averting death. If "happiness-prone" people can be expected to live longer on average than the miserable because they are less likely to commit suicide and more likely to take good care of themselves than the latter, they will tend to be overrepresented among the elderly. This selection phenomenon might offset an age-related decline in the happiness of these survivors, making them highly reluctant to die. In fact, as shown in figure 5.1, survey statistics indicate that the percentage of people who are "very happy" is greater among octogenarians than among people in their thirties or forties.[29] This is a further illustration of the pervasiveness of selection bias in explaining the attitudes and behavior of elderly people.

Another reason why the old can be expected to display as much as or even more aversion to death than the young is that the sacrifice of an old person is likely to confer a smaller expected gain on other people than the sacrifice of a young person. A warrior who sacrifices himself in combat may, by doing the risky deed that has led to his death, have contributed to the survival of his nation, comrades, family, and way of life, and by contributing have obtained an altruistic benefit. The risking of life by a deed done by one too old to be effective in combat is less likely to produce a compensating gain. It might seem that the social loss from the sacrifice of

28. See, for example, William M. Landes and Richard A. Posner, *The Economic Structure of Tort Law* 187–188 (1987); Marvin Frankel and Charles M. Linke, "The Value of Life and Hedonic Damages: Some Unresolved Issues," 5 *Journal of Forensic Economics* 233, 236 (1992).

29. The source for figure 5.1 is the General Social Survey for 1988–1993. See chapter 4, note 44.

(%)

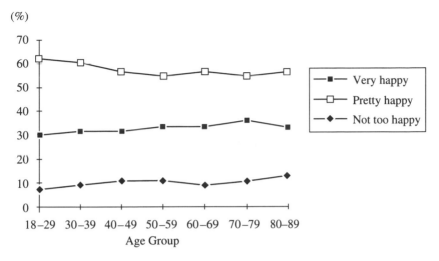

Figure 5.1 Self-report of happiness as a function of age

the old person would also be less; the warrior who survives can fight another day. But the old may have social value other than as fighters—for example as counselors, priests, or judges—so that their lives are not free goods to the society, to be flung away recklessly.

Moreover, as between two persons, one old, one young, facing what would be the same risk if they were the same age (maybe both are equidistant from a drowning child), the risk of death or serious injury is apt to be much greater to the old person because of his physical frailty.[30] This would tend to make the expected cost of risky activity higher to old people than to young ones even if the old did not dread death more than the young.

And rarely is the issue life versus *certain* death or *certain* serious injury. Cowardice is unwillingness to *risk* one's life in circumstances in which honor requires assuming such a risk; it is not (in our culture anyway) unwillingness to commit suicide. If the young are more optimistic about the outcome of risky choices than the old, this would make the disutility of the objectively same risk of death greater to an old person than to a young one.

30. Lloyd Cohen, "Toward an Economic Theory of the Measurement of Damages in a Wrongful Death Action," 34 *Emory Law Journal* 295, 332 (1985); see also Erin Ann O'Hara, "Hedonic Damages for Wrongful Death: Are Tortfeasors Getting Away with Murder?" 78 *Georgetown Law Journal* 1687, 1717–1718 (1990). For evidence, note that the distribution by age of death of pedestrian fatalities in automobile accidents is highly skewed toward old people. Robert Arking, *Biology of Aging: Observations and Principles* 35 (1991) (fig. 2–12). See also the discussion of driving in the next chapter.

A further point is that as the end of life approaches, other sources of utility besides continuing to live recede. With the marginal value of competing goods, such as sex, travel, rich food and drink, and strenuous exercise, falling, the rational old person will reallocate resources to life-extending investments in medical care and in safety.[31] He will become more cautious than a young person because what he gives up in alternative consumption by being cautious is worth less to him. Equivalently, he has less to gain from taking risks than a young person would.

"Our life resembles the Sibylline Books: the less there is left of it, the more precious it becomes." So Goethe. There are two interpretations. One is that the nearer the prospect of death is, the keener is the appreciation of what death does. When death is remote, we may take life for granted, not dwelling on its joys and rewards; and what we take for granted we tend to value less. Second, remaining life, like other inputs into activity, may have scarcity value. As the end of life approaches, additional months or even weeks may have great value in enabling a person to arrange his affairs, to make farewells, and, by thinking over his life, to achieve an aesthetically and psychologically pleasing sense of completeness or roundedness; this is an aspect of the Nietzschean idea (or at least an idea attributed to Nietzsche) of conceiving of one's life as a work of art.

A final point is that it is arbitrary to suppose that the only thing lost through death is future living. There is the destruction of the complex of memories that constitutes a person. Until senility destroys many of those memories, the old person has a greater stock of them than a young person, which may somewhat offset, as a source of utility, the young person's greater life expectancy.[32] This is implicit in Aristotle's concept of the knowledge shift. Conversely, however, that richer stock may give the old person a greater sense of having fulfilled his potential for living, at least if he has time (my previous point) to arrange his memories into a pleasing pattern.

Taken together, these points show how life-endangering risk-taking by

31. Isaac Ehrlich and Hiroyuki Chuma, "A Model of the Demand for Longevity and the Value of Life Extension," 98 *Journal of Political Economy* 761, 776–777, 780–781 (1990); see also Cohen, note 30 above, at 332. Such a reallocation is particularly likely, of course, if the life-extending choice is subsidized but the alternative choices are not. It is therefore not surprising that an estimated 28 percent of Medicare expenditures are for the treatment of people who are in their last year of life. Dennis W. Jahnigen and Robert H. Binstock, "Economic and Clinical Realities: Health Care for Elderly People," in *Too Old for Health Care? Controversies in Medicine, Law, Economics, and Ethics* 13, 29–30 (1991). This figure is for 1978; I have not found more recent figures.

32. On the utility derived from the recollection of pleasurable or exciting experiences, see Jon Elster and George Loewenstein, "Utility from Memory and Anticipation," in *Choice over Time* 213, 229–231 (George Loewenstein and Jon Elster, eds., 1992).

the old might be at once less beneficial and more costly than such risk-taking by the young, provided that the expected utility of the remaining years of life is not the dominant factor in the fear of death.[33] But we must not go overboard, and forget the higher suicide rates of old than of young people (see next chapter) or neglect afterlife concerns, which generally carry heavier weight for the old than for the young. The influence of such concerns on behavior in the face of danger depends, however, on the nature of a person's religious beliefs. If he thinks himself likely to go to Hell, this should increase his dread of death. But if he thinks himself likely to be punished in the afterlife for cowardice if he does not behave courageously, this should reduce his dread of dying as a result of a courageous act. And if he is convinced of his salvation, he may not think he is giving up much by dying.

Even if cowardice in the particular sense of reluctance to encounter physical danger is a characteristic of old people (not of all, of course), it is balanced, as Aristotle neglects to point out, by a form of courage unknown to the young—courage in facing old age without flinching. Long before I thought of writing about old age, I had remarked that Justice Holmes "faced the indignities and deprivations of old age . . . with great courage and gallantry, so that his last years completed a circle with the military heroism of his youth." [34] Holmes, in this as in other respects luckier than most, had a chance to prove his courage on two fields of human endeavor. For most of us, old age will be the only field in which we have that chance.

Clemenceau, when asked in his old age what he would do now, replied, "I am going to live till I die." [35] In like vein, Holmes ended a radio address celebrating his ninetieth birthday with the following free translation of a line from an anonymous medieval Latin poet: "Death plucks my ears and says, Live—I am coming." [36] I have mentioned the downbeat poems about old age that Yeats wrote when he was in his early sixties. Old age continued to be a major theme of Yeats's poetry until his death at the age of 73, but

33. For evidence that it is not, see Edmund C. Payne et al., "To Die Young, To Die Old: Management of Terminal Illness at Age 20 and at Age 85: Case Reports," 8 *Journal of Geriatric Psychiatry* 107 (1975).

34. *The Essential Holmes: Selections from the Letters, Speeches, Judicial Opinions, and Other Writings of Oliver Wendell Holmes, Jr.* xv (Richard A. Posner, ed., 1992) (editor's introduction). The selections in chapter 1 of *The Essential Holmes* ("Aging and Death") document this claim.

35. Quoted in *The Art of Growing Older: Writers on Living and Aging,* note 1 above, at 177.

36. *The Essential Holmes,* note 34 above, at 21. See the exchange of letters between Holmes and Frederick Pollock, May 4 and 15, 1931, in *Holmes-Pollock Letters: The Correspondence of Mr. Justice Holmes and Sir Frederick Pollock 1874–1932,* vol. 2, pp. 285–286 (Mark DeWolfe Howe, ed., 1941).

the tone became increasingly defiant and even triumphal. Not in the sense of Tennyson's Ulysses, of hoping still to accomplish against all odds some great work, let alone a sense of peace or wisdom attained; in most of the poems of his old age, Yeats depicts the wisdom of the old as bitter, as pure disillusionment—indeed as the answer to the question that furnishes the title of one of those poems, "Why Should Old Men Be Mad?" What informs Yeats's late poems is Nietzsche's idea that man makes his own reality. The idea recalls the philosophy of self-sufficiency of the stoics, to whom Nietzsche, and through him Yeats, were in fact indebted.[37] Or as Hamlet put it (and we know that Shakespeare, too, was influenced by the stoics), "there is nothing either good or bad, but thinking makes it so." [38] Even old age is what we make of it. In "A Prayer for Old Age" Yeats prays "That I may seem, though I die old, / A foolish, passionate man." And in "The Spur," he is unmoved that "You think it horrible that lust and rage / Should dance attention upon my old age . . . They were not such a plague when I was young; / What else have I [now] to spur me into song?"

We are not all Holmes, Clemenceau, or Yeats; we cannot all expect to be stoics of either the stolid or the triumphalist variety in our old age. Especially those of us who are men. For the "cowardice" of the old of which Aristotle speaks may be related to the common observation that as people age the men tend to become more like women and the women more like men.[39] The men tend to become more nurturant and less aggressive, the women less nurturant and more assertive. These changes in the direction of gender convergence should not be thought of purely in terms of deterioration. As we shall see in chapter 9, they equip the elderly to find new social niches for themselves.

Although I do not want to denigrate the courage that so many people display in the face of the indignities of old age and the imminence of death, I feel bound to point out that as life draws to a close considerations of posthumous reputation loom larger in the rational individual's utility function. Not only is the posthumous state closer, but alternative investments to

37. On Nietzsche's influence on Yeats, see references in Richard A. Posner, *Law and Literature: A Misunderstood Relation* 150 n. 29 (1988). On the influence of the stoics on Nietzsche, see Martha C. Nussbaum, *The Therapy of Desire: Theory and Practice in Hellenistic Ethics* 4–5 (1994).

38. *Hamlet,* act II, sc. ii, ll. 251–252. Yeats's late poem "Death" ends, "Man has created death;" and another late poem, "A Dialogue of Self and Soul," ends, "When such as I cast out remorse / So great a sweetness flows into the breast / We must laugh and we must sing, / We are blessed by everything, / Everything we look upon is blest."

39. See, for example, David Gutmann, *Reclaimed Powers: Toward a New Psychology of Men and Women in Later Life* (1987); also Costa, McCrae, and Arenberg, note 6 above, at 191–192.

creating posthumous reputation are less feasible. One's deportment in the face of death is an important part of most people's posthumous reputation; their brave words, their stoical demeanor, may be long remembered. Admirable as these things are, we should recognize that their benefit-cost ratio rises as death approaches; that they are in a sense "selfish" behaviors.

Physical and Mental Decline as Factors in the Psychology of the Elderly

Decline of faculties and loss of powers do not play a large role in Aristotle's depiction of the psychology of old age, at least explicitly. He attributes almost all the distinctive traits of the old to what I have been calling the knowledge shift, which he does not attribute to any deterioration in the mental abilities of the old. His approach both explains and is explained by his choice of age 50 as the onset of old age. By then a person has seen enough of life to have lost his youthful optimism; and it is doubtful that the typical 50-year-old Athenian of the fourth century B.C. was mentally or physically decrepit. But as I have remarked previously, it is a puzzle why if there is no age-related decline the knowledge shift should involve loss as well as gain. The elderly would be more pessimistic, but realistically so. They would have both imagination and knowledge, the young only imagination. Aristotle seems to have believed that experience displaced rather than supplemented imagination, a sound belief because there is, though not remarked by him, an age-related decline in fluid intelligence.

Once the threshold of old age is raised to a more realistic level than Aristotle's, the importance of age-related decline in explaining the characteristic psychology of the elderly becomes inescapable. It helps to explain not only their "cowardice" but also their hesitation and tentativeness. One way to compensate for diminished physical or mental capability is by investing more time in doing tasks. So old people walk more slowly, drive more slowly, and make decisions more slowly. The point is not that they are incapable of walking fast, and so on, although that is also true, at least in the sense that the exertional (not just expected-accident) cost of speed is higher for older people, and sometimes prohibitive. "Behavioral slowing" over a broad range of behaviors is a marked characteristic of aging organisms, animal as well as human; not all of it is a volitional response to a changing environment of costs and benefits.[40] But the point I want to make

40. James E. Birren, Anita M. Woods, and M. Virtrue Williams, "Behavioral Slowing with Age: Causes, Organization, and Consequences," in *Aging in the 1980s: Psychological Issues* 293, 302–303 (Leonard W. Poon, ed., 1980).

is that taking more time is also a rationally chosen adaptation to diminished capability. An old person has a greater risk of falling than a young person does. He has poorer balance and eyesight and slower reflexes, and being more frail is also more likely to be injured if he falls. The benefits of using more inputs of time are therefore greater to him, so he makes a deliberate choice to walk and drive more slowly than he is capable of doing. The cost of time is also likely to be less to an old than to a young person, and this will increase the tendency of the old to substitute inputs of time for other inputs into their activities.

Age-related decline helps explain why old professionals and academics do not keep up with the literature in their fields as assiduously as the young do. The cost of absorbing new information is higher to the old than to the young because of the erosion of their fluid intelligence, and the benefit is smaller because they have fewer periods remaining in which to earn a return on any new human capital that they do acquire. The broader point is that, because of this changing balance between cost and benefit, the old are less receptive to new ideas than the young. This is the kernel of validity to the cruel aphorism (a "smoking gun" of age discrimination cases) that "you can't teach an old dog new tricks." The old dog is rational in not wanting to take the time to learn new tricks, as the cost will be greater and the benefit smaller than in the case of a young dog. An additional cost is that of abandoning habitual behaviors and settled beliefs. The older a person is, the more deeply entrenched and hence more costly to change are his practices, attitudes, and responses, just as the more addicted a person is to some activity, whether smoking cigarettes or listening to classical music, the more he will suffer from withdrawal symptoms if he abandons the activity even if, as in the case of music, the addiction to it is purely psychological.

This analysis of the costs and benefits to the old of novelty adds a further dimension to the aversion of the old to risk-taking activity. Often a proposed course of action is risky in the sense of being quite likely to fail merely because it involves doing something new. Were it merely the repetition of an old action, the likelihood of its succeeding would be easy to estimate because there would be a track record. The risk of failure would be minimized. So if, because of the decline of fluid intelligence or the cost of breaking old habits, the old have trouble absorbing new ideas, it will be difficult for them to evaluate risky choices.

Not taking risks or doing new things imparts to a person's conduct a conservative, rote style. We should expect it to be a more common style among the old than among the young. A study of military leadership found that, after correction for other factors, older generals are less likely than younger ones to adopt an offensive rather than a defensive strategy.[41] The point again is not that the old are incapable of taking risks, absorbing new ideas, and so forth, though that is sometimes the case, but that often it is rational for them to shun such activities as not worth the cost, which is higher to them than to the young.

Additional considerations come into play when we consider the well-known aversion of the old to *financial* risk, in the sense of variance of expected returns about the mean. The older a person is, the larger will be the fraction of his total wealth that is constituted by financial rather than human capital; indeed, at retirement, labor-market human capital is in effect written off. So variance in the income on an old person's financial assets will impart greater variance to his total income than in the case of a younger person. A less technical way to put this is that older people have less capacity to bear risk than younger people because they do not have wages with which to cover losses resulting from the taking of investment risks. Hence the optimal investment strategy of the older person is more conservative.[42] This is reflected in the rule of thumb that the percentage of bonds in one's portfolio of bonds and common stocks should be equal to one's age—a 20-year-old should have only 20 percent of his portfolio in bonds, an 80-year-old 80 percent.

Religion, Voting Preferences, and Speaking

We should not be surprised to find that old people are on average[43] somewhat more religious than young people (in belief, not practices, since the incapacities associated with old age may limit church attendance).[44] As I

41. Dean Keith Simonton, "Land Battles, Generals, and Armies: Individual and Situational Determinants of Victory and Casualties," 38 *Journal of Personality and Social Psychology* 110, 115 (1980).

42. Burton G. Malkiel, *A Random Walk down Wall Street, Including a Life-Cycle Guide to Personal Investing,* ch. 13 (5th ed. 1990); David P. Brown, "Multiperiod Financial Planning," 33 *Management Science* 848, 859–860 (1987).

43. I keep repeating this qualification, but perhaps not frequently enough. As we shall see in chapter 13, the essence of age discrimination is refusal to recognize the *variance* in the attitudes, behaviors, and so forth of middle-aged and elderly people. Here as in most of the book, indeed as in most of economics, I am generally concerned with the mean of the distribution rather than with the entire distribution.

44. See, for example, Cary S. Kart, *The Realities of Aging: An Introduction* 344–349 (3d ed. 1990); David O. Moberg, "Religiosity in Old Age," in *Middle Age and Aging: A Reader in Social Psychology* 497, 508 (Bernice L. Neugarten, ed., 1968); Dan Blazer and Erdman Palmore, "Religion and Aging in a Longitudinal Panel," 16 *Gerontologist* 82 (1976); John M. Finney and Gary R. Lee, "Age Differences on Five Dimensions of Religious Involvement," 18 *Review of Religious Research* (1976); Rodney Stark, "Age and Faith: A Changing Outlook or an Old Pro-

remarked in chapter 3, the afterlife, being more imminent for the old, has a greater weight in their thoughts and decisions. A slightly subtler prediction is that among the old, religiosity will be negatively related to health, because the unhealthy old have a shorter life expectancy.[45]

We might expect old people to be on average selfish, single-issue voters. Like politicians with short terms of office, the old have truncated horizons and therefore would be irrational to take the long view. This point is only superficially in tension with the point about religiosity, which extends the horizons of many old people but does so in a way that affects their perceived self-interest; it need not make them altruistic voters. A deeper problem is that since a rational person knows that his vote will not swing the election, why shouldn't he vote his convictions?[46] What is the cost? The answer may be that most people are convinced that what is good for themselves is good, period. This is a rational conviction to hold since they would gain nothing from being tugged in different directions by principle and by self-interest. They avoid the pain of cognitive dissonance, and at trivial cost.

Familial altruism is not the answer either. The old are better off supporting than opposing policies that transfer wealth to them from the young as a group, since they can always give some of that wealth back to their own children and grandchildren. This is a clue to why, as we shall see in chapter 11, it is possible to obtain widespread political support for laws reducing social security retirement benefits in the distant future. The old have nothing to lose from laws that will bite after they are dead, and they may have an altruistic desire to lighten the burden of taxation on the younger members of their own families.

The greatest objection to the idea that old people invariably are selfish voters is that it disregards disinterest. To the extent that the aged are in the process of disengaging from the world, they have less stake in redistributive

---

cess?" 29 *Sociological Analysis* 1 (1968). Data from the General Social Survey for 1988–1993 (see note 29 above) generally confirm these studies. The elderly respondents exhibit on average much stronger religious affiliation and somewhat stronger feelings of "nearness to God" than younger persons, but no greater belief in an afterlife. That may be because the afterlife is a source of fear as well as hope—or because beliefs in such things are not in fact dominated or even heavily influenced by wishful thinking.

45. For evidence, see Bradley C. Courtenay et al., "Religiosity and Adaptation in the Oldest-Old," 34 *International Journal of Aging and Human Development* 47, 54 (1992).

46. For that matter, why should he vote at all? This is a profound question in economics and political science. I return to it in the next chapter.

policies than younger persons do. In this respect old people resemble judges (many of them old), whom we assume to be more impartial than other decision-makers because the rules of judicial ethics require that they have no family or financial stake in the cases they judge.

This point requires us to qualify Aristotle's insistence that the old are more self-centered than the young. Even if they are, their "self" may be less affected by various decisions and policies than the selves of younger persons. Although the young may be less selfish than the old when the cost of being selfless is the same, the cost of voting selflessly may be higher for the young because they have more to gain or lose from the governmental policies at issue in the election, having a much longer period over which gains and losses can accrue to them.

From Nestor to Polonius, Montaigne, and beyond, a frequently observed characteristic of old people is loquacity.[47] I suggested in the Introduction that this could be explained by reference to the lesser value of privacy, consideration, and new information to the old than to the young. Another factor is the difficulty of interpersonal transfer of lived experience. If the knowledge that comes through experience were easy to transfer through books or conversation (some of it is easy to transfer that way), there would be no socially useful age-related attribute called "experience" or "judgment." The young would pick up these things by reading about them. To the extent that lived experience is imperfectly transferable (it is *literally* nontransferable, of course), we should expect older people to resort to elaborate, protracted speech in an effort to overcome the obstacles to communication.

Not all old people are loquacious; some, indeed, are more taciturn than they were when they were young. This may reflect the effect of another element of the psychology of the elderly, their reluctance to take risks. A further point is that much speech is reciprocal: I tell you something in the hope of being told something useful in return. This kind of speech exchange is related to transacting and is therefore less valuable to old people. So we might expect not that old people on average are more loquacious

---

47. See, for example, Cicero, note 3 above, ch. XVI, § 55. For empirical evidence, see Dolores Gold et al., "Measurement and Correlates of Verbosity in Elderly People," 43 *Journal of Gerontology* P27 (1988). I am not concerned here with the pathological "off-target verbosity" that afflicts a minority of old people as a result of a specific brain dysfunction. Tannis Y. Arbuckle and Dolores Pushkar Gold, "Aging, Inhibition, and Verbosity," 48 *Journal of Gerontology* P225 (1993). Or with gossip—but it is a plausible inference that because the old have lower opportunity costs of time they gossip more than young people.

than young people, but that there is greater dispersion along the loquacity-taciturnity continuum among the old than among the young.

As this last example suggests, the psychology of the old is not simple; but economics, with help from evolutionary biology and the literary examples with which this chapter is sprinkled, can help to make it intelligible. I have argued, for example, that if, as is plausible, most people are innately optimistic, the knowledge shift emphasized in previous chapters—the tendency of people as they get older to substitute reasoning based on experience for reasoning based on imagination—implies that as people age they become more pessimistic. A supporting point, one with independent significance, is that the decline of fluid intelligence with age, and the effects of habit, cause aging people to have difficulty accepting and taking full advantage of all the improvements associated with "progress," while at the same time they are more conscious of all the accompanying losses than the young because they will have experienced them and not merely read about them. Progress implies substitution of new for old services, products, activities, and so forth, and thus loss as well as gain, even though the latter predominates (this is implied by the concept of "progress")—but it may not predominate in the eyes of the old. Averseness to novelties gives a conservative cast to old people, but it is rational conservatism, based on changes in the cost of absorbing novelty, not merely a mindless standpattism. It is reinforced in the financial arena by the fact that when a person stops working, variance in the return on his financial assets imparts greater variance to his total income because that return is now a larger part of his total income.

The tentativeness and hesitation that are characteristic of old people are also rational adaptations to the increased risks that they face as a consequence of age-related decline. The self-preoccupation that is also characteristic of many old people, and characteristic features of the conversation of the old that can be summed up by saying that old people tend to be inconsiderate conversationalists, are mutually related consequences of the diminished benefits of transacting to the old. The other side of this particular coin, however, is that the old may be more disinterested than the young because, as a consequence of their truncated horizon, they have less to gain from selfish behavior. As for the puzzling "dread of death" of old people, this is explicable by reference to the *absence* of a genetic program for old age, as a consequence of which the instinctual dread of death that promotes inclusive fitness in the young but not the old has not been eliminated in the old by natural selection, and to a number of strictly economic factors as well. These include the fragility of the old, the paucity of uses for their resources other than to prolong life, and the related but distinct fact that the opportunity cost of resources devoted to averting imminent death may be zero, since in the absence of a bequest motive the resources will be useless to the owner if he dies.

6

Behavioral Correlates of Age

I want to consider what economic sense can be made of typical behaviors of the old regarding residence, driving, crime, suicide, sex, employment and retirement, voting and jury service. Some of these topics are treated in other chapters as well, and an area of particular interest—productivity in a broad sense, embracing creativity, leadership, and other forms of achievement—I do not discuss in this chapter at all but devote the whole of the next two chapters to. My purposes in this chapter are to illustrate the utility of economic theory in explaining a wide variety of behavioral differences between young and old and to lay additional foundations for the analysis of policy in later chapters.

Driving

Old people on average drive much less than young people and have a higher accident rate than all but the very youngest drivers.[1] The simplest life-cycle model, in which the only significance of aging is that it brings a person nearer to a finite horizon, might be thought to explain the higher accident

1. Leonard Evans, "Older Driver Involvement in Fatal and Severe Traffic Crashes," 43 *Journal of Gerontology* S186 (1988); Donald W. Kline et al., "Vision, Aging and Driving: The Problems of Older Drivers," 47 *Journal of Gerontology* P27, P33 (1992); Richard A. Marottoli et al., "Driving Cessation and Changes in Mileage Driven among Elderly Individuals," 48 *Journal of Gerontology* S255, S258 (1993); Joan E. Rigdon, "Older Drivers Pose Growing Risk on Roads as Their Numbers Rise," *Wall Street Journal* (midwest ed.), Oct. 29, 1993, pp. A1, A6. Unless otherwise indicated, the data in this chapter are limited to the United States.

rate simply by reference to reduced longevity: the old have less to lose. But this would be inconsistent with the psychology of aging discussed in the preceding chapter and with the low level of criminal activity of the old (of which more shortly). And it would leave the reduction in driving by the old unexplained, for while it is true that retired people are not commuters, many of the leisure activities in which people engage are driving-intensive.

I believe that the driving patterns of the old are decisively influenced by age-related decline. The characteristic age-related erosion of visual acuity, reflexes, and concentration has a marked effect on capability for driving safely.[2] But it would be a mistake to infer that the accident rate of the old would rise *proportionately* to the decline in relevant physical and mental skills.

An age-related decline in driving skills raises the expected cost of driving—both the expected cost of being injured (or incurring property damage) in an accident and the expected cost of liability for injuring someone else (or inflicting property damage). Both costs are a positive function of the probability of an accident, and that probability is greater, other things remaining unchanged, the older the driver. The expected cost of being injured also rises with age because old people are more fragile and therefore more likely to be injured if they are involved in an accident.

We can expect two types of response to the higher expected accident costs of old drivers: an activity response, and a care response.[3] One way to reduce the expected costs of accidents is by driving less—cutting out marginal trips that are no longer cost-justified when expected accident costs rise—or not at all, if those costs become so high that they exceed the benefit of any driving. A parallel phenomenon in the workplace—the tendency for older workers to leave jobs in which age-related sensory and motor decline would make them prone to accidental injury—may explain the negative correlation between age and industrial accidents.[4]

The other response to higher expected accident costs of driving—driv-

2. See, for example, Rudolf W. H. M. Ponds, Wiebo H. Brouwer, and Peter C. van Wolffe-laar, "Age Differences in Divided Attention in a Simulated Driving Task," 43 *Journal of Gerontology* P151 (1988).

3. A fundamental distinction in the economic analysis of torts. See William M. Landes and Richard A. Posner, *The Economic Structure of Tort Law* (1987); Steven Shavell, *Economic Analysis of Accident Law* (1987).

4. Mildred Doering, Susan R. Rhodes, and Michael Schuster, *The Aging Worker: Research and Recommendations* 79 (1983). For evidence that the decisions of elderly people regarding whether and how much to drive are heavily influenced by expected accident costs, as my analysis predicts, see Marottoli et al., note 1 above, esp. S258–S259.

ing more carefully—is possible for the aged driver simply by driving more slowly. This gives him more time to focus eyes and mind and to react to a threatening situation. Since the opportunity cost of time is lower for the old, it is not a costly substitution, so one is not surprised that old people are involved in fewer accidents that are due to excessive speed (by them) than are younger people.[5] I am led to predict that the accident rate of old people will rise more slowly than the decline in their driving skills. It might seem that if the cost of time fell faster than the decline in driving skill, the accident rate of the old might actually decline. But this is unlikely for three reasons. First, time is not a perfect substitute for skill; otherwise a blind person could drive safely. Second, difference in vehicle speeds, as well as high speed, is a risk factor in accidents; that is why high-speed highways are often posted with minimum as well as maximum speeds. Third, driving slowly increases the amount of time one spends in automobile travel, so if such travel is more likely to involve an accident than the activity that would be substituted for it, there will be a partial offset to the effect of driving slowly in reducing the risk of accident.[6]

Driving more slowly is not the only care response of the old to a greater risk of being involved in an accident. They are also less likely to drive under the influence of alcohol.[7] The reader will recall from the preceding chapter that quite apart from increased fragility, the old are likely to devote more resources than the young to preserving their lives because the opportunity costs of life-extending measures are lower to the old than to the young. A pertinent example is that the costs of reducing the amount of liquor consumed are lower to the old because their bodies are less able to tolerate liquor anyway.

Because care and activity changes are not perfect substitutes for reflexes and other driving skills adversely affected by age, the elderly have a higher accident rate than younger drivers, and since very young drivers also have an abnormally high accident rate the function that relates driving safety to age has the familiar inverted U shape. A plausible interpretation is that safety grows with experience but at a diminishing rate eventually overcome by age-related decline.

It would be a mistake to infer from the high accident rate of old people that their driving ought to be curtailed by more stringent licensing requirements. This would overlook the value to them of their inframarginal driv-

---

5. Kline et al., note 1 above, at P33.

6. Cf. Landes and Posner, note 3 above, at 238 n. 17.

7. Isaac Ehrlich and Hiroyuki Chuma, "A Model of the Demand for Longevity and the Value of Life Extension," 98 *Journal of Political Economy* 761, 781 (1990) (tab. 5).

ing—the driving they continue to do despite its dangerousness—and the fact that so long as insurance companies are permitted to adjust their premiums for age, as they are, the risks posed by old drivers can be internalized without need for governmental intervention beyond the provision of a tort law system. A high accident rate, moreover, does not necessarily imply a high degree of risk to other users of the roads. An accident rate is a rate per mile driven. The total number of miles driven per year by the elderly is much smaller than in younger age groups,[8] both because there are fewer elderly and because (the activity point) they drive on average less than younger people. Hence the elderly are not nearly so big a source of automobile accidents *to others* as their accident rate would suggest. The qualification is vital. Because the old are fragile, they are more likely than the young to be killed in automobile accidents; they are also more likely to be pedestrian fatalities.[9] But they are less likely than the young to inflict fatalities. For example, male drivers aged 65 cause only 32.8 percent as many pedestrian deaths as male drivers aged 40 and only 11.8 percent as many as 20-year-old male drivers.[10] And the rate of total vehicle crash involvements per number of licensed male drivers decreases monotonically with age, with just a slight uptick at age 85 and above. Even in that age group, the rate is one-fourth the teenage male crash involvement rate and one-half the rate of male drivers aged 25 to 29.[11]

The fact that the old are not responsible for a large number of accidents does not prove that letting them drive is a cost-justified policy. Elderly drivers may not be a major threat to highway safety; yet if miles driven are a good index of the benefits of driving, the low aggregate accident costs that the elderly inflict on other users of the road would be balanced by low

8. For example, in 1990 drivers aged 75 to 79 drove 26.3 million miles, compared to 141.6 million for drivers aged 50 to 54. Ezio C. Cerrelli, "Crash Data and Rates for Age-Sex Groups of Drivers, 1990" 10 (U.S. Dept. of Transportation, National Highway Traffic Safety Administration Research Note, May 1992) (tab. C). For evidence that rational behavior of the elderly with respect to safety is consistent with their having higher injury rates, see next footnote.

9. Id., p. 6; U.S. Dept. of Transportation, National Highway Traffic Safety Administration, "Traffic Safety Facts 1992: Older Population" 3 (n.d.). See also Dawn L. Massie and Kenneth L. Campbell, "Accident Involvement Rates by Age and Gender," *UMTRI Research Review,* March-April 1993, p. 1. In 1992, persons 70 and older, though less than 9 percent of the U.S. population, accounted for 11.8 percent of all deaths of occupants of motor vehicles and 17.9 percent of all pedestrian deaths. "Traffic Safety Facts 1992: Older Population," above, at pp. 1, 3. For empirical evidence that elderly pedestrians respond rationally to the greater risk of being injured or killed by exercising greater care than younger, less vulnerable people, see W. Andrew Harrell, "Precautionary Street Crossing by Elderly Pedestrians," 32 *International Journal of Aging and Human Development* 65 (1991).

10. Evans, note 1 above, at S192 (tab. 1).

11. Cerrelli, note 8 above, p. 7 (fig. 1).

aggregate benefits to the elderly. But I doubt that those benefits are low. Given the incentive of elderly drivers to reduce their driving, both for their own protection and to minimize liability-insurance costs, it is likely that the driving they do confers large benefits on them. Indeed, to conclude otherwise would cast doubt on the proposition that changes in activity level are a socially valuable method of accident prevention. Suppose that railroads are inherently much more dangerous than canals, and as a result the pricing of transportation services to reflect accident risks as well as all other costs causes most freight to be carried by canal. The logical inference would be that the remaining rail transportation, that for which canal transportation is not substitutable even when accident costs are taken into account, must confer very large benefits on shippers; else these shippers would be induced to switch to canals too. A similar inference seems warranted in the case of elderly drivers. This is one more example of the importance of selection bias in illuminating (and, in this example, in enabling a social valuation to be placed on) the behavior of the elderly. The elderly who continue driving are in effect selected for the high value of their driving.

If this analysis is correct, it would be bad policy to curtail driving by the old by requiring the elderly driver, as a condition of retaining his or her license, to demonstrate a level of skill equal to that of a young driver. A less skilled elderly driver may be able to come up to the same level of care as the young simply by driving slowly, and may well derive benefits from driving that are large enough to offset the higher risk of an accident to others that his driving does create. Yet it is equally a mistake to propose measures to increase the safety of elderly drivers or pedestrians, such as increasing the pedestrian-crossing time allowed by traffic lights, without considering the cost of the measures to other users of streets.[12]

The Involvement of the Elderly in Crime as Victims and as Offenders

The elderly crime victim. Although the aged are overrepresented in the statistics of traffic deaths, they are underrepresented in the statistics of criminal victimization. Persons 65 or older were victims in only 5 percent

---

12. As in Russell E. Hoxie and Laurence Z. Rubenstein, "Are Older Pedestrians Allowed Enough Time to Cross Intersections Safely?" 42 *Journal of the American Geriatric Society* 241 (1994).

of the murders committed in 1992 and only 2 percent of all crimes committed that year, even though they comprise more than 12 percent of the population.[13] Because older persons are frailer than younger ones, the expected cost to them of a criminal encounter is greater,[14] so we expect them to take greater precautions. The cost of these precautions is, properly speaking, a cost of crime; statistics of victimization therefore understate those costs. But this is true for everyone, and it is not obvious that, despite their greater frailty and hence greater vulnerability to crime, the elderly incur higher costs (nonpecuniary as well as pecuniary, of course) of avoiding becoming victims of crime. For the cost of precautions is lower to elderly than to young people. The elderly are less active and mobile anyway, so it costs them less to avoid going out at night or living or working (they don't work, most of them) in dangerous areas. The large disparity between traffic and crime fatalities to older people suggests, plausibly enough, that it is more costly for the old to avoid automobile travel or crossing streets than to avoid places where criminals lurk. Differences in the cost of avoiding activities are no doubt also one explanation for why the ratio of fatal traffic accidents to fatal nontraffic accidents is much lower among elderly than middle-aged persons.[15] It is more costly for the elderly to avoid activities that create a danger of a fall or a burn (the most common types of nontraffic accident to elderly people)[16] than those that create a danger of an automobile accident or a criminal assault. Even a person who never leaves his residence faces a risk of falling or of scalding himself or of being injured in a fire.

13. U.S. Dept. of Justice, Bureau of Justice Statistics, "Elderly Crime Victims: National Crime Victimization Survey" (NCJ-147002, March 1994). There is, no doubt, underreporting of intrafamilial violence against the old, most of it committed by spouses. Karl Pillemer and David Finkelhor, "The Prevalence of Elder Abuse: A Random Sample Survey," 28 *Gerontologist* 51 (1988). But no one seems to know whether it is greater than the underreporting of intrafamilial violence directed against younger persons, particularly children. And a recent study suggests that the prevalence of physical abuse of elderly persons has been greatly exaggerated. Beletshachew Shiferaw et al., "The Investigation and Outcome of Reported Cases of Elder Abuse: The Forsyth County Aging Study," 34 *Gerontologist* 123 (1994).

14. This may explain why a number of states make assault and battery a more serious crime when the victim is elderly. Annotation, "Criminal Assault or Battery Statutes Making Attack on Elderly Person a Special or Aggravated Offense," 73 A.L.R.4th 1123 (1989).

15. William Wilbanks, "Trends in Violent Death among the Elderly," 14 *International Journal of Aging and Human Development* 167, 170 (1981–1982) (tab. 2).

16. See, for example, Harmeet Sjögren and Ulf Björnstig, "Unintentional Injuries among Elderly People: Incidence, Causes, Severity, and Costs," 21 *Accident Analysis and Prevention* 233 (1989); Jeanne Ann Grisso et al., "Injuries in an Elderly Inner-City Population," 38 *Journal of the American Geriatric Society* 1326 (1990).

An alternative explanation for the low rate of criminal victimization of the elderly is that they have an irrational fear of crime and therefore take excessive precautions, as by becoming hermits. Although popular, this view appears to be exaggerated.[17] Survey data do reveal, however, that elderly people are more afraid to walk at night in their neighborhoods than young people are.[18]

It is noteworthy that between 1973 and 1992, a period when the overall rate of crimes of violence was essentially constant, the rate of crimes of violence against persons 65 or older fell by almost 50 percent, while the rate of thefts from persons in that age group fell more slowly than the overall rate of personal theft.[19] These trends may be related to the rapidly growing income of elderly people during this period, which both facilitated their choice of residential and activity patterns in which the risk of violence would be minimized and made them more attractive targets for acquisitive crimes.

The elderly offender. The low rate of criminal victimization of the elderly is matched and in fact exceeded by their remarkably low crime rate. Of total arrests in the United States in 1992, only 0.7 percent were of persons aged 60 to 64; persons 65 and over accounted for an identical percentage.[20] The total for both groups was thus only 1.4 percent, even though persons aged 60 and older constitute more than 20 percent of all Americans 15 years old or older. As one would expect, the percentage of arrests of persons 65 and over for the most serious crimes of violence—murder, forcible rape, robbery, and aggravated assault—is lower than for serious property crimes such as burglary, larceny-theft, motor vehicle theft, and arson. But the difference is small—0.6 versus 0.8 percent—and there is no difference when we drop down to the 60 through 64 year olds. The meagerness of the difference between the violent and nonviolent crime rates of the el-

17. Randy L. LaGrange and Kenneth F. Ferraro, "The Elderly's Fear of Crime: A Critical Examination of the Research," 9 *Research on Aging* 372 (1987).

18. According to data from the General Social Survey (see chapter 4, note 44), 60 percent of persons in their eighties are afraid, compared to only 36.7 percent of those in their forties.

19. U.S. Dept. of Justice, Bureau of Justice Statistics, *Criminal Victimization in the United States: 1973–92 Trends* 1, 13 (NCJ-147006, July 1994).

20. The statistics in this paragraph are from U.S. Dept. of Justice, Federal Bureau of Investigation, *Uniform Crime Reports: Crime in the United States 1992* 228 (1993) (tab. 38). Arrest statistics are imperfect proxies for crimes committed, but I have found no data on the age of persons who commit crimes but are not arrested. For an excellent review of the literature on elderly criminality, see Kyle Kercher, "Causes and Correlates of Crime Committed by the Elderly: A Review of the Literature," in *Critical Issues in Aging Policy: Linking Research and Values* 254 (Edgar F. Borgatta and Rhonda J. V. Montgomery, eds., 1987).

derly and near-elderly is surprising, especially since one might expect violent criminals to be particularly likely to be killed before they reached the threshold of old age.

We shall see that arrest statistics probably underestimate the amount of criminal activity of the old. Nevertheless, that amount must be small.

Elderly criminality was found, in the only economic study of the subject that I have discovered, to be "rational" in the sense of being responsive to legitimate employment opportunities and other factors bearing on the costs and benefits of alternative uses of one's time.[21] The study did not, however, attempt to explain the striking difference between the crime rates of old and young.

The fact that the violent and nonviolent crime rates of the elderly are so close suggests that enfeeblement is not the principal factor in the remarkable law-abidingness of old people. Another reason to doubt this is that the crime rate is already very low for persons in the 55 to 59 age group; only 1.1 percent of total arrests are of persons in that group.[22] No doubt enfeeblement plays some role, a controversial example being the propensity of elderly sex offenders to commit offenses against children rather than adults.[23] And there are more old women than old men, and criminality is much less common among women than among men. But enfeeblement and the falling sex ratio can together explain only a part of the age-related decline in criminality.

The decline challenges the simple life-cycle model of incentives and behavior, especially in a system such as ours in which the principal method of punishing crimes is imprisonment. Even a very long prison term is unlikely to be an effective deterrent to the commission of crimes by persons unlikely to survive more than a small part of the term, especially because it has long been the practice to release very old prisoners rather than compel them to die in prison. And since old people are likely to seem rather "harmless," concerns with recidivism do not play a large role in the sentencing

21. Donald J. Bachand and George A. Chressanthis, "Property Crime and the Elderly Offender: A Theoretical and Empirical Analysis, 1964–1984," in *Older Offenders: Perspectives in Criminology and Criminal Justice* 76 (Belinda McCarthy and Robert Langworthy, eds., 1988).

22. U.S. Dept. of Justice, note 20 above, at 228 (tab. 38).

23. E. A. Fattah and V. F. Sacco, *Crime and Victimization of the Elderly* 39–48 (1989); cf. William Wilbanks, "Are Elderly Felons Treated More Leniently by the Criminal Justice System?" 26 *International Journal of Aging and Human Development* 275, 282 (1988) (tab. 3). For evidence that "opportunistic" pedophilia—substituting a child as the victim of a sexual offense because the offender is too feeble to rape an adult—is rare, see A. Nicholas Groth, *Men Who Rape: The Psychology of the Offender* 144–145 (1979); Marc Hillbrand, Hilliard Foster, Jr., and Michael Hirt, "Rapists and Child Molesters: Psychometric Comparisons," 19 *Archives of Sexual Behavior* 65, 69 (1990).

of the old—another reason to expect their punishments to be too slight to deter effectively.[24] The puzzle is deepened when the concept of multiple selves is brought into the picture. To the extent that the young self can be regarded as a separate person from his old self, the segment of a long prison sentence that will be served when the criminal is old is tantamount to punishment for a different, albeit closely related, person's crime.

In light of these points, how are we to explain the low crime rate of the elderly? There are several explanations. To an economist, crime is a form of work, and productivity in any line of work is a function, in part at least, of investment in human capital. We therefore would not expect elderly people to invest heavily in the acquisition of criminal skills; and without those skills, the probability of apprehension and conviction is greater. Since the expected cost of punishment is approximately the present disutility of punishment times the probability that punishment will be imposed, a drop in the former term can be offset by an increase in the latter term.

The offset is particularly likely if criminal skills differ significantly from those employed in lawful occupations. The decline of fluid intelligence increases the cost of learning new skills. Thus, not only are the benefits of investing in the acquisition of criminal skills truncated by the short life expectancy of the old; the cost of making the investment is higher than in the case of young people. Such skills are therefore unlikely to be acquired late in life, and without them the probability of apprehension and conviction, and so the cost of becoming a criminal, will soar. If for these reasons the demand for criminal activity by old people is slight even when the severity of punishment is also slight, the lenient treatment of elderly offenders by the criminal justice system may be optimal.

The severity with which elderly criminals are punished may, moreover, be greater than an exclusive focus on the truncation of prison sentences would suggest. The reasons are twofold, and were suggested in earlier chapters. First, one's time may actually become more valuable (in terms of utility, not earnings) as one ages. Although at some point the difference

24. For evidence that elderly criminals are in fact punished lightly, see Fattah and Sacco, note 23 above, at 72–75; Dean J. Champion, "The Severity of Sentencing: Do Federal Judges Really Go Easier on Elderly Felons in Plea-Bargaining Negotiations Compared with Their Younger Counterparts?" in *Older Offenders: Perspectives in Criminology and Criminal Justice,* note 21 above, at 143; John H. Lindquist, O. Z. White, and Carl D. Chambers, "Elderly Felons: Dispositions of Arrests," in *The Elderly: Victims and Deviants* 161 (Carl D. Chambers et al., eds., 1987). However, Wilbanks, note 23 above, presents evidence that elderly felons are not treated more leniently by the California criminal justice system when other factors besides age are controlled for. On the bearing of the federal sentencing guidelines on lenient treatment of the elderly offender, see discussion in chapter 12.

between freedom and confinement becomes pretty academic—one is not much freer in a nursing home than in a prison, and indeed the differences between a nursing home and a prison geriatric ward may be slight—few enfeebled elderly are capable of committing crimes.

Second, not everyone's future is bounded by his life. If old people are more likely than young ones to believe in an afterlife in which the good are rewarded and the wicked punished, they are less likely to think that any punishment visited on them for criminal acts will be truncated by the death of the body. Likewise if they want to leave a good name. Although few of us believe any more that the sins of the father are visited upon the children even unto remote generations, families do have reputations, good or bad, that affect the terms on which their members can engage in advantageous transactions. The notion of "bringing disgrace upon one's family" is not entirely archaic. An old person who is altruistic toward the members of his family who are likely to survive him will incur disutility if by committing a crime he imposes a reputation cost on those younger members. And the older he is, the larger will the bequest motive—including a "reputation bequest" motive—and other forms of posthumous utility loom in his utility function, as other sources of utility fall away.

My analysis predicts that, other things being equal, the elderly crime rate will be greater (1) the more severely the particular type of offense is punished (because the truncation of punishment due to the imminence of death will be greater the longer the sentence), and (2) the less new skill is required for its commission. So we would expect, for example, more arrests for drunk driving (per mile driven) among old people relative to young than for counterfeiting, because driving is not a new skill for old people. But we would still expect fewer arrests for drunk driving among old than among young drivers, because the expected accident cost from drunk driving is greater for the elderly than for the young. My prediction about the age incidence of different crimes is borne out by the statistics on arrests of the elderly. Recall that only 0.7 percent of all arrests are of persons 65 or older. For driving under the influence, however, the percentage rises to 1.3 (which is still far below the percentage of elderly persons in the population), and for forgery and counterfeiting it falls to 0.3.[25]

I have been discussing the costs to the elderly of committing crimes. Another reason for the low crime rate of the elderly, though one likely to be operative in only a small fraction of cases, is that for crimes that yield benefits over a long period of time (killing a hated enemy, perhaps?), the

25. Computed from U.S. Dept. of Justice, note 20 above, at 228 (tab. 38).

benefits are greater the younger the criminal. Such a crime is, in effect, an investment and we know that the return on investments is truncated for elderly people because of their short life expectancy.

The career criminal. I have thus far been considering the case of people who were law-abiding until they became old. What of career criminals? Why do they seem to burn out when they get old?[26] These are people whose skills are specialized to criminal activity, who have already blotched the family escutcheon, and who are less likely than the law-abiding to be religious.[27] It might seem, given the decline with age in fluid intelligence, that it would be as difficult to switch out of criminal activity at an advanced age as to switch into it at an advanced age. Many criminal occupations are strenuous and dangerous, however, and such occupations take a toll on a person's health, leading to earlier retirement than in softer, safer jobs; recall the relation of stress to burnout discussed in chapter 4. A less obvious point is that arrest and prosecution have a sorting effect. The less skillful criminals are caught repeatedly and learn from this that they aren't very good at what they do; so they tend eventually to drop out, thinning the ranks of older criminals. The more skillful avoid frequent arrest or conviction, and hence are underrepresented in statistics of older criminals, which are based on arrest. This point implies that the elderly are not quite so law-abiding as one would infer from arrest statistics alone.

Possibly the most important factor in the very early "retirement" of criminals is that every time a person is caught and convicted, the probability that he will be caught and convicted the next time he commits a crime is increased. He now has a criminal record, which will make the police more likely to suspect him; and if a criminal defendant testifies in his own defense, his prior convictions can be used to undermine the credibility of his testimony. This prospect discourages defendants with a record of convictions from testifying, and by doing so increases the probability of their conviction (though presumably less than if they did testify), since, although instructed otherwise, jurors frequently infer guilt from a defendant's failure to testify. Not only is the recidivist thus easier to catch and convict (at least if we ignore the fact, discussed below, that he is apt to be more experienced than a first offender); he is bound, as a recidivist, to receive a heavier sen-

---

26. Not all of them, of course; and as human-capital theory predicts, the "professional" criminal who invests in his criminal skills remains a criminal longer than the amateur. Evelyn S. Newman et al., *Elderly Criminals* 8–11 (1984).

27. Lee Ellis, "Religiosity and Criminality: Evidence and Explanations surrounding Complex Relationships," 28 *Sociological Perspective* 501 (1985).

tence. On both counts the expected punishment cost of the already con-victed is higher than that of the first offender, and the cost mounts with every successive conviction. Eventually the expected punishment cost is so high, even with the truncation effect, that the career criminal is deterred, "retires," unless he has exceptional skills which enable him to avoid being caught; on either count we expect age and known criminal activity to be negatively correlated even for career criminals.

We might even speculate that one reason for punishing recidivists more heavily than first-time criminals is to maintain constant deterrence in the face of the age-related decline, due to the truncation effect, in the deterrent effect of punishment. There is a parallel to the backloading of compensa-tion in order to offset the last-period problem, discussed in chapter 3. The expected cost of imprisonment, as of being fired from one's job, declines as one gets closer to retirement from life and from work, respectively. The decline can be offset, up to a point anyway (an important qualification, to which I return in chapter 12), by lengthening the prison sentence of re-peat offenders, who by virtue of being "careerists" are likely to continue committing crimes to an advanced age. A further justification for the heavier punishment of recidivists is that it is necessary to counteract learn-ing by doing, that is, the reduction in the probability of being apprehended and hence in the expected cost of punishment as a criminal gains more experience.

This discussion of the career criminal helps to show why the reported crime rate of the elderly is so *very* low. Both an aging effect and a selection effect are at work. For those who start out straight, the benefit-cost ratio of switching into criminal activity when old is adverse. For those who start out crooked, few survive as criminals to old age unless they are so good that they are never caught and convicted, in which event they do not show up in the statistics of elderly crime.

Suicide

While crime rates decline with age, male suicide rates rise monotonically with age after declining in early adulthood.[28] If crime and suicide are

28. U.S. Senate Special Committee on Aging et al., *Aging America: Trends and Projections* 115 (1991 ed.). In 1990, for example, the suicide rate was 34.2 per 100,000 for white men aged 65 to 74, 60.2 for those aged 75 to 84, and 70.3 for those aged 85 and older, compared to only 25.3 for those aged 35 to 44. U.S. Bureau of the Census, *Statistical Abstract of the United States 1993* 99 (113th ed.) (ser. 137). This pattern appears to hold in most other nations as well, al-though in Finland, which has the highest suicide rate of any Western country, the suicide rate peaks at ages 55–64, and in Denmark and Germany there is a dip between that and the next age

thought to be merely different manifestations of a propensity for violence, this divergence is puzzling. Not so if an economic approach is taken. The utility of living, net of disutility due to suffering, bereavement, and other losses, declines with age. A falling present value of remaining life intersects a rising curve of suffering. Gary Becker and Rebecca Kilburn emphasize two further points.[29] First, since perceptions of welfare are relative, aging may cause a sharp drop in utility even for persons who are "objectively" well off, because they will compare their present state to their own earlier state rather than just to that of other persons. Second, one component of expected utility for a young person—the "option" value of continued living, a value generated by the possibility that the quality of one's life will improve significantly at some future time—is greatly diminished in old age. Aging reduces both the objective likelihood of such an improvement and, because of the effect of aging in boiling away the optimism of youth, the subjective likelihood as well. And if there is an improvement, there will be less time to enjoy it. For all these reasons, aging reduces the option value of living on.

Family altruism, as well as fear of death and other costs of suicide (of which more in chapter 10), may deter the elderly person from ending his life even if his net expected utility of continuing to live would otherwise be negative. Or may not. The stigma of suicide is less than that of crime, and in some circles is nil, at least when committed by an elderly person in poor health. Hence the effect of suicide on the family's "good name" may not be great. In some cases family altruism will actually increase rather than reduce the net expected benefit of suicide, by accelerating the inheritance of the elderly person's property. By reducing his consumption to zero, the elderly person who, having inheritable wealth, ends his life enables greater consumption by his heirs unless he is a much more efficient saver than they.

Since utility is a positive function of income, and since the incomes of the elderly have risen dramatically in recent decades, we should not be surprised that the white male elderly suicide rate has fallen in the last half

---

group (65–74), although the peak rate is, as in the United States, in the 75-and-over group. See World Health Organization, *World Health Statistics Annual,* various years. For an excellent discussion of the U.S. and foreign statistics on suicide by the elderly, see John McIntosh, "Epidemiology of Suicide in the Elderly," in *Suicide and the Older Adult* 15 (Antoon A. Leenaars et al., eds., 1992).

29. Gary S. Becker and M. Rebecca Kilburn, "The Economics of Misery" (unpublished, University of Chicago Dept. of Economics, Dec. 19, 1993).

century.[30] This explanation for the data is too pat, however, because the 65-and-over suicide rate rose during the 1980s[31] even though the prosperity of elderly Americans was continuing to grow. The rise was not merely the result of the higher number of people in the very oldest age groups, for whom the utility of life might be especially meager; the suicide rate of white males aged 65 to 69 rose between 1981 and 1989.[32]

An alternative, noneconomic explanation for the high suicide rate of the elderly is that depression increases the risk of suicide and is more prevalent among the elderly.[33] But it is unclear whether depression really is more prevalent among them[34] unless we give "depression" a circular definition that makes it a mysterious something that predisposes people to suicide. Depression is difficult to distinguish operationally from rational, clear-eyed evaluation of declining quality and prospects of life; that is, from "depressive realism" (see chapter 5). A study that ascribes elderly suicide to depression also recommends such "treatments" as furnishing elderly people with pets.[35] As a cat lover of the most abjectly sentimental sort, I would be the last person in the world to question the value of "pet therapy." But it is more accurately if less impressively described as a method of increasing happiness, and thus reducing the incentive to self-destruction, than as a "treatment" for "clinical depression."

The high rate of suicide among the elderly is especially striking because of selection bias, the omnipresent problem in attempting to infer the

30. Patricia L. McCall, "Adolescent and Elderly White Male Suicide Trends: Evidence of Changing Well-Being?" 46 *Journal of Gerontology* S43, S44 (1991) (fig. 1); Dan Blazer, "Suicide Risk Factors in the Elderly: An Epidemiological Study," 24 *Journal of Geriatric Psychiatry* 175, 177 (1991); James R. Marshall, "Changes in Aged White Male Suicide: 1948–1972," 33 *Journal of Gerontology* 763 (1978).

31. Nancy J. Osgood, *Suicide in Later Life: Recognizing the Warning Signs* 10–13 (1992); Mark S. Kaplan, Margaret E. Adamek, and Scott Johnson, "Trends in Firearm Suicide among Older American Males: 1979–1988," 34 *Gerontologist* 59 (1994).

32. Calculated from Bureau of the Census, *Vital Statistics of the United States,* 1965–1989.

33. See, for example, Kalle Achté, "Suicidal Tendencies in the Elderly," 18 *Suicide and Life-Threatening Behavior* 55, 57 (1988).

34. See James C. Anthony and Ahmed Aboraya, "The Epidemiology of Selected Mental Disorders in Later Life," in *Handbook of Mental Health and Aging* 27, 42, 46 (James E. Birren et al., eds., 2d ed. 1992); Blazer, note 30 above, at 182–183; Gerda E. Gomez and Efrain A. Gomez, "Depression in the Elderly," *Journal of Psychosocial Nursing,* no. 5, p. 28 (1993). In addition to the difficulty discussed in the text, many of the symptoms of depression—such as apathy, loss of appetite, and sleeplessness—are equally symptoms of physical disorders of old age.

35. Nancy J. Osgood, Barbara A. Brant, and Aaron Lipman, *Suicide among the Elderly in Long-Term Care Facilities* 115, 140 (1991). On the difficulty of fitting the conventional psychiatric criteria of depression to "depression" in elderly people, see Dan G. Blazer, "Affective Disorders in Late Life," in *Geriatric Psychiatry* 369, 370–371 (Ewald W. Busse and Dan G. Blazer, eds., 1989).

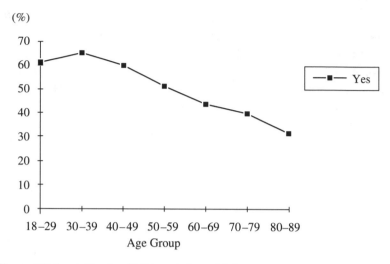

Figure 6.1 Is suicide okay if disease is incurable?

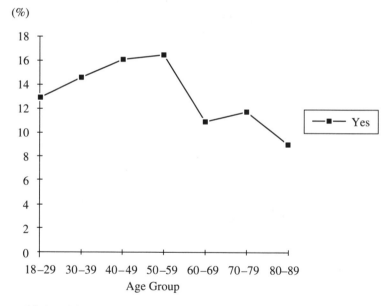

Figure 6.2 Is suicide okay if tired of living?

effect of age on behavior from comparisons between old and young. The most suicidal people can be expected to commit suicide at relatively young ages, with the result that the elderly represent a population sample biased against suicide. This may explain the puzzling fact that, as shown in figures 6.1 and 6.2, older people are much more likely than young or middle-aged ones to believe that it is wrong to commit suicide just because one has an incurable disease or is tired of living.[36]

Selection bias has a further significance in explaining the pattern of elderly suicides. It implies that the suicide attempts of the elderly are likely to be more deliberated, less impulsive, and more likely to succeed than those of the young, because those prone to commit suicide impulsively are likely to have done so before reaching old age. (For evidence, see chapter 10.) A related implication is that elderly suicides are less likely to be the product of clinical depression (unless such depression really is more common among old than among young people, despite the doubts that I have expressed), because a disproportionate number of persons suffering from depression will have committed suicide before reaching old age.

The steep age gradient for suicide is limited to men. Not only is the female suicide rate much lower, but it does not increase as much with age. The ratio of male to female suicide rates is 6.10 among persons 65 and older, compared to only 3.81 in the population as a whole.[37] Proneness to suicide is thus an area in which there is a greater difference between men and women in old age than at earlier ages. There is no generally accepted explanation for either the divergence in suicide rates between men and women or the increase in that divergence with age.

Penny-Pinching

Fortunately, unsafe driving, crime, and suicide are not the principal activities of elderly persons. The principal activities are work, recreation, and household production, including care of self.[38] A minor but extremely curious activity of the old is penny-pinching—as seen in coupon-shopping and bargain-hunting generally. Young people are amazed at the lengths to which the old will go to save a few dollars. But this behavior is rational. The cost of time is very low for retired people; and penny-pinching, as by careful shopping, is a time-intensive activity. Furthermore, retired people generally have a lower income than when they were working, implying (by the assumption of diminishing marginal utility of income) that they value the extra dollar more in retirement than when they were working. Since the costs of penny-pinching are lower to the old and the benefits greater, we

36. The source of the data for figures 6.1 and 6.2 is the General Social Survey. See note 18 above. The possibility that a cohort effect is at work cannot be excluded, however.

37. Robert Travis, "Suicide in Cross-Cultural Perspective," 31 *International Journal of Comparative Sociology* 237, 241, 244 (1990) (tabs. 1, 2). Figures are for the United States in 1986.

38. I discussed the consumption and savings behavior of the elderly in chapter 4.

should expect them to engage in this behavior more than young people do. An additional reason is that penny-pinching is a game (how much money can I save), and its entertainment value is greater to people whose alternative entertainments have been curtailed by age. It also provides an occasion for demonstrating the retention of mental acuity.

It could be objected that a rational person who derives more utility from a dollar when old than when young will through saving reallocate dollars from his young to his old self until the utility of the marginal dollar is equalized at all ages; this will maximize his total lifetime utility. But this assumes that the young self, who controls the allocation of income over the life cycle (the old self cannot do anything to reduce the income or consumption of his young self), will treat the welfare of the old self equally with his own; and it is by no means certain that he will, for the reasons explored in the discussion of the concept of multiple selves in chapter 4.

Sex

The Kinsey reports found that sexual activity declines in men from about the age of 30 and in women from about the age of 40.[39] More recent survey data suggest that the age of onset of the decline, at least when measured by the percentage of persons sexually inactive for the past year, is the fifties for men but only the twenties for women. Although the percentage of sexually inactive women remains below 20 percent until the fifties, by the late fifties it exceeds 40 percent, compared to less than 16 percent of men. Many elderly men and women continue to be sexually active, some to extremely advanced ages. In the 65–69 age group, almost 80 percent of men, and 40 percent of women, remain sexually active, while even in the 80–84 age group more than 40 percent of men do, though fewer than 10 percent of women.[40] As part of normal aging, sexual desire declines in both sexes,

39. Alfred C. Kinsey, Wardell B. Pomeroy, and Clyde E. Martin, *Sexual Behavior in the Human Male* 220–221 (1948) (tab. 44 and fig. 34); Kinsey et al., *Sexual Behavior in the Human Female* 548 (1953) (tab. 153). The Kinsey samples for elderly men and, especially, elderly women are very small, however.

40. Edward O. Laumann et al., *The Social Organization of Sexuality: Sexual Practices in the United States* 88, 90, 92–93 (1994) (tab. 3.4 and fig. 3.1). The source for the data on persons 60 and older in *The Social Organization of Sexuality* is the General Social Survey. See note 18 above. The data for younger persons are from the National Health and Social Life Survey conducted by the University of Chicago. Unfortunately, that survey—the most comprehensive representative survey of the sexual behavior of the American people that has ever been conducted—was limited to persons between the ages of 18 and 59.

For other estimates of levels of sexual activity of elderly people, see Ananias C. Diokno, Morton B. Brown, and A. Regula Herzog, "Sexual Function in the Elderly," 150 *Archives of*

but rarely to zero.[41] The ability to have an orgasm also declines, but far more in men than in women. Why then are old men so much more likely than old women to be sexually active? There appear to be two reasons. Since women cease being fertile at a much earlier age than men, one expects on genetic grounds, and finds, that on average (the vital qualification) elderly women are less attractive sexually to men of all ages than elderly men are to women of all ages.[42] And there are far more elderly women than elderly men because of the much greater longevity of women in modern societies.

The effect of these two factors (relative attractiveness and number) is to make the "effective sex ratio," which is to say the ratio of sexually available and desired males to sexually available and desired females, very low among the elderly. Among young people a low effective sex ratio is associated with male promiscuity, with low levels of rape and child sexual abuse (because willing adult females are not in short supply), with a low female marriage rate, and with a high rate of births out of wedlock.[43] Among the elderly a low effective sex ratio has different implications, not only because of the effects of aging on sexual desire and performance and on fertility, but also because the sexual opportunities of the elderly are a function in part of choices they made when young. Because of the costs, relative to the benefits, of forming new relationships in old age (see chapter 3), we expect (and find) that the sexual activity of the elderly is highly correlated with marriage, especially for women.[44] This correlation is unfavorable to elderly women, because so many more elderly women than elderly men are widowed or divorced. In 1989, 78.4 percent of men aged 65 to 74 were married and living with their spouse, while only 51.4 percent of women in that age group were. And for the 85-and-over group the disparity was much greater—48.2 percent of men versus only 9.1 percent of

---

Internal Medicine 197 (1990); Judy G. Bretschneider and Norma L. McCoy, "Sexual Interest and Behavior in Healthy 80- to 102-Year-Olds," 17 *Archives of Sexual Behavior* 109 (1988); Edward M. Brecher et al., *Love, Sex, and Aging: A Consumers Union Report* (1984); John W. Lorton and Eveleen L. Lorton, *Human Development through the Lifespan* 497–499 (1984).

41. For good discussions, see Arshag D. Mooradian and Vicki Greiff, "Sexuality in Older Women," 150 *Archives of Internal Medicine* 1033 (1990); David L. Rowland et al., "Aging and Sexual Function in Men," 22 *Archives of Sexual Behavior* 545 (1993).

42. See, for example, Mary B. Harris, "Growing Old Gracefully: Age Concealment and Gender," 49 *Journal of Gerontology* P149, P156 (1994). Of course, there are exceptions. See Lois W. Banner, *In Full Flower: Aging Women, Power, and Sexuality: A History* (1992). I am offering merely a statistical generalization.

43. Richard A. Posner, *Sex and Reason* 136–141 (1992).

44. Stephen J. Weiler, "Aging and Sexuality and the Myth of Decline," in *Aging: Stability and Change in the Family* 317 (Robert W. Fogel et al., eds., 1981); Bretschneider and McCoy, note 40 above, at 126–127.

women.[45] Some gerontologists have seriously proposed that polygynous marriage be permitted to the elderly as a way of alleviating the shortage of men.[46] There is a bit of evidence that elderly women may turn to homosexual relationships ("opportunistic homosexuality") because of the shortage of men, and more evidence that they turn to masturbation.[47] Despite these substitutions, it is apparent that the ratio of sexual activity of men to that of women is higher among old than among young people.[48]

The picture changes somewhat if we turn from elderly male heterosexuals to elderly male homosexuals. The traditional view was that the aging male homosexual was a pathetic individual because of a cult of youth in the homosexual subculture.[49] This view has been challenged by more recent scholarship.[50] Yet there is persuasive evidence that homosexual men, like heterosexual men (to whom they are similar in most respects other than sexual orientation), place a greater premium on youth than women do.[51] One consequence is that elderly homosexual men appear to have fewer unpaid sexual opportunities than elderly heterosexual men.[52] Another is that a higher percentage of elderly homosexual men than elderly heterosexual men live alone.[53]

---

45. U.S. Senate Special Committee on Aging et al., note 28 above, at 184 (tab. 6–1). For more detailed statistics, see Jacob S. Siegel, *A Generation of Change: A Profile of America's Older Population* 300–311 (1993).

46. Diana K. Harris and William E. Cole, *Sociology of Aging* 234–235 (1980).

47. See Brecher et al., note 40 above, at 215; Catherine G. Adams and Barbara F. Turner, "Reported Change in Sexuality from Young Adulthood to Old Age," 21 *Journal of Sex Research* 126, 133–134, 139 (1985).

48. Lorton and Lorton, note 40 above, at 499; Maj-Briht Bergström-Walan and Helle H. Nielsen, "Sexual Expression among 60–80 Year Old Men and Women: A Sample from Sweden," 27 *Journal of Sex Research* 289, 291 (1990); see also Adams and Turner, note 47 above. This is particularly true in the oldest age groups; recall the figures on the relative percentage of sexually active men and women in the 80–84 age group.

49. See, for example, John H. Gagnon and William Simon, *Sexual Conduct: The Social Sources of Human Sexuality* 149–151 (1973).

50. See, for example, Mary Riege Laner, "Growing Older Male: Heterosexual and Homosexual," 18 *Gerontologist* 496 (1978); Heather Gray and Paula Dressel, "Alternative Interpretations of Aging among Gay Males," 25 *Gerontologist* 83 (1985).

51. See, for example, Gray and Dressel, note 50 above, at 84–85; John Alan Lee, "What Can Homosexual Aging Studies Contribute to Theories of Aging?" 13 *Journal of Homosexuality* 43, 62 (1987).

52. Cf. Brecher et al., note 40 above, at 225; Douglas C. Kimmel, "Life-History Interviews of Aging Gay Men," 10 *International Journal of Aging and Human Development* 239, 245 (1979). Raymond M. Berger, *Gay and Gray: The Older Homosexual Man* 159–160, 164, 185 (1982), confirms that older homosexual men (over 40) have limited social contacts with younger men.

53. Compare Jean K. Quam and Gary S. Whitford, "Adaptation and Age-Related Expectations of Older Gay and Lesbian Adults," 32 *Gerontologist* 367, 370 (1992) (more than 63 percent of male homosexuals in sample of male and female homosexuals aged 50 to 73 lived alone), and

The cost of forming new relationships in old age has other implications for sexual activity. It may be a factor in the tendency that I noted earlier for older men to substitute child sexual abuse for other forms of sexual crime and also in their tendency to substitute masturbation for intercourse.[54] The broader point is that we should expect to observe among the unmarried elderly some tendency to substitute "spot" for "relational" contracting in the sexual "market" because of the high cost of forming new relationships.

Work and Leisure

The discussion in chapter 4 of the factors bearing on the timing of retirement was not exhaustive. Other important factors include the structure of retirement benefits. For example, the receipt of social security retirement benefits is, until the age of 70, contingent on the recipient's not having significant income from work. The effect is that of a heavy tax on the income of persons eligible for those benefits until they reach 70. Even without regard to the more favorable income-tax treatment of social security benefits than of "earned" income, and the fact that there is no social security tax on them, a person who is earning $30,000 in a job when he could retire and receive social security benefits of $20,000 is in effect paying a two-thirds tax on his earned income. The lower the age of eligibility for social security and the greater the benefits, the greater the incentive to retire early. And people who retire at age 65 are unlikely to reenter the work force five years later when they could do so without giving up any of their social security benefits;[55] their work skills will have deteriorated.

Kimmel, note 52 above, at 242 (10 out of 14 male homosexuals between the ages of 55 and 81 lived alone), with the figure in the text that 78.4 percent of men aged 65 to 74 were married and living with their spouses, implying that a maximum of 21.6 percent in this older (presumably mostly heterosexual) group were living alone. (See also A. J. Lucco, "Planned Retirement Housing Preferences of Older Homosexuals," 14 *Journal of Homosexuality* 35, 50 [1987].) The actual figure is undoubtedly lower than 21.6 percent, since some of these men must have been living with someone other than a spouse. However, a smaller percentage of women in the homosexual sample were living alone (41 percent) than the percentage of women in the 65 to 74 age group who were not married and living with their spouse (48.6 percent). Since most people do not like to live alone, this is consistent with other evidence (see, for example, Posner, note 43 above, at 306–307) that lesbians tend to be happier than male homosexuals. Another study of aged lesbians, however, found that only 18 percent (9 out of the 50 in the sample) were at present in a "committed relationship." Monika Kehoe, "Lesbians over 65: A Triply Invisible Minority," *Journal of Homosexuality,* May 1986, p. 139.

54. Simone de Beauvoir, *Old Age* 322–323 (1972); Lorton and Lorton, note 40 above, at 498–499.

55. See generally William J. Wiatrowski, "Factors Affecting Retirement Income," *Monthly Labor Review,* March 1993, p. 25.

But the effect of the social security program on the labor-force participation of the elderly probably is swamped by the effect of private pension plans, which generally create strong inducements to retire no later than at 65 and often substantially earlier.[56] It is true that, unlike social security retirement benefits, private pension benefits (and for that matter most public pension benefits other than social security—for example military pensions and pensions of public school teachers, police officers, judges, and other civil servants) are not conditioned on cessation of all work. They are conditioned on cessation only of full-time work for the employer in whose employ the benefits were earned. So we expect and find that some retirees seek second careers. They are especially likely to do so if they retired before they became eligible for social security retirement benefits. But these careers are mostly in "dead-end" jobs.[57] The reasons should be obvious from previous chapters. The decline in fluid intelligence with age makes it costly for the older person to acquire new skills, and his benefits from doing so are reduced because the payback period for any new investment that he does make in his human capital will be truncated. (The metaphor "dead end" is peculiarly apt.) Since dead-end jobs pay low wages, most elderly people prefer the leisure of retirement even when their pension entitlement does not (as it does in the case of social security) levy in effect a tax on those wages.

This discussion has implications for the job security of the aging worker. To the extent that his wage reflects an investment in his human capital that is specific to his present employer, it may well exceed the wage he could expect to obtain were he fired, since it is unlikely that he would make a similar investment in a different firm. The difference is likely to be especially great for the middle-aged worker, whose wage may be rising because of experience so that he is still building human capital,[58] yet whose experience may not be transferable to another employer because the human capital he is building or renewing is firm-specific human capital. Until that capital begins to depreciate more rapidly than it is being replaced, he will be increasingly valuable to the firm. That is one reason he is able to command a higher wage than he could hope for in another job. Another reason

56. Laurence J. Kotlikoff and David A. Wise, *The Wage Carrot and the Pension Stick: Retirement Benefits and Labor Force Participation* (1989). I discuss early-retirement incentives further in chapter 13.

57. Robert L. Kaufman and Seymour Spilerman, "The Age Structures of Occupations and Jobs," 87 *American Journal of Sociology* 827, 839 (1982).

58. Donald P. Schwab and Herbert G. Heneman III, "Effects of Age and Experience on Productivity," 4 *Industrial Gerontology* 113 (1977).

is that as he gets older his ability and incentive to acquire human capital specific to a different firm decline, and this makes him less likely to quit and by quitting wipe out his present employer's investment in him. Beyond some point, however, the older he gets, the less valuable he becomes to his present firm at the same time that he is becoming ever less employable elsewhere, even though he may be years short of retirement. The precarious position of the older worker makes it easy to see why unionization is generally believed to be more attractive to older than to younger workers (see chapter 3) and helps explain the push behind the age discrimination in employment law, which I shall examine in detail in chapter 13.

Average age at retirement differs across occupations, and is one factor in the different age profiles of different occupations.[59] The more strenuous or dangerous the occupation and the smaller the optimal investment in human capital in the occupation, the earlier the age of retirement. Both points are illustrated by military careers. Retirement is generally earlier for low-ranking soldiers than for high-ranking officers. The former have by and large the most strenuous and dangerous jobs, and, partly because it does not pay to invest as much human capital in a worker who is likely to be killed or disabled, their value ceases to grow significantly with experience after a relatively short period of time. Senior officers, in contrast, have less strenuous and dangerous assignments, so the age-decay curve is less steep; and they employ more complex skills, requiring a larger investment in human capital to bring to a peak. With military employment coming more and more to resemble modern civilian employment (a trend aptly if exaggeratedly captured in the phrase "push-button warfare"), the traditional system of retirement (half pay after twenty years of service)[60] is increasingly being questioned.[61]

The algorithm that the Social Security Administration uses to determine whether applicants for social security disability benefits are totally disabled conclusively presumes that an older worker with limited education is totally disabled if he has a severe impairment, whereas if he were younger additional evidence of disability would have to be considered or a more severe impairment established. This makes good sense. An older worker with limited general human capital (a limitation proxied by lack of formal education) has especially poor employment prospects. Almost his

59. For an interesting discussion, with data, see Kaufman and Spilerman, note 57 above.

60. See Headquarters, Department of the Army, "Handbook on Retirement and Services for Army Personnel and Their Families" 5–1 (Pamphlet No. 600–5, Aug. 1, 1982).

61. See, for example, "Military Retirement: The Administration's Plan and Related Proposals" (American Enterprise Institute Legislative Analysis, 1980).

only human capital—specific human capital—is nonportable, and it is too late for him to acquire new capital with a new employer.

Self-employed persons—but taxicab drivers and tailors more than lawyers and doctors—tend to retire later than employees.[62] A superficial explanation is that the self-employed are not "forced" to choose between full-time work and retirement, so they gradually reduce the amount of time they work, thus postponing (full) retirement. But with the doubtful exception (see chapter 13) of mandatory retirement at fixed ages, people retire because they consider themselves better off not working, not because they are dragged kicking and screaming from the workplace. And their decision to retire has nothing directly to do with whether they are self-employed or employed by someone else.

Another unconvincing explanation for later retirement by the self-employed is that self-employment tends to attract risk-takers, and risk-takers do not like a common form of retirement pension—the defined-benefit plan, in which all investment risk is borne by the employer (see chapter 12). But an employee who wants more risk in his financial assets than a defined-benefit plan confers will usually be able to achieve his desired level of risk by borrowing more heavily than he would otherwise do or by investing his savings in more risky vehicles than he would otherwise find attractive.

The most convincing explanation for later retirement by self-employed workers is that a reduction in hours worked is less costly to the worker (or his employer) when he does not occupy expensive space, use expensive equipment, or enjoy fringe benefits that are independent of the precise number of hours worked. The lower these costs are, the less the hourly cost of his work will rise as the number of hours he works falls. Consider a worker who receives a wage of $10 an hour for a 40-hour week and uses equipment that costs the employer $200 a week, making the hourly cost of employing this worker $15 ($10 + $200/40). If he works only 20 hours a week with no reduction in wage and no possibility of another worker's using the equipment the other 20 hours, the hourly cost of employing him will rise to $20 ($10 + $200/20).

Self-employed professionals, such as doctors and lawyers, often have expensive equipment the cost of which is independent of how many hours they work. This will make their net income fall disproportionately to any reduction in hours. In the previous example, if the self-employed profes-

62. Kaufman and Spilerman, note 57 above, at 837–838.

sional's gross income is $15 an hour (with $5 representing the cost of amortizing his equipment), that income will fall to $7.50 per hour if he reduces his hours by half, and the result will be a 75 percent decline in his net income (from $10 to $2.50), since his equipment cost is unaffected. (Chapter 4 noted the positive correlation between hours worked and hourly wage.) If the professional's equipment, though expensive when purchased, has little resale value and has been paid in full, the reduction in hours of work will not be costly to him. But today most doctors and lawyers must make substantial continuing outlays on books and equipment to remain effective practitioners.

This analysis may explain why, even though their jobs generally are less strenuous, self-employed professionals retire earlier on average than self-employed tailors, barbers, and taxicab drivers, who can reduce their hours of work without substantially reducing their hourly pay. Another reason, however, may be the higher incomes of self-employed professionals. And one group of professionals—judges—constitute the most geriatric occupation in the United States; we shall seek an explanation in chapter 8.

Residence

When there were no pensions, most retired people had no income, so they had perforce to live with their children or other family members. This pattern of "coresidence" has changed dramatically. Most retired persons live either by themselves or in nursing homes, though intermediate institutions (retirement homes with nursing-home facilities available on demand) are becoming increasingly common. The change from coresidence to individual residence is sometimes deplored as condemning people to a bitter and lonely old age and depriving the young of the wisdom of the aged. But it is important to distinguish between independent and institutional living. The trend to the former is more convincingly understood as a voluntary joint decision by children and parents than as the abandonment of the latter by the former. For several reasons, the cost of coresidence has risen. With old people living longer, the costs to children of providing them with housing, food, companionship, and other goods and services are incurred for a longer period. With family size shrinking, there are fewer children to share the burden of aged parents; a fixed (and growing) cost is spread over fewer people. And with the great expansion in women's job opportunities, the opportunity cost of household production, which includes taking care of elderly relatives, a time-intensive activity, has been rising.[63] At the same time, the benefits of coresidence, both to the young and to the elderly members of families, have declined. Mass education, and rapid social and technological change, have reduced the value to the young of elderly relatives' wisdom.

Since the incomes of the elderly have been rising rapidly, it is likely that if they wanted to live with their children they could reimburse them for the full cost. They must not want to live with their children badly enough to pay the price that would make the children indifferent between coresidence and independent residence. As just noted, in our rapidly changing society the benefits of association between persons in different age groups are reduced because of a dearth of common experiences. In addition, there is a good deal of evidence that privacy is a superior good.[64] As the incomes of the elderly rise, they want more privacy and therefore value coresidence less.[65] Eventually, infirmity forces many elderly people into nursing homes, where there is little privacy. The immobility of the infirm forces them to choose between companionship and privacy. Although the elderly value privacy, the analysis in chapter 5 suggests that they value it less than the young do, because the value of privacy to a person (other than a recluse) is positively related to the person's transactional activity.

"Older persons, both owners and renters, resist moving," and as a result frequently live in houses that are "too large" for their needs, or in neighborhoods that are unsafe.[66] But this pattern makes perfectly good economic sense. Moving requires adaptation to new circumstances, and the costs of such adaptation are higher for older than for younger persons. A slightly less obvious point is that the benefits of a move tend to be lower

63. Cf. Kiyosi Hirosima, "The Living Arrangements and Familial Contacts of the Elderly in Japan," in *The Elderly Population in Developed and Developing World* 68, 75 (P. Krishnan and K. Mahadevan, eds., 1992).

64. See my book *Overcoming Law*, ch. 25 (1995).

65. For empirical evidence, see Robert T. Michael, Victor R. Fuchs, and Sharon R. Scott, "Changes in the Propensity to Live Alone: 1950–1976," 17 *Demography* 39 (1980); Saul Schwartz, Sheldon Danziger, and Eugene Smolensky, "The Choice of Living Arrangements by the Elderly," in *Retirement and Economic Behavior* 229, 243 (Henry J. Aaron and Gary Burtless, eds., 1984); Jeffrey A. Burr and Jan E. Mutchler, "Nativity, Acculturation, and Economic Status: Explanations of Asian American Living Arrangements in Later Life," 48 *Journal of Gerontology* S55 (1993); but see Fred C. Pampel, "Changes in the Propensity to Live Alone: Evidence from Consecutive Cross-Sectional Surveys, 1960–1976," 20 *Demography* 433 (1983), esp. p. 445. Another reason for the decline in coresidence is discussed in chapter 9.

66. Siegel, note 45 above, at 574. The inertial character of the living arrangements of elderly people is emphasized in Axel H. Börsch-Supan, "A Dynamic Analysis of Household Dissolution and Living Arrangement Transitions by Elderly Americans," in *Issues in the Economics of Aging* 89 (David A. Wise, ed., 1990).

for old persons. The benefits will be received over a shorter period, and therefore the costs of relocating are less likely to be fully amortized even if they are no higher than for young persons. But as I have said, they are higher.

I mentioned the loss of privacy in nursing homes. Another cost of institutionalized living is "atmospheric." The concentration of infirm elderly persons, a high percentage of them senile, is depressing even when efforts are made, as they often are, to segregate the most senile residents. It is no surprise that income has been found to have a strong negative effect on the probability of becoming a nursing-home resident, implying that living in a nursing home is considered to be inferior to independent living.[67] The same study found, after correcting for other factors, that the probability of becoming a nursing-home resident is positively related to age (of course) and negatively related not only to income but also to number of children and to being married, and that independently of all these factors the probability has been increasing. With longevity increasing and family size and the marriage rate decreasing, and given the unrelated time trend just noted toward nursing-home residence—a trend that may reflect a growing disinclination of family to take care of elderly members[68]—we can expect the percentage of elderly people who live in nursing homes to continue to increase unless retirement incomes also continue to increase in real (that is, inflation-adjusted) terms. Since nursing-home living is unpopular, we might expect people to increase their savings for old age in order to reduce the probability of such a destiny—but maybe not, as we shall note in chapter 11, if they are not highly altruistic toward their future old, infirm self.

In discussing the costs of nursing homes I may have seemed to overlook the most important cost—that of their large staffs. To include it, however, would be implicitly to compare the cost of maintaining an elderly person who is healthy enough to live by himself with the cost of maintaining an elderly person whose infirmities are such as to drive him into a nursing home. If physical and mental condition is held constant, the cost of institutionalized living is plainly less than the cost of living in a private residence, since there are economies of scale in institutionalized living. Indeed, were this not so, no one who was not extremely senile would enter a nursing home, because of the loss of privacy and the "atmosphere" costs. This point is important because it is the foundation of the

---

67. Börsch-Supan, note 66 above, at 102.
68. For the same reasons that coresidence is declining.

discussion in chapter 11 of what may be the most serious long-term problem created by the aging of the population: the cost of home care, which is much higher than the cost of institutional care because the economies of scale are lost.

Voting and Jury Service

Voting in political elections is an important activity of elderly people. I shall try to explain why, as shown in tables 6.1 through 6.4, the old have a greater propensity to vote than the young.[69]

The first two tables show that since 1986 a higher percentage of elderly persons has been voting, despite infirmities and institutionalization, than any other age group and that the percentage has increased since the early 1970s, while the voting percentages of all the other age groups have decreased, although the changes are not great. The disparity in voting propensities of different age groups is particularly marked in off-year congressional elections (table 6.2), where we find 76.5 percent of the elderly voting in 1990 compared to only 39.9 percent of the youngest eligible age group. The greater propensity of elderly persons to vote persists when other demographic variables are corrected for. A careful multivariate study concludes that "*aging, by itself, produces not a decline but an increase in turnout. The rate of increase in voting begins to level off at around age fifty-five but turnout continues to rise, at an increasingly slower pace, through the seventies.*"[70]

What are we to make of this? Because the probability that a major election will be decided by one vote is vanishingly close to zero, voting in such elections is not realistically interpreted as an instrumental activity, an investment. It is apparently a consumption activity,[71] which I have compared elsewhere to applauding; people derive utility from expressing a

69. The sources of the data for tables 6.1 through 6.4 are two papers by Jerry T. Jennings: "Voting and Registration in the Election of November 1992" (Current Population Reports, Population Characteristics, Series P20–466, 1993) (tab. A, p. v, and app. A, pp. A1–A7), and "Voting and Registration in the Election of November 1990" (Current Population Reports, Population Characteristics, Series P20–453, 1991) (tab. B, p. 2, and app. A, pp. 77–82).

70. Raymond E. Wolfinger and Steven J. Rosenstone, *Who Votes?* 47 (1980) (emphasis in original); see also G. Bingham Powell, Jr., "American Voter Turnout in Comparative Perspective," in *Controversies in Voting Behavior* 56, 67–73 (Richard G. Niemi and Herbert F. Weisberg, eds., 1993).

71. See, for example, Anthony J. Nownes, "Primaries, General Elections, and Voter Turnout: A Multinomial Logit Model of the Decision to Vote," 20 *American Politics Quarterly* 205 (1992).

Table 6.1 Percentage of Each Age Group That Voted in Presidential Elections, 1964–1992

Age	1964	1968	1972	1976	1980	1984	1988	1992
18–24	50.9	50.4	49.6	42.2	39.9	40.8	36.2	42.8
25–44	69.0	66.6	62.7	58.7	58.7	58.4	54.0	58.3
45–64	75.9	74.9	70.8	68.7	69.3	69.8	67.9	70.0
65+	66.3	65.8	63.5	62.2	65.1	67.7	68.8	70.1

Table 6.2 Percentage of Each Age Group That Voted in Off-Year Congressional Elections, 1966–1990

Age	1966	1970	1974	1978	1982	1986	1990
18–24	44.1	40.9	41.3	40.5	42.4	42.0	39.9
25–44	67.6	65.0	59.9	60.2	61.5	61.1	58.4
45–64	78.9	77.5	73.6	74.3	75.6	74.8	71.4
65+	73.5	73.7	70.2	72.8	75.2	76.9	76.5

view on a performance or contest.[72] But it is not a costless consumption activity, and herein, I believe, lies the clue to the greater propensity of elderly people to vote.[73] The principal cost—the time it takes to vote, and to acquire minimum information about the candidates (akin to the time spent in watching the performance that you are going to applaud at the end)—is modest. But it is not negligible, especially if the candidates are obscure, as they often are for the lesser offices. That is one reason why elections for such offices often have very low turnouts, even though the instrumental value of a vote is greater in a local than in a national election.

With time the principal cost of voting, we can formulate an economic explanation for why elderly people are more likely to vote than younger people, why the gap is greater in congressional than in presidential elections, and why it has been growing. The opportunity cost of time is lower to elderly

72. *Overcoming Law,* note 64 above, ch. 3. The extensive literature on voter turnout is illustrated by Steven J. Rosenstone and John Mark Hansen, *Mobilization, Participation, and Democracy in America* (1993); *Controversies in Voting Behavior,* note 70 above, pt. 1; Jan E. Leighley and Jonathan Nagler, "Individual and Systemic Influences on Turnout: Who Votes? 1984," 54 *Journal of Politics* 718 (1992); *Political Participation and American Democracy* (William Crotty, ed., 1991); and references in note 75 below.

73. Wolfinger and Rosenstone, note 70 above, at 60, offer the alternative suggestion that the greater propensity of old people to vote reflects the fact that "exposure to life in general and politics in particular" increases people's interest in voting.

people. Although their physical mobility may be restricted, and hence other costs of voting besides the opportunity cost of a unit of time may be higher to them than to the young,[74] the political parties compete for their favor by offering them free transportation to the polling place; and, increasingly, polling places are being established in nursing and retirement homes.

The difference in the opportunity costs of voting of elderly compared to young persons is greater, the less publicized and more obscure the election, because a greater investment in finding out about the candidates is required. This may explain why the relative turnout of the elderly is even greater in congressional than in presidential elections.[75]

Voting is not only cheaper for older than for younger people, but also more valuable. Not because the old have more to gain from the political process; they may, but that is no reason for an individual old person to vote, since his vote is not going to decide the election. Rather it is because the old have a limited menu of activities to choose from. Not only work, but also the more strenuous recreational activities, are largely barred to them. This is not just another way of saying that the opportunity cost of a few hours of their time every year or two is low. The point is rather that the benefit derived from an activity is apt to be greater the fewer the alternatives. Voting, like penny-pinching, is a more *exciting* pastime to people whose alternative pastimes are distinctly unexciting.

The greater interest that voting holds for the elderly, their low opportunity costs of time, and a truncated horizon that tends to occlude their view of issues not closely related to their own particular concerns (though altruism may, as we saw in chapter 3, lengthen their horizon) combine to make the elderly a voting bloc unusually focused on a relative handful of issues. This enhances their influence by making it difficult for politicians to win their votes without promising to protect their interests and fulfilling their promises. Although the percentage of the population that is elderly is not always a good predictor of the economic welfare of the elderly, it is in the political system of the United States.[76]

74. One of these other costs is a time cost. If it takes longer for the old person to get to the polls because of his physical infirmities, his time cost may be greater than that of the young person even if the cost of time is less to him than to the young person per unit of time.

75. The suggestion that the costs of voting are lower in heavily publicized elections is supported by the fact that turnout tends to be higher in such elections. John H. Aldrich, "Rational Choice and Turnout," 37 *American Journal of Political Science* 246, 266–268 (1993); Gary W. Cox and Michael C. Munger, "Closeness, Expenditures, and Turnout in the 1982 U.S. House Elections," 83 *American Political Science Review* 217 (1989).

76. John B. Williamson and Fred C. Pampel, *Old-Age Security in Comparative Perspective* 116, 196, 220 (1993).

All this does not explain why the ratio of older persons' propensity to vote to younger persons' has increased. One possibility is that the opportunity costs of the time of older people have declined because a higher percentage of older people are retired.

Since the percentage of the population that is 65 or older has been growing at the same time that the percentage of that age group which votes has been growing, the percentage of votes cast by the elderly has been growing more rapidly than either statistic. This is shown in the next two tables. By 1992, when 12.6 percent of the U.S. population was 65 or older, they were casting about 50 percent more votes in the presidential election than their percentage of the population (close to two-thirds more, in the congressional elections of 1990). The disproportion is much smaller when their voting percentage is compared with their percentage of the voting-age population, as done in these tables. But the adjustment obscures the fact that parents of minors are more or less adequate representatives of their children's interests, and few elderly persons have minor children. I come back to this point in chapter 11.

Comparisons between the voting behavior of old and of young must be interpreted cautiously because of the possibility of cohort effects. When one compares 18-year-olds and 65-year-olds in 1992 one is not comparing groups that differ only in age, being otherwise random draws from the same population. They are different vintages—the class of 1974 (the year of birth of the 18-year-olds) and the class of 1927—and have therefore had

Table 6.3 Votes Cast by Persons 65 and Over as Percentage of Total Votes, Presidential Elections 1964–1992
(Percentage of Voting-Age Population in Parentheses)

1964	1968	1972	1976	1980	1984	1988	1992
14.9	15.4	14.9	15.8	16.8	17.7	19.4	19.0
(14.8)	(14.8)	(15.0)	(15.3)	(15.7)	(16.1)	(16.6)	(17.0)

Table 6.4 Votes Cast by Persons 65 and Over as Percentage of Total Votes, Congressional Elections 1966–1990
(Percentage of Voting-Age Population in Parentheses)

1966	1970	1974	1978	1982	1986	1990
16.0	16.6	17.0	18.5	19.1	21.1	22.0
(14.8)	(14.9)	(15.1)	(15.5)	(15.9)	(16.4)	(16.9)

different experiences. This makes it difficult to assess the popular view that older voters are more "conservative" than younger ones, an issue to which I return in subsequent chapters.

The hypothesis that low costs of time and a paucity of other "entertainments" explain the high voter turnout of elderly persons may seem inconsistent with the fact that turnout is low among the unemployed, even after correction for other factors.[77] The unemployed, it might seem, have plenty of time, and a relative paucity of other distractions. But this is not true. The term "unemployed" generally and in the relevant studies refers to people who are looking for a job, rather than people who have dropped out of the labor force. People looking for a job are busy—looking for a job; and are likely to be preoccupied with that search to the exclusion of taking much interest in the relatively remote realm of politics.[78]

Jury service is another form of private participation in the political process. Since such service is time-intensive and the elderly have lower costs of time than younger people, we might expect them to be overrepresented on juries. It is widely believed that juries *are* dominated by retirees, but on the contrary retirees appear to be underrepresented on juries. Although almost 12 percent of the U.S. adult population is 70 years old or older, a study of federal and state juries in eight cities found that only 4 percent of jurors were that old.[79] Jury service requires greater mobility and greater overall fitness, mental as well as physical, than voting does; so we should not be surprised that a smaller percentage of the elderly serve on juries than vote. Another reason is that most employers continue their employees' regular salary during (modest) periods of jury service, thus reducing the opportunity costs to the young (who are more likely to be employed than the old) of serving on juries.

Persons 60 or older accounted for 17.8 percent of the jurors in the study, which is much closer to their percentage of the adult population (23 percent) than in the case of the 70-and-over jurors, though still below it. This is additional evidence that, as I have been emphasizing throughout this book, there is indeed a pronounced age-related decline in physical and (or) mental ability.

77. Rosenstone and Hansen, note 72 above, at 273 (tab. D-1), 282 (tab. D-5); Wolfinger and Rosenstone, note 70 above, at 29. But see Wilma Smeenk, "Non-Voting in the Netherlands and the United States" 10 (unpublished, Nijmegen University [Netherlands], Dept. of Sociology, n.d.), finding that after correction for other factors unemployment does not reduce the likelihood of one's voting.

78. See Rosenstone and Hansen, note 72 above, at 81–82, 135.

79. Computed from Washington Project Office, "The Relationship of Juror Fees and Terms of Service to Jury System Performance" D-1 (National Center for State Courts, March 1991).

Both the preceding chapter and this one have been largely although not entirely devoted to trying to explain puzzling phenomena concerning the elderly, ranging from penny-pinching to loquacity. The preceding chapter focused on paradoxes in attitude, disposition, and mind set, such as the apparent negative relation between dread of death and expected utility. In the present chapter the focus shifted to differences in behavior. The paradoxes here are numerous. Among them: high vehicular accident rates of elderly people, both as injurers and as injured, and high suicide rates (a form of violence in which injurer and victim coincide) coexist with low rates of criminal conduct and victimization; the frequency of male sexual activity relative to female sexual activity increases with age even though male sexual performance deteriorates with age more rapidly than female does; higher elderly incomes make the elderly less rather than more welcome to live in their children's households; and high voter turnout among the old coexists with low juror turnout.

Age-related decline in vision, hearing, reflexes, and other neuromotor capacities is the key to understanding the higher automobile accident rate of older people. I argued that their driving safety declines less rapidly than their underlying capabilities because it is possible up to a point to compensate at reasonable cost for deteriorating capabilities with greater care and with a reduction in the amount of driving. (And this implies that such driving as the elderly do is probably high-valued—a selection effect—albeit dangerous.) It may be more costly to reduce "pedestrianizing" to the same extent; this may explain why the age gradient of the pedestrian death rate is even higher than that of the vehicle occupant's death rate.[80] And it probably is much less costly to reduce exposure to situations in which one is likely to become a victim of crime than situations in which one is likely to be the victim of a traffic accident, which may explain the extremely low rate of criminal victimization of the old. I attribute their low crime rate— at first glance a paradox, because old age truncates the expected disutility of a long prison sentence—not to feebleness but primarily to a low rate of elderly entry into crime and a high rate of exit. The elderly avoid entering the criminal "job market" from a lawful activity for the same reasons that they avoid other career-switching—the age-related cost of acquiring new human capital—and age-related attrition is steep because of the heavy punishment of recidivists. Selection bias is also at work. The most experienced elderly criminals may elude arrest, and estimates of the crime rates of different age groups are based primarily on statistics of arrest.

80. See note 9 above.

The aversion to risk and danger that marks elderly behavior with respect to accidents and crime is not inconsistent with the high suicide rate of elderly men, once we realize that impulsive suicide is more common among the young, and deliberated among the old.[81] Among the young, suicide is part of a spectrum of risky behaviors. Among the old, it is a more or less straightforward response to situations of negative expected utility, once circular definitions of "depression" are rejected as explanations for the high elderly suicide rate.

The key to understanding differences in the frequency of sexual behavior of elderly men and women is the concept of the effective sex ratio—the ratio of sexually available and desired males to sexually available and desired females. The ratio drops with age both because male mortality is higher than female and because the sexual attractiveness of men to women declines less steeply with age than the sexual attractiveness of women to men. I also argued that the rising cost of forming new friendships in old age (discussed in chapter 3) will lead some unmarried elderly persons to substitute "spot" for "relational" sexual contracting.

One might suppose that the secular growth in the incomes of elderly people relative to the incomes of the young would result in an increase rather than a decrease in "coresidence" (different generations living under the same roof); the elderly would be in a better position to pay their children or other young relatives to defray the cost of the additional space and services required. They *are* in a better position to pay for these things, but they do not want them. Privacy is a superior good, so the demand for coresidence falls as elderly incomes rise. The cost of coresidence has been rising in recent decades for the further reason that the opportunity cost of female caretaking of elderly relatives has increased with the improvement in the marketplace job opportunities of women. I also gave an economic reason for why the tendency of many old people to remain in houses that are "too big for them" is consistent with rationality.

The paradox that elderly people vote disproportionately to their share of the adult population but are (contrary to popular belief) underrepresented on juries is explained by the different costs to elderly people of these two forms of participation in civic life. Jury service requires greater mobility and greater mental as well as physical fitness than voting, and employers frequently pay their employees who are on jury duty, whereas retired people on jury duty have no similar source of compensation and

81. For evidence, see Kalle Achté, "Suicidal Tendencies in the Elderly," 18 *Suicide and Life-Threatening Behavior* 55 (1988).

therefore are less likely to be willing to serve.[82] The fact that the voting rate of elderly people has been increasing may reflect the long-term decline in the rate of participation by the elderly in the labor force. This decline has reduced the opportunity costs of time spent both in voting itself and in preparing for voting by obtaining information about candidates and issues.[83]

I also examined additional factors, besides those considered in earlier chapters (especially chapter 4), bearing on the age of retirement. This enabled me to offer an economic explanation for differences in the age of retirement of different types of self-employed worker and for the peculiar structure of military retirement, and to explore the effect of both social security and private pensions on the age of retirement.

82. Although jury service is compulsory, people can and do get out of it either by not responding to jury summonses (enforcement of such summonses being sporadic in most jurisdictions) or by responding to questions in jury questionnaires or in the voir dire of prospective jurors conducted by the judge or the lawyers at the outset of trial in ways that cause them to be disqualified.

83. This analysis implies a rising rate of jury participation by the elderly as well, but I do not know of any time-series data on jury service by different age groups.

7

Age, Creativity, and Output

Retirement is the most dramatic age-related change in work, but it is purely quantitative. In this chapter I consider two other age-related changes in work. The first is change from one kind of work to another, rather than from work to leisure as in retirement. The second is change in the quantity or quality of one's work over the course of one's working life. The second type of change is related to retirement because it affects the value of the worker to his employer and thus the date of retirement. But it is distinct, not only because it can occur long before retirement but also because it can be positive as well as negative. I shall be discussing both points—change in the kind of work and change in the quality or quantity of work within the same line of work—together. I shall therefore have much to say about the different peak ages of productivity in different fields.

Productivity and Age: Creativity versus Leadership

I begin with an example of age-related change from one kind of work to another. Academics at research universities, as they get older, often reallocate more and more of their working time from producing scholarship to assisting in the administration of the university. Call this an age-related substitution of "leadership" activity for "creative" activity. Because the opposite pattern, in which an academic begins his career heavily involved in academic administration and later reallocates time from administration to scholarship, is almost never observed, it is unlikely that the age-related substitution of leadership activity for creative activity is a matter of sorting.

Were it merely the case that when an academic was starting his career no one could tell whether he was better at scholarship or at administration—that it took several years of observation to determine which type of work he was better at—there would be as many cases in which an academic started in administration and later switched to scholarship as the reverse.

The key to understanding the phenomenon of age-related change from one kind of work to another is that different kinds of work have different age profiles of productivity. It has been suggested that the shift from scholarship to administration reflects a decline in creative output caused by diminishing investment in human capital over the life cycle.[1] But this cannot be the entire explanation. The simple life-cycle model does not explain why the investment profile for *leadership* human capital should be different from that for *creativity* human capital. And the extensive sociological and psychological literature on peak ages of creativity identifies in fields such as mathematics and theoretical physics average peak ages that are too low—in the thirties or even twenties—to be explained by the reduction in investment in human capital that is induced by proximity to death.[2] If we ignore age-related decline, as the simple life-cycle model does, a 35-year-old particle physicist would have an expected payback period of roughly

1. Arthur M. Diamond, Jr., "The Life-Cycle Research Productivity of Mathematicians and Scientists," 41 *Journal of Gerontology* 520 (1986); Sharon G. Levin and Paula E. Stephan, "Research Productivity over the Life Cycle: Evidence for Academic Scientists," 81 *American Economic Review* 114 (1991); Daniel L. Rubenson and Mark A. Runco, "The Psychoeconomic Approach to Creativity," 10 *New Ideas in Psychology* 131 (1992). See also John M. McDowell, "Obsolescence of Knowledge and Career Publication Profiles: Some Evidence of Differences among Fields in Costs of Interrupted Careers," 72 *American Economic Review* 752 (1982).

2. The major study of the age profile of creativity remains Harvey C. Lehman, *Age and Achievement* (1953). The foremost contemporary contributor to the literature is Dean Keith Simonton. Among his many works, see especially *Genius, Creativity, and Leadership: Historiometric Inquiries,* ch. 6 (1984) ("Age and Achievement"); "Age and Outstanding Achievement: What Do We Know after a Century of Research?" 104 *Psychological Bulletin* 251 (1988); *Scientific Genius: A Psychology of Science* 66–68 (1988); and "Age and Creative Productivity: Nonlinear Estimation of an Information-Processing Model," 29 *International Journal of Aging and Human Development* 23 (1989). See also Jock Abra, "Changes in Creativity with Age: Data, Explanations, and Further Predictions," 28 *International Journal of Aging and Human Development* 105 (1989); Michael D. Mumford, Kimberly A. Olsen, and Lawrence R. James, "Age-Related Changes in the Likelihood of Major Contributions," 29 *International Journal of Aging and Human Development* 171 (1989); Simone de Beauvoir, *Old Age* 384–444 (1972); Wayne Dennis, "Creative Productivity between the Ages of 20 and 80 Years," 21 *Journal of Gerontology* 1 (1966); Evelyn Raskin, "Comparison of Scientific and Literary Ability: A Biographical Study of Eminent Scientists and Men of Letters of the Nineteenth Century," 31 *Journal of Abnormal and Social Psychology* 20 (1936). Illustrative of this literature, a careful study of the productivity (as proxied by number of publications in a refereed journal) of professors of finance found that the peak was in the late thirties with an almost 50 percent decline by the fifties. Robert M. Soldofsky, "Age and Productivity of University Faculties: A Case Study," 3 *Economics of Education Review* 289 (1984).

40 years for any new investment that he made in his human capital. Even at the age of 45 he would have more than a 30-year expected payback period,[3] and at ordinary discount rates there is only a small difference in present value between a 30-year annuity and a 40-year annuity (or a 40-year and a 50-year annuity, if we are comparing the incentives to invest of a 25-year-old physicist and of a 35-year-old one), each yielding the same annual income to the annuitant. At a discount rate of 10 percent, the present value of the 30-year annuity will be 96.4 percent as great as that of a 40-year one. Even at a discount rate of 5 percent, the present value of the 30-year annuity will be 89.6 percent of the present value of the 40-year annuity.[4]

It is true that, quite apart from any effect of aging on the ability to develop or maintain intellectual skills, the opportunity costs of investing in human capital will rise with hourly income, and hence (up to a point) with age, since most investing in human capital is time-intensive. But although a 35-year-old is therefore likely to have higher opportunity costs of investing in human capital than a 20-year-old, early peaking implies that the optimal investment in human capital in the activity in question probably is modest. So a diminished incentive to continue investing, whether the diminution is caused by rising opportunity costs or by the shortening of the payback period, is unlikely to explain the decline of performance from the peak. Physicians who specialize rarely complete their training before they reach 30. The result is to push their peak age of earnings way back. Fields with low age peaks are fields that, unlike medicine, require relatively little training, with the exception of fields such as musical performance, figure skating, and tennis, where training begins in childhood. The less human capital (other than innate ability) required in a particular activity, and hence the lower the cost of acquiring the necessary human capital, the less sensitive will investment in it be to the proximity of death. An octogenarian might invest in the knowledge required to play poker or bingo even though the payback period for his investment would be short because of his age.

If we are to explain differences in peak ages of productivity, both generally and with specific reference to the difference in those ages between leadership and creative work, we must, as in other chapters, move beyond the simplest economic life-cycle model. The first thing to note is that the

---

3. The sum of age and remaining life expectancy increases with age, since every year lived transforms a probability of surviving that year into a certainty.

4. The higher discount rate seems plausible, since investments in human capital are risky. The lower discount rates used in chapter 4 were riskless rates.

very concept of a peak age of productivity is misleading in suggesting that all careers have a sharp peak. There are careers with early peaks and careers with late ones, but also careers in which the peak, whenever attained, is sustained without a significant decline virtually till death. Let us call these "sustained peak" careers, as distinct from "early peak" careers and "late peak careers." Sustained-peak careers can in turn be divided into "early peak, sustained" and "late peak, sustained," thus giving us a fourfold division: early peak, not sustained; early peak, sustained; late peak, not sustained; late peak, sustained. Examples of the first category (early peak, not sustained) are most fields of professional athletics,[5] along with mathematics, theoretical physics,[6] chess,[7] heavy manual labor, and—the analysis in chapter 6 implied—most criminal "careers." In the case of physically demanding activities, risk of injury plays a role; it is more difficult to sustain peak performance in football than in dance.

Examples of the second category (early peak, sustained) are literature, economics (other than the severely mathematical), musical composition (including choreography), painting and sculpture (consider Michelangelo, Titian, Picasso, and O'Keefe, among others), and musical performance. An example of the third category (late peak, not sustained) is the senior management of large firms, where the peak age will often be in the late fifties, followed by retirement in the early sixties;[8] perhaps most leadership is in this category. The fourth category (late peak, sustained) is illustrated by judging, discussed in the next chapter. History, theology, literary criticism and scholarship, and philosophy appear to straddle the second (early peak,

5. See, for example, Neil Charness and Elizabeth A. Bosman, "Expertise and Aging: Life in the Lab," in *Aging and Cognition: Knowledge Organization and Utilization* 343, 369–374 (Thomas M. Hess, ed., 1990). A careful study of professional baseball players finds their peak age to be 27, with a decline in performance from the peak of 22 to 24 percent by age 30, 84 percent by age 36, and 99.5 percent by age 40. Bill James, *The Bill James Baseball Abstract 1982* 196 (1982).

6. The natural sciences in general are early-peak fields. A telling statistic is the average age at which Nobel-prize-winning scientists did the work for which they received the Nobel prize: 37.5. Only 5.6 percent of the Nobel prize winners were over the age of 50 when they did their prize-winning work. Paula E. Stephan and Sharon G. Levin, *Striking the Mother Lode in Science: The Importance of Age, Place, and Time* 55 (1992) (tab. 4–2). As for math, here is what a distinguished mathematician, G. H. Hardy, had to say: "Mathematics, more than any other art or science, is a young man's game. To take a simple illustration at a comparatively humble level, the average age of election to the Royal Society is lowest in mathematics." Hardy, *A Mathematician's Apology* 70–71 (1940).

7. Charness and Bosman, note 5 above, at 352–360.

8. The average chief executive officer of a major U.S. corporation is 56 or 58 and plans to retire at 64. Sunita Wadekar Bhargava, "Portrait of a CEO: What's the Typical Boss Like? Here Are the Vital Statistics," *Business Week,* Oct. 11, 1993, p. 64; Michael J. McCarthy, "A CEO's Life: Money, Security and Meetings," *Wall Street Journal* (midwest ed.), July 7, 1987, p. 27.

sustained) and fourth (late peak, sustained) categories. The fourfold matrix is displayed in table 7.1 with a few examples.

A more complete analysis would distinguish not only among different fields but also among different activities within the same field. Within the field of professional athletics, for example, performance has an early peak, but coaching does not. There is a close parallel in academia: research generally has an earlier peak than teaching, and the rate of decline from the peak is also faster than for teaching. Even more refined distinctions are possible: for example, between teaching advanced subjects and teaching basic ones. Since the heartland of a field changes less rapidly than the frontier, teaching the heartland requires less investment in acquiring new human capital. Older teachers are therefore more likely to teach basic than advanced subjects. When, as is common in some fields, older and younger scholars collaborate, the younger tend to bring mathematical and other techniques to the collaboration, the older the insights enabled by experience. Such a collaboration marries fluid and crystallized intelligence.

To explain early peaking with greater precision, we need to recall figure 4.1, in which mental and physical capability to perform a task was correlated with age, negatively so in the region to the right of the peak age (m in that diagram), the region, that is, of the downward-sloping curve that relates capability to age (d). Human capital in the conventional sense, that is, leaving out innate ability, is only one factor that affects the location and shape of that curve. This point is obvious if we consider an early-peak activity such as professional basketball. Peak age is low in such an activity in part because the investment in human capital (including experience, an important source of human capital) required to reach peak proficiency either is small or is concentrated in one's very early years, in part because the activity involves abilities that age rapidly for purely biological reasons, and in part because minimum capability is very close to peak capability. Or consider chess. Serious players generally start to play before the age of ten.

Table 7.1 Careers with Different Age Profiles

	Early Peak	*Late Peak*
Not Sustained	Mathematics, Basketball	Corporate management
Sustained	Painting, Musical composition	Judging

capability

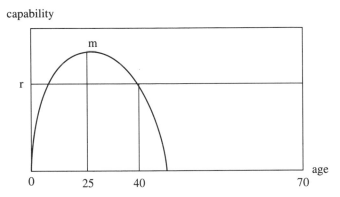

Figure 7.1 Activity with low peak age

Although their speed (important in tournament chess, where there are time limits on moves) begins to decline in their twenties, at first this decline is offset by growing experience, which even after the player reaches his peak, usually in his early thirties, will retard the net rate of decline in performance until his sixties, when most players stop participating in tournament play.[9]

Early peaking is depicted in figure 7.1. The proximity of r (minimum required capability) to m (peak capability) identifies the hypothetical activity depicted in the figure as an elite one. Elite activities are more challenging; that is, they draw on more of a person's ability than routine ones do. If an elite activity does not require a large investment in human capital and if the biological abilities on which it draws peak at an early age, the decline in capability can be precipitous, as in many sports. In academic fields in which these conditions obtain, we can expect substitution into administration early in a scholar's career—provided of course that administration does not have the same age profile. It does not. For example, Harvey Lehman found much later age peaks in activities (including political and judicial office) that he classified as leadership positions.[10] Yet it is important to note that a nonelite activity can have a very low age peak, too, if, even though r lies far below m, the age-decline curve is extremely steep, as in heavy manual labor, where the worker wears out rapidly.

Why should leadership have a later age peak than creativity? Here are five mutually compatible possibilities. First, the ratio of fluid to crystallized intelligence is higher in creative tasks, and we know that fluid intelligence

---

9. Charness and Bosman, note 5 above, at 354–360.
10. Lehman, note 2 above, at 286 (tab. 50).

ages more rapidly than crystallized intelligence. Although leadership usually requires some problem-solving abilities, much of it (especially in the
kind of leadership dubbed charismatic by Max Weber, as distinct from
more routine management) consists of evaluating, matching, and motivat-
ing other people. These are interpersonal skills not well correlated with
problem-solving ability. They may even in some cases be negatively correlated with it. Superior intelligence can be an impediment to effective
leadership if the gap in intelligence between leader and followers is so wide
as to retard mutual understanding.[11]

Second, effective leadership often requires having a wide network of
acquaintances—persons one can trust as aides or allies. Such a network, an
important form of relational human capital discussed in chapter 3, tends to
grow with age, and there may be very little depreciation until retirement is
imminent.

Third, experience is an important input into most forms of leadership.
Being the knowledge that accrues from living and working, as opposed to
reading or studying, experience grows with age, though in some activities
only up to a point: after a point early reached in living or working, one does
not become better at tying one's shoe laces or tightening a bolt on an as-
sembly line. If experience is more valuable in leadership than in creative
activity, it is easy to see why the peak age for leaders might be later than
that for scientists or poets.

Fourth, most people mature with age, though only up to a point. I am
speaking of a process that is different from the accumulation of experience;
that is emotional as much as cognitive; and that is largely complete by the
onset of middle age and may actually reverse itself in old age ("second
childhood") even in people who do not become senile—for many elderly
people who are not senile are labile, self-centered, excessively stubborn,
and rather simple-minded. The process of maturation that I am describing
involves more than anything the shucking off of childish traits, traits such
as selfishness, stubbornness, disregard of convention, and "ask[ing] questions that adults usually have stopped asking."[12] Though inimical to most

11. Dean Keith Simonton, "Land Battles, Generals, and Armies: Individual and Situational
Determinants of Victory and Casualties," 38 *Journal of Personality and Social Psychology* 110,
112 (1980); Ralph M. Stogdill, *Handbook of Leadership: A Survey of Theory and Research* 43–
45 (1974). This is one reason why Felix Frankfurter, contrary to expectations, failed to play an
effective leadership role in the Supreme Court.

12. Howard Gardner, "The Creators' Patterns," in *Changing the World: A Framework for
the Study of Creativity* 69, 76 (David Henry Feldman, Mihaly Csikszentmihalyi, and Howard
Gardner, eds., 1994); see also Gardner, *Creating Minds: An Anatomy of Creativity Seen through
the Lives of Freud, Einstein, Picasso, Stravinsky, Eliot, Graham, and Gandhi* 365–366 (1993).

forms of leadership, these traits may actually foster creative activity in the arts and sciences.[13]

Fifth, leadership implies responsibility. An academic who is a flop as teacher or scholar can be fired (unless he has tenure), and little harm has been done. Even if he has tenure and cannot be fired, his ineptitude will do relatively little harm. But a leader who is a flop may cause serious harm to many other people; a bad leader can wreck a successful organization. It is therefore natural to require that he demonstrate his competence in advance by success at the next lower rung of the administrative ladder, and the necessity of climbing the ladder makes it likely that senior leaders will be of mature age. To put this differently, the costs of failed leadership tend to be greater than those of failed creativity, implying the need for a more careful screening of leaders than of creative workers. One dimension of care is minimization of the adverse consequences of an incorrect assessment, as by requiring that candidates for a top leadership position rotate through a series of progressively more responsible assignments rather than being selected for the position on the basis of performance at the bottom of the ladder. Careful screening of leaders may, as a result, require many years.

The suggested contrast between the costs of failure as a leader and as a creative worker may be somewhat overdrawn. The uncreative researcher may discourage promising young people from entering his field, vote against the advancement of the able, or be occupying a place that a creative researcher might have occupied instead. But the first two consequences have limited significance as long as the uncreative researcher, and others like him, are outnumbered by able colleagues. And as for the displaced creative researcher, he probably will find a different position and make as great or almost as great a contribution as he would have done in the position from which he was blocked. The failed leader does more harm than merely blocking an opportunity for a superior leader to emerge.

There is a puzzle still. Why must some things be learned by doing rather than by studying, given that study takes so much less time? In the case of "physical" tasks (using the word loosely) such as riding a bicycle, or mixed physical-mental tasks such as driving a car, or even such "purely" mental tasks as learning to speak a foreign language, the answer is that the task, to be done right, requires a degree of speed in responding to stimuli that can be achieved only by habit-inducing drill. These are areas of what philosophers call "tacit" knowledge—knowledge, largely unconscious, inarticulate, and incommunicable, of how to do things (including how to

---

13. As argued by Gardner in the works cited in the preceding footnote.

produce and comprehend sentences) as distinct from knowledge of rules, algorithms, and other propositions. Instruction may help a little in these areas but it cannot just take the form of issuing the trainee a set of instructions that he can use to accomplish the task, in the way that he could use a set of instructions on how to assemble a bookcase to assemble the bookcase.

Most leadership positions do require rapid decision-making. Not being able to make up one's mind, which is to say being slow at making decisions, is a common cause of failure in leadership. The ability to make responsible decisions rapidly comes, usually, only with experience. But this is not the complete solution to the puzzle. The reason that physicists peak early is not that they operate without a substantial knowledge base but that they can absorb the essential parts of the base by a relatively brief course of reading, practice, and being instructed.[14] Why could not a social scientist, through careful study of the writings of political and management theorists, psychologists, politicians, and business leaders, assemble a course of readings that would impart to students all the principles of effective leadership, so that after a brief course of study the student would know everything that seasoned politicians and managers knew? It is only a partial answer that institutions differ in significant detail.[15] That just implies having to supplement the general course of instruction in the principles of leadership with a handbook applying them to the particular institution (university, business firm, nation, or whatever) in which the student wanted to make his career of leadership. Once the handbook was memorized, the fledgling leader could make confident decisions rapidly.

Why does that seem a quixotic suggestion? Literally, of course, one person's experience cannot be "transferred" to another person; one's experience is by definition what has happened to oneself. And while even a lifetime's experience can be summarized or narrated in readable form, the summary will not provide much in the way of useful guidance to a different person who is at an earlier point in his own life cycle. Why there should be such a tremendous loss in transmission—why some forms of knowledge

14. Cf. Harriet Zuckerman and Robert K. Merton, "Age, Aging, and Age Structure in Science," in *Aging and Society,* vol. 3: *A Sociology of Age Stratification* 292, 302–306 (Matilda White Riley, ed., 1972), noting that the various sciences differ in the degree to which they are "codified"—where "codification refers to the consolidation of empirical knowledge into succinct and interdependent theoretical formulations"—and that "experience should count more heavily in the less codified fields." Id. at 303. Law, as we shall see in the next chapter, is one of those less codified—that is, incompletely theorized—fields.

15. This is Aristotle's point that practical wisdom requires knowledge of particulars. See chapter 5.

should depend on the knower's own experience rather than on his knowledge of the experience of his predecessors—is a deep mystery, though one that the field of artificial intelligence may eventually dispel (or transcend). It is not enough to say that leadership is one of those activities about which we do not know enough to lay down rules and are therefore left to grope our way as best we can by employing analogies to past experiences. For why could not all the potential analogies, or at least the most important ones, be neatly laid out in a book for the young leader to consult when he came upon a new problem?

I offer several suggestions, though it may seem that to the extent they dispel the central mystery they merely bring other mysteries into view. First, for reasons not well understood it is difficult to learn how to deal with people effectively from books, and the essence of leadership is dealing with people effectively. Second, effective leadership of a particular group (nation, firm, university, whatever) often requires that the leader know a number of specific people well, and this will take time. This is a point about relational human capital again (see chapter 3), but here my emphasis is on the fact that by its nature it cannot be sold or otherwise transferred. I do not put too much emphasis on the point, however, because leaders are often appointed from other institutions rather than from the ranks of the institution they are to lead.

Third, leadership like warfare is often though not always a strategic activity in the game-theoretic sense: every move invites a countermove, so the leader who merely repeats the moves of previous leaders is easily thwarted because predictable. Fourth, a point that carries beyond leadership, the ability to choose the apt analogy from the array in front of one may require "judgment" based somehow on experience rather than on the mastery of some analogy-selecting algorithm. (But there is reason to question this point, as we saw in chapter 5 and will see again later in this chapter.) Fifth, there may be genetic reasons, having to do with optimal family structure, and age-grading, in the evolutionary period of human development (see chapter 9), why it is "natural" for younger persons to look for leadership to older ones. I suggest one of those reasons below.

I do not want to exaggerate. There is instruction, not all of it wasted, in techniques of management. And not all leaders have been old. Alexander the Great and Napoleon Bonaparte are conspicuous counterexamples, but ones easy to explain. Both were military leaders at a time when successful military leadership required considerable daring and fitness, and both ascended to power in settings in which the usual sorting process was infeasible. Alexander became King of Macedonia because he was the king's son, and Napoleon became a general at a time when the ordinary process for promotion had been disrupted by the French Revolution. Both, moreover, were charismatic leaders, although Napoleon had, and Alexander seems rather to have lacked, considerable managerial skills as well. Successful management normally requires patience, self-control, and willingness to suffer fools gladly, qualities more common among middle-aged than among young people because age tends to boil away tempestuous emotion, though uncommon among the elderly too because such qualities require the suppression of ego.

Differences in Peak Age between and within Fields

We saw earlier that within the class of creative fields (broadly defined, to include for example engineers as well as scientists) there are large differences in the age profile of productivity. Some of these differences can be explained in terms of the different rates at which fluid and crystallized intelligence decline with age, or of the different levels of required investment in human capital. Mathematics and physics (especially theoretical physics) involve both high ratios of fluid to crystallized intelligence and low levels of investment in human capital. The stock of knowledge they employ can be conveyed through books and instruction economically, with relatively little learning by doing required. As the cliché has it, each generation of scientists can see farther because it is standing on the shoulders of giants.[16] It is no surprise that these are early-peak, not-sustained, fields. Nor is it surprising that experimental scientists have a later peak than theoretical ones. Not only are the demands on their fluid intelligence somewhat less, but experimentation involves team work, hence some people skills and therefore leadership in a broad sense. Most modern economists employ formal modeling skills that depend heavily on fluid intelligence. But experience of social life is important too, and it accrues with age, so that economists lacking frontier skills may still be able to do frontier work. Some modern economists, such as Ronald Coase and Thomas Schelling, have managed to make important contributions to economics without any use of formal models. Economics thus appears to be an early-peak, sustained, field.

In architecture and engineering, the visualization of objects in their spatial relations is an important skill. This is an element of fluid intelli-

---

16. Michael D. Mumford, "Age and Outstanding Achievement: Lehman Revisited," 25 *Journal of Vocational Behavior* 225, 231 (1984).

gence, and one that has been found specifically to decline with age.[17] So it is not surprising that architecture and engineering are early-peak, not-sustained, fields, though less so than more mathematical fields.[18] Invention (which is related to engineering) seems, surprisingly, to be a late-peak field.[19] This should allay concerns that the aging of the population threatens to reduce the rate of inventive activity, and with it the economic growth that is due to that activity. The threat is slight in any event, since the rate of inventive activity depends on the number of inventors rather than on the fraction of the population that is "age eligible" to engage in the activity, and that number should grow as the population grows.

History and literary criticism are fields that traditionally have required large investments in human capital. Practitioners have to master large bodies of text or other information that cannot be reduced to a handful of principles. And aspects of crystallized intelligence, in particular skills of exposition, play a much larger role in these fields, relative to fluid intelligence, than is true in scientific and social scientific fields. Expository skills—not only writing skills narrowly conceived but also the organizing skills required in the composition of books as distinct from articles—tend to improve with experience for a very long time, and then plateau rather than sink.

Lehman found lyric poetry to be an early-peak field. This may seem surprising. It is, of course, a branch of writing, although it involves less organization, and therefore less experience, than scholarly writing, epic poetry, or fiction (novels and short stories) because the unit of composition is so much smaller. One explanation that has been offered for the early peaking of poetic ability is that it is positively correlated with psychiatric illness, which is likely to disable the poet at an early age.[20] But so many lyric poets have *not* suffered a creative decline with age (familiar examples are Yeats, Stevens, Whitman, and Frost) that the field should probably be classified with fields in which early peaks are sustained. Such a classi-

17. Timothy A. Salthouse, "Age and Experience Effects on the Interpretation of Orthographic Drawings of Three-Dimensional Objects," 6 *Psychology and Aging* 426 (1991).

18. Paul R. Sparrow and D. R. Davies, "Effects of Age, Tenure, Training, and Job Complexity on Technical Performance," 3 *Psychology and Aging* 307 (1988); Dennis, note 2 above, at 2–4.

19. Id. at 3 (tab. 2). See also Naomi Stewart and William J. Sparks, "Patent Productivity of Research Chemists as Related to Age and Experience," *Personnel and Guidance Journal,* Sept. 1966, p. 28. Another study, however, finds a significant positive correlation between the percentage of young adults in the population and the number of patents awarded. Mumford, Olsen, and James, note 2 above.

20. Dennis, note 2 above; Raskin, note 2 above, at 29–30.

fication would be consistent with the centrality of writing skill to poetic achievement *and* the dispensability of substantial life experience to the writing of poetry, as distinct from the writing of novels, where we would expect the peak to be reached later but, again, sustained indefinitely.

Musical creativity, both in composition and in performance, follows a pattern similar to that of poetry—early-peak sustained. Why this should be so in the case of musical performance is unclear. A concert pianist or violinist is engaged in an elite activity, that is, one in which required capability is close to peak capability; and the capability in question has a physical dimension. One might expect, therefore, that even if the age-related decline in the requisite physical skills were slight, aging concert performers would be quickly supplanted by equally able youngsters. Yet there are innumerable examples of pianists, violinists, other soloists, and conductors who continued to perform with distinction and undimmed popularity to a very old age. (Think of Horowitz, Heifetz, Casals, and Toscanini.) Maybe experience can compensate for the relatively slight physical decline. Music is richly expressive of emotion, and a person's emotional repertoire changes with age.

An additional point, though relevant to the continued popularity rather than to the performing quality of famous elderly performers, is that a person who achieves celebrity becomes an object of interest independent of his current capability. People will go to see rather than to hear him. This point suggests, incidentally, an explanation that does not depend on the costs of information for the frequency with which a good reputation, personal or institutional, persists long after the qualities that originally gave rise to it have disappeared. A person or institution once prized for real capacities or achievements continues to be prized as a memento. People wanted to meet Winston Churchill even in his dotage, and they still visit the tomb of Napoleon.

The sustained peak in philosophy may seem a mystery, since the ratio of fluid to crystallized intelligence in the activity of philosophers is, or at least might seem to be, very high. The peak is early, and not sustained, for philosophers whose work borders on science or mathematics (Bertrand Russell for example). But Wittgenstein had peaks in his twenties (when he was doing logic) *and* in his fifties; and many philosophers, ranging from Plato and Kant to Dewey and Sartre, and, among the living, Willard Quine, Donald Davidson, John Rawls, Hilary Putnam, Stanley Cavell, Nelson Goodman, Judith Jarvis Thomson, Bernard Williams, Richard Rorty, and a number of others, have remained highly creative in their sixties or even later. To complicate the picture further, a number of distinguished philosophers have had late peaks, as distinct from early peaks sustained; examples are Kant, Rawls, and Goodman.

I suggest two explanations for the fact that age seems to take only a light toll of nonmathematical, nonlogician philosophers. The first is that literary skills are far more important in philosophy than in, say, mathematics. The distinction of many philosophers, including Plato, Wittgenstein, Nietzsche, James, Quine, and Rorty, is owed in no small part to those skills. Metaphors ("language game," "veil of ignorance," "cash value," "tribunal of sense experience," etc.) and other striking turns of phrase (such as Kuhn's "normal science" and "paradigm"), neologisms ("grue"), parables (Plato's cave, Neurath's boat, "turtles all the way down"), dialogues (Plato again), and even poetry (Lucretius, Nietzsche) have been employed in philosophy to striking effect.

I am not comfortable with this point. Although metaphor is usually conceived to be a verbal skill, it is similar to analogy,[21] which plays an important part in scientific discovery[22] and seems, therefore—this power of discovering the similar in the dissimilar—work for the fluid intelligence.[23] Yet while scientific reasoning, presumably including the scientist's use of analogy as a tool of discovery, is an example of abstract reasoning—reasoning that abstracts from particulars in its search for universal laws or at least of a form of cognition seemingly far removed from the literary, metaphor is usually thought to illustrate, even to typify, the concreteness of literary expression.[24] So metaphor and analogy seem both like and unlike each other. Maybe the explanation for the difference between the correlations of age with use of metaphor and with use of scientific analogy is that while both devices draw on the fluid intelligence, metaphor is also a verbal phenomenon and so draws on skills that tend not to decline with age and may even improve with it.

---

21. See, for example, D. A. Boswell, "Metaphoric Processing in the Mature Years," 22 *Human Development* 373, 382 (1979). In the words of a famous literary critic, "The essence of poetry is metaphor and metaphor is finally analogical rather than logical." Cleanth Brooks, *The Well Wrought Urn: Studies in the Structure of Poetry* 248 (1947).

22. See, for example, John H. Holland et al., *Induction: Processes of Inference, Learning, and Discovery* 289–295 (1986); Mark T. Keane, *Analogical Problem Solving* 11–18 (1988); Brenda E. F. Beck, "Metaphors, Cognition, and Artificial Intelligence," in *Cognition and Symbolic Structures: The Psychology of Metaphoric Transformation* 9, 15 (Robert E. Haskell, ed., 1987). Beck, indeed, treats analogy as a form of metaphor.

23. There is evidence that skill in analogical reasoning is indeed one of the intellectual capacities that declines markedly with age. See Douglas H. Powell (in collaboration with Dean K. Whitla), *Profiles in Cognitive Aging,* ch. 4 (1994).

24. See, for example, W. K. Wimsatt, Jr., *The Verbal Icon: Studies in the Meaning of Poetry* 79–80 (1954).

A second reason for the sustained peaking of philosophers but not of highly mathematical scientists is that philosophy is less progressive than the scientific disciplines. Because the problems addressed by philosophers and the analytic tools used to solve them change much less rapidly than in the case of physics or mathematics, philosophers' human capital depreciates less rapidly than scientists' and therefore requires less new investment to maintain it. The decline of their fluid intelligence is also less hampering if they do not have to address new problems but can continue worrying the old ones, for the ratio of fluid to crystallized intelligence employed is higher the newer the problem being addressed is to the person addressing it.

We can model some of these points by expressing output at age a (O_a) as a function of the peak-age output (O_p), the rate at which output declines from the peak (d),[25] and the number of years that has elapsed since the peak age ($a - p$), as in

$$O_a = O_p[(1 - d)^{a-p}]. \tag{7.1}$$

So if, for example, the peak is reached at age 25, the individual whose current output we are interested in measuring is now 30 (so that $a - p = 5$), and his output declines by 2 percent a year (making $1 - d$ .98), his current output will be roughly 90 percent of his peak output.

If $a = p$, that is, if we are evaluating output at the peak age, equation 7.1 reduces to $O_a = O_p$. If $p > a$, meaning that the individual has not yet reached his peak age, then the rate of decline of output is negative, so the equation becomes $O_a = O_p[(1 + d)^{a-p}]$, or equivalently (since now $a - p < 0$), $O_a/O_p = 1/(1 + d)^{p-a}$. The right side of this equation is larger than zero and smaller than one, which shows that pre-peak output, just like post-peak output, is below peak output.

An alternative formulation is possible, based on the equation in chapter 3 relating earnings (or output) to time: $E(t) = a + b_1t - b_2t^2$ (equation 3.1). If t^* is the peak year, and y the number of years that the individual is past the peak, then the amount by which his output in the peak year will exceed his output in the current year (E) is approximated by

$$E = y[(2t^* + y)b_2 - b_1]. \tag{7.2}$$

Recall that b_2 is depreciation (here, age-related decline) and b_1 is investment in human capital (for present purposes, experience). The greater the

---

25. A constant rate of decline is assumed for simplicity. A more realistic assumption would be that the rate increases with age.

rate of decline, and the less important continued experience is, the higher will the excess of peak over current output be. And unless experience is terribly important, it will be higher the older the individual is.[26]

Suppose that the production of the individual's output requires three inputs (besides time and effort, which I will ignore): problem-solving ability, writing ability, and some "installed base" of information and techniques. Then d (in equation 7.1) or b_2 (in equation 7.2) will be an average of the rate of decline or depreciation of these inputs, weighted by their relative importance in the production function. Suppose the average scientist combines in fixed proportions 1 unit of problem-solving ability and 1 unit of knowledge base (with only negligible amounts of writing ability), and that both depreciate (net of any new investment) at a high rate— problem-solving ability because it is an aspect of fluid intelligence and the knowledge base because of rapid advances in scientific knowledge. Suppose that the average philosopher, in contrast, combines 1 unit of problem solving ability, which depreciates at the same rate as the scientist's, with 1 unit of writing ability, which does not depreciate at all, and with 1 unit of knowledge base which depreciates very slowly because the problems that philosophers address are not changing and the corpus of significant philosophical literature is growing very slowly. Then the rate of decline of the philosopher's output as a function of age will be much lower than the scientist's. It may even be negative if writing ability increases with age or if experience is a large component of philosophical human capital, as it may well be in such incompletely theorized areas (compared to logic) as political and moral philosophy. A related consequence if experience and writing skill are important to the philosopher's output will be to postpone the peak age of creativity; and, other things being equal, this will also postpone the age at which the ratio of current to peak output falls to the point where the individual is no longer making significant contributions. He will remain productive longer.

As the ratio of current to peak output falls, the opportunity set facing the creative worker changes. Suppose that the best journals in some scientific field will not publish articles that reflect a capability of less than 90 percent of the peak capability of average practitioners, and Dr. Y is average. When his capability falls below 90 percent of his peak, he will no

---

26. An admittedly odd implication of equation 7.2 is that E will be higher the older the peak age (t^*). The reason is that in the model which underlies this equation earnings increase at the same rate with every year of experience until the peak earnings year is reached, so the longer it takes to reach the peak the higher the peak earnings will be relative to current earnings.

longer be able to publish in such journals. He may respond by publishing in lower-quality journals.[27] Since there is some substitutability between quality and quantity—though I am assuming not enough to enable Dr. *Y* to continue publishing, albeit at a lower rate, in the best journals—maybe he will write more articles for the lower-quality journals than he previously wrote for the best ones.[28] Or, borrowing a leaf from the philosopher's book, he may decide to concentrate his research efforts on old problems rather than on new ones; or he may decide to become a popularizer rather than a creator of science; or he may decide to collaborate with a younger scholar. Whichever of these courses he chooses, he will be making less use of his fluid intelligence.[29]

Another reason for the aging scientist to adopt a conservative research agenda is that a bold agenda might bring into question the validity of his earlier work, the work on which his reputation is based.[30] A young scientist by challenging received wisdom threatens the reputation of other scientists, not his own reputation, for he has none. It is otherwise for the older scientist. But I doubt that this is an important influence on the research of older scientists. If one's earlier research is unsound this is bound to be discovered sooner or later, and if you are your own unmasker you will get credit for courage as well as for intelligence. Trying to protect a reputation created by one's early work should be distinguished from the resistance to new ideas that is caused by age-related decline in fluid intelligence and by disinvestment in human capital.

The incentive of the older scientist to concentrate on old problems is paralleled by the incentive of the younger to concentrate on new ones. It is not only that the younger scientist has a superior ability to deal with new problems (or with old problems in new ways) because he has up-to-date training and undiminished fluid intelligence. It is also that he would be at a

27. He could be thought to be "retiring" from his primary career and taking up a less demanding form of work as a second career.

28. A. M. Diamond, Jr., "An Economic Model of the Life-Cycle Research Productivity of Scientists," 6 *Scientometrics* 189, 194 (1984).

29. Arthur M. Diamond, Jr., "Age and the Acceptance of Cliometrics," 40 *Journal of Economic History* 838, 839 (1980). Diamond argues that these adaptations to aging may explain why older scientists are slower to adopt new theories than younger scientists, although his own research has found that the negative effect of age on the acceptance of new scientific theories has been exaggerated. Id. at 839, 841; Arthur M. Diamond, Jr., "The Polywater Episode and the Appraisal of Theories," in *Scrutinizing Science* 181 (A. Donovan et al., eds., 1988); David L. Hull, Peter D. Tessner, and Arthur M. Diamond, "Planck's Principle: Do Young Scientists Accept New Scientific Ideas with Greater Alacrity than Older Scientists?" 202 *Science* 717 (1978). We shall note a possible explanation for this surprising finding in the last section of this chapter.

30. See, for example, Rubenson and Runco, note 1 above, at 141.

comparative disadvantage in following the groove planed by the older generation—that is, in using established techniques to deal with familiar problems—because he would lack the experience of the older scientist. He is therefore led to pursue problems, or use methods, for which the older scientist's experience is not an asset. So, even within the same field, there is a generational division of labor; and this is why intergenerational collaboration can be fruitful.

I suggested that the aging scientist might decide to reallocate research and writing time to administration.[31] Here I add that this tendency will be accelerated if his accumulated experience enables him to obtain a high salary in an administrative post. By raising his potential earnings in an alternative activity (administration), experience increases the opportunity cost of his remaining a researcher. Another thing that increases that cost is—success. Successful scientists and other successful creative people are invited, sometimes even badgered, to give prestigious lectures, accept honorary degrees, serve on boards and committees, consult, advise, write popular papers, give memorial addresses, appear on television, write letters of recommendation, and so forth, and to the extent that they yield to these importunings, as most of them do (because these activities produce psychic and sometimes pecuniary income), they have less time for research. A partially offsetting factor is that the successful, prominent person is in a better position to obtain criticisms from other able people; indeed, his success, his prominence, may make him a target for criticism—which he can learn from, if he does not dismiss it as a product of envy. But that is what he is apt to do. I am led to predict that creative people who remain obscure throughout their lifetime will reach their creative peak later than those who are successful in their lifetime (of course the causality could run both ways—some people are obscure throughout their lifetime *because* they are very late bloomers).

On similar grounds one might expect applied economists to peak earlier than mathematical economists. The former have better consulting opportunities, which increase with age (an academic needs an academic reputation before he can "cash in" as a consultant). A countervailing consideration, however, is that the applied economist uses more experience and less fluid intelligence in his work than the mathematical economist, implying a later peak and lower rate of decline. Another reason why the rate of decline probably is lower for the applied economist is that his

31. For evidence, see Soldofsky, note 2 above, at 296; Zuckerman and Merton, note 14 above, at 318–321.

knowledge base depreciates more slowly, given the rapid advances in mathematics. Cutting back the other way again is that the experience acquired by the applied economist may be more transferable to administrative tasks.

A final observation is that people may tend for a variety of reasons to exaggerate the rate at which elders' skills erode. One reason is that the cost of acquiring a new skill may exceed its benefit to someone who possesses the old skill for which the new one is a replacement, even though the new skill is an improvement over the old one and the cost of acquiring it, even to an older economist, is not great. Suppose that mathematical economists develop—this is happening all the time—a more compact and elegant method of formulating some problem, yet the older method is adequate. Young economists will be trained in the new method; older economists will not think it worthwhile to acquire it because, the older method being adequate, the incremental benefit from the acquisition would be slight to them. They will continue in the old way, and hence will strike the younger generation as old-fashioned. But if the old method is indeed adequate, the ability of the older economist to compete with younger ones may not be adversely affected by his refusal to learn the new technique. Age-related decline is an important theme of this book, but economic analysis can help us identify some areas where that decline is *not* at work.

Changes with Age in the Character of Creative Work

We should consider not only age-related decline in the quality of creative work but also age-related quality-independent changes in the character of creative work. In such fields as painting and sculpture, musical composition, and law—fields in which age-related declines in quality tend to be slight, zero, or even negative—as well as in the careers of exceptional poets, such as Yeats, who remained unabatedly productive until his death, there is nevertheless change—a tendency, dubbed the *Altersstil* (old-age style), toward boldness, clarity, and directness, and away from artifice. Dean Simonton remarks the "concise directness" of the late works of the composers in his large sample,[32] and Martin Lindauer finds support for "those descriptions of the late-life style which emphasize a holistic per-

---

32. Dean Keith Simonton, "The Swan-Song Phenomenon: Last-Works Effects for 172 Classical Composers," 4 *Psychology and Aging* 42, 45 (1989); Simonton, *Greatness: Who Makes History and Why* 208–209 (1994).

spective, a broader brush stroke, and an unconcern over detail," [33] while a sixteenth-century Chinese remarked of an earlier Chinese artist, Ni Tsan, that "in his old age he followed his own ideas, rubbed and brushed and was like an old lion, walked alone without a single companion." [34] Sophocles, Yeats, Verdi, Stravinsky, Richard Strauss, Leonardo da Vinci, Michelangelo, Titian, Bernini, Matisse, and Oliver Wendell Holmes, Jr.[35] illustrate the tendency in their different fields.

There are plenty of skeptics about the *Altersstil*.[36] But I take it that there is *some* such tendency of the kind described above, enough to invite an effort at explanation. Economics suggests two possibilities. First, the diminishing value of transactions as the end of life nears reduces the cost of outraging an audience's expectations, as by blunt speaking. This point is only superficially inconsistent with the remarks in chapter 5 about the tendency toward loquacity in elderly people: bluntness and loquacity are merely different examples of speech that violates the hearer's expectations. Inconsiderate communication may reveal more about the speaker than the more careful and often more reticent speech typical of younger people, who are concerned with maximizing their transactions. Since blunt, straight-from-the shoulder speaking or writing can be a social good, this suggests that the problem of the "last period" (see chapter 3) can have an up side; we shall see another example of this in the next chapter.

Second, fame may confer license. If a person has done valued work in the past, this increases the probability that his current work is also valuable and induces the audience to suspend its disbelief. He can therefore afford to thumb his nose at the crowd.[37] This is merely the obverse of the "shame-

33. Martin S. Lindauer, "Creativity in Aging Artists: Contributions from the Humanities to the Psychology of Old Age," 5 *Creativity Research Journal* 211, 223 (1992); see also id. at 216.

34. Quoted in Jerome Silbergeld, "Chinese Concepts of Old Age and Their Role in Chinese Painting, Theory, and Criticism," *Art Journal*, Summer 1987, pp. 103, 105. For other examples of the literature on the *Altersstil*, see Beauvoir, note 2 above, at 404–406; David Gutmann, "Age and Leadership: Cross-Cultural Observations," in *Aging and Political Leadership* 89, 93–94 (Angus McIntyre, ed., 1988); *Symposium on "Old-Age Style," Art Journal*, Summer 1987, p. 91.

35. Another example from law is Judge Learned Hand. His biographer remarks the "extreme, stark position" that Hand took in the lectures on the Bill of Rights that he wrote and deliv ered at the age of 86—"a more extreme position than he had taken earlier." Gerald Gunther, *Learned Hand: The Man and the Judge* 665 (1994). More on Hand in the next chapter.

36. See, for example, Catherine M. Soussloff, "Old Age and Old-Age Style in the 'Lives' of Artists: Gianlorenzo Bernini," *Art Journal*, Summer 1987, pp. 115, 119; Julius S. Held, "Commentary," *Art Journal*, Summer 1987, pp. 127, 129; Avis Berman, "When Artists Grow Old: Secure in the Mastery of Their Craft, They Can't Stop 'Looking for a Breakthrough,' " *Art News*, Dec. 1983, pp. 76, 81.

37. See Beauvoir, note 2 above, at 488–492.

lessness" of the old, which Aristotle discussed. Peter Messeri argues in this vein that "senior scientists are better situated than younger scientists to withstand adverse consequences of public advocacy of unpopular positions," and that this factor may explain why the tendency for older scientists to resist new theories is, in fact, weak.[38] And remember Kenneth Dover's negative verdict on old age (chapter 5)? He offered one qualification: "There just aren't any [aspects of old age which compensate for its ills]—except, maybe, a complacent indifference to fashion, because people no longer seeking employment or promotion have less to fear." [39]

This point suggests that the use by scholarly journals of blind refereeing is a mistaken policy. It may cause them to turn down unconventional work to which they would rightly have given the benefit of the doubt had they known that the author was not a neophyte or an eccentric.[40]

Finally, as fluid intelligence declines, the cost of complexity rises,[41] inducing the creative worker to substitute toward less complex forms of creation and expression.[42] It might seem that if there is value in simple works, the younger creative worker would produce them even though he was capable of creating more complex works. But it may be difficult to

38. Peter Messeri, "Age Differences in the Reception of New Scientific Theories: The Case of Plate Tectonics Theory," 18 *Social Studies of Science* 91, 96 (1988).

39. Kenneth Dover, *Marginal Comment: A Memoir* 243 (1994). But why must it be complacent?

40. I am not aware that this hypothesis has been tested in the literature on the effects of blind refereeing. The most systematic study that has come to my attention finds very few effects of blind (technically, "double-blind" – "single-blind" just means that the author is not told the referee's identity) refereeing. Rebecca M. Blank, "The Effects of Double-Blind versus Single-Blind Reviewing: Experimental Evidence from *The American Economic Review*," 81 *American Economic Review* 1041 (1991).

41. "The tendency for the magnitude of age differences in cognitive performance to increase with the complexity of the task" has been well documented. Timothy A. Salthouse, *Theoretical Perspectives on Cognitive Aging* 308 (1991); see also D. B. Bromley, "Aspects of Written Language Production over Adult Life," 6 *Psychology and Aging* 296, 306–307 (1991); Leah L. Light, "Interactions between Memory and Language in Old Age," in *Handbook of the Psychology of Aging* 275, 285 (James E. Birren and K. Warner Schaie, eds., 1990); James E. Birren, Anita M. Woods, and M. Virtrue Williams, "Behavioral Slowing with Age: Causes, Organization, and Consequences," in *Aging in the 1980s: Psychological Issues* 293, 303 (Leonard W. Poon, ed., 1980); Patricia K. Alpaugh and James E. Birren, "Variables Affecting Creative Contributions across the Adult Life Span," 20 *Human Development* 240 (1977).

42. An extreme example is the "unembarrassed reductiveness" of the painting of William de Kooning after he became senile, a style that one critic has called, apparently without irony, "the senile sublime." Quoted in David Rosand, "Editor's Statement: Style and the Aging Artist," *Art Journal*, Summer 1987, pp. 91, 92. Of Matisse's late work it has been remarked that "in his seventies and eighties, when his hands became too crippled to hold a brush, he produced wonderful collages made of cut-out paper shapes, working in a simplified style, all excess stripped away." Hugo Munsterberg, "The Critic at Seventy-Five," *Art Journal*, Spring 1994, p. 64.

make simple works that are of high quality, so that the worker economizes by producing complex works until no longer capable of doing so.

Yeats made my essential points in his poem "The Coming of Wisdom with Time," which ends, "Through all the lying days of my youth / I swayed my leaves and flowers in the sun; / Now I may wither into the truth." Yeats's late poetry is candid, unadorned, bawdy, strident, violent in diction, and often celebratory of actual violence. It goes to the heart of the matter (as he sees it, rightly or wrongly) without any effort to conciliate readers who might be shocked at the old man's "lust and rage."[43] The example of Yeats shows, incidentally, that simplicity should not be equated with popular appeal. The stripping away of artifice, the abandonment of decorum, may shock a public accustomed to artifice and decorum.

Admittedly Yeats may be a special case among lyric poets. He was a great poet in his youth and yet in the judgment of most critics his poetry got continuously better until sometime in his fifties ("Easter 1916," written in 1916, when he was 51, surpasses any poem that he had written previously), at which point it reached a plateau that was sustained until his death. The character of the poetry of Yeats's late sixties and his seventies was different from that of his earlier poetry but not inferior. In part he maintained the quality of his poetry into his old age by making old age a subject of poetry; and while we know that young people can write feelingly and insightfully about old age, presumably it is a subject in which old people have a comparative advantage that can offset, up to a point anyway, an age-related decline in ability. Another example is *Oedipus at Colonus,* Sophocles' great play of old age, written shortly before his death at the age of 90.[44] Resisting the ravages of age by making age one's subject is not an option available in all fields. But Simonton gives the example of a chemist who, having switched to gerontology in his nineties, published his last scientific paper at the age of 102![45]

I have not suggested, and do not believe, that the "old-age" or "late-life" style is characteristically superior to the artist's or other creative worker's prime-of-life style; and this raises the question why some creative people keep going, while others retire (E. M. Forster for example). Of

43. See generally *Yeats: Last Poems: A Casebook* (John Stallworthy, ed., 1968); also Douglas Archibald, *Yeats* 233–235 (1983).

44. There is a story, though it is not well authenticated, that one of Sophocles' sons tried to get his father declared incompetent and that Sophocles refuted the charge by reciting *Oedipus at Colonus,* which he had just written, to the court. Cicero, *De Senectute,* ch. VII, §§ 22–23; F. J. H. Letters, *The Life and Work of Sophocles* 53–54 (1953).

45. Dean Keith Simonton, "Creativity in the Later Years: Optimistic Prospects for Achievement," 30 *Gerontologist* 626, 627 (1990).

course part of the reason is simply that people age at different rates. Yet even in the case of someone who aged slowly, one might suppose that long before his abilities fell below some minimal level the rising costs to him of continued work would cross the declining benefits to him of continued work. Creative people tend to be people who derive enormous psychic income from possessing or even from hoping to possess posthumously a large reputation. The more one has done, the less contribution one more work or several more works, likely to be of somewhat diminished and in any event no greater quality than one's previous works, will make to one's reputation; and there is a cost in forgone leisure, as well as, in the usual case, a higher cost of production because of the effects of age. Hence one expects that the creative workers who persist in working into their old age will be those who have limited retirement income, derive psychic income, unrelated to reputation, from working, disvalue leisure, have aged very slowly, or have aged from a very high peak (so that their residual ability is likely to be high).

I find the leisure disvaluers particularly interesting, and will give two examples. The first is Justice Holmes, who in a radio address on the occasion of his ninetieth birthday said:

> The riders in a race do not stop short when they reach the goal. There is a little finishing canter before coming to a standstill. There is time to hear the kind words of friends and say to one's self: "The work is done."
>
> But just as one says that, the answer comes: "The race is over, but the work never is done while the power to work remains."
>
> The canter that brings you to a standstill need not be only coming to rest. It cannot be while you still live. For to live is to function. That is all there is in living.[46]

This is the essential Calvinist outlook (all there is in living is the performance of duty), and hence of course not peculiar to Holmes. The passage I have quoted from his radio address could almost have been a paraphrase of a passage from Tennyson's "Ulysses": "How dull it is to pause, to make an end, / To rust unburnished, not to shine in use! / As though to breathe were to live."

---

46. Holmes, "Radio Address (1931)," in *The Essential Holmes: Selections from the Letters, Speeches, Judicial Opinions, and Other Writings of Oliver Wendell Holmes, Jr.* 20–21 (Richard A. Posner, ed., 1992).

The essential findings of this chapter can be summarized very briefly. Fields of human endeavor, ranging from poetry to burglary and from theoretical physics to military generalship, can be divided into four classes defined by their peak age of productivity and by the rate at which productivity declines from the peak. The classes are early peak, not sustained; early peak, sustained; late peak, not sustained; and late peak, sustained. I used the economic model developed in earlier chapters—especially chapter 4, which emphasizes age-related decline along with familiar features of the economic model of the life cycle—to fix the location of a number of fields in the fourfold matrix and also to explain characteristic career switches within fields, such as from academic research to academic administration, and different peaks within fields (the obscure versus the prominent practitioner, and the theoretical versus the applied economist). As in the example of the academic's switch from a creative to a leadership job, I laid particular stress on the difference in age profiles between leadership and creativity, a difference that turns in part on the rather mysterious incommunicability of life experiences. Finally, I pointed out that the economic model can be used not only to explain differences in rates of aging across different fields but also to provide an account—one that emphasizes both last-period "irresponsibility" (in a good sense) and decline of fluid intelligence of the distinctive "old-age style" found in some artists.

8

Adjudication and Old Age

The judiciary is the nation's premier geriatric occupation. But it must not be considered in isolation from the rest of the legal profession. The different branches of the profession are interdependent. For example, precisely because judicial creativity or achievement continues to a later age than is the case in most academic fields, a major determinant of the peak age of creativity of law professors can be expected to be the degree to which the law professor's work is closer to that of a judge, on the one hand, or to that of a nonlegal academic, on the other. Especially but not only at elite law schools, recent decades have seen a pronounced shift in academic scholarship from the judicial to the academic model, implying an earlier peak for academic legal careers. Cutting the other way, however, is the fact that the judicial model of legal scholarship was a better preparation for administrative work than the academic model is. It is remarkable how many university presidents and provosts are former law professors, many removed from scholarship at an early age because of the demand for their administrative skills. Maybe the peak age of academic legal creativity is indeed falling but the rate of decline from the peak is also falling because fewer legal academic careers will be truncated by entry into academic administration.

The practice of law is in general a "late peak, sustained" activity, although the strenuous demands of a trial practice make litigation more of a late-peak, not-sustained, activity, and some young lawyers have had notable success in trials because jurors like young lawyers. As a consequence of the incompletely theorized nature of law as an activity, experience plays a larger role in successful lawyering than abstract reasoning does. The following summation of studies that find significant age-related decline in the power of abstract reasoning would be embraced by many an elderly lawyer or judge as a *favorable* description, on the whole, of himself: "The old person is more literal, more concrete, more concerned with tangible and immediate impressions, less able to detach himself from the particular example and consider the general class or principle, less able to ignore the individual fact in order to think in hypothetical terms."[1] In addition, the difficulty that even sophisticated corporate clients encounter in assessing lawyers' performance makes reputation created over many years an important asset. Since appellate advocacy is a more theoretical activity than trial practice, negotiation, or counseling, we should expect (and I have observed) that appellate advocates are on average younger than other lawyers.

How Productive Are Older Judges?

Article III of the U.S. Constitution appears to forbid imposing a mandatory retirement age on federal judges. Yet this is only an intermediate and incomplete reason why the average age of American judges is so much higher than that of other professionals. The framers of the Constitution could have imposed an age ceiling; and Congress could if it wanted lure judges off the bench with generous early-retirement offers, as private employers often do even when they are constrained by a law forbidding mandatory retirement or other "discrimination" on account of age, as we shall see in chapter 13. Any employer can pay an employee to quit. And states can and do fix retirement ages for their judges, but state judges are not youngsters either.[2]

The remarkable thing about judges, moreover, is not that they hang on to their jobs to such advanced ages but that they perform them creditably, and indeed sometimes with great distinction, at advanced ages. This fact is masked nowadays by the prevalence of judicial ghostwriting—the delegation of opinion writing to law clerks—which is enabling a small number of senile judges, and a significant number of judges who are well past their prime though not yet senile (merely "senescent"), to continue in office. But long before law clerks were a significant factor in the judiciary, judges such as Holmes, Brandeis, Hughes, and Learned Hand performed with dis-

1. D. B. Bromley, *The Psychology of Human Ageing* 189 (1974), quoted in Timothy A. Salthouse, *Theoretical Perspectives on Cognitive Aging* 276 (1991).
2. See, for an admittedly unusual example, Roger M. Grace, "Court of Appeal Presiding Justice Lester Wm. Roth, 96, to Retire Oct. 15," *Metropolitan News-Enterprise* (Los Angeles), Oct. 4, 1991, p. 1.

tinction into their eighties; and even after some judges started leaning heavily on clerks, others, who did not, such as Felix Frankfurter and Henry Friendly, turned in distinguished performances in their late seventies, and in the case of Friendly early eighties as well. It is not unusual for lawyers to be appointed to the federal appellate bench who are in their early sixties and have had no previous judicial experience (a distinguished recent example is Guido Calabresi), yet who are realistically expected to perform creditably in their new career for at least fifteen years. This was true even before the era of law clerks and geriatric fitness. Holmes and Cardozo were over 60 when appointed to the Supreme Court, though both had judicial experience; and while Cardozo, because of ill health, lasted only a few years on the Court, Holmes performed with great distinction for almost 30 years, though he faded some toward the end. Most lesser judges, as we shall see, also continue to be productive well beyond the normal retirement age. Finally, although the delegation of responsibilities to law clerks is full of problems, it is also a method of compensating, in part anyway, for age-related deterioration in a judge's ability. Simonton points out that in a number of fields, including painting and science, the elderly creative worker can "adjust to this effect of aging [i.e., the age-related slowing in the rate of processing information] by judicious use of assistants." [3] Why should this not be true in judging?

The impression that the quality of judging is not highly sensitive to age is just that, an impression, based on a handful of examples. I want to try to be more systematic by using as a proxy for judicial quality the average number of judicial citations to a judge's opinions. It is a rough proxy, with many drawbacks, but at least when it is used only to compare judges within the same court system in the same era it has sufficient validity to be serviceable for my purposes here. [4] Table 8.1 counts the average number of citations in published decisions of the federal courts of appeals to published cases decided in different periods by different cohorts of federal court of appeals judges. Specifically, the population from which the cited cases are drawn consists of the signed, published majority opinions of federal court of appeals judges who were still sitting in 1993 but who had been appointed between 1955 and 1984. [5] As the average age of appointment was virtually

3. Dean Keith Simonton, "Creativity in the Later Years: Optimistic Prospects for Achievement," 30 *Gerontologist* 626, 627 (1990).

4. For evidence and discussion of the validity of number of citations as a tool of judicial evaluation, see Richard A. Posner, *Cardozo: A Study in Reputation,* ch. 5 (1990).

5. All federal court of appeals judges appointed in this interval who were still sitting in 1993 were included in the sample. The sample was created for purposes unrelated to this book by a

Table 8.1 Average Number of Citations to Judicial Opinions of Different Age Cohorts

Period of Case Cited	Cohort					
	1955–59 (n = 6)	1960–64 (n = 5)	1965–69 (n = 19)	1970–74 (n = 21)	1975–79 (n = 29)	1980–84 (n = 60)
1960–64	2.693	3.005				
1965–69	4.780	4.263	4.736			
1970–74	6.865	3.969	6.406	5.322		
1975–79	7.446	5.284	7.825	7.187	7.835	
1980–84	6.212	3.681	7.172	7.044	7.811	6.922
1985–89	5.346	4.000	6.041	6.582	6.666	7.565

unchanged throughout this period (it varied from 50 to 54, with no trend), the different appointment cohorts (five year intervals between 1955 and 1984) correspond to different age groups.

I have limited the citing opinions to those issued within eight years after the beginning of each period. So the number 2.693 in the first cell of the table means that opinions written between 1960 and 1964 by judges appointed between 1955 and 1959 were cited an average of 2.693 times in opinions published between 1960 and 1968. Thus, reading across the table provides an index of the quality of the decisions rendered by the different age cohorts in the same period, and so should help us identify both an aging and an experience effect. Not only identify, but (when we read down as well as across) distinguish between. For while the oldest and also the most experienced judges are at the left, and the youngest and least experienced at the right, as we move down the table the most experienced judges become older. If judging is like other jobs, then at first the experience effect would be expected to dominate the aging effect, so that the older judges would have more citations than the younger ones, but eventually the aging effect would overtake the experience effect, so that the very oldest judges, like the younger ones, would have fewer citations than the middle-aged ones.

Neither the aging nor the experience effect is consistently observed (the significance of the qualification implicit in "consistently" will be con-

research team at the University of Chicago Law School headed by William Landes and Lawrence Lessig; the data used to construct tables 8.1 and 8.2 are drawn from this sample. According to data furnished me by the Statistics Division of the Administrative Office of the United States Courts, in 1993 the average age of federal court of appeals judges was 58.9 and the average years of service as a court of appeals judge were 9.2.

sidered shortly). For example, judges appointed between 1955 and 1959 had more experience in the period 1960–1964 than judges appointed in that period, and were still relatively young by judicial standards (late fifties or early sixties), yet the fledglings' opinions were cited more often (3.005 versus 2.693) than the experienced judges' opinions. In the last two rows in the table, the oldest judges, although by now pretty long in the tooth, were garnering more citations for their current opinions than the younger but still highly experienced judges of the 1960–1964 cohort.

I am particularly interested in the aging effect. None at all is perceptible until the last two periods. By the middle 1980s, the eleven judges in the sample who had been appointed between 1955 and 1964 (first two columns) were in their eighties; and the citations to the decisions they wrote in the period 1985–1989 are indeed fewer than the citations to the decisions written by the younger judges in that period. Still, considering the table as a whole, one is struck by how slight the effect of aging on quality, at least as measured by citations, appears to be.

Two qualifications are necessary. The first is that if citations per opinion are increasing over time, perhaps because a rapid expansion in the number of decisions is increasing the "demand" for citations to earlier decisions, this might mask an aging effect. Reading the table diagonally from left to right compares the average number of citations to the decisions of the different cohorts at approximately the same age (for example, the first cohort after ten years, the second after ten years, the third after ten years, and so on). This comparison does reveal an upward trend,[6] but this is a reason only for not attaching much significance to the trend within each column, that is, to the time trend of each age cohort's citations. When, instead, the comparison is across rows, that is, when what is compared are the citations to the different age cohorts in the same period, the time trend in citations drops out.

A more important qualification concerns the effect of aging on quantity, and indirectly on quality (depending on precisely how "quality" is defined). This effect is explored in table 8.2, where the average annual number of opinions written by the different age cohorts in the different periods is compared.

The number of opinions in the first period of each age cohort is artificially depressed, since some of the judges would have been appointed to-

6. The fall off in the last row is misleading; the count of citations ended with the end of 1993, so that many decisions rendered in the 1985 to 1989 period could not accrue a full eight years of citations.

Table 8.2 Average Annual Number of Judicial Opinions, by Age Cohorts

Period of Opinion	Cohort					
	1955–59 (n = 6)	1960–64 (n = 5)	1965–69 (n = 19)	1970–74 (n = 21)	1975–79 (n = 29)	1980–84 (n = 60)
1955–59	28.6					
1960–64	34.1	16.6				
1965–69	27.8	24.3	14.7			
1970–74	23.2	21.8	28.1	16.4		
1975–79	17.1	17.5	26.7	29.3	11.9	
1980–84	15.3	17.6	24.3	28.3	33.6	20.2
1985–89	11.3	6.9	21.0	21.4	32.9	28.6

ward the end of the period and would therefore not have had an opportunity to produce a full five years' worth of opinions. Ignoring the first period, therefore, and reading down the columns, we see that the production of opinions does appear to decrease with age. Reading diagonally from left to right, we see that this is not because the caseload per judge has been decreasing. Reading diagonally compares the output of the different age cohorts at roughly the same age. For example, in its third period the third age cohort wrote an average of 26.7 opinions, while the fourth cohort wrote 28.3 opinions in its third period, and the fifth 32.9 in its. This trend reflects the fact that caseload per federal appellate judge has been increasing over the entire period covered by the tables.

In the case of the first and second age cohorts, a substantial decrease in output sets in either in the third period after appointment, for the first cohort, or in the second period, for the second cohort. In the case of the third cohort very little decrease is observable until the fourth period, when most of the judges would have been in their early or middle seventies.

The quantity effect of age is related to the interesting institution of "senior status." Federal judges are eligible either to retire at full pay, or to take senior status (reduced workload, also at full pay), if they are at least 65 years old and the sum of their age and their years of service is at least 80; thus a 68-year-old could retire or take senior status with only 12 years of federal judicial service. There is no vesting, however, and therefore no early retirement except for disability. A retired judge as distinct from one who takes senior status is released from all restrictions on the outside activities of federal judges. He can, if he wants, practice law. But of course he can no longer exercise any federal judicial authority, and he is not entitled, as a senior judge is, to participate in any general pay raise that federal judges may receive during his lifetime, as distinct from cost of living increases, which the retirees do receive.

Judges have a strong financial inducement to take senior status at the earliest possible opportunity. The pay of a senior judge is deemed "unearned" for purposes of social security, and therefore the senior judge does not pay social security tax on his judicial income. Nor does that income affect his eligibility for social security benefits (for which all judges who take senior status are eligible, since the earliest age at which senior status can be taken, other than in cases of total disability, is 65), as earned income would until the judge reached 70. Yet despite this—a benefit easily worth $100,000 to a judge eligible to take senior status at 65—only 16 percent of the 371 current senior judges took senior status on their earliest eligibility date.[7] This is powerful evidence that federal judicial service confers substantial nonpecuniary benefits. The average age at which judges take senior status in recent years has varied between 67 and 69. This is substantially higher than the average retirement age in this country—and it is not retirement. Most federal judges do not retire completely before they reach the age of 80, and many keep going until their middle or even late eighties.

The work of a federal district judge (trial judge) is harder than that of a federal circuit judge (appellate judge) because it requires much more time in court. So it is not surprising that of the 21 federal judges who took senior status on their earliest eligibility date in the period 1991 through 1993 all but one were district judges and that the district judges had on average fewer years of service (13.4) than the years of service of the lone circuit judge (17.0). Obviously the circuit judge "sample" is too small to be meaningful, but if we consider all federal judges who took senior status in this period—17 circuit judges and 82 district judges—the disparity in years of service is even greater. The circuit judges had on average 20.2 years of service, the district judges only 15. Yet even district judges have sometimes remained in active status to extraordinarily advanced ages—Judge Edward Weinfeld of the Southern District of New York, for example, until his death at the age of 86.

Since senior status encourages judges to take a reduced caseload at advanced ages, it helps explain the age effect on quantity shown in table 8.2. Yet although the quantity of the older judges' output is smaller,

---

7. The statistics in this paragraph and the next were furnished me by the Statistics Division of the Administrative Office of the United States Courts. The figure 371 includes senior district as well as senior circuit judges.

the quality, at least as proxied by average citations per opinion, holds up remarkably well compared to other occupations. Granted, most of the judges in our sample whose performance had suffered severely because of age would have been nudged into retirement—once a federal judge takes senior status, his continued sitting is at the sufferance of the chief judge of his court and the judicial council of his circuit—before the aging effect was too conspicuous. As I pointed out in chapter 4, the failure to consider this selection phenomenon explains (and greatly undermines) the findings in some studies that age has no effect on workers' quality. Nevertheless, unlike the handful of older workers in other fields of employment, the older cohorts in the tables represent in the aggregate a significant fraction of the federal appellate judiciary rather than a tiny handful of freaks who have managed to defy the aging process. Most of the 51 judges in the sample who had been appointed before 1975, constituting more than a quarter of the federal appellate judiciary today, had reached normal retirement age before or during the 1985–1989 period—yet had not retired, although most of them were carrying a significantly reduced caseload.

Another form of selection bias is at work as well, however. People hired for new jobs in their fifties or later are not a random draw from their age cohort with regard to health and energy. They are likely to have aged less than the average member of their cohort, and are therefore likely to be productive to an older age than the average. Had Holmes been a dodderer at 61, he would not have been appointed to the U.S. Supreme Court. The point can be generalized: the older a class of workers is on the date of their initial hire, the more "youthful" they are likely to be relative to their contemporaries. This makes it both less surprising that elderly judges perform as well as they do and perilous to generalize from that performance to the vocational capabilities of the elderly in general.

The most serious objection to concluding that age takes only a slight toll of judges lies in the problematic character of trying to distinguish between "quality" and "quantity." If by working more slowly an elderly automobile worker could assemble two cars a day rather than his quota of 10, it would be odd to commend him for the "quality" of his work even if the cars he assembled were as sturdy as those assembled by younger workers. His productivity would be only 20 percent as great as theirs. Elderly judges who produce fewer opinions per year than their younger colleagues are similarly less productive unless their opinions are better, which no one suggests is the case. Presumably these judges, despite their diminished output (weighting quantity by quality), are not replaced because Article III of the Constitution would make that difficult or impossible to do, because the federal judiciary does not have to compete in the marketplace and therefore is not constrained to maximize productivity, and because increased turnover of judges could impose social costs (of which more shortly). Still, there are many activities in which elderly people could not duplicate the performance of younger ones even if allowed to take more time, and we shall have to consider why that seems not to be the case with judging, at least within broad limits. But this does not affect my conclusion that there is an aging effect.

Further evidence both that there is an age-related decline in judging and that it may not set in until an unusually advanced age is presented in table 8.3, which summarizes a citation study of Judge Learned Hand's 38-year career as a federal court of appeals judge, ending with his death in 1961 at the age of 89.[8] He took senior status in 1951, at the age of 79. The table presents data on citations to Hand and his colleagues in five- or six-year slices.[9] The order of the judges in each time slice is the order of the total rather than average number of citations, in all years (through 1992), to the signed, published, majority opinions that each judge wrote in the five-year period.[10] In effect I am weighting quantity (number of opinions) by quality (number of citations per opinion). But I also give the average number of citations, as well as a measure of the *durability* of a judge's opinions—the total number of citations to them in the most recent five-year period for which data are available (1988 through 1992).

Hand's distinction, at least as proxied by citation analysis, is great; but there is a pronounced aging effect. Hand leads in total number of citations in every period until he took senior status and in total citations within the last five years in all but one such period. In average citations he loses the lead three times during his active period, but in two the winning judges wrote so few opinions that their victories are not meaningful. For reasons suggested earlier, total citations is in any event a more meaningful measure of value of output than average citations, since it weights quality by quantity. Hand continued to perform with distinction during the first half of his period of senior status, despite his great age. He led in average citations, although because the number of opinions he wrote dropped substantially he lost the lead in total citations and in citations

8. The source of table 8.3 is my essay "The Learned Hand Biography and the Question of Judicial Greatness," 104 *Yale Law Journal* 511, 536–539 (1994) (tab. 1).

9. The reason for the two six-year slices is to prevent the period in which Hand was in senior service from overlapping his period of active service.

10. The universe of citations is, as with the previous tables, limited to citations by federal courts of appeals.

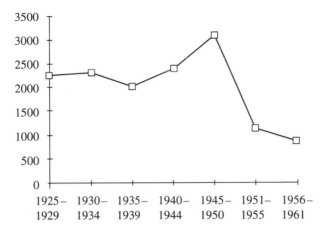

Figure 8.1 Total citations to different vintages of Learned Hand's opinions

within the last five years (the latter also being a total rather than an average number). In the last period of his career, between the ages of 84 and 89, his annual output of opinions dropped slightly,[11] and his average number of citations markedly. The result was a substantial decline in total citations (quantity weighted by quality), as shown graphically in figure 8.1. Yet the most productive period in Hand's entire career as a federal court of appeals judge came just before he took senior status; and he was 73 when that last period of regular full-time service, 1945–1950, began and 78 when it ended.[12]

The results of the study are not altered significantly by two adjustments routinely made to make citation counts a better proxy of judicial output—subtracting self-citations and confining the count to citations by other circuits than Hand's, which were not bound as a matter of precedent to cite Second Circuit opinions. (Hand was a judge of the Second Circuit, which covers New York, Connecticut, and Vermont.) When the study is redone with self-citations omitted, the only change is that Hand jumps from third to second in average citations in 1940–1944. And when the count is rerun to exclude citations in Second Circuit opinions—so that what is being counted are citations by judges not bound as a matter of precedent to follow the opinions of the judges in my sample, and therefore free to choose the best opinions to cite—Hand does even better. Now he leads in both total

11. He wrote 84 in the last period, compared to 82 the period before, but the last period is longer, because he was on senior status for a total of 11 years.

12. This was another "long" period, but scaling the total figures in it down to a normal five-year period would not change the conclusion that it was his most productive period.

Table 8.3 Citations to Learned Hand and His Colleagues

			1925–1929	
Judge	*Opinions*	*Citations*	*Citations per Opinion*	*1988–1992 Citations*
Hand	**244**	**2269**	**9.3**	**46**
Manton	291	1560	5.4	11
Swan	121	790	6.5	7
Hough	141	680	4.8	8
Rogers	66	660	10.0	19
A. Hand	85	417	4.9	4
Chase	17	77	4.5	3
			1930–1934	
Judge	*Opinions*	*Citations*	*Citations per Opinion*	*1988–1992 Citations*
Hand	**257**	**2300**	**8.9**	**72**
Swan	245	1529	6.2	15
Manton	306	1251	4.1	9
A. Hand	216	1071	5.0	14
Chase	223	916	4.1	4
			1935–1939	
Judge	*Opinions*	*Citations*	*Citations per Opinion*	*1988–1992 Citations*
Hand	**244**	**2025**	**8.3**	**81**
Swan	236	1250	5.3	18
Manton	268	1213	4.5	21
A. Hand	216	1043	4.8	21
Chase	209	830	4.0	9
Clark	21	192	9.1	4
Patterson	25	152	6.1	6
			1940–1944	
Judge	*Opinions*	*Citations*	*Citations per Opinion*	*1988–1992 Citations*
Hand	**215**	**2436**	**11.3**	**39**
Clark	193	2287	11.8	49
Frank	140	1822	13.0	39
Swan	211	1430	6.8	27
A. Hand	191	1180	6.2	16
Chase	183	948	5.2	13
Patterson	33	178	5.4	3

Table 8.3 (*continued*)

	1945–1950			
			Citations per	*1988–1992*
Judge	*Opinions*	*Citations*	*Opinion*	*Citations*
Hand	**224**	**3149**	**14.1**	**119**
Frank	191	1624	8.5	52
Clark	198	1595	8.1	23
Swan	202	1372	6.8	16
Chase	179	1164	6.5	22
A. Hand	144	808	5.6	12
	1951–1955			
			Citations per	*1988–1992*
Judge	*Opinions*	*Citations*	*Opinion*	*Citations*
Frank	147	1535	10.4	50
Clark	167	1415	8.5	27
Swan	113	1188	10.5	20
Hand	**82**	**1049**	**12.8**	**42**
A. Hand	74	731	9.9	22
Chase	102	714	7.0	22
Medina	54	500	9.3	27
Harlan	23	252	11.0	17
Waterman	3	22	7.3	0
Hincks	32	0	0.0	0
	1956–1961			
			Citations per	*1988–1992*
Judge	*Opinions*	*Citations*	*Opinion*	*Citations*
Friendly	91	1825	20.1	107
Waterman	155	1642	10.6	61
Clark	169	1454	8.6	64
Medina	127	1283	10.1	62
Hand	**84**	**645**	**7.7**	**41**
Swan	70	562	8.0	22
Moore	68	399	5.9	23
Smith	28	356	12.7	12
Hincks	95	304	3.2	7
Frank	35	265	7.6	2

and average citations in every period—until he took senior status. The aging effect is not erased.

Causes of the Productivity of Older Judges

Explaining the results in the previous section is a challenge. Lehman lists judging as a leadership job and so is not surprised to find a high average age of judges.[13] That doesn't seem right. Chief judges, especially the Chief Justice of the United States, exercise some leadership functions, and the collegial nature of appellate decision-making places some premium on interpersonal skills, but these things have figured in the reputations of only a handful of the "great" judges. If judicial staffs, which are still small, continue to expand, leadership may some day become an important dimension of judicial performance—and if so that will be a boon to older judges, both directly through the increased assistance provided by a larger staff and indirectly by enabling them to employ their mature leadership skills. But that is in the future. The highly reputed judges of the past do not owe their reputation to leadership skills, with the exception of a few Chief Justices, such as John Marshall, William Howard Taft, Charles Evans Hughes, and Arthur Vanderbilt (the last a chief justice of New Jersey's supreme court).

Judges, especially in a common law system, rely heavily on reasoning by analogy, conventionally a branch of practical reasoning, hence arguably less dependent on fluid intelligence than exact reasoning is. But we have considered this argument in previous chapters, and found it wanting. Reasoning by analogy draws on the fluid intelligence, and declines with age.

Most people would say that judges can perform creditably at advanced ages because to be a good judge requires good judgment, and judgment is a function of age and experience. Judges are "wise men," and the wise are old, their wisdom being the product of lived experience. It is difficult to make sense out of this claim. Judges in a mature legal system, especially appellate judges (and all the distinguished elderly judges whom I have mentioned, except Edward Weinfeld, were appellate judges), are not mediators or conciliators. They are rule appliers and, to a limited extent, rule makers. Why extensive lived experience, or even long experience in one or more of the nonjudicial branches of the legal profession, should enhance the quality of their output is therefore not obvious. But I think there is some merit to the popular view, though not to the thinking behind it. The rules of judicial ethics and the institutional characteristics of appellate judging limit

13. Harvey C. Lehman, *Age and Achievement* 286 (1953) (tab. 50).

the information that filters up to the judges about the cases they are hearing. In particular, the facts of a case tend for a variety of reasons to become bleached and deformed en route to the appellate court, and lawyers are very bad at filling in the judges with the background of practices and usages out of which the case arises. It is therefore important for an appellate judge to bring to his job a background of knowledge about the behaviors out of which the cases he will be judging arise: to be, in short, "experienced." [14] This point, however, is more relevant to the optimum age of appointment than to a comparison of judges of different amounts of judicial experience. I shall come back to this distinction.

Another important asset of a judge is disinterest; and judges are less likely to decide cases with a view toward maximizing their future career opportunities, and are therefore more likely to decide cases impartially, the less of a future they have.[15] We want judging to be a terminal job rather than a springboard to another career. This implies that judges should be appointed at an age sufficiently advanced to make it unlikely that they will change careers. The feasibility of such a strategy is reinforced by the "cliff" nature of the federal system of judicial pensions. The absence of any vesting before the earliest retirement age (65) means that as that age approaches, the discounted cost of resignation in lost pension rights rises steeply. The cost drops to zero or even turns negative when the judicial pension finally vests, but the age-decline curve that I have emphasized throughout this book implies that few 65-year-olds will seek new careers. Granted that the practice of law is not quite a "new" career for a judge— most judges practiced law before their appointment to the bench—its rigors and risks in comparison to senior status are sufficiently daunting that the judge who for the sake of his pension rights sticks to judging until the age of 65 is unlikely to retire then and seek employment elsewhere.[16] The younger the judge is when appointed, the less influenced he will be in deciding whether to remain a judge by the prospect of losing all his pension benefits if he resigns.

14. To the extent that "book learning" is a substitute for lived experience, we can expect judges appointed from academia to be somewhat younger than judges appointed from practice.

15. Cf. David Gutmann, "Age and Leadership: Cross-Cultural Observations," in *Aging and Political Leadership* 89, 95–96 (Angus McIntyre, ed., 1988), discussing the role of the presumed disinterest of aged lawyers in bringing down both Senator Joseph McCarthy and President Nixon.

16. Between 1990 and 1992, 113 federal judges either took senior status or retired, but only 7 (all of them retirees, of course) went into private practice. Emily Field Van Tassel, *Why Judges Resign: Influences on Federal Judicial Service, 1789 to 1992* 40 (Federal Judicial Center 1993). The average age of the 58 federal judges who have resigned since 1950 for reasons other than bad health or criminal conviction is only 52. Computed from id. at 126–127.

Experience and disinterest are important elements of "wisdom," unfortunately one of the vaguest concepts going.[17] Anthony Kronman calls wisdom the defining trait of "lawyer-statesmen," a category that in his view includes the best judges.[18] His concept of wisdom involves a combination of cognitive and emotional skills not always easy to distinguish (which is "empathy," for example?). The wisdom of the judge includes such attributes as the capacity to understand from within the plans and projects of other people, the capacity to project in the imagination the probable consequences of alternative approaches and outcomes, habituation to the practices and folkways of the legal profession, deliberative ability, the capacity to avoid becoming emotionally involved with the issues or the litigants, thereby losing perspective, and the ability to put aside one's own personal or career interests in the outcome of the case. In short, a mature professional judgment is central to the concept of a wise judge, and the intellectual and dispositional qualities that go to create such a judgment plainly improve with age up to a point (a "wise child judge" would be a considerable oxymoron) and then plateau until senility. The traditional association of age, wisdom, and judging is therefore plausible. I do not mean to disparage brilliance in judges; but the brilliance of the great judges, like Holmes, Hand, and Cardozo, is, as we shall see, different from the brilliance of a great scientist.

A further point to consider in evaluating the effect of age on a judge's quality is the backward-looking character of the judicial process. Recall Aristotle's time line, according to which, as we age, the focus of our thinking shifts from imagining the future to recalling the past. If one desideratum in judging is to maintain continuity with the past—to enforce settled understandings, traditional rights, and old compacts such as the U.S. Constitution—it may be good to have as judges people whose cognitive orientation is toward the past rather than the future. The backward-looking emphasis of adjudication is summarized in the principle of stare decisis: judges are to adhere to precedent. We should expect therefore that the more a judicial system emphasizes stare decisis, the older its judges will be on average. This may be one reason why judges in Anglo-American judiciaries are older on average than Continental judges (indeed, Continental

17. Cf. Douglas H. Powell (with the collaboration of Dean K. Whitla), *Profiles in Cognitive Aging*, ch. 9 (1994).

18. Anthony T. Kronman, *The Lost Lawyer: Failing Ideals of the Legal Profession* (1993). The issue of wisdom pervades Kronman's book, so I do not give specific page references. Kronman does not associate wisdom in his sense with any particular age. He distinguishes between tyros and seasoned professionals but does not investigate the actual age profile of professional ability.

judges begin their judicial careers right after law school): stare decisis is a more important principle in the Anglo-American legal system. But I do not find this suggestion entirely convincing. The very fact that decisions are precedents in the Anglo-American system requires the judge in that system to look forward to the consequences of his decision in future cases. He must look forward *and* backward. The causality, moreover, might run from the age of the judges to the character of adjudication rather than from the character of adjudication to the age of the judges. The orientation of Anglo-American law may be backward-looking, with more emphasis on adherence to precedent than on forward-looking policy-making, in part because law's administrators are inclined because of their age to take a backward-looking approach to law.

Those who assign a balance-wheel function to the judiciary—the function of reducing the amplitude of swings in public policy—will welcome an aged judiciary. There is some evidence that, as popularly believed, older people are politically more conservative than younger ones even after correction is made for cohort effects.[19] But another and probably more salient dimension of elderly conservatism is that, consistent with characteristics of aging emphasized in this book, in particular the age-related cost of assimilating new ideas, "older persons retain many of the political attitudes and orientations they developed earlier in life."[20] Presumably this is true of judges as well as of voters. So if society swings to the left of where it was when the judges were young they will want to tug it right, and if it swings to the right of where it was when they were young they will want to tug it left. The effect will be to enhance political stability. Of course, just as when comparing the effects of fixed versus floating exchange rates, we must consider long-run as well as short-run stability; they may go in opposite directions. If judges attempt to resist the tides of social change, they may be swept away in a flood—one interpretation of what happened when the aged Justices of the Supreme Court challenged the New Deal. Although the adventurism of the Court during the chief justiceship of Earl Warren may seem a dramatic counterinstance, it is arguable that the liberal justices of the "Warren Court" were enacting the values they had acquired in their

19. Anne Foner, "The Polity," in *Aging and Society,* vol. 3: *A Sociology of Age Stratification* 115, 132–136 (Matilda White Riley, ed., 1972).

20. John B. Williamson, Linda Evans, and Lawrence A. Powell, *The Politics of Aging: Power and Policy* 106 (1982). For evidence, see Duane F. Alwin, Ronald L. Cohen, and Theodore M. Newcomb, *Political Attitudes over the Life Span: The Bennington Women after Fifty Years* 90–96 (1991), and other studies cited there; also M. Kent Jennings, "Residues of a Movement: The Aging of the American Protest Generation," 81 *American Political Science Review* 367 (1987).

youth—which for many of them coincided with the New Deal. The unseemly haste with which German judges adopted the values of the Third Reich may reflect the concordance between those values and the conservative values of the judges' youth.[21] In both cases, that of the Warren Court and that of the Nazi judiciary, judges amplified rather than moderated a social revolution.

A mundane but important consideration in the continued productivity of very old judges is the bearing of boredom. Many judges in this country are people who began a substantially new career when they were in their fifties. If it takes (at a guess) about 30 years of working at the same job to make boredom a substantial cost of working, we should not expect it to push most judges into retiring at the earliest opportunity, or to degrade the quality of their work substantially until they are well past the earliest age at which they can retire.

My discussion of the congruence of age and adjudication may seem to have overlooked the last-period problem. What is to keep judges on the beam when they are in the last period of their lives? But this question reveals a misunderstanding of the last-period problem (which is perhaps misnamed). The last period is a problem in large part because it is not *really* the last period; it is simply the last period in which the individual is subject to a particular set of incentives. The employee who soldiers on the job or steals from the till because the only feasible sanction available to his employer is to fire him and he is about to leave anyway has an incentive to misbehave only because he will still be living after he leaves his job. If the job were literally terminal, he would lack that incentive. So to the extent that judicial employment approximates terminal employment, the judges' incentive to misbehave will be limited. Judges will not only have nothing to lose from deciding a case in a particular way, but nothing to gain either. The hope is that with incentives to self-interested behavior in the usual sense[22] out of the picture, the judge will render a genuinely public-interested decision. The older the judge, other things the same, the more likely this hope is to be realized. But it is just a hope, because with self-interest out of the picture the penalty for whimsical or arbitrary action is

---

21. See Ingo Müller, *Hitler's Justice: The Courts of the Third Reich* (Deborah Lucas Schneider, trans., 1990); Richard A. Posner, *Overcoming Law*, ch. 4 (1985).

22. An important qualification for some judges—those who derive satisfaction from using their judicial office to advance a political philosophy. But below the Supreme Court level, they are a minority. See Richard A. Posner, "What Do Judges and Justices Maximize? (The Same Thing Everybody Else Does)," 3 *Supreme Court Economic Review* 1 (1994), reprinted in *Overcoming Law*, note 21 above, ch. 3.

removed along with the reward. Admittedly this is an exaggeration, since judges may care about their posthumous reputation.

I have said that wisdom, and by implication judicial capability, do not decline with age. But this, too, is an exaggeration, as we saw in connection with Learned Hand's career, and I have now to consider the issue more carefully. Experience in the sense of first-hand engagement with the law in operation ceases to grow the moment the judge is appointed and thereby withdraws from that world. This implies net depreciation of his professional human capital from that moment forward. But judicial experience creates judicial human capital, enabling the judge to increase his quality-weighted output of decisions and thereby offset, for a time anyway, the inevitable age-related decline in mental energy and acuity. Judging is a learning-by-doing sort of job. The experience of reading many briefs and hearing many oral arguments increases the speed at which the judge can extract the gist of a case from the briefs and arguments of the lawyers. Speed is important in judicial work. As in certain forms of leadership (see chapter 7), judges have to make many decisions in a limited amount of time, and speed and confidence in judicial decision-making are functions of experience.

In addition, the work that a judge puts into preparing to hear a case and afterward writing the opinion in it (if he is the judge on the panel who is assigned the case to write) teaches him something about the field or sub-field of law involved; so the next time he has a case in the same area he can master it more quickly. This is important because most judges were engaged in more specialized work before they ascended the bench. Most American judges are generalists, most lawyers and law professors specialists. So judges must acquire much of their judicial knowledge base as judges.

If judges acquire new human capital while judging, one might expect the quantity and the quality of a judge's work actually to *increase* as he ages in the job, rather than just not to decrease. But the judge's pre–judicial experience will be depreciating even as his judicial experience is appreciating, as will his energy. His fluid intelligence will be diminishing as well. Since such diminution is an increasing function of age, and since the cost of acquiring judicial experience like other new human capital is higher for older than for younger people, we might expect the quality-weighted output of judges appointed at younger ages to increase for a time after their appointment before leveling off and eventually declining, while the output of work of judges appointed at more advanced ages would remain constant until the eventual decline. But tables 8.1 and 8.2 reveal no correlation between judicial output and judicial experience. The explanation may lie in the peculiar terms of federal judicial employment. The reason that an experience-related increase in an employee's productivity is expected to lead to an increase in his output is that his employer can reward him for the larger output in a higher salary or fire him if he produces a smaller output. Both carrot and stick are missing in the case of federal judges, all of whom (of the same rank) are paid the same and can be removed only for gross malfeasance. There is nothing to prevent a federal judge from transforming an increase in his productivity due to increased experience into leisure. His output remains the same, but is produced in less time, allowing him more leisure. This interpretation of the tables is consistent with the argument I have made elsewhere that leisure is an important element of the average judge's utility function.[23] The interpretation is weakened if judges would derive additional utility from additional output. Some would. Many would not. They derive utility from "doing their job" but not from doing more.

Another factor that may explain the low rate of decline of judicial ability (the first was the acquisition of judicial capital)—and it is the decisive factor in the high quality of exceptional judges at advanced ages—is the importance, to judicial distinction, of writing. The distinguishing feature of most great judges, even those rightly pronounced "brilliant," has not been exceptional analytical power; it has been exceptional rhetorical power.[24] The volume, variety, and random sequence of cases, the committee character of judicial decision-making, the essentially interpretive rather than creative character of the judicial function, and the sheer age of the judges make it unlikely that judicial decisions, even of the ablest judges, would display a high order of intellectual creativity. Most of the ideas expressed in judicial opinions come from outside, from lawyers, legislators, law professors, and scholars in other fields, such as economics, political science, and philosophy, or in the case of intellectual judges like Holmes, Brandeis, or Frankfurter from ideas that they had developed before they became judges. What lifts a judicial opinion out of the commonplace, apart from the accidents of historical significance over which the judge has no control, is the vividness, compactness, and, in short, memorableness of his exposition. Even so famous an example of judicial "creativity" as Learned Hand's formula for negligence,[25] a landmark in the economic analysis of

---

23. See id.

24. Posner, note 4 above, at 133–137.

25. $B < PL$, where B is the burden (cost) of avoiding an accident, P the probability that the accident will occur unless precaution B is taken, and L the loss (cost) that the accident will cause if it occurs. The formula was announced in Hand's opinion in United States v. Carroll Towing Co., 159 F.2d 169, 173 (2d Cir. 1947).

law, is merely a restatement in algebraic form of the conventional tort standard of negligence; it is algebra as metaphor, not as mathematical analysis.

Writing ability, which in the best judges can fairly be termed literary, is an aspect of crystallized intelligence, and is one of the aspects least likely to decline with age until senility sets in. It is true that creative writers often run out of things to say, with the result that many writing careers have an early peak.[26] But not all by any means, as we saw in the preceding chapter; and running out of fresh ideas is unlikely to be a problem for judges, because they are given a fresh topic, as it were, in every case; they don't need to draw on an internal stock of ideas that might run down. Comparison of the writing style (not intellectual creativity) of the same person at different ages often reveals steady improvement to a quite advanced age, with no decline from that late peak until shortly before death. Holmes's most eloquent opinion, his dissent in the *Abrams* free-speech case,[27] was written in his late seventies, and Learned Hand wrote the "Hand formula" opinion in his middle seventies.

Not every student of adjudication will agree with my analysis of the elements of judicial distinction. But I do not think that my conclusion that there is an age-related decline in judicial performance, but that it does not set in until a relatively very advanced age, is highly sensitive to that analysis. Judge Friendly, whom I have mentioned, once listed four elements of "outstanding [judicial] quality": "analytical power," "legal learning," "general culture," and "the ability to write graceful and powerful English." [28] The first of these—but only the first—is likely to decline with age.

The Effect of Increased Longevity

Despite the many examples of distinguished performance by old judges, and the reasons that explain them, continuing increases in longevity may have a negative impact on the performance of the federal judiciary if the rules governing the retirement of federal judges remain unchanged. Even if the age-decline curve is very gradual for judges, their performance must eventually decline; and of course the decline is more rapid for some judges

26. Dean Keith Simonton, "Age and Creative Productivity: Nonlinear Estimation of an Information-Processing Model," 29 *International Journal of Aging and Human Development* 23 (1989), proposes a model in which the researcher begins his career with a fixed creative potential and draws down this endowment over the course of his career. See also Simonton, *Genius, Creativity, and Leadership: Historiometric Inquiries* 109–112 (1984).

27. Abrams v. United States, 250 U.S. 616, 624 (1919).

28. Henry J. Friendly, Book Review (of *Learned Hand's Court,* by Marvin Schick), 86 *Political Science Quarterly* 470, 471 (1971).

than for others. So if increased longevity increases the percentage of judges who are very old, the quality of judicial output could suffer unless the effect of increased longevity on capability were perfectly offset by a reduction in the age-decline rate, which is unlikely. A negative effect of increased longevity on judicial performance is especially likely if our society continues to change very rapidly, causing the problems thrown up to the judiciary for solution to change rapidly as well. Such change would increase the rate at which judicial performance declines because of age. A partial offset, however, is the increased size of judicial staffs, which, as I have noted, enables some elderly judges to produce a larger quality-weighted output than they could have done in the old days. A further point is that a rising average age of retirement for judges implies, unless the average age of appointment rises by the same amount, a reduction in judicial turnover, and this may be a good thing if a high value is placed on legal stability.

The effect of longevity on judicial performance would have little significance if the average age of judicial retirement could not be expected to rise as judges' longevity increases. But it may rise. Judicial employment generates substantial psychic income[29] not offset by substantial nonpecuniary costs until the elderly judge becomes incapable of putting forth the modest amount of effort required for a judicial performance of minimum respectability. In other words, I_o in equation 4.2 is strongly positive for most judges—and we recall that this reduces the likelihood of retirement at the earliest possible opportunity, especially where, as in the case of the federal judiciary, retirement is strictly voluntary. The effort costs of remaining a judge at an advanced age have fallen in recent decades because of better health and the increase in judicial staffs. Both developments have probably conduced to increased productivity by elderly judges. If it nevertheless is desired that judges retire no later than they do now, the terms of retirement can be made even more attractive than they are now. This has been the response of the private market to the law's curtailment of mandatory retirement at fixed ages.

An alternative approach to the problem (if it is a problem) of an aging judiciary would be to replace our system of generalist courts with one of specialized courts. Generally, the more specialized a worker is, the less new human capital he need acquire in order to be able to do his job creditably. The acquisition of new human capital is costly for the old because of the age-related decline in fluid intelligence, and a generalist judge is one who has to keep investing in human capital as new fields of law come within his

---

29. See Posner, note 22 above.

purview. But boredom is more likely to set in sooner, the more specialized the job. So a specialized judiciary may not be the best way to accommodate the predictable increase in judicial longevity.

As should be plain from this discussion, the age profile of judicial achievement, and the factors that determine the profile, have implications for the structure of the judicial system. These implications are explored further in chapter 13. The essential points in the present chapter have been, first, to use citation analysis to evaluate the proposition that adjudication is an example of a late peak, sustained, activity and, second, if it is, to explain why. The citations analysis confirmed that appellate adjudication has the predicted properties. But it also shows that there is an aging effect; that even so distinguished and long-lived a judge as Learned Hand eventually experienced a pronounced decline in output as proxied by total citations, which, properly, weight quality by quantity. As far as the causality of the judicial age profile is concerned, we saw that the major cause appears to be the character of legal reasoning, with its heavy emphasis on practical reason in a sense that identified it as an aspect of crystallized intelligence. Notice that as well as using the concept of practical reason to account for the result of the citation analysis, I have argued that that analysis supported the proposition that practical reason is indeed the lifeblood of legal reasoning, rather than—as a surprising number of judges and law professors continue to believe—logic or some other method of abstract reasoning. Other factors that help explain the age profile of the judicial profession include the policy of adhering to precedent in the Anglo-American judicial system, the (related) desire for the judiciary to act as a stabilizing rather than innovative force in social and political life, the positive correlation between old age and disinterestedness, and the late age of judicial appointment, which both reduces the likelihood that boredom will drive judges to retire and selects for persons more youthful than the average of their age cohort.

9

The Status of the Old
and the Aging of Institutions

I have been considering the old mostly from their own standpoint and that of their employers rather than from the standpoint of society as a whole or even of the families of aged people. But the way in which nonelderly members of society, including both relatives and nonrelatives, regard and treat the elderly has great significance for both positive and normative analysis of aging. There is an instructive analogy to the social valuation of children. Because children are dependent on adults, the status of children—including how many there are and what investments are made in their human capital—reflects the interests of the adult population. Families will be smaller when children are costly to raise and do not provide extensive services to their parents, and larger when they are cheap to raise and do provide extensive services to their parents, as in traditional agricultural societies.[1] The dependent old are in a parallel position. They exist at the sufferance of the dominant age groups, including their own adult children.

I want to consider the factors that from a rational-choice perspective are likely to influence the treatment that the elderly will receive from society. Such a perspective seems, if anything, even more apt to the treatment of the old than to the treatment of the young. People appear to be genetically programmed to feel protective toward children; why else do we find children, and the young of animals, "cute," appealing, even adorable?[2] We

1. On the economics of the family, see Gary S. Becker, *A Treatise on the Family* (enlarged ed. 1991).

2. A point by no means inconsistent with even widespread infanticide, abortion, and neglect. Richard A. Posner, *Sex and Reason* 143–144 (1992). The optimum and the maximum number of

do not appear to be genetically programmed to feel as protective toward old people in general; while most children love their parents even when the parents are old, they do so generally with diminished intensity. This asymmetry makes biological sense. Inclusive fitness is unlikely to be promoted by the devotion of huge resources to the survival of persons who, by reason of advanced age, are not reproductively or otherwise productive, either actually or (like children) potentially. Postreproductive individuals may contribute to the survival of their offspring and thus be productive; because of this, respect for old people in general and for one's parents and grandparents in particular may be instinctual. But these feelings are less intense than the counterpart feelings toward the young because the old make a smaller contribution to inclusive fitness. We can therefore expect the dominant groups in a society, because they are not being tugged as powerfully by the genes, to be more calculating about the very old than about the very young members of the society, even when the very old are their own parents and grandparents. Indeed, we can expect the old themselves, altruistically inclined by their genes to favor the younger members of their families, to cooperate to a certain extent (depending on circumstances, as we shall see) with policies that promote the interests of the young at the expense of the old.

The status of the old, as measured by offices occupied, wealth controlled, and respect accorded, varies greatly both across societies[3] and, within societies—including, as we shall see, our own—across time. Some ancient and primitive societies have killed their old people,[4] sometimes

---

children are not the same, as too many children may endanger the survival of all. As I noted in chapter 1, this is a possible explanation of menopause.

3. For a good summary, see John B. Williamson, Linda Evans, and Lawrence A. Powell, *The Politics of Aging: Power and Policy,* pt. 1 (1982). Case studies are numerous. A representative anthology is *Aging in Cross-Cultural Perspective: Africa and the Americas* (Enid Gort, ed., 1988). A somewhat dated but incomparably vivid summary of the anthropological literature on old age is Simone de Beauvoir, *Old Age,* ch. 2 (1972); another excellent summary is Jack Goody, "Aging in Nonindustrial Societies," in *Handbook of Aging and the Social Sciences* 117 (Robert H. Binstock and Ethel Shanas, eds., 1976); while for a wealth of data concerning the status of the aged in primitive societies, see Leo W. Simmons, *The Role of the Aged in Primitive Society* (1945).

4. Some 20 percent of primitive societies in two studies based on data in the Human Relations Area Files. Jennie Keith, "Age in Social and Cultural Context: Anthropological Perspectives," in *Handbook of Aging and the Social Sciences* 91, 92 (Robert H. Binstock and Linda K. George, eds., 3d ed. 1990). See also Steven M. Albert and Maria G. Cattell, *Old Age in Global Perspective: Cross-Cultural and Cross-National Views* 224–228 (1994). In one of the studies, elderly were "forsaken," "abandoned,"or "killed" in 59 percent of the societies sampled. Anthony P. Glascock and Susan L. Feinman, "A Holocultural Analysis of Old Age," 3 *Comparative Social Research* 311, 323 (1980) (tab. 7). It should be plain that geronticide is no more inconsistent with an instinctual filiality than infanticide is inconsistent with an instinctual affection for children. See note 2 above.

with the convenient rationalization that dying a natural death impairs one's prospects in the afterlife;[5] others have neglected them; others have revered them. Despite charges of "ageism" leveled by representatives of the elderly and by some radical egalitarians (who see discrimination everywhere), it is doubtful that there has ever been a society in which old people as a whole have been as politically influential, as materially well-off, and, probably, as happy as they are in modern American society, although they are not revered. Apart from their wealth and number, and the extraordinary medical resources devoted to their health and longevity, old people occupy a range of important positions in government, business, and the nonprofit sector. We saw in the preceding chapter that judging is an old person's profession; and we know that the legal profession in general, and the courts in particular, are more powerful in the United States than in any other country. How to explain the dramatic differences in the status of the old across societies is the main challenge of this chapter. I acknowledge that the term "status" is vague in this setting, but it will do for now and I shall clarify it later.

Primitive and Agrarian Societies

Determinants of elderly people's status. Since I shall be talking a lot about "primitive" societies, and the term is likely to raise hackles, I should explain what I mean and assure the reader that no pejorative or demeaning connotation is intended. Nineteenth-century explorers, ethnographers, and anthropologists discovered that a large number of cultures scattered around the world were preliterate, were extremely poor by Western standards, and were subsisting at an essentially Stone Age level of technology, with very little contact with the inhabitants of the industrialized world. These cultures (now extensively "contaminated" by contact with technologically advanced cultures) have been studied intensively and a good deal of data about them have been collected in forms that enable, though with great difficulty, the kind of comparative empirical study reported later in this chapter. So "primitive" should be understood as a technical term, just as when it is used to denote the style of painting of Grandma Moses.

A preliterate society is unlikely, course, to know the precise chronological age of its elderly members. (Even today, we saw in chapter 2, the number of the very oldest Americans is not known with precision.) How does this cut, so far as status is concerned? Both ways. On the one hand,

5. See, for example, James George Frazer, *The Dying God* (part 3 of *The Golden Bough*) 10–14 (1913):

chronological age cannot be used as a proxy for ability to perform particular tasks, so "mandatory retirement," which forces the ablest old to retire on the basis of the average capability of their age cohort, is unlikely to be practiced. Statistical discrimination against the aged (see chapter 13) is less feasible if there are no statistics. On the other hand, lacking a precise knowledge of chronological ages, people may be classified as "old" on the basis of superficial characteristics, such as the amount of grey in their hair or the number of creases in their skin, that are only loosely related to age in either a chronological or a functional sense. By the same token, some young-looking people will be classified as young even though they are functionally and chronologically old. They will benefit from the absence of records. The effect of that absence on the position of elderly persons in a society is thus indeterminate on the level of theory.

In an extremely poor society, the maintenance of the old, if they can no longer maintain themselves, may be prohibitively costly. The cost of a good or service in real as distinct from pecuniary terms is what is given up in its consumption; that is why, as we saw in chapter 5, old people are willing to spend so much money on modest extensions of life. What is given up depends on scarcity. If a society is so poor that food is very scarce, the cost of feeding an old person may be the starvation of a young one, and in such a case the society is likely to allow the old person to starve, or even kill him outright. The anthropological literature contains examples of primitive societies in which elderly people acquiesce in their society's gerontocidal norms, even to the point of going to their deaths gaily.[6] Is this a product of socialization so intense that it succeeds in overcoming the instinctual dread of death? Perhaps so, but an alternative hypothesis is that where the choice is between survival of a person who is past reproductive age and survival of his descendants who still have reproductive potential, the genes will incline the older family member to sacrifice himself for the younger.

This analysis suggests that, other things being equal, the poorer a society is, the more likely it will be to kill or let die its oldest members. Other things may not be equal, however. An important variable is the ratio of the nonworking old (and any other nonworkers, such as children, but I shall ignore this point in order to simplify the analysis) to the working part of the population. The lower that ratio, the less each worker will need to contribute from his output in order to support the old. Also militating against

6. See, for example, Simmons, note 3 above, at 236–238; Lucy Mair, *African Societies* 197 (1974).

the neglect or mistreatment of the elderly is the effect on the last-period problem. If a person knows that he will die as soon as he reaches the threshold of old age, this knowledge will affect his incentives while he is still young. He will be less likely to work hard, help others, and be honest, because the punishments and rewards for his conduct will be severely truncated. Particularly if effort, honesty, or other dimensions of conduct are difficult to monitor, society will have a reason for preserving the lives of old people that is similar to that underlying the "wage-bonding" theory (discussed in chapter 3), in which compensation is backloaded as a way of increasing the expected punishment cost of a worker's performing his job indolently or dishonestly.

It has long been thought that even though memory is impaired by age, the memories of old people are potentially of great value to a preliterate society, a society whose only "records" are the recollections of its members.[7] To evaluate this belief, we must distinguish between the society that is static, in the sense that technology and social practices change very slowly in them, and the dynamic society. If it is static, as most primitive societies are, there might seem to be little utility to a long memory: the old would be remembering and recounting the same kind of things that the young are experiencing in the present. Yet if the society were dynamic (though still primitive—admittedly an unlikely combination), what the old remembered from the old days would not be of much assistance in responding to the challenges of the present. This point does help explain why the old are indeed not revered in dynamic societies, such as our own. But it is not a complete explanation. The very fact of rapid social change might cause people to value the old as living links to a receding, perhaps nostalgically regarded or even heroic, past ("the War," "the Fifties"). However, the old are at a disadvantage in a dynamic society for another reason besides the diminished value of their memories to the young. As a consequence of the age-related decline in fluid intelligence and the age-related truncation of the expected returns from investing in human capital, old people are unlikely to make a successful switch to a new type of job. If demands change rapidly, many old people will find themselves on the shelf.

7. For an example, see Austin J. Shelton, "The Aged and Eldership among the Igbo," in *Aging and Modernization* 31, 45 (Donald O. Cowgill and Lowell D. Holmes, eds., 1972). And recall the African motto quoted in chapter 2 about the death of an old man being equivalent to the burning down of a library. The qualification—even if memory is impaired by age—is probably not important. Few "old" people in primitive societies are so old as to be likely sufferers from serious age-related cognitive impairments.

The argument that a long memory is unlikely to be a valuable social asset is far more persuasive with regard to a dynamic society than with regard to a static one. For a static society is as likely as any other to be subject to shocks that occur infrequently; the shocks indeed may be more numerous and more severe. Famine, invasion, eclipse, plague, flood, drought, the irruption of charismatic personalities, a run of multiple or deformed births, and other alarming or challenging events may be sufficiently rare that when they occur only the old people in the society can recall a parallel instance. Perhaps no young person has ever seen an eclipse of the sun but the old can reassure the young that it is not a new thing and that the last time it happened there were no untoward consequences. Literacy, and education more broadly, greatly reduce the value of old people's memories as a record of past events.[8]

Memory plays a further role in a static society. The immediate cause of a society's remaining static is that its strategy for coping with the challenges that face it is to adhere to its existing practices—to "tradition"—rather than to seek new solutions. The reason may be that as an aspect of a general paucity of knowledge, problem-solving skills are not well developed. We can observe the strategy in ourselves when we do not understand the principles underlying an activity. In such cases, once one has hit on a method that works, one is reluctant to deviate from it. I, for example, not understanding the principles of computers, am very reluctant to alter my accustomed routines even when I have no reason to believe that an alteration would cause the computer to "crash." If the characteristic method of "progress" in a primitive society is trial and error, followed by rigid adherence to the first successful procedure that the method yields, there will be little scope for the employment of problem-solving skills. The characteristic intellectual attributes of youth—flexibility, imagination, problem-solving ability, mental quickness, openness to new ideas, and powerful short-term memory—will confer few social benefits and therefore will not be highly valued. They may even be perceived as dangerous.

Another reason to expect the knowledge value of the elderly to be great in a primitive society is that, as we saw in chapter 1, life expectancies are short in such societies. Most of the "elderly" will probably be only middle-aged by our standards, hence only one generation removed from young

8. For examples, see Maria G. Cattell, "Knowledge and Social Change in Samia, Western Kenya," in *The Elderly Population in Developed and Developing World* 121, 139 (P. Krishnan and K. Mahadevan, eds., 1992); Charles Edward Fuller, "Aging among Southern African Bantu," in *Aging and Modernization,* note 7 above, at 51, 60.

adults, to whom the "elderly" will be imparting concrete advice on the performance of adult tasks rather than merely a generalized "wisdom" of the aged.

We can expect preliterate societies to allocate tasks and social roles on the basis of age (this is known as "age grading")[9] to a greater extent than literate societies do, even when the absence of written records creates uncertainty about precise ages. Preliterate societies face high information costs,[10] including costs of matching workers to jobs. Everyone may know everyone else in a small-scale society yet still have great difficulty appraising their marginal product in alternative employments, especially when performance in some of the employments (warfare, for example, or magic) is intermittent or difficult to evaluate. It is natural in such a situation to use crude proxies, such as age and parental occupation, for capacity to perform particular jobs. So one is not surprised at the emergence of customs that assign all the young men to be warriors, the middle-aged to be leaders, the king's son to be king, and the old to occupy judicial,[11] sacral, or consultative roles, in which wisdom and experience, plausibly if only crudely correlated with age, dominate strength and mental quickness. In such a system the old are not in competition with the young, and this may give them a secure niche in the social structure. The "feminizing" of old men, remarked in chapter 5, contributes to this reallocation of roles by reducing competition between old and young men for the same social positions, while the "masculinizing" of aging women equips them, when age has freed them from having to tend their own children, to exercise a leadership role in their extended family.[12]

The less a vulnerable segment of the population, such as the old, can rely on legal and political rights to secure their survival, the more resources they will devote to cultivating the goodwill of the powerful. So we can expect parents in a primitive society to spend more time inculcating filial piety, or a more general respect for the elderly, in their children than parents

9. See, for example, Keith, note 4 above, at 101–102; Nancy Foner, *Ages in Conflict: A Cross-Cultural Perspective on Inequality between Old and Young* 17–24 (1984); Bernardo Bernardi, *Age Class Systems: Social Institutions and Polities Based on Age* (1985).

10. As emphasized in my book *The Economics of Justice,* ch. 6 (1981) ("A Theory of Primitive Society").

11. See, for example, Walter H. Sangree, "Age and Power: Life-Course Trajectories and Age Structuring of Power Relations in East and West Africa," in *Age Structuring in Comparative Perspective* 23, 28 (David I. Kertzer and K. Warner Schaie, eds., 1989); Albert and Cattell, note 4 above, at 70.

12. The importance of "sex-role turnover" in preserving a valuable place of elderly men and women in primitive societies is emphasized in David Gutmann, *Reclaimed Powers: Toward a New Psychology of Men and Women in Later Life* (1987).

in a modern society bother to do.[13] This piety, this "filiality,"[14] takes the place of legal enforcement in guaranteeing performance of the implicit (and sometimes quite elaborate) intergenerational contract in which parents support children when young in exchange for support by the children in the parents' old age.[15] To the extent that efforts at inculcating filiality succeed, the elderly will be more respected than they are in a society in which fewer such efforts are made.

Odd as it may seem, an exogenous increase in longevity, other things remaining constant, should increase the incentive of parents to inculcate filial piety in their children, and might even increase their target number of children, because they could anticipate a longer period of dependency on their children.[16] Adult adoption, common in societies ranging from ancient Rome to modern Japan, is a device by which the childless obtain a surrogate assurance (contractual rather than emotional) of support in old age.[17]

13. Parents "may want to be taken care of when old or ill, but cannot have a contract with their children to help out. However, they can try to shape the formation of children's preferences to raise their chances their children will help voluntarily." Gary S. Becker, "Habits, Addictions, and Traditions," 45 *Kyklos* 327, 336 (1992). See also Jeffrey B. Nugent, "The Old-Age Security Motive for Fertility," 11 *Population and Development Review* 75, 78–79 (1985). Nugent points out that a culture of arranged marriage promotes filial piety by reducing the likelihood that a child will redirect his affections from his parents to his spouse. Id. at 91 n. 16. For some evidence that inculcating filial piety really "works," see Les Whitbeck, Danny R. Hoyt, and Shirley M. Huck, "Early Family Relationships, Intergenerational Solidarity, and Support Provided to Parents by Their Adult Children," 49 *Journal of Gerontology* S85 (1994).

14. The Confucian ideal. See Benjamin I. Schwartz, *The World of Thought in Ancient China* 71, 100–101 (1985); "Editor's Preface," in *The Hsiao Ching* v (Paul K. T. Sih, ed., 1961); cf. Kyu-Taik Sung, "Motivations for Parent Care: The Case of Filial Children in Korea," 34 *International Journal of Aging and Human Development* 109 (1992). For a vivid but possibly unreliable description of Japanese filiality, see Ruth Benedict, *The Chrysanthemum and the Sword: Patterns of Japanese Culture* 51–52, 101–102, 121 (1946).

15. See, for example, Laura J. Zimmer, "'Who Will Bury Me?': The Plight of Childless Elderly among the Gende," 2 *Journal of Cross-Cultural Gerontology* 61 (1987), esp. pp. 76–77. On the importance of children as a source of support for their parents in poor societies, see the careful empirical study, Daniel C. Clay and Jane E. vander Haar, "Patterns of Intergenerational Support and Childbearing in the Third World," 47 *Population Studies* 67 (1993). For evidence that children are indeed treated better by their parents in cultures in which the parents look to their children for old-age support, see Margaret F. Brinig, "Finite Horizons: The American Family," 2 *International Journal of Children's Rights* 293 (1994). To the extent that family altruism is "two-sided," that is, children are altruistic toward their parents (as I have suggested is biologically plausible) as well as vice versa, parents will be more generous to their children because more likely to be repaid in their old age. See Peter Rangazas, "Human Capital Investment in Wealth-Constrained Families with Two-Sided Altruism," 35 *Economics Letters* 137 (1991).

16. Isaac Ehrlich and Francis T. Lui, "Intergenerational Trade, Longevity, and Economic Growth," 99 *Journal of Political Economy* 1029, 1046 (1991). This is on the assumption that the increase in longevity does not result merely in a higher fraction of children surviving to adulthood, but, also or instead, in an increase in the likelihood of reaching, or the length of, old age.

17. Richard A. Posner, *Sex and Reason* 405–406 (1992), and references cited there.

In nineteenth-century America, childless elderly persons would sometimes contract for nursing and other services in exchange for a promise to will property to the caretaker.[18]

A society's location on the static versus dynamic continuum is not a completely exogenous factor in the status of the old. One can imagine a society—perhaps mandarin China was it—in which the old enjoy a dominant influence because the politically dominant groups in the society *want* the society to remain static. Just as the pace of social change might be slowed by a powerful judiciary employing the characteristically backward-looking techniques of legal reasoning, so might it be slowed by having old people occupy the major political and social positions. This is doubtless a factor in the gerontocratic structure of governance of the Roman Catholic and Mormon churches.

I have said that a low ratio of old to young helps the old by reducing the per capita cost of supporting them. A further point is that the smaller the proportion of the population that survives to an advanced age, the more likely society is to attribute extraordinary powers to those who do survive. The tougher the obstacle course the old have had to run in order to survive into old age, moreover, the sturdier they are likely to be when they get there; this selection effect will strengthen the impression that very old people have exceptional powers. But it is essential to distinguish between exogenous and endogenous influences on the ratio of old to young. The ratio might be low because of the prevalence of diseases to which the old were particularly vulnerable[19] or because the society had decided not to support its old people. Obviously if the ratio were low for the latter reason it would not be evidence that the society had a high regard for the old— unless, perhaps, the old were *willing* to sacrifice themselves for the sake of the young, as in fact they seem to be in some primitive societies.

The bearing of agriculture. We can also expect the status of the old to be influenced by the character of the society's economy, and, specifically, to be higher in an agricultural society than in a hunter-gatherer society.[20] An agricultural society is likely to have, other than in times of famine

---

18. See, for example, Slater v. Estate of Cook, 67 N.W. 15 (Wis. 1896); Brady v. Smith, 28 N.Y. Supp. 776 (Super. Ct. 1894); Stockley v. Goodwin, 78 Ill. 127 (1875).

19. Conversely, we saw in chapter 2 that the Black Death in medieval Europe, by sparing the old, raised the dependency ratio.

20. For evidence, see Gordon E. Finley, "Modernization and Ageing," in *The Elderly Population in Developed and Developing World,* note 8 above, at 87. Among primitive societies, geronticide is far more common in hunter-gatherer economies than in agricultural economies. Albert and Cattell, note 4 above, at 225.

(when we can expect the old to fare very poorly), a larger food output per productive persõn, and this will reduce the cost, in foregone consumption, of maintaining an old person.[21] If the economy is sufficiently productive, the old may have been able to save enough from current income when young to support themselves when old, reducing to zero the cost imposed on other people, at least if the others do not consider confiscating the savings of the old an attractive policy, because of the last-period problem.

The part of the output of an agricultural society that is not required for the subsistence of the producers also enables the support of specialists in activities, such as dispute resolution, religion, and magic, that are within the capacity of the old to perform. Since, moreover, agricultural societies are stationary rather than nomadic, the reduced mobility of the old imposes a lesser cost on the young; they don't have to be carried from camp to camp. In addition, the labor of the elderly is more valuable in such a society because there are more light agricultural tasks (such as tending sheep) than there are light hunting-gathering tasks, and the old can perform light but not heavy labor. Many old people in our society love to garden, and horticultural tasks are broadly similar to agricultural ones.[22]

An agricultural economy has a further significance for the status of the old beyond generating a surplus for consumption by the elderly and providing them opportunities for employment. An agricultural economy revolves around a stock of durable assets, namely arable land, and the control and devolution of that stock present difficult problems from the standpoint of political stability and economic efficiency. The story of King Lear is instructive. Because of his advancing age, Lear wishes to divest himself of responsibility for his kingdom ("unburden'd crawl toward death," as he puts it), and he proposes therefore to divide the kingdom among his three daughters, reserving a right of support for himself. But a division of the kingdom is a recipe for civil war, as King Lear learns to his sorrow. (We can see here a metaphor for the inefficiency of breaking up a large estate into small farms.) And the right to support that he had reserved turns out to be unenforceable.

21. Though, as Malthus argued, much of the food surplus may go to supporting a larger population, without significantly increasing per capita wealth.

22. Even today, labor-participation rates are higher in agricultural economies because agriculture provides more employment opportunities for elderly persons than most other economic activities do. Robert L. Clark and Richard Anker, "Cross-National Analysis of Labor Force Participation of Older Men and Women," 41 *Economic Development and Cultural Change* 489 (1993). In the United States, a disproportionate number of employed elderly men are farmers or farm laborers. Herbert S. Parnes and David G. Sommers, "Shunning Retirement: Work Experience of Men in Their Seventies and Early Eighties," 49 *Journal of Gerontology* S117, S122 (1994).

The interest in keeping an agricultural estate intact across the generations, or even within a generation, in a society in which contracts may be difficult to enforce, argues for simple rules of property, such as the eldest male owns everything, and mechanical rules of succession, such as that the property passes intact at the owner's death to his eldest son. (The parallel to hereditary monarchy is obvious.) Such rules favor the old by concentrating the ownership of property in their hands. In a society in which the economic rent of land is a large fraction of all income, owners of property will not experience a decline in income when they get old, unlike the situation in a modern economy, where most people's most valuable capital assets are various forms of human capital, which depreciates with age. The patriarchal principle is thus a natural though not an inevitable corollary of an agrarian economy in which the costs of transactions are inherently high because of the absence of a commercially sophisticated legal system and in which, therefore, the rules governing ownership and transfers must be kept simple.

So in a society at once agricultural and preliterate (and hence almost certain both to be static and to lack a commercially sophisticated legal system), we have optimum conditions for old people to attain a high social status. If status increases monotonically with age, we may get ancestor worship, the extrapolation of a positive correlation between age and importance beyond the lifetime. Ancestors are not only the *very* old; they are also predecessors. Predecessors are apt to be venerated more the more static the society; their contributions are less likely to be obsolete. So a static society is likely to value ancestors both directly, as specimens of the (very) old, and indirectly, as predecessors whose contributions have not faded with time.

But before concluding that the situation of the old in the type of premodern society that I have been describing is optimal, we must remind ourselves not only of the poverty by our standards of everybody in such a society, young and old, but also of the likelihood of a severe maldistribution of wealth and status among the old. If the ownership of land is concentrated, the patriarchal class will be small even relative to the small total number of old people in a premodern society; most old people may be condemned, therefore, to extreme penury. Indeed, the wealth and power of the patriarchal class may engender resentment against old people in general (this is especially likely in societies that permit polygyny, which favors wealthy older men), and the resentment may be taken out against the weakest of them.

I must defend my assumption, heretofore tacit, that there is some mechanism by which policies that are beneficial to a society are adopted by it. Democratic societies have such mechanisms, though they are subject to deformation by pressure from interest groups; so, for that matter, do nondemocratic societies, provided they have a government. The issue of the mechanism is more challenging when one is speaking of a prepolitical society, a society that lacks formal institutions of government. How does the fact that old people might have a valuable role to play in the intergenerational transmission of useful knowledge get translated into arrangements for supporting old people rather than letting them starve when they get too old to pitch in? I do not have the answer. But it is enough for my purposes to point out that prepolitical societies do have extensive, law-like, apparently socially beneficial or functional customs. However deep the mysteries of the provenance and persistence of such customs may be, they are no greater with regard to the customary treatment of old people than with regard to the other customs of such societies.

An empirical study. We can try to test the economic model of the status of the elderly in primitive and early societies more systematically with the aid of data on 71 primitive societies culled by Leo Simmons from the Human Relations Area Files, a compendium of anthropological and ethnographic materials.[23] Simmons reported data on more than a hundred variables, including several that measure or proxy the status of elderly men (Simmons's data on the status of elderly women are meager), along with many demographic, political, and economic variables. The tables that follow attempt to group the variables in meaningful categories and to display the relations among them.

Preliminary tables not published here reveal strong positive correlations on the one hand among hunting, gathering, and fishing, and on the other hand between agriculture and herding, as modes of production. These correlations enable societies to be classified according to the relative predominance of these two polar classes of modes of production. Table 9.1 correlates the status of the old with the society's mode of production, ranging from "AGR" (predominantly agricultural or herding, or some combination of the two) to "HUNT" (predominantly hunting, fishing, or gathering, or, again, some combination). The middle row and middle column represent intermediate categories. The percentages are the percentages of

---

23. See Simmons, note 3 above. Simmons's bibliography lists 336 books and articles as the sources for his data. Id. at 294–308. The empirical study whose results I summarize here was conducted under my direction by my research assistant Mark Fisher, and he deserves the principal credit for such merit as the study may have.

Table 9.1 Status of Elderly Men as a Function of the System of Production

	AGR	Mixed A/H	HUNT
High	40%	43%	38%
	(8)	(9)	(8)
Medium	35%	33%	24%
	(7)	(7)	(5)
Low	25%	24%	38%
	(5)	(5)	(8)

Table 9.2 Status of Elderly Men as a Function of the Social System

	INDIV	Mixed I/C	COMM
High	38%	35%	50%
	(6)	(11)	(8)
Medium	25%	39%	25%
	(4)	(12)	(4)
Low	38%	26%	25%
	(6)	(8)	(4)

the particular class of society (classified by mode of production) in each of the status categories. (The numbers in parentheses are the number of societies; they do not sum to 71 because of missing data.) As expected, the status of the old is higher in a higher fraction of societies with much or some agriculture (columns 1 and 2) than in societies with a strong predominance of hunting, fishing, and (or) gathering. For example, in only 25 percent of the agricultural societies, but in 38 percent of the hunting societies, do the elderly have a low status. But the correlations are weak.

The next two tables correlate the status of the elderly with the type of social system—whether it emphasizes individuality ("INDIV") or community ("COMM") (table 9.2), and whether market or nonmarket methods of resource allocation ("MKT" or "NONMKT") predominate (table 9.3).

It is not surprising that the elderly tend to have a high status in societies that emphasize communal values, since one expects the family to be a strong institution in such societies. It may seem surprising, however, that they also tend to have a high status in societies that emphasize nonmarket rather than market allocation of resources. Societies that emphasize market

Table 9.3 Status of Elderly Men as a Function of the Economic System

	MKT	Mixed M/N	NONMKT
High	25%	50%	41%
	(5)	(8)	(9)
Medium	25%	44%	32%
	(5)	(7)	(7)
Low	50%	6%	27%
	(10)	(1)	(6)

Table 9.4 Mode of Production as a Function of the Social System

	INDIV	Mixed I/C	COMM
AGR	50%	33%	19%
	(9)	(11)	(3)
Mixed A/H	28%	33%	38%
	(5)	(11)	(6)
HUNT	22%	33%	44%
	(4)	(11)	(7)

allocation might be expected to have a more secure system of property rights, enabling people to accumulate property and retain it in their old age. But without the free and easy transferability of property rights that is a hallmark of a market economy, a patriarchal system of land ownership may be, as suggested earlier, the only efficient system of property rights in an agrarian society's most important resource. The relative weight of these opposed factors is an empirical issue.

A potential problem with all these correlations is that if the independent variables (mode of production, social system, and economic system) are correlated with each other, the effects of each one on the status of the aged may be difficult to separate out. For example, if agricultural societies tend to emphasize communal values, it would be unclear whether the positive correlation between the status of elderly men on the one hand and the predominance of agricultural and communal features in the social landscape on the other was due to agriculture or to communal values; or it might be that the latter came from the former, and so was not an ultimate cause of a high social status of elderly men. In fact, as shown in tables 9.4 and

Table 9.5 Mode of Production as a Function of the Economic System

	MKT	Mixed M/N	NONMKT
AGR	58%	30%	14%
	(14)	(6)	(3)
Mixed A/H	25%	55%	29%
	(6)	(11)	(6)
HUNT	17%	15%	58%
	(4)	(3)	(12)

9.5, there are strong correlations between mode of production on the one hand and the social and economic system of the society on the other. The agricultural (and herding) mode of production is correlated with the predominance of individual and market values, the hunting (and gathering and fishing) mode with the predominance of communal and nonmarket values. Since the agricultural mode is negatively correlated with both communal and nonmarket values yet positively correlated with the status of elderly men, we can infer that the likely cause of the positive correlation is not any of the values associated with an agricultural society but the fact that such a society generates a surplus that makes it less costly on a per capita basis to support the aged; incurs fewer costs in transporting the elderly, because its way of life is less nomadic; and can make more productive use of the elderly.

It might be thought that the status of the aged would be higher in a warrior society than in a pacific one. The aged would, it is true, have little value in actual combat, but warfare would tend to weed out the weaker men, so that the men who survived into old age would tend to be ones who had been successful warriors. They would be prestigious survivors, admired for their deeds (Othello); their memories of earlier wars would provide a valuable stock of information for meeting fresh military challenges (Nestor); and their experiences and maturity would make them valued as leaders and counselors (Nestor again). Table 9.6, in which incidence of warfare is correlated with treatment of the aged, provides some, but rather slight, support for the hypothesis that the aged tend to be better treated in the more warlike societies.

Not only are the correlations in table 9.6 weak, but they may reflect the fact that there is a positive correlation between the incidence of warfare and the presence of agriculture, as shown in table 9.7. Presumably this is be-

Table 9.6 Status of Elderly as a Function of the Incidence of Warfare

	High Incidence	Medium Incidence	Low Incidence
High status	43%	29%	46%
	(13)	(5)	(6)
Medium status	33%	35%	23%
	(10)	(6)	(3)
Low status	23%	35%	31%
	(7)	(6)	(4)

Table 9.7 Incidence of Warfare as a Function of the Mode of Production

	High Incidence	Medium Incidence	Low Incidence
Societies with agriculture	74%	42%	33%
	(26)	(8)	(4)
Societies without agriculture	26%	58%	66%
	(9)	(11)	(8)

cause there is better plunder in an agricultural society and also more surplus to support warriors. We have already seen that the status of the aged tends to be higher in agricultural than in nonagricultural societies. A reason in addition to those discussed earlier may be that an agricultural society tends to engage in warfare a lot, and warfare is a positive factor in the status of the elderly.

Last, table 9.8 explores the relation between the status of the aged and the prevalence of polygyny. The pattern is nonlinear. The status of elderly men tends to be high in societies in which polygyny is either frequent or nonexistent, but low in societies in which there is some but not much polygyny. Polygyny favors older men because it facilitates their employing their accumulated resources to compete with young men for young women.[24] It is therefore resented by young men. If polygyny is com-

24. Who in turn become the supports of the men in their old age. Nugent, note 13 above, at 80–81.

Table 9.8 Status of Elderly Men as a Function of the Prevalence of Polygyny

	Polygyny Frequent	Some Polygyny	No Polygyny
High status	46%	18%	50%
	(12)	(3)	(9)
Medium status	38%	35%	22%
	(10)	(6)	(4)
Low status	15%	47%	28%
	(4)	(8)	(5)

mon, the resentment is exacerbated, but the fact that it *is* common suggests that older men have a commanding position in the society, implying high status. If polygyny is nonexistent, this source of resentment is removed, while if there is some but not much polygyny, this implies that older men do not have the power to universalize the institution, and yet its very existence will be an affront to young men. So the status of older men might indeed be lowest in such societies, as table 9.8 suggests.

Because of the small size of the samples, the unreliability of much of the data, and difficulties of classification (as in deciding whether a society has "frequent" or merely "some" polygyny), the empirical results presented in this chapter are merely suggestive. But they do provide some grounds for thinking that the rational model of human behavior may have considerable applicability to primitive societies in general and to the treatment of their aged members in particular.[25]

Modernity and Symbolic Status

The transition to a modern mixed economy with mass education reduces the social worth of the elderly. Mass education reduces the value of old

25. For other examples of the application of the rational-choice model to primitive societies, see Gary S. Becker and Richard A. Posner, "Cross-Cultural Differences in Family and Sexual Life: An Economic Analysis," 5 *Rationality and Society* 421 (1993), and references cited there; Bruce L. Benson, "Legal Evolution in Primitive Societies," 144 *Journal of Institutional and Theoretical Economics* 772 (1988); Vernon L. Smith, "The Primitive Hunter Culture, Pleistocene Extinction, and the Rise of Agriculture," 83 *Journal of Political Economy* 727 (1975). On the high status of the elderly in static agricultural societies, see the careful empirical analysis of rural India in Mark K. Rosenzweig, "Risk, Implicit Contracts and the Family in Rural Areas of Low-Income Countries," 98 *Economic Journal* 1148, 1168 (1988).

people's memories; industrial labor places physical demands on workers that old people cannot meet; advances in medicine, nutrition, and sanitation prolong life and by doing so increase the dependency ratio; and the greater dynamism of the modern economy exacerbates the adverse impact on the productivity of the old caused by the age-related decline in fluid intelligence and in investment in human capital. It is true that education and literacy might, by enabling the young to learn what the old already know, reduce the mutual incomprehension of the generations. But if society is changing rapidly, the rational young may not be much interested in what the old know; the value of that knowledge may have depreciated to nothing. It is also true that in a postindustrial economy such as ours the physically demanding and dangerous jobs characteristic of industrialization (such as railroad and factory work) tend to give way to light service jobs, and the tendency expands the opportunities of elderly workers. Many service jobs, moreover, put a premium on relational human capital, which depreciates less slowly than other forms of human capital. But these effects may be offset by the increased rapidity of technological change associated with the postindustrial economy, since it is more difficult for older workers to acquire new human capital.

Paradoxically, age grading reasserts itself in a modern society, though it is social rather than occupational. In a patriarchal family, even in its modified nineteenth-century form (Thomas Mann's Buddenbrookses or John Galsworthy's Forsytes), there is constant intergenerational association, and often coresidence, within a family. This changes with modernity, as the increasing pace of cultural and technological change that is associated with modernity drives the generations apart, making separate communities of different age groups, particularly the old.[26]

Yet the picture of the impact of modernization on the status of the old that I have limned so far is severely incomplete. The factors adverse to the position of the elderly in a modern society are offset by, first and foremost, the enormous increase in productivity that modern social and economic arrangements, including mass education and technological innovation, make possible. That increased productivity greatly facilitates making adequate provision for consumption by the nonproductive. For example, it enables the individual to reallocate consumption from youth to old age without great sacrifice, because his level of consumption is so high.

The political arrangements of modern societies tend also to work in

26. The theme of Arlie Russell Hochschild, *The Unexpected Community* (1973), a distinguished sociological field study of old age in America. See esp. ch. 4. See also Howard P. Chudacoff, *How Old Are You? Age Consciousness in American Culture* (1989).

favor of the old. Political democracy, the characteristic if far from universal regime of modern societies, is sometimes thought to be simply a civilized, or an economist might say cheap, method for registering power— civilized and cheap because it does not require that the powerful exercise their muscle to prove they really are the powerful. This was the view of Oliver Wendell Holmes, Jr. and James Fitzjames Stephen,[27] among others. It is an oversimplification. Universal adult suffrage and the secret ballot combine to confer political and therefore social and economic power on naturally weak groups, provided they have sufficient education to be motivated to vote and sufficient agreement on objectives to constitute an effective bloc. This describes the old in the wealthy nations of Europe and North America today. Numerous, and adequately educated, for reasons largely although not entirely exogenous to their electoral power, the old in these nations have enough political power to obtain wide-ranging governmental support and protection,[28] even though in a state of nature or under a different political system they would have little or no power. Yet even before the old became a politically powerful group, increased family wealth shielded most of them from poverty during the industrializing era of U.S. history. "In contrast to an assumption common to both observers in the past and present, the great majority of aged persons [in the United States] have never been impoverished or isolated." [29]

We must probe more deeply the ambiguous term "status," distinguishing in particular between pecuniary income, political power, health, and longevity, on the one hand, and affection, respect, and veneration, on the other. These two aspects of social status—the material and the symbolic— may, in the case of the old, actually be negatively correlated in a modern society.[30] The reason is related to the earlier point about the inculcation of filial piety. The more the old are emancipated by their political power from dependence on the young, the less they have to gain, when raising their children, from inculcating filial piety. So the less such piety their children

27. Holmes, "The Gas-Stokers' Strike," 7 *American Law Review* 582 (1873), reprinted in *The Essential Holmes: Selections from the Letters, Speeches, Judicial Opinions, and Other Writings of Oliver Wendell Holmes, Jr.* 120 (Richard A. Posner, ed., 1992); Stephen, *Liberty, Equality, Fraternity* 70 (1967 [1873]).

28. We shall consider in chapter 11 whether they have received "too much" support and protection in some intelligible sense.

29. Carole Haber and Brian Gratton, *Old Age and the Search for Security: An American Social History* 172 (1994). Haber and Gratton's book (especially chapter 2) provides convincing documentation for this conclusion, to which I return in chapter 11.

30. Cf. Aaron Lipman, "Prestige of the Aged in Portugal: Realistic Appraisal and Ritualistic Deference," 1 *Aging and Human Development* 127 (1970).

will feel. Also, it becomes harder to feel sorry for old people as their incomes rise, though an offsetting consideration is that the old are less likely to be—and to be resented as—a financial albatross to their children. With young people better off, moreover, the old are less willing to make sacrifices for them; so the young have less to be grateful for to the old.

Not only are the benefits of cultivating filial piety fewer when parents do not expect to look to their children for support in their old age; the benefits of having children are fewer. We can therefore expect smaller families as filial support to aged parents declines.[31] This shrinkage increases, in turn, the cost to each of the children of providing care to their aged parents, since there are fewer of them to spread the cost among. An equilibrium involving support for the elderly by both the state and the family may therefore be precarious, if state support leads to smaller families, which in turn increases the cost to families of supporting their elderly members. An important factor is the growing participation of women in the labor force, which is both effect and cause of shrinking families. In most societies, daughters and daughters-in-law are the primary family caregivers to the elderly,[32] partly at least because their opportunity costs of time are lower than those of men as a consequence of limited opportunities in the market. Women's opportunity costs of family caregiving rise as the demand for their services in the market rises. This increased demand also raises the opportunity costs of having children, reinforcing the trend to smaller families which in turn, as I have noted, raises the cost to each child of providing care for his or her elderly parents.[33]

Large families are generally considered "warmer" and closer-knit than small ones, and this should benefit the elderly members. But the greater warmth of the large family may be a consequence in part of the fact that less is demanded of each child—family obligations, while possibly more extensive, are also more widely shared. And large family size may be the product in part of a high value that is placed on close intrafamilial relations in the environment in which the family finds itself. The causality

31. For evidence, see, for example, Alice Munnings, "Intergenerational Interdependence: A Cross-Cultural Study of the Care of Elderly Parents," in *Heterogeneity in Cross-Cultural Psychology* 561, 572 (Daphne M. Keats, Donald Munro, and Leon Mann, eds., 1988).

32. See, for example, Rhonda J. V. Montgomery and Yoshinoro Kamo, "Parent Care by Sons and Daughters," in *Aging Parents and Aging Children* 213, 216–217 (Jay A. Mancini, ed., 1989); Hal L. Kendig and Don T. Rowland, "Family Support of the Australian Aged: A Comparison with the United States," 23 *Gerontologist* 643, 647 (1983).

33. For evidence that these factors erode the sense of filial obligation, see Nancy J. Finley, M. Diane Roberts, and Benjamin F. Banahan, III, "Motivators and Inhibitors of Attitudes of Filial Obligation toward Aging Parents," 28 *Gerontologist* 73, 74, 77 (1988).

thus may run from warmth to large families rather than from large families to warmth.

The undependability of filial obligation as a protection for the elderly is evidenced by the fact that most states have laws requiring children to support (if they can) their destitute parents.[34] These laws date back to the sixteenth century in England, when the system of poor support was rudimentary and it was natural to require families to take care of their own members to the extent possible. The laws have ceased to be of any importance in this country, given social security and welfare; we shall consider in chapter 11 the justice of allowing families to shift some of the burden of supporting their elderly members to the taxpaying public. If my analysis of filiality is correct, laws requiring children to support their parents would, but for the existence of a generous social security program, be more needful today than they were in the sixteenth century.

In addition to being liked or at least reverenced less, both generally and by their own younger relatives, the old in our society, being numerous, are no longer such objects of fascination as they once were.[35] Octogenarians used to be prized for their rarity; someone who lived so long seemed specially blessed. Now that they are a dime a dozen they have ceased to fascinate. Selection bias is relevant here, as I have already suggested. The tougher the obstacle course, the tougher the winners. This, along with scarcity, may explain the evidence that, on average, blacks respect old people more than whites do.[36] Because blacks receive on average poorer medical care than whites (and possibly for other reasons as well), a substantially smaller fraction of blacks than of whites survive to old age.[37] Their old people thus are more rare than in the case of whites, and maybe tougher as well,[38] and therefore more impressive. The point has nothing to do with

34. Marvin B. Sussman, "Law and Legal Systems," in *Family and Support Systems across the Life Span* 11, 26–28 (Suzanne K. Steinmetz, ed., 1988).

35. The scarcity of the old as a factor contributing to the honor in which they are held is stressed in David Hackett Fischer, *Growing Old in America* 29, 33 (1977).

36. See, for example, Finley, Roberts, and Banahan, note 33 above, at 77; Elizabeth Mutran, "Intergenerational Family Support among Blacks and Whites: Response to Culture or to Socioeconomic Differences," 40 *Journal of Gerontology* 382, 388 (1985); cf. Amasa B. Ford et al., "Race-Related Differences among Elderly Urban Residents: A Cohort Study, 1975–1984," 45 *Journal of Gerontology* S163, S169 (1990); Colleen L. Johnson and Barbara M. Barer, "Families and Networks among Older Inner-City Blacks," 30 *Gerontologist* 726 (1990).

37. Of the adult (>18) white population, 18.0 percent is over the age of 65 and 1.8 percent over the age of 85; the corresponding percentages for blacks are 12.1 percent and 1.1 percent. U.S. Bureau of the Census, *Current Population Reports,* ser. P-25, p. 2 (1991) (tab. 1). See also Jacquelyne Johnson Jackson, *Minorities and Aging,* ch. 4 (1980).

38. Donald S. Shepard and Richard J. Zeckhauser, "The Choice of Health Policies with Heterogeneous Populations," in *Economic Aspects of Health* 255, 308 (Victor R. Fuchs, ed.,

race as such. Edmund Wilson remarked that the "consecrated authoritative role" that the nation assigned to Justice Holmes was due in part to "the prestige of longevity when the ancient has retained his faculties."[39]

In a society as dynamic as ours, workers are probably becoming obsolete at younger and younger ages; it is a factor in the falling age of retirement. And the political power of the old—a factor in their high material status in our society—is a source of resentment to the young. The resentment is exacerbated by the fact that the greatly improved market opportunities of women have, as I have mentioned, increased their opportunity costs of caring for the elderly members of their families. And the more the rate of aging seems under conscious human control by virtue of advances in medical understanding, the more the infirmities of old age seem almost culpable, rather than inevitable. We are increasingly apt to think that a *decrepit* old person is such because he failed to follow the advice of doctors and nutritionists concerning a healthful style of living. The diminished symbolic or prestige status of the old is thus the price they have paid for their improved material status.

I have deliberately not emphasized the growing specialization of economic activities in modern economies as a factor in this diminution. It is true that the more work is specialized, the fewer are the opportunities for the old to make a productive contribution in a new field after altered conditions of demand and supply have ejected them from their former specialty. But a countervailing consideration is that, as I noted in the preceding chapter, specialist work is easier for old people to perform productively than generalist work. A generalist must be adept at adapting to changed conditions; a specialist need only continue planing his accustomed groove—though he may become bored more quickly than the generalist.

What has been the impact of modernity on the distribution of income or wealth within the ranks of the old, as distinguished from between old and young? As I have already suggested, one would expect that in an agrarian society, such as that of colonial America, some elderly men, especially landowners, would be wealthy and powerful but many others

---

1982). Elderly blacks actually have a longer life expectancy, and possibly better health, than elderly whites. Rose C. Gibson, "The Age-by-Race Gap in Health and Mortality in the Older Population: A Social Science Research Agenda," 34 *Gerontologist* 454 (1994); Bert Kestenbaum, "A Description of the Extreme Aged Population Based on Improved Medicare Enrollment Data," 29 *Demography* 565, 572 (1992); Ford et al., note 36 above, at S167–S168. This supports the "toughness" hypothesis.

39. "Justice Oliver Wendell Holmes," in Edmund Wilson, *Patriotic Gore: Studies in the Literature of the American Civil War* 743, 795 (1962).

would not be.[40] Even though the average income of the elderly relative to that of middle-aged and younger people has increased since colonial times, the position of the wealthiest old relative to the wealthiest middle-aged has probably deteriorated. This change is due in part to estate taxation, which creates incentives for wealthy people to distribute a large portion of their estate before they die, and in part to the declining importance of land—a form of wealth that does not depreciate with the age of the owner—relative to human capital, a form of wealth that does decline with age. As wealth shifts from land and other forms of physical capital to human capital, moreover, the ability of elderly parents to extract services from their children by threatening to withhold bequests decreases;[41] human capital is not transferred by bequest. Societies differ, incidentally, in the extent to which they allow the use of threats to disinherit. In England and the United States, for example, people are free to disinherit their heirs; in France, they are not. We can expect that the more influential the elderly are in a society, the more reluctant the society will be to limit disinheritance, a tool by which elderly people can extract services from the young.

The Bearing of Ideology

I have emphasized the role of economic factors in influencing both the material and the symbolic status of the old, but other factors may also be important. For example, the difference between the ancient Greek and the early Christian view of old age seems to reflect religious rather than economic factors, though underlying the religious differences may have been an intensely practical difference between a warrior and a civilian outlook, a difference that made the Greeks set a higher value on physique. On the whole the Greeks were not so committed to mind-body or soul-body dualism as the Christians. They did believe that the spirit survived the death of the body. But especially though not only in Homer and the tragedians, it was a weak, pitiable, inglorious spirit, fit only for Hades. The Christian conception of the soul (greatly influenced, to be sure, by a Greek—Plato) endowed it with much greater dignity. Consistent with this difference, Greek art celebrates the beauty of the body, and Christian art (until the

40. For evidence, see Fischer, note 35 above, ch. 1, esp. pp. 58–66.

41. Paul H. Rubin, James B. Kau, and Edward F. Meeker, "Forms of Wealth and Parent-Offspring Conflict," 2 *Journal of Social and Biological Structures* 53 (1979). Not only can a person threaten to cut off his heirs; he can, as noted earlier, make a legally enforceable promise of a bequest to another person in exchange for a legally enforceable promise of support in his old age. See note 18 above and accompanying text.

Renaissance) apologizes for the body—depicting it as etiolated beneath copious garments calculated to conceal its shape—and for bodily functions, such as eating and sex, notwithstanding the doctrine of bodily resurrection. The more the physical aspect of man is prized, the greater the contempt and revulsion that old age is likely to produce, in the same way that gourmets are more likely to be distressed by poor food than people for whom the only function of eating is sustenance. The more the body is disprized, the greater the reverence for old age, seen as the transitional period in which the stripping away of the accidental and even shameful attributes that human beings share with animals prepares the soul to meet God.

But we should not exaggerate the importance of religious factors in the changing status of the old. Although the Christian Middle Ages provided a dignified retirement for some old people—those received into monasteries—the lot of the run-of-the-mill old, especially those who lived in cities or did not have living children (and there were many, owing to high death rates among the young), was not a happy one. Society was not prepared to devote substantial resources to their survival. A straw in the wind was the *charivari*—the practice, widely condoned, by which young bachelors harassed widowers who remarried, protesting against the tendency of wealthy older men to monopolize the marriageable women.[42]

Darwinism may have had a greater impact than Christianity on the status of elderly people. Before Darwin, it was common to think that the world was regressing rather than progressing. The present was thought to mark a decline from a Golden Age located in the dim past; and nonhuman primates, rather than being thought of as man's predecessors, were thought to be degenerate versions of man. In effect the outlook was that of the typical elderly person—the world is going to the dogs (see chapter 5). A society in which such an outlook was common would provide a congenial environment for the elderly, while a society such as ours in which progress is anticipated by most people will be more congenial to the young because they are more forward-looking and optimistic.

David Fischer, in his comprehensive study of changing attitudes in America toward old age, identifies the period 1770–1820 as a crucial period of change.[43] Before then, Americans venerated the old, even to the

---

42. See, for example, Natalie Zemon Davis, "The Reasons of Misrule: Youth Groups and Charivaris in Sixteenth-Century France," 50 *Past and Present* 41 (1971). The high death rate of women in childbirth during the Middle Ages enabled some men to practice a form of serial polygyny despite the prohibition against divorce.

43. Fischer, note 35 above, ch. 2. His thesis has not gone unchallenged. For a summary of the criticisms, see Haber and Gratton, note 29 above, at 5–8.

point that American men exaggerated their age and dressed to look older than they were. Afterward, youth was celebrated, people tried to look younger rather than older than their chronological age, mandatory retirement was imposed on (nonfederal) judges, and the valence of words referring to old people, such as "gaffer," changed from honorific to pejorative. During this period the nation was changing in ways consistent with the economic explanation of attitudes toward age. The nation was becoming less agrarian and more industrial and old people were becoming more plentiful. But Fischer argues that the reversal of attitudes toward old age was too abrupt to be explained by these very gradual economic and demographic trends. He attributes the reversal to the libertarian and egalitarian ideas of the American and French Revolutions.[44] Americans, he thinks, became restive with traditional hierarchies, including that of age. Consistent with his conjecture, it has been argued that the extreme emphasis on filial piety in Confucian China was motivated in part by hope that habits of deference and subordination inculcated in the family would radiate into people's political attitudes and behavior.[45]

Even today, and even if attention is confined to the wealthy nations, the status of elderly people differs across nations; the analysis in this chapter has pointed to possible explanatory factors. Might it be possible to develop an empirical test of the relative status, or influence, of the elderly in different nations? Perhaps so. We might expect that, other things being equal, "young selfish" societies, in which the preferences of old selves are given little weight, would have higher social discount rates than societies in which old selves are given equal or greater weight. The latter societies, to the extent that they were guided by a consistent conception of the public interest rather than tugged hither and yon by competing interest groups, would presumably use lower social discount rates in evaluating projects having deferred payoffs, for example certain kinds of environmental projects. A potentially important qualification, however, is that the truncated horizon of "old selfish" societies may cause them to discount very drastically the benefits of projects that will not come "on line" until the current young are old, since by then the current old will be dead. So we might expect that "old selfish" societies would have lower social discount rates than "young selfish ones" but that the gap would narrow (and the lines might even cross) the more distant the future being discounted.

44. Fischer, note 35 above, at 108–112.
45. See Schwartz, note 14 above, at 100–101.

The Institutional Life Cycle

Fischer's analysis relates attitudes toward aging to institutional age. Generalizing, we might conjecture that a "young" nation, perhaps any "young" institution, will orient itself toward the values of youth rather than of age and therefore that the age of an institution and the age of its leaders will be positively correlated. It is a plausible conjecture. Revolutionary political leaders, for example, generally are much younger than other political leaders.[46] Most of our "founding fathers" were young men, though the appellation suggests a persisting respect for mature wisdom. Other examples of the correlation between individual and institutional age are the generally youthful leadership of young companies in young industries, such as the computer-software industry, and the generally old leadership of declining institutions, such as American labor unions. Established religious sects, ranging from Orthodox Judaism to the Roman Catholic Church, tend to have old leaders, new sects young ones.

A young in the sense of a new organization entails risk-taking, because the mortality rate of young organizations is high,[47] much like that of infants before modern medicine. Since older people have more trouble than younger people in finding new jobs, the risk of having to search for a new job because one's present employer has folded is more costly to older than to younger employees. So we can expect new firms to attract more young workers than old ones. And for two other reasons as well. A new organization is apt to require new skills and ideas, which tend to be properties of the young. And a new organization if successful will be growing[48]—for it is unlikely to have reached its mature size at the date of initial entry—and a growing organization is likely to have a younger age distribution than a static or declining one. For it will be hiring more new employees; and most hires are of young people, the older having firm-specific human capital that would be wiped out by their switching to new jobs. So if young organizations tend to be growing organizations, and old ones tend to be static be-

---

46. Dean Keith Simonton, *Genius, Creativity, and Leadership: Historiometric Inquiries* 102–103 (1984).

47. Boyan Jovanovic, "Selection and the Evolution of Industry," 50 *Econometrica* 649 (1982); Howard Aldrich and Ellen R. Auster, "Even Dwarfs Started Small: Liabilities of Age and Size and Their Strategic Implications," 8 *Research in Organizational Behavior* 165, 177 (1986) (tab. 1); Michael T. Hannan and John Freeman, "The Ecology of Organizational Mortality: American Labor Unions, 1836–1985," 94 *American Journal of Sociology* 25, 32–33, 42 (1988).

48. For evidence that young firms grow faster than old ones, see David S. Evans, "Tests of Alternative Theories of Firm Growth," 95 *Journal of Political Economy* 657 (1987). See also Jovanovic, note 47 above.

cause they have grown to a size where further growth would encounter diseconomies of scale, young organizations will have a higher percentage of young employees independently of the different qualities or attitudes of young and old workers. The causality can run in both directions, however: a firm may be growing because it has a youthful age distribution, or static because it does not.

The analogy between the individual and the institutional life cycle must not be pressed too hard. The life-cycle theory of the firm, proposed by Michael Spence and other economists, predicts that young firms will seek to maximize revenue and capacity in an effort to obtain permanent advantages of cost or demand over competitors and to deter new entrants.[49] That theory has no fruitful applications to aging that I can see. And "learning by doing" has different implications for the individual than for the collective; can explain, for example, the secular improvement in athletic records without implying that the individual athlete will continuously break his own records.[50] Furthermore, although the "birth," "growing," and "prime" stages in the growth of a living person have close counterparts in organizations, the life-cycle analogy fails completely when we consider the "elderly" organization. There is no reason in principle why organizations cannot be for all practical purposes eternal; consider the Roman Catholic Church, now almost two millennia old. It may be that as an organization grows larger it becomes less adaptable to a changing environment because the chain of communication that connects stimulus with response is longer.[51] Yet this negative effect of size and hence of age may be offset by the greater hardiness of a large organization, due in part to its superior ability to diversify, compared to a small one. In any event, my interest here is in the pure effect of age on survival rather than in the effect that is due to the fact that age is positively correlated with size; and it appears that, altogether unlike the human situation, that effect is positive. Old firms, unlike

49. See, for example, Joseph H. Anthony and K. Ramesh, "Association between Accounting Performance Measures and Stock Prices: A Test of the Life Cycle Hypothesis," 15 *Journal of Accounting and Economics* 203 (1992), and studies cited there. On life-cycle theories of organizations generally, see, for example, Douglas D. Baker and John B. Cullen, "Administrative Reorganization and Configurational Context: The Contingent Effects of Age, Size, and Change in Size," 36 *Academy of Management Journal* 1251 (1993); Herbert Kaufman, *Time, Chance, and Organizations: Natural Selection in a Perilous Environment* (1985), esp. ch. 4.

50. See William Fellner, "Specific Interpretations of Learning by Doing," 1 *Journal of Economic Theory* 119 (1969).

51. Michael T. Hannan and John Freeman, "Structural Inertia and Organizational Change," 49 *American Sociological Journal* 149, 163 (1984); Aldrich and Auster, note 47 above, at 169. See generally Jitendra V. Singh and Charles J. Lumsden, "Theory and Research in Organizational Ecology," 16 *Annual Review of Sociology* 161, 168–169, 180–182 (1990).

old human beings, have a higher likelihood of continued survival than young ones.[52] This is why they are more attractive to older workers.

We should distinguish between workers (up to middle management) and leaders. Although old firms in decline (hence not hiring any or many new workers) are likely to have old workers, their leaders will sometimes be young. It may be that the decline of the firm can be reversed only by turning the firm in a completely new direction; and if, thus, the firms needs a "revolution," it will need revolutionary leaders, and they tend to be young, as we have seen. Also, if a firm seems likely to fail anyway, the expected cost of bad leadership may be much less than the expected benefit of good leadership. In that event, recruiting an older leader, one who has survived a patient screening of future leaders by being rotated through a variety of gradually more responsible jobs in the corporate hierarchy, may not be the best strategy. This screening method is designed more to weed out persons who might fail in top leadership and by failing wreak heavy damage on a stable and successful enterprise than to identify the person most likely to rise to a daunting challenge requiring bold, original thought.

If individuals and institutions age, so can whole fields of scholarship or creativity. Kuhn's distinction between revolutionary and normal science[53]—the first involving a paradigm shift, the second working within a paradigm—is germane. We might say, translating Kuhn into age-speak, that a field is new, or young, or renewed, or rejuvenated, when a new paradigm (Copernican, Newtonian, or Einsteinian cosmology, for example) emerges; is middle-aged when scientists work incrementally within an unchallenged paradigm; and is old when the accumulating anomalies of the current paradigm make it ripe to be overthrown. We would expect a science in its revolutionary phase or phases to be attractive to the young, because older scientists will incur higher costs of developing and adapting to a new paradigm, and normal science to be attractive to older scientists, whose accumulated knowledge will give them an edge in dealing with problems within its domain.

Admittedly, the causality runs in both directions; a science that happens to attract young persons is more likely to experience a paradigm shift. But not every science, or other field of endeavor, is at all times ripe for a

52. Michael T. Hannan and John Freeman, *Organizational Ecology,* ch. 10 (1989); David S. Evans, "The Relationship between Firm Growth, Size, and Age: Estimates for 100 Manufacturing Industries," 35 *Journal of Industrial Economics* 567 (1987). It is true that infants in most societies have had high death rates, but the comparison in the cited study is not infant versus mature, but younger versus older, firms.

53. See Thomas S. Kuhn, *The Structure of Scientific Revolutions* (2d ed. 1970).

paradigm shift. Constraints deriving from the relation between existing resources (money, techniques, and so forth) and the natural or social phenomena that the field seeks to explain often make paradigm shifts infeasible in particular fields at particular times. We should expect such fields to
be less attractive to the young at such times, especially to the adventurous
and creative young. These fields, if they want to maintain their staffing, will
have to accept less creative applicants.

My emphasis in this chapter has been on two senses of social status, the
material and the honorific. We have seen, with reference to the elderly, that
the two senses need not coincide. In primitive societies they tend to coincide, but the resulting status of the elderly can be very high or very low, or
anywhere in between. The association of reverence for the elderly with
primitive man is spurious; many primitive societies kill, abuse, or seriously
neglect their elderly. I presented some evidence that a key variable in the
power and respect accorded elderly people in premodern societies is the
degree to which the society is agrarian, because the value of the old is, for
a variety of reasons, greater in agrarian societies than in other societies at
the same level of development.

In modern societies, notably that of the United States, the material and
honorific status of the elderly tend to diverge. The material status of elderly
Americans is without historical precedent and is high relatively as well as
absolutely, in part because of the tendency of democratic politics to am-
plify the power of "naturally" weak groups. But the honorific status of
elderly Americans is lower today than it was when the nation was founded.
Plausible explanatory factors are numerous. One is the increased rate of
social and technical change, which because of the characteristic resistance
of the elderly to novelty has widened the gap between the generations. Others are the diminishing incentive of parents to instill filial piety in their
children (because the parents' welfare in old age is no longer crucially dependent on their families), the greatly increased number and proportion of
elderly persons in the population, the decline of coresidence, and the
shrinking size of families. That shrinkage, in conjunction with the increased number of elderly persons and the increased market opportunities
of women, has increased the cost of personal caregiving to old by young
family members, making the maintenance of close relations with elderly
family members increasingly irksome. Cutting the other way, however, is
the greater wealth of today's old people, which makes them less of a financial burden to the young and increases the probability of a bequest or other
gifts to the young.

I took a brief look at institutional aging. Although old age has no clear counterpart in the life cycle of institutions, youth does. Moreover, there are economic reasons to believe that the age of institutions is positively correlated with the age of their staffs, with the causality running in both directions.

Part Three

Normative Issues

10

Euthanasia and Geronticide

The previous chapters have elaborated an explanatory and predictive theory of old age as a social phenomenon, a theory that I consider to have social scientific value in its own right but that I shall now employ to evaluate present and proposed policies concerning old people. This chapter and the next analyze policies in which moral and political concerns predominate over legal ones, although the line is blurred; assisted suicide, for example, is a crime in many states—with no exception for *physician*-assisted suicide, the focus of this chapter.

Definitions

Physician-assisted suicide is an aspect of a larger issue, that of euthanasia. Immediately one is plunged into a terminological thicket. Euthanasia can be voluntary, a form of suicide in a broad sense, or involuntary—the sort of thing the Nazis practiced, as have a number of primitive societies, as we saw in the preceding chapter. I am not interested in involuntary euthanasia, other than where an individual is in a vegetative state or otherwise incapable of giving consent to die. That is an important case for the issue of geronticide, the euthanasia of old people, since many very elderly individuals are severely demented; and I shall touch upon it. But mostly I shall be using the term "euthanasia" as shorthand for "voluntary euthanasia" and interchangeably with "physician-assisted suicide." In so doing, I shall be ignoring not only the distinction between voluntary and involuntary euthanasia but also the distinction often made between euthanasia in a narrow sense as a physician's administering drugs intended to kill the patient and physician-assisted suicide narrowly defined as a physician's helping the patient to kill himself. I shall treat both as simply different modalities of physician-assisted suicide (or euthanasia, or voluntary euthanasia).

A further complication is that euthanasia as I am defining it is merely a subset of medical events (or nonevents) that have the effect of bringing on death earlier than is medically inevitable. The other subsets are withholding or withdrawing medical treatments that are considered useless because they cannot prolong conscious life significantly; administering painkillers likely to shorten the patient's life; and acceding to a patient's refusal to accept further medical treatment or to take food or water.[1] The entire set has been dubbed "MDEL" (medical decisions at end of life). Even in the Netherlands, where euthanasia or, equivalently in my though not in the Dutch terminology, physician-assisted suicide is not punishable if proper guidelines are followed, it accounts for only a small fraction of the total number of deaths due to MDEL.[2] I have not found reliable estimates for the United States. One might expect MDELs other than physician-assisted suicide to be more common in this country (a substitution effect)—or to be less common because the hostility to physician-assisted suicide may reflect a desire to prolong life at all costs. We shall see that MDELs are being facilitated in this country by the recognition of the living will and the durable health-care power of attorney.

The issue of physician-assisted suicide transcends the elderly, but concerns them more than most simply because they are much more likely to be terminally or otherwise terribly ill than younger people.[3] That is not to say that the *rate* of physician-assisted suicide is higher among the elderly when—the essential qualification—state of health is held constant. It may well be lower.[4] There are several reasons. One is that with many persons of very advanced age there is uncertainty about their ability to give a valid consent. And they will often be so frail that the dosage of painkillers re-

1. For an excellent discussion, see G. K. Kimsma and E. van Leeuwen, "Dutch Euthanasia: Background, Practice, and Present Justifications," 2 *Cambridge Quarterly of Healthcare Ethics* 19 (1993).

2. Id. at 27–28.

3. Hence the term "geronticide," as in Stephen G. Post, "Infanticide and Geronticide," 10 *Ageing and Society* 317 (1990). And recall from chapter 6 that the suicide rate is highest among elderly persons. In the Netherlands, 38 percent of MDELs involve persons aged 65 to 79. Kimsma and van Leeuwen, note 1 above, at 27. I do not have a separate figure for euthanasia.

4. Some evidence for this conjecture is that euthanasia is said to be rare after the age of 75 and especially after 85. Gerrit van der Wal and Robert J. M. Dillmann, "Euthanasia in the Netherlands," 308 *British Medical Journal* 1346, 1347 (1994).

quired to subdue their pain (most cases of euthanasia in the Netherlands involve cancer patients) will kill them. Because the very elderly have reached a "natural" age of death, moreover, physicians may not think it necessary to report death as being due to euthanasia. Selection bias is also at work: the elderly population is likely to contain a disproportionate number of people who have a very strong will to live. A related point is that for people so old that they must have adjusted to a greatly reduced utility of living, the further drop entailed by the prospect of entering the terminal stage of life may not register with as much vividness as the same prospect would for a young person.

I shall distinguish between suicides in which the intention is formed and executed at more or less the same time and suicides in which the execution is substantially deferred (*A* decides at time *t* that he wants his life to end at time *t* + *k,* where *k* might be many years), and within the first category between suicides in which there is assistance from another person and those in which there is no assistance. I focus on the assisted suicide because if a person who wants to end his life can do so without the assistance of another person, the right to assist in the suicide without incurring criminal liability has limited practical importance, though not none, as we shall see. For a reason to be explained, I exclude assisted suicide where the assistance is rendered by someone other than a physician.

By referendum in November 1994, Oregon became the first American state to authorize physician-assisted suicide. (The law was supposed to go into effect on January 1, 1995, but at this writing has been delayed by a court challenge.) Subject to elaborate safeguards, physicians will be authorized to prescribe "suicide pills" to patients expected to live no more than six months. The six-month limitation is problematic, not only because estimates of how long a dying person has to live are fraught with error, but also because some of the strongest cases of rational suicide involve people who face an indefinite lifetime of paralysis, severe pain, or other terrible disability. Even so, experience with Oregon's new law may eventually provide decisive evidence concerning the merits of physician-assisted suicide. In the meantime, as debate intensifies in other states, economic analysis has a significant and unrecognized contribution to make.

An Economic Analysis of Physician-Assisted Suicide in Cases of Physical Incapacity

Benefits and costs. I have narrowed my focus to physician-assisted suicide in cases of severely disabling and debilitating, usually though not always terminal, illness.[5] These are the cases in which the patient is likely to lack the capacity to commit suicide on his own, at least without experiencing prohibitive pain or fear; the cases therefore in which the demand for physician-assisted suicide is greatest; the cases of most importance to elderly people; and the only cases in which physicians are likely to be willing to assist people to commit suicide. I set to one side religious objections to suicide, not because I consider them unanswerable,[6] but because they belong to the domain of individual choice rather than to that of social policy. My conception of the appropriate scope of legal regulation is that of John Stuart Mill: the only voluntary activities of competent adults with which government can properly interfere are those that impose tangible harms, as distinct from causing merely disapproval or even revulsion. The fact that X's committing suicide with the assistance of Y is contrary to Z's religious beliefs is therefore not a good reason for having a law against assisting suicide.

The main nonreligious objection to *generally* making suicide easier than it is, whether by permitting the sale of suicide pills and suicide kits or just by authorizing physicians to assist in the suicide of persons who are dying or hideously impaired, is that many suicides are impulsive, the product of a bout of depression, intense grief or shame, bad news that may be wrong (as in *Romeo and Juliet*), or other transient causes that, ex ante, the affected individual might want to prevent from affecting him. Efforts to discourage such suicides, as by making them more costly by punishing people who assist in them, can be loosely analogized to the prohibition of extortion (as in "your money or your life"), in which a class of transactions yielding a short-term gain (when you buy your life by giving the robber your money) is denied legal sanction because the vast majority of people would consider themselves better off if the occasion for such a transaction never arose. A prohibition against assisting suicide cannot be persuasively defended on this ground in cases in which the person who wants to end his life is incapable of doing so. The condition that makes it infeasible for the individual to take his own life furnishes a rational motivation for suicide.[7]

5. Almost three-quarters of euthanasia cases in the Netherlands involve cancer, and in 83 percent the patient was estimated to have less than a month to live. Van der Wal and Dillmann, note 4 above, at 1347. Nevertheless, as I point out in the text, it is doubtful that imminent death should be a precondition to allowing physician-assisted suicide.

6. See David Hume, "Of Suicide," in Hume, *Essays: Moral, Political, and Literary* 577 (Eugene F. Miller, ed., rev. ed. 1987). For philosophical arguments pro and con, see *Suicide: Right or Wrong?* (John Donnelly, ed., 1990).

7. "The Elder Pliny . . . regarded suicide as the greatest gift given to man amid life's sufferings." Miriam Griffin, "Philosophy, Cato, and Roman Suicide: 2," 33 *Greece and Rome* 192, 193

A recent judicial decision invalidated, as an arbitrary deprivation of the liberty protected by the due process clause of the Fourteenth Amendment, a state statute criminalizing physician-assisted suicide.[8] Setting to one side the question of the legal merits of the decision (which has since been reversed), a reader cannot fail to be moved by the court's harrowing description of the situations of the three terminally ill plaintiffs (two elderly). Contrary to widespread belief, in our society dying people usually experience significant pain or other unpleasant symptoms;[9] the "peaceful" death celebrated in Victorian fiction continues to be rare, or at least is not to be counted on. It is easy to see that an individual who is soon to die anyway and anticipates extraordinary pain or suffering in the interval that remains may have a negative expected utility of living.[10] We need only recall Kent's comment when signs of life are noted in the dying Lear: "Vex not his ghost: O! let him pass; he hates him / That would upon the rack of this tough world / Stretch him out longer."[11]

A right to seek assistance in committing suicide has value to the holder even if he never exercises it. The right of suicide is an option,[12] and options have value independent of the value of exercising them, just as insurance has value for people who never have occasion to file a claim with an insurer. Knowing that if life becomes unbearable one can end it creates peace

---

(1986). "Every day, rational people all over the world plead to be allowed to die." Ronald Dworkin, *Life's Dominion: An Argument about Abortion, Euthanasia, and Individual Freedom* 179 (1993). I suggested in chapter 6 that elderly suicide is less likely to be impulsive than youthful suicide; more on this later.

8. Compassion in Dying v. Washington, 850 F. Supp. 1454 (W.D. Wash. 1994), rev'd, 49 F.3d 586 (9th Cir. 1995). The U. S. Supreme Court had earlier held that a person has a constitutional right to refuse medical treatment even though death will result. Cruzan v. Director, Missouri Dept. of Health, 497 U.S. 261, 278–279 (1990).

9. Robert Kastenbaum and Claude Normand, "Deathbed Scenes as Imagined by the Young and Experienced by the Old," 14 *Death Studies* 201, 212 (1990). Physicians know this best— and it is well known that many of them keep "stashes" of lethal drugs on hand so that they can kill themselves if they find themselves in the terminal stage of an illness. In a recent study in which terminally ill patients were allowed to refuse to eat or drink, and as a result died of a combination of dehydration and starvation, only 13 percent were judged to have experienced discomfort during their dying period. Efforts, apparently mostly successful, were made to relieve dry mouth, thirst, and other symptoms of these modes of death. Robert M. McCann, William J. Hall, and Annmarie Groth-Juncker, "Comfort Care for Terminally Ill Patients: The Appropriate Use of Nutrition and Hydration," 272 *JAMA* (*Journal of the American Medical Association*) 1263, 1265 (1994).

10. "It will generally be found that, as soon as the terrors of life reach the point at which they outweigh the terrors of death, a man will put an end to his life." Schopenhauer, "On Suicide," in *Essays of Arthur Schopenhauer* 399, 403 (T. Bailey Saunders, trans., 1902).

11. *King Lear*, act V, sc. iii, ll. 314–316.

12. An argument that goes back at least to Seneca. For a modern version, see C. G. Prado, *The Last Choice: Preemptive Suicide in Advanced Age*, ch. 7 (1990).

of mind and so makes life more bearable. This is important, in any cost-benefit analysis of permitting physician-assisted suicide, as a reminder that the benefits of euthanasia are not limited to the relatively small number of people who actually undergo it. The fact that the benefits are not limited to those people is an offset to the concern that the costs will not be so limited either—that authorizing assisted suicide, in however circumscribed a set of cases, will inevitably encourage other suicides, and perhaps, by making life seem cheaper, murders as well. Later I shall give reasons and data that suggest that this concern is in any event exaggerated.

While on the subject of the third-party effects of allowing physician-assisted suicide, I should address the argument that even if an individual really and truly wants to die, his family may not want him to die and therefore his death will impose a cost on uncompensated third parties. I do not think this argument can survive a careful consideration of the relations of altruism that connect the members of a loving family. In deciding whether he wants to die, an individual will consider the effect of the decision on the members of his family; and in deciding whether and in what spirit to accept that decision, the family members will consider the cost to him if he is forced to prolong his life. The decision he makes is therefore likely to maximize the utility of the family as a whole.

It has been argued that "preemptive suicide on grounds of age actually amounts to a kind of perverse faith that we can predict our own future, that we can know what sources of unexpected meaning life has in store for us." [13] We cannot know for certain. But we can have a pretty good idea; human choices, including the irreversible ones, are made on the basis of probabilities, not certainties. We shall see that the presence of uncertainty is actually an argument *for* a right of physician-assisted suicide.

It has been argued that since most elderly people who commit suicide "have emotional or psychological illnesses," their decision to commit suicide is irrational and should not be respected.[14] The principal illness mentioned is depression. Anyone who decides to kill himself must find his life depressing, and, with "suicidal ideation" and the like used to diagnose depression, it is apparent that one would have to assume that suicide is irrational in order to be justified in declaring a suicide irrational *because* the person who committed suicide was depressed.[15] The argument is circular.

13. Harry R. Moody, " 'Rational Suicide' on Grounds of Old Age?" 24 *Journal of Geriatric Psychiatry* 261, 274 (1991).

14. Thomas J. Marzen, " 'Out, Out Brief Candle': Constitutionally Prescribed Suicide for the Terminally Ill," 21 *Hastings Constitutional Law Quarterly* 799, 811–812 (1994).

15. Recall the discussion of the suicide-depression circle in chapter 6.

Another common argument against allowing physicians to assist in the suicide of a patient, one that is also made against the right of abortion, is that it is bad for society if physicians are used to kill as well as to save; by blurring their mission, it may make them less committed to healing. Yet if their healing efforts sometimes, perhaps often, place people in a situation of such ghastly pain or incapacity that they are desperately eager to be dead, physicians may become ambivalent about healing. It is also argued— by opponents of capital punishment as well—that any policy which facilitates the ending of human life as a deliberate choice undermines respect for human life. The argument is especially weak in the case of capital punishment, when it is confined to murderers and can therefore be defended as showing respect for the lives of the victims. We shall see in a moment that a "life-saving" rationale may also be available to defend euthanasia, improbable as that may seem. But in addition the argument that euthanasia is inconsistent with a proper sense of the dignity of human life overlooks the relation of dignity to quality. Respect for human life must have *something* to do with perceptions of the value, not wholly metaphysical, of that life. The spectacle of nursing homes crowded with frail and demented old people, or of hospital wards crowded with dying people so heavily sedated as to be barely sentient or so twisted with pain as to be barely recognizable, might be thought rather to undermine than to enhance a sense of the preciousness of life. The better the quality of lives, the greater the perceived value of preserving them. Doctors and nurses who talk about "watering the vegetables" on their rounds have not been made sensitive, by their exposure to the practical consequences of sacrificing quality of life, to the desire to prolong life regardless.

Voluntary euthanasia has been practiced openly in the Netherlands since the early 1970s,[16] yet the Dutch have not become more violent or callous than other Europeans, let alone Americans. The Dutch murder rate is only one-tenth that of the United States; more to the point, it is well below the average of the European Union.[17] Later we shall see that the

16. The extensive literature on euthanasia in the Netherlands is illustrated by Kimsma and van Leeuwen, note 1 above; van der Wal and Dillmann, note 4 above; John Griffiths, "Recent Developments in the Netherlands concerning Euthanasia and Other Medical Behavior That Shortens Life," 1 *Medical Law International* 347 (1995); G. van der Wal et al., "Euthanasia and Assisted Suicide, 1, How Often Is It Practised by Family Doctors in the Netherlands?" 9 *Family Practice* 130 (1992); Paul J. van der Maas et al., "Euthanasia and Other Medical Decisions concerning the End of Life," 338 *Lancet* 669 (1991); M. A. M. de Wachter, "Active Euthanasia in the Netherlands," 262 *JAMA* (*Journal of the American Medical Association*) 3316 (1989).

17. United Nations Development Programme, *Human Development Report 1994* 186 (1994) (tab. 30). The statistics are for murders by males only, but most murderers are male.

practice of euthanasia in the Netherlands appears not to have increased the suicide rate either.

Carlos Gomez argues on the basis of 26 case studies of euthanasia in the Netherlands[18] that there are insufficient controls over the practice to ensure that it is always voluntary. Only one of his case studies (one of three that he describes as "even more troubling" than the other 23)[19] provides even a modicum of support for his thesis: a young woman dying of leukemia may not have been told that there were less painful alternative treatments to chemotherapy.[20] Then again she may have been told—Gomez doesn't know. During a one-year remission from the disease, she and her husband had spoken with their family doctor many times about euthanasia,[21] but he may not have been conversant with the full range of alternative therapies.

Gomez's fear of doctors' rushing patients to their death[22] has not been substantiated[23] and does not appear realistic. Such behavior would go against the grain of the medical profession, which strongly favors treatment, however unlikely of success. It might also be contrary to the profession's financial self-interest, although this depends on the method of financing medical services. If doctors are paid for services rendered—the payment method that prevails in the United States—the incentive is to give patients too much rather than too little treatment. (This point implies that physicians should be forbidden to specialize in assisting suicide, as that would realign their financial incentives. Apparently no such specialty has emerged in the Netherlands.) Yet even in the United States, many patients are not treated on a fee-for-services basis. This is true not only of people enrolled in health maintenance organizations (HMOs) but also of other people, veterans for example, who receive medical care from salaried physicians. Here the financial incentive is to avoid expensive end-of-life treatments, for which euthanasia might be a cheap alternative.

Also pertinent in evaluating the danger of a rush to death is the hospice movement, which is hostile to euthanasia. It holds that the terminal phase

18. Carlos F. Gomez, *Regulating Death: Euthanasia and the Case of the Netherlands* 64–89 (1991).

19. Id. at 111.

20. Id. at 112.

21. Id. at 79.

22. As in Waugh's burlesque of euthanasia. Evelyn Waugh, *Love Among the Ruins: A Romance of the Near Future,* ch. 2 (1953).

23. Another case study of euthanasia in the Netherlands found no serious abuses. G. van der Wal et al., "Euthanasia and Assisted Suicide, 2, Do Dutch Family Doctors Act Prudently?" 9 *Family Practice* 135 (1992).

of a person's life can be made bearable and therefore need not be shortened by suicide. A hospice offers an alternative to a dying person who considers suicide, and hence it offers competition to physicians who provide assistance in committing suicide.

The danger of the abuses that Gomez fears can be minimized by relatively simple regulations, such as a requirement that the patient's consent to euthanasia be witnessed or in writing, that the physician performing euthanasia report any case in which he performs it to a hospital committee, and that before performing it he consult with a duly certified specialist in the ethics of dealing with dying patients.[24] The feasibility of such regulations, and the culture of the medical profession, are reasons why allowing physician-assisted suicide does not as a matter of logic entail allowing non-physicians to assist in suicides. Fear that many so-called "mercy" killings are nothing of the kind, that they lack the consent whether explicit or reasonably implied of the person killed, is weakly grounded when the person doing the killing is a physician not related to or otherwise personally involved with the person killed.

More questionable than anything recounted by Gomez is a case in which a Dutch doctor was acquitted of a criminal charge for assisting in the suicide of a middle-aged woman who was neither physically nor mentally ill but who was determined to die and had attempted to commit suicide before, and who the doctor was persuaded would try again and eventually succeed.[25] The case goes beyond any measure legalizing euthanasia that I would be inclined to support. It was not a case in which the person requesting assistance had a terminal illness or other progressively disabling condition that might incapacitate her from taking her own life when her suffering became unbearable. But I do not believe on the basis of a single Dutch case that by authorizing physician-assisted suicide in cases of physical incapacity as I have defined it the United States would be taking an irreversible step toward unregulated assisted suicide.

Fewer and later suicides? So far I have suggested merely that the opponents of physician-assisted suicide underestimate the benefits and exaggerate the costs. I have taken for granted that one consequence is that there

24. See Franklin G. Miller et al., "Regulating Physician-Assisted Death," 331 *New England Journal of Medicine* 119 (1994).

25. *Office of Public Prosecutions v. Chabot,* translated and analyzed in John Griffiths, "Assisted Suicide in the Netherlands: The *Chabot* Case," 58 *Modern Law Review* 232 (1995). The Dutch Supeme Court reversed the acquittal, but only because there had not been an independent examination of the woman by another physician; and the court waived punishment.

will be more suicides and a net loss of years of life. The bearing of this on a Millian analysis of the right to physician-assisted suicide is unclear. If the number of suicides rose as a consequence of legalizing physician-assisted suicide (in appropriate cases, subject to appropriate safeguards), this might indicate nothing more than that many people place a negative value on extending the period in which they are dying. An alternative possibility, however, which makes investigating the impact of allowing physician-assisted suicide on the suicide rate worth pursuing even for a Millian, is that a rise in the rate might indicate—though it would not prove—that people were indeed being rushed to their deaths by selfish relatives and callous physicians. So it becomes relevant to point out, as I shall, that permitting physician-assisted suicide limited to what I am calling cases of physical incapacity might actually *reduce* the number of suicides and *postpone* the suicides that occur. Gomez argues in effect that there will be more deaths (and they will come sooner) than those attributable to a genuine and fully informed choice by the patient to die. The argument I shall be exploring is that there will be fewer deaths (and later) than under a regime in which physician-assisted suicide is unlawful.

Of course, if this is correct, aggregate medical costs might rise, since seriously ill people who decide not to end their life immediately are bound to incur substantial medical costs as a consequence of their decision. To the extent that these costs are borne by third parties rather than by the person making the decision to live—and this is a pervasive feature of our health-care system—it becomes difficult to say whether allowing physician-assisted suicide would be socially cost-justified. Mill's approach enables us to exclude (as a strictly economic or utilitarian analysis would not) the disutility that third parties experience merely as a consequence of abhorring suicide. But it does not entitle us to disregard the tangible costs borne by people who through their taxes, health-insurance premiums, or doctors' bills are forced to pay other people's medical expenses. I shall not attempt to estimate those costs; and to that extent the analysis presented in this chapter must be considered tentative.

Suppose an individual learns that he has a progressive disease that will reduce him to a state in which he would consider himself better off dead than alive because of acute suffering unredeemed by any hope of recovery or improvement or by the diminished utility from living in this state. He realizes, let us further assume, that at some point the progress of the disease will incapacitate him from committing suicide. This may be one reason why elderly suicide attempters tend to use more lethal methods, such as firearms instead of drugs, than younger ones, and have a higher success rate.[26] The elderly person fears that if his attempt fails, he may be incapable of repeating it; the cost of failure is greater to him. An alternative explanation is that elderly suicides are more deliberated for the reasons discussed in chapter 6, and the deliberative as distinct from impulsive attempted suicide is more likely to choose an effective means. Fair enough; but by implying that elderly suicides are more likely to be rationally considered than the suicides of younger persons, the point provides additional support for a right of physician-assisted suicide.

To make the case more realistic, assume that our hypothetical sufferer is not certain that the disease will progress to a point where he will prefer to be dead, though he is certain that if it does progress to that point he will be incapable of killing himself without assistance. The possibility that he will recover after all, at least recover sufficiently to be glad that he is still alive, or at the very least that he will live longer than he expected and in circumstances less oppressive than he anticipated—the possibility, in short, of a mistake about the future course of his disease—is omnipresent in suicide situations and is one of the objections that I listed earlier to making suicide easy. A surprising number of people have had the experience of being misinformed that they had a terminal illness.[27]

We need to compare alternative regimes for our hypothetical case. In the first, physician-assisted suicide is forbidden. So when the individual first learns his probable fate he must choose between two courses of action: one in which he commits suicide now, at a cost (in dread of death, pain, moral compunctions, whatever) of c; the other in which he postpones the decision to a time when, if he still wants to commit suicide, he will be unable to do so. The question is which course will confer greater utility on him. If he commits suicide now, he will have utility of $-c$. He will experience neither positive nor expected utility from living, because he will be dead, but he will incur the cost of getting from the state of being alive to

26. John L. McIntosh and John F. Santos, "Methods of Suicide by Age: Sex and Race Differences among the Young and Old," 22 *International Journal of Aging and Human Development* 123 (1986); Ellen Mellick, Kathleen C. Buckwalter, and Jacqueline M. Stolley, "Suicide among Elderly White Men: Development of a Profile," *Journal of Psychosocial Nursing*, no. 2, 1992, p. 29.

27. One of my grandfathers was told in his forties by a reputable medical specialist that he had a fatal kidney disease but could eke out another year or two of life if he gave up meat. He did not give up meat and he died at the age of 85 of an unrelated ailment. This was a long time ago, but the problem persists. Like other professionals, doctors sometimes speak with greater confidence than the facts warrant.

the state of being dead. If he decides not to commit suicide now, he avoids incurring c and obtains whatever utility, positive or negative, continued life confers upon him. Because of uncertainty, that utility is an expected utility; it is equal to the weighted average of his negative utility in the doomed state, $-U_d$—the disutility that he will incur if it turns out that he really does have a terminal or otherwise horribly painful or disabling illness— and his positive utility in the healthy or at least relatively healthy state that he will be in if he recovers to the point of wanting to live after all: U_h.

Each expected utility must be weighted by the probability (p or $1 - p$) that the individual will in fact find himself in the doomed or in the healthy state. He reasonably expects the former, but not with certainty: that is, $1 > p > (1 - p)$. The sum of these utilities is $p(-U_d) + (1 - p)U_h$, and must be compared with the utility of committing suicide ($-c$). I assume that $U_d > c$, an important assumption that will be relaxed later.[28]

With these assumptions, our hypothetical individual will commit suicide if

$$pU_d > (1 - p)U_h + c \qquad (10.1)$$

—in words, if the expected utility of death now, which is to say the disutility averted by death now, exceeds the expected utility of life plus the cost of suicide. The loss of that expected utility, and the cost of suicide, are the costs that he incurs by committing suicide now.[29] If $c = 0$, he will commit suicide if $pU_d > (1 - p)U_h$, that is, if the expected (that is, probability-weighted) disutility of living in what I am calling the doomed state exceeds the expected utility of living in the healthy state.

Since the doomed state is more likely—that is, $p > (1 - p)$—the anticipated disutility of that state need not be so great as the anticipated utility of the saved (healthy) state for suicide to be a rational decision; indeed, if p is high enough, the disutility of living in the doomed state could be considerably smaller than the utility of living in the saved state without making the decision to commit suicide an irrational one. This also depends on the size of c, however. If the cost of committing suicide is great enough, an individual will refrain from committing suicide even if he would consider himself much better off dead than alive. So c is a type of transaction cost, a one-way ticket to oblivion.

28. It is because c usually is high and because, even so, often $U_d > c$ that suicide can be and has been regarded both as courageous and as cowardly. For an interesting discussion, see Miriam Griffin, "Roman Suicide," in *Medicine and Moral Reasoning* 106, 122–123 (K. W. M. Fulford, Grant R. Gillett, and Janet Martin Soskice, eds., 1994).

29. I ignore, as inessential to the analysis, the discounting of these future values to present values.

Contrast the situation in which the individual has a choice between committing suicide now, again at cost c, and committing it later, at the same cost, with a physician's assistance. It is a real choice because, by virtue of the possibility of assistance (assumed to have been legalized), the individual can postpone the decision to commit suicide.[30] If we assume for simplicity that the unbearable suffering that gives rise to $-U_d$, the disutility of the doomed state, will begin at some future time when the individual will know for certain that he will not recover into the relatively healthy state U_h, the assumption that suicide is possible later at a cost of c implies the substitution of c for U_d in inequality 10.1. That is, as soon as the doomed state sets in, the individual (with assistance, for I am assuming that the onset of the doomed state will incapacitate the individual from committing suicide without assistance) will substitute for it a lesser disutility, the cost of committing suicide.

With this substitution into 10.1, our hypothetical individual will commit suicide now, rather than postpone the decision, only if

$$pc > (1 - p)U_h + c \qquad (10.2)$$

or equivalently if $-U_h > c$—which makes clear that he will not commit suicide now, since both U_h and c are positive. Even if discounting to present value is ignored, the cost of committing suicide with probability 1 must exceed that cost when multiplied by a probability of less than one and offset by some expectation of entering a state in which continued life will yield net utility. Indeed the cost of suicide now must exceed the *expected* cost of suicide later (since c is assumed constant and exceeds pc), even if the expected utility from living is ignored.

The analysis implies that if physician-assisted suicide in cases of physical incapacity is permitted, the number of suicides in the class of cases that I have modeled will be reduced by $1 - p$, the percentage of cases in which the individual contemplating suicide is mistaken about the future course of his disease or its effect on his desire to live. Moreover, in the fraction of cases in which suicide does occur (p), it will occur later than if physician-assisted suicide were prevented. Weeks, months, or even years of life will be gained, and with it net utility.

The intuition behind these results is straightforward. If the only choice is suicide now and suffering later, individuals will frequently choose sui-

---

30. According to the physician in one of Carlos Gomez's case studies, "the availability of euthanasia gave the woman [his patient] enough assurance to at least try one round of chemotherapy." Gomez, note 18 above, at 111.

cide now. If the choice is suicide now or suicide at no greater cost later, they will choose suicide later because there is always a chance that they are mistaken in believing that continued life will impose unbearable suffering or incapacity on them. They would give up that chance by committing suicide now. The possibility of physician-assisted suicide enables them to wait until they have more information before deciding whether to live or die. Another way to put this is that the availability of physician-assisted suicide increases the option value of continued living. We noted in chapter 6 that the diminution in that value with age is one of the factors that contributes to the high suicide rate of elderly people.

The general point—that the availability of a service can reduce rather than, as one might expect, increase the utilization of the service—is neither inconsistent with assuming rational behavior by persons facing horrific choices nor limited to suicide. Suppose that you get a sharp pain in your abdomen on Friday afternoon. If your physician's office is closed on weekends, you may rush to the office on Friday, lest your condition worsen during the weekend. But if the office is open on weekends you may decide to wait and see whether the pain gets better or worse. In most cases it will get better, so there will be fewer total visits, in the class of cases represented by the example, if the physician is more available.

The effect of physician-assisted suicide in reducing the number of suicides will be amplified if, as is plausible, physician-assisted suicide is less costly to a person contemplating suicide than unassisted suicide would be rather than, as I have been assuming, just as costly. The difference in cost will increase his incentive to wait because physician-assisted suicide is not permissible in my analysis until the patient has become incapable of taking his own life. Paradoxically, then, cheaper suicide may result in less suicide. But this depends on the assumption in the model that $c < U_d$, the cost of suicide is less than the utility of the dying state. Suppose that unassisted suicide (c_u) is so costly (in search for the requisite means, in pain, in fear of failure, and in the expected consequences of failure) that many a person who anticipates with certainty a life of utter misery will nevertheless not attempt to commit suicide unless he can have the assistance of a physician. (That is, $c_u > U_d$.) Then if physician-assisted suicide (c_a) at a sufficiently lower cost that $c_a < U_d$ is available when the period of misery begins, he will terminate his life then if, and only if, physician-assisted suicide is permitted. That the cost of suicide is an important factor in the suicide rate, especially for older people, is shown by the fact that the suicide rate of elderly English people fell when cooking gas was detoxified; putting one's head in a gas oven had been a favorite (and very easy) method of suicide, especially for middle-aged and elderly persons.[31]

Physician-assisted suicide could also increase rather than reduce the number of suicides if people systematically underestimate either the probability or the severity of the doomed outcome and as a result do not commit suicide when they first learn their probable fate. When they wise up it is too late if physician-assisted suicide is not permitted. Notice however that if the analysis in chapter 5 is correct, this problem of foolish optimism is less likely to be acute with old than with young people.

Even in the case where $c_u > U_d > c_a$, it is possible that allowing physician-assisted suicide would, as before, lower rather than raise the suicide rate. With physician-assisted suicide cheaper than unassisted, persons contemplating suicide will tend to choose physician-assisted over unassisted. This implies that before committing suicide they will consult with a physician. The delay required by such a consultation will reduce the number of impulsive suicides; others will be avoided by the physician's identifying a treatable mental illness. The frequently remarked difficulty of diagnosing suicidal tendencies in elderly patients[32] is reduced when patients have an incentive to disclose those tendencies because they are seeking help in killing themselves. Physician-assisted suicide thus lowers the cost not only of suicide but also of interventions that can avoid suicide. This effect is not limited to cases of physical incapacity, but is not, I think, large enough to justify a broader right to physician-assisted suicide. I base this judgment not only on the *Chabot* case,[33] which may of course be unrepresentative, but also on the fact that a general right of physician-assisted suicide could (though needn't, as I have just suggested) reduce the cost of impulsive as well as of deliberated suicides. I pointed out earlier that people may not want to make it easier for themselves to commit suicide impulsively.

It may be objected that my entire analysis violates the economist's Law

---

31. Dan G. Blazer, "The Epidemiology of Psychiatric Disorders in Late Life," in *Geriatric Psychiatry* 235, 251 (Ewald W. Buse and Dan G. Blazer, eds., 1989); see also George Winokur and Donald W. Black, "Suicide—What Can Be Done?" 327 *New England Journal of Medicine* 490 (1992); Bijou Yang and David Lester, "The Effect of Gun Availability on Suicide Rates," 19 *Atlantic Economic Journal* 74 (1991).

32. See Carmelita R. Tobias, Raymond Pary, and Steven Lippmann, "Preventing Suicide in Older People," 45 *American Family Physician* 1707 (1992); Yeates Conwell and Eric D. Caine, "Rational Suicide and the Right to Die: Reality and Myth," 325 *New England Journal of Medicine* 1100, 1101–1102 (1991).

33. See note 25 above and accompanying text.

of Demand; that lowering the price of a good or service—here, suicide—must increase rather than reduce the demand for it. This is not the correct way to frame the issue. We have two goods, not one: unassisted suicide, and physician-assisted suicide. They are substitutes, so lowering the price of the second (by legalizing it) will reduce the demand for the first, and nothing in economics teaches that this reduction must be fully offset by the increased demand for the second good. A razor blade that retains its sharpness for ten shaves is a substitute for one that retains it for only one shave, but if the former takes over the market the total number of razor blades produced and sold will decline even if the longer-lasting blade is no more expensive than the other blade.

Although I have been stressing the physician's role in reducing the cost of suicide, he also has an important role to play in reducing the benefits, in particular by administering effective painkillers, which by reducing U_d reduce the likelihood of suicide. The two roles merge when, as is common, the physician administers painkillers in potentially lethal doses. In such a case U_d is eliminated either by killing the patient's pain or by killing the patient.

Notice, finally, that if my analysis is correct, physicians in a fee-for-service health-care system, the dominant system in the United States, should support a change in the laws to authorize physician-assisted suicide. Such a change would increase the demand for physicians' services both directly, and, if it is true that the laws would reduce the suicide rate of sick and elderly people and postpone the suicides of such people that do occur, indirectly by prolonging the life of people who have very grave diseases requiring protracted and expensive medical attention.

Evidence. The question whether allowing physician-assisted suicide in cases of physical incapacity would increase or reduce the suicide rate can be studied empirically. Table 10.1 regresses state suicide rates in the United States on state per capita income, the percentage of the state's population that is black (blacks have much lower suicide rates than whites), and a dummy variable that takes a value of 1 if a state has a law criminalizing physician-assisted suicide and 0 otherwise.[34]

---

34. More than half the states have such laws. Data on suicide rates and per capita income are from the *Statistical Abstract of the United States* for 1993. Data on race are from Kathleen O'Leary-Morgan et al., *1991 State Rankings: A Statistical View of the 50 United States* (1991). Data on assisted-suicide laws are from Julia Pugliese, "Don't Ask—Don't Tell: The Secret Practice of Physician Assisted Suicide," 44 *Hastings Law Journal* 1291, 1295 n. 20 (1993).

Table 10.1 Regression of Suicide Rate on Assisted-Suicide
Law and Other Variables (t-statistics in parentheses)

Per Capita Income	Percentage Black	Assisted-Suicide Law	R^2
−.0005	−.1287	−.7601	.31
(−3.388)	(−2.999)	(−0.951)	

The coefficients of the income and percentage-black variables are negative and highly significant statistically, and these two variables explain a good deal of the variance across states in the suicide rate. The coefficient of the law variable is also negative, implying that states that forbid physician-assisted suicide do have lower suicide rates than states that permit it. But it is not statistically significant, though perhaps only because most suicides are not committed by terminally ill or otherwise desperately ill people and thus do not come within the scope of the hypothesis that I am trying to test. Although these results do not suggest that repealing an assisted-suicide law is a sound method of reducing a state's suicide rate, they cast at least some doubt on the hypothesis, which I have been questioning despite its intuitive appeal, that making suicide easier is likely to lead to more suicides.

But I stress "some" doubt. If assisted-suicide laws are rarely enforced against physicians, this would suggest that such laws probably have very little deterrent effect. (The alternative hypothesis, that there is little enforcement because of perfect compliance, is hardly credible; there is considerable, and cumulatively persuasive, anecdotal and survey evidence that physician-assisted suicide is not rare in the United States.)[35] Or if, though such laws are commonly enforced in states that have them, states that do not have them punish physician-assisted suicide as ordinary homicide,[36] the absence of a special law would not be expected to make much difference, unless juries were willing to convict physicians of assisted suicide but not of homicide.

In fact it appears that neither type of law is used with any frequency against physicians who assist their patients to commit suicide. I have found

35. See id. at 1305–1306.
36. See David R. Schanker, "Of Suicide Machines, Euthanasia Legislation, and the Health Care Crisis," 68 *Indiana Law Journal* 977, 985–992 (1993).

only three published judicial opinions involving such conduct since 1950, all involving Dr. Jack Kevorkian[37]—surely a special case in view of his decision to conduct his activities in the open, and indeed in the glare of publicity. I have found only four American cases, other than those involving Kevorkian, in which a physician was prosecuted for assisting a patient to commit suicide.[38] No doubt there are more, but the total must be very slight in relation to the number of physician-assisted suicides. This makes it unlikely that a law criminalizing physician-assisted suicide would actually increase the suicide rate, although it helps explain the absence of a statistically significant effect of such laws. And yet the existence of an unenforced prohibition, whether its source is a special statute on assisted suicide or the general law of homicide, could increase the suicide rate by retarding the development of legal and ethical norms that regulate, and by regulating limit, the practice.

Another bit of evidence concerning the effect on the suicide rate of laws relating to physician-assisted suicide is presented in figure 10.1, which graphs the trend in the suicide rate of elderly males (75 years old and older), relative to that of all males, in the Netherlands and other northern European countries. That rate was very high in the Netherlands before euthanasia became common in the early 1970s and has fallen since, both absolutely and relatively to the other countries in the sample.[39]

Deaths caused by euthanasia, however, including physician-assisted suicides, are not counted as suicides in the Dutch statistics. One article, it is true, refers to incurably ill elderly patients who "request euthanasia or physician-assisted suicide," in a context suggesting that if their requests are granted they are counted as suicides.[40] But this is wildly implausible (and in fact incorrect), since the estimated number of annual deaths due to

---

37. People v. Kevorkian, 527 N.W.2d 714 (Mich. 1994); People v. Kevorkian, 517 N.W.2d 293 (Mich. Ct. App. 1994); Hobbins v. Attorney General, 518 N.W.2d 487 (Mich. Ct. App. 1994).

38. See H. Tristam Englehardt, Jr., and Michelle Malloy, "Suicide and Assisting Suicide: A Critique of Legal Sanctions," 36 *Southwestern Law Journal* 1003, 1029 (1982); Michael Winerip, "Prosecutor Ponders Mercy for a Mercy-Killing Doctor," *New York Times* (national ed.), Nov. 25, 1986, p. B4; Lawrence K. Altman, "Jury Declines to Indict a Doctor Who Said He Aided in a Suicide," *New York Times* (national ed.), July 27, 1991, p. 1. Only one of the four cases resulted in a conviction; the defendant pleaded guilty to manslaughter. Assisted suicide is rarely prosecuted even when the person rendering assistance is not a physician. Catherine D. Shaffer, Note, "Criminal Liability for Assisting Suicide," 86 *Columbia Law Review* 348, 369–371 (1986).

39. The source of the data for figure 10.1 is World Health Organization, *World Health Statistics Annual,* various years. The pattern with respect to female suicide is similar though with an uptick for Dutch suicides in the most recent period.

40. A. J. F. M. Kerkhof et al., "The Prevention of Suicide among Older People in the Netherlands: Interventions in Community Mental Health Care," 12 *Crisis* 59, 63 (1991).

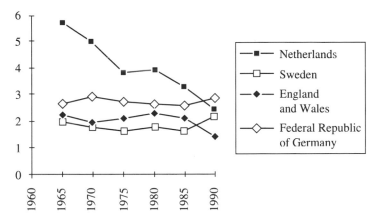

Figure 10.1 Suicide rate of elderly males as a multiple of the total male suicide rate, 1965–1990

euthanasia (2,700, of which 400 are physician-assisted suicides) exceeds the total number of reported Dutch suicides, which is less than 2,000.[41] The Dutch count as "suicide" for statistical reporting purposes only a fraction of deliberate efforts by persons to bring about their immediate death. Lacking as we do a time series for euthanasia, we cannot infer from figure 10.1 that the total number of elderly suicides in the broadest sense has fallen in the Netherlands since euthanasia became common. It is possible that, consistent with my analysis, what has happened is a substitution of euthanasia for conventional suicide.

It has been argued, we saw, that allowing euthanasia would encourage suicide (as well as murder) at all ages by undermining the sanctity of life. If so, we might expect the Dutch suicide rate to have risen since the early 1970s. It did rise by 25 percent between 1974 and 1988, but the average increase in the other member nations of the European community was 36.25 percent; the Dutch increase was the fourth lowest out of 12.[42]

41. See id. at 59; Kimsma and van Leeuwen, note 1 above, at 27–28; Netherlands Central Bureau of Statistics, *Statistical Yearbook 1993 of the Netherlands* 418 (1993) (tab. 43). A phone call to the Netherlands Central Bureau of Statistics confirmed that no cases of euthanasia are included in the Dutch suicide statistics.

42. Computed from Colin Pritchard, "Is There a Link between Suicide in Young Men and Employment? A Comparison of the UK with Other European Community Countries," 160 *British Journal of Psychiatry* 750, 753 (1992) (tab. 3). The table from which I have derived these data lists Scotland and Northern Ireland separately from England and Wales. I have included the figure for Scotland, but not for Northern Ireland—a distinct outlier with its 206 percent increase in the suicide rate.

Voluntary Euthanasia with Implementation Deferred

I turn now to the case in which there is a nontrivial interval between the decision to die and the carrying out of the decision. I shall consider two versions of this case. The first is where *A,* having acquainted himself with the facts about old age, decides that the physical decrepitude of that state is such that he would greatly prefer not to enter it; but fearing that he will have different preferences when he reaches that age, he wants to commit himself now to die at age 75, which he regards as the threshold of too old age. In the second case, *B* is anxious not about old age as such but about senility, which he considers a living death. He knows that if he becomes senile it may be too late for him to terminate his life voluntarily, so like *A* he wants somehow to commit to die if and when he becomes senile, at whatever age. *B*'s anxiety about becoming senile cannot be considered neurotic or irrational. Senile dementia afflicts a substantial fraction of old people, as we saw in chapter 1, causing grievous and degrading cognitive impairment. The risk of becoming severely demented, especially for people in their eighties or nineties, is great enough to be a source of understandable dread to many aging people.

The case of physical decrepitude. The economic argument for giving *A* what he wants is that we permit people to make irrevocable commitments about their future—to foreclose any realistic prospect of becoming a doctor by going to law school instead of to medical school, or, coming closer to home, to impair one's longevity by adopting an unsafe or unhealthy mode of life. Suicide can be regarded in that light. But there is a counterargument when the decision to commit suicide is made many years before the intended execution of the decision. For it can be argued, as we saw in chapter 4, that the self at time t and the self at time $t + k$ are actually two persons, A_t and A_{t+k}, at least when k is a substantial number. What is a person? By hypothesis A_t and A_{t+k} have different preferences concerning the fundamental issue of life versus death. The younger self has of course a degree of control over the older, and the older has no control at all over the younger, simply because time runs forwards but not backwards. It may be impossible as a practical matter to make A_t a fiduciary of A_{t+k}.[43] But it does not follow that the law should affirmatively assist in the younger self's destructive designs against the older self, as by enforcing a contract be-

---

43. With a limited exception discussed below; and notice the analogy to cases in which a pregnant woman is punished for not taking adequate care of herself and thus endangering the fetus.

tween A_t and some third party to kill A at time $t + k$. For on what ground shall the younger self be adjudged more authentic than the older self? The problem of picking the authentic self is a standard one in multiple-selves analysis.[44] Perhaps the game theorists can help us, by modeling the outcome of bargaining between one's current and one's future self. Perhaps; but at present no satisfactory solution has been suggested to the problem of arbitrating the conflict among successive selves. I find it odd therefore that Prado should think it an argument in *favor* of "preemptive" suicide that in old age we may cease "to be the persons we are" and "adjust to what even a few months before we would have rejected as intolerable."[45]

This analysis might seem to support a much stronger position, that suicide should always be prevented if prevention is feasible, since when A_t kills himself he is also killing A_{t+k}, who may have positive utility from living. Yet one can easily imagine a case in which A_t kills A as it were impartially, because even though he knows that his future self will derive a positive utility from living (that is, $UA_{t+k} > 0$), the sum of present and future utilities is negative $(-UA_t + UA_{t+k} < 0)$; the disutility to A_t of living (maybe his life is blighted by fear that he will end up in a nursing home,[46] which he may consider the equivalent of a concentration camp) exceeds the utility to A_{t+k} of living. In such a case, suicide will be utility maximizing even if the present self weights the future self's utility equally with its own.

So multiple-selves analysis need not condemn all suicide—at least if we are utilitarians, a big "if" for many people. Yet even if we *are* utilitarians, willing to trade off one "person's" life against another's, the implications of the analysis for the permissible scope of governmental interference with individual choices are disquieting to anyone who believes in liberty. For example, if our future self has a moral claim as great as a fetus (another potential person) even if not so great as our present self, the argument for forbidding a pregnant woman to smoke becomes an argument for forbidding anyone but a dying person to smoke.

The argument for forbidding suicide commitments cannot be dismissed out of hand as paternalistic even by those who reject all paternalis-

---

44. See, for example, Thomas C. Schelling, *Choice and Consequence: Perspectives of an Errant Economist* 67–68, 98, 152–156 (1984).

45. Prado, note 12 above, at 119; see also id. at 124–125.

46. Although, contrary to the popular impression, most nursing-home stays even for elderly people are relatively short, whether they end in death or in return to the noninstitutionalized community, "nearly 25 percent of all women who enter a nursing home will spend three years there." Andrew Dick, Alan M. Garber, and Thomas A. MaCurdy, "Forecasting Nursing Home Utilization of Elderly Americans," in *Studies in the Economics of Aging* 365, 392 (David A. Wise, ed., 1994).

tic grounds for interference with choices made by competent adults;[47] the person is not choosing for himself if his future self is a different person from his present self. Nevertheless the pragmatic objections to the argument are similar to the pragmatic objections to paternalistic arguments for government interference with personal liberty. In particular, even if the younger self is not a perfect agent of the older self, how likely is it that the state will be a better agent, or more precisely will better balance the competing claims of the two selves? In just the same way, even though parents are not perfect agents of their children, we assume that except in the extreme cases which we call by such names as neglect and abuse they are apt to be better agents than the state. We observe that people do make provision for their old age and also for their other contingent selves—they buy disability insurance, for example, rather than simply writing off their possible disabled self that may come into being after an accident. They are not wholly neglectful of their future selves. The question is whether they are sufficiently neglectful to warrant government intervention, with all its costs.

The case of senility. B's case, in which the younger self wants to kill the older only if the older becomes severely demented, differs from A's because there is a question whether B_{t+k} is a person. If he is not, the question whether he is a *separate* person, entitled to some protection against B_t, does not arise. For there is a distinction between identity and personhood.[48] B_{t+k} has the same name and other indicia of identity as B_t, but if personhood requires some degree of mentation[49] and not merely a functioning brain stem, B_{t+k} may not be a person and therefore may not be entitled to any protection.

I am not comfortable with this argument.[50] Dan Brock, who is, acknowledges that his "view of personhood implies that infanticide need not

47. On the difference between paternalistic arguments and arguments based on the concept of multiple selves, see discussion in next chapter of the compulsory character of social security.

48. See, for example, Dan W. Brock, *Life and Death: Philosophical Essays in Biomedical Ethics*, ch. 12 (1993).

49. Signally including "autobiographical memory" in the elementary sense of knowing who one is and was. See D. B. Bromley, *Behavioural Gerontology: Central Issues in the Psychology of Ageing* 231 (1990). This, the reader will recall from chapter 5, is part of the reason why an old person may be eager to postpone his death even if only for a short time.

50. Dworkin, note 7 above, at 232, expresses ambivalence about it in the case where it appears that the demented individual is happy despite his state. A further concern, which I shall not discuss, is the use of guardianship and procedures for involuntary civil commitment to confine to institutions or otherwise impair the autonomy of elderly persons who are not in fact incompetent, but merely an inconvenience to their relatives. See George J. Alexander, "Age and the Law," in *Perspectives on Aging: Exploding the Myths* 45, 54–66 (Priscilla W. Johnston, ed., 1981).

wrong a newborn infant and that infants lack any serious moral right not to be killed." [51] Brock's speculations have carried him beyond the gravitational field of American morality. The immorality of infanticide is not up for reconsideration, and it is equally unthinkable that a suicide contract would be enforced and a person dragged to his death against his will because he had signed a contract and was now deemed incompetent to repudiate it, or even that it would be enforced by the forfeiture of a bond or by some other monetary sanction. We happen to have unshakable moral intuitions concerning the wrongfulness of infanticide and of enforcing suicide contracts. These intuitions precede and inform, rather than following and being informed by, philosophical analyses of personhood. If the case for allowing a person to arrange in advance for his death should he some day become senile stands or falls on whether infanticide is just, or whether a monkey or a computer should be deemed more of a person than a severely demented or profoundly retarded human being, we shall make no progress in dealing with the senile case, for we shall be up against immovable intuitions concerning the priority of human beings over animals and machines.[52] I do not mean to suggest either that all of our unshakable moral intuitions are universal[53] or even that they are permanent within our society. Many of them seem in fact rather local and fluid. But they are not changeable by reasons, in part because they are not founded on reasons. Because of our genetic programming, and because of the material conditions of our society discussed in the preceding chapter, we have more regard for the lives of infants than for the lives of the senile. That is a good enough ground, even though it is not a "rational" ground, for decoupling the issues, although not to the extent of enforcing suicide contracts.

All this talk of unshakable moral intuition may seem inconsistent with my commitment announced at the outset of this chapter to John Stuart Mill's theory of limited government. There is no inconsistency, once the concept of multiple selves enables us to see that a decision by the current occupant of one's body to kill a future occupant is "other regarding" in Mill's sense, that is, it imposes a cost on one who has not consented to bear it. The problem is not serious in the case of physical incapacity, with which I began. Remember that the vast majority of Dutch euthanasia cases involve persons with less than a month to live. They are not making decisions

---

51. Brock, note 48 above, at 385 n. 14.

52. On the priority of intuition over analysis in moral judgments, see my book *The Problems of Jurisprudence* 76–77, 339–340 (1990).

53. There are societies (premodern Japan is an example) in which old men are revered and infanticide tolerated. Cf. chapter 9.

for a future self so remote, so likely to have different values and preferences, that it can plausibly be regarded as a different person.

At the level of nonphilosophical practice, the issues of infanticide and geronticide have been decoupled to a limited extent. Although contracts of assisted suicide are unenforceable, people have a limited power to bring about, through the devices of the living will and, especially, the durable power of attorney for health care, a state of affairs in which they are unlikely to survive for long in a severely demented state.[54] But the emphasis belongs on the word "limited"—and not only because it appears that, as recently as 1989, less than a quarter of the elderly population had living wills and an even smaller percentage had granted durable powers of attorney for health care.[55] (Undoubtedly the percentage has increased, but I have no current figures. Nor do I know what percentage of the people *who need living wills the most* have them, dying people for example; perhaps it is large.) The more fundamental problem is that the living will is designed for the case in which "death is imminent except for death delaying procedures" (I am quoting from the form approved in Illinois), and this point will not be reached until very late in the progression of the dementia. The power of attorney is broader, authorizing the holder of the power (again I quote from the Illinois form) "to make any decision you could make to obtain or terminate any type of health care, including withdrawal of food and water." But like the living will, the power of attorney is revocable as long as the grantor of the power remains competent, and it may be difficult to determine when that point has been reached in the progress of the dementia. And until the demented patient has entered the vegetative state, the holder of the power will be reluctant to authorize measures that amount to inflicting death by starvation or dehydration, although it appears that these deaths can be made relatively painless.[56]

A number of states now have "surrogate decision-making statutes," whereby medical decisions, including cessation of treatment, can be made by a surrogate (normally a close relative) of a patient who is comatose or otherwise incapable of making decisions and does not have a living will or

54. For background on living wills and durable powers of attorney, see Barry R. Furrow et al., *Bioethics: Health Care Law and Ethics* 263–279 (1991); Peter J. Strauss, Robert Wolf, and Dana Shilling, *Aging and the Law,* ch. 22 (1990), and Supplement thereto, ch. 10 (1991). And for a model statute that reflects the latest thinking on the subject, see National Conference of Commissioners on Uniform State Laws, "Uniform Health-Care Decisions Act" (1993).

55. Wayne Moore, "Improving the Delivery of Legal Services for the Elderly: A Comprehensive Approach," 41 *Emory Law Journal* 805, 812–813 (1992).

56. See McCann, Hall, and Groth-Juncker, note 9 above.

a health-care power of attorney.[57] The combination of living wills, health-care powers of attorney, and surrogacy statutes has reduced the problems involved in prolonging the life of comatose patients to manageable proportions, and I shall not discuss it further. The problem with using these devices to terminate the life of a severely demented person is that such a person is not comatose and usually does not appear to be suffering unbearably.

Notice that by facilitating MDELs other than euthanasia—which as we saw at the beginning of this chapter are substitutes for physician-assisted suicide—the living will, the durable health-care power of attorney, and surrogate decision-making could all be considered substitutes for, or way stations toward, the legitimization of physician-assisted suicide. When, pursuant say to a living will, a physician facilitates a patient's voluntary death of dehydration by giving him salves to relieve the discomfort of cracked lips incident to dehydration, it is difficult to distinguish what the physician is doing from assisting in a suicide. Yet the Dutch experience suggests that MDELs, other than physician-assisted suicide itself, are not a perfect substitute for physician-assisted suicide. If they were, there would be no reason to authorize physician-assisted suicide.

Although enforcing a contract of suicide against a person who has changed his mind about being killed is patently inconsistent with the moral feelings of our society and not required by Millian liberalism, I feel bound to point out that the refusal to enforce such contracts may increase the suicide rate and, what I have explained is qualitatively similar, reduce the average age of suicide. People in the early stages of senile dementia often both know that they have the disease and know that it will get worse. These people may have several pretty good years before their dementia progresses to the point at which, ex ante, they would consider themselves better off dead. Unable to "schedule" death to occur at that cross-over point, however, and fearful that when the point is reached they will lack the will or the means to kill themselves, they may decide to kill themselves earlier,[58] thus losing valuable years of life in order to prevent a more than offsetting loss of expected utility. Those years would be saved if they could make an

57. Strauss, Wolf, and Shilling, note 54 above, at 607–614; Supplement, note 54 above, at 234–238. See generally James Lindgren, "Death by Default," *Law and Contemporary Problems,* Summer 1993, p. 185.

58. An actual case is discussed in Christine K. Cassel and Diane E. Meier, "Morals and Moralism in the Debate over Euthanasia and Assisted Suicide," 323 *New England Journal of Medicine* 750 (1990).

enforceable agreement to be killed painlessly when a responsible judgment is made that their quality of life has fallen below the level at which they would (if capable of making a rational judgment) want to continue living.

The main conclusions of this chapter can be summarized briefly. In cases of terminally ill, pain-wracked, or severely impaired people who are or anticipate shortly becoming physically incapable of committing suicide, Mill's theory of the proper limits of government suggests, although it does not prove, that a right of physician-assisted suicide should be recognized (subject to appropriate safeguards, and to details[59] of design and implementation that I have not discussed) and that therefore the laws forbidding the practice should be repealed. The fear that under such a regime physicians will hustle their patients to a premature and undesired death seems greatly exaggerated; indeed, the suicide rate might actually fall if physician-assisted suicide were permitted in the subset of cases that I have described. I do not believe, however, that a broader right of physician-assisted suicide, for example a right to make an enforceable contract to die when one becomes senile, can be justified on Millian grounds once the concept of multiple selves is brought into the analysis, as it should be.

I want to close with one of those details of implementation.That is the political level at which reform should be implemented. I believe that it should be at the state rather than at the federal level. Today more than ever the United States is a morally heterogeneous country, and some of the moral boundaries approximate the boundaries of states. A midwestern or far-western state inhabited mainly by persons of northern European origin may occupy a different moral universe from that of most of our southern states, at least with regard to a number of issues heavily freighted with religious and emotional meaning, including issues of life and death.[60] I cannot think of a compelling reason why, whether through congressional action or judicial interpretation of the provisions of the Constitution that are applicable to the states, the views of a national majority (or the political or intellectual elites from which federal courts, especially, often take their

59. Including such minute but important details as whether physician-assisted suicide would, if made legal, still count as "suicide" within the meaning of life insurance policies that contain an exception (usually limited, however, to the first two years in which the policy is in effect) for self-inflicted death. Cf. Robert J. Kovacs, "Insurance Issues in Physician-Assisted Suicide," *New Jersey Lawyer,* Sept. 26, 1994, p. 15. A number of living-will statutes provide that death which results from the honoring of the decedent's living will is not a suicide. Legal Counsel for the Elderly, *Decision-Making, Incapacity, and the Elderly* 24 (1987).

60. Notice that Dworkin bracketed abortion and euthanasia in his book *Life's Dominion,* note 7 above.

cues) concerning such a matter as physician-assisted suicide should be imposed on the entire nation. As I mentioned at the outset of this chapter, Oregon recently became the first state to authorize a form of physician-assisted suicide; a bill is pending in the Connecticut legislature that would do the same thing;[61] legislative activity in other states can be anticipated; in still other cases the cause is and will long remain hopeless. This pattern, this ferment and variety, is as it should be. Each state should be allowed to decide, and premature nationalization (illustrated by *Roe v. Wade,* which interrupted and preempted a liberalizing tide of state abortion laws) avoided.

61. 1994 Conn. Sen. Bill No. 361.

11

Social Security and Health

The question whether to permit people in general and the elderly ailing in particular to end their lives draws on ethical and economic arguments that turn out to be helpful in resolving other policy issues concerning the elderly, as I hope to show in this chapter. The most important of these policies, and the ones on which I shall focus, are the social security program of retirement benefits and the public provision of health care (comprising expenditures on medical research as well as on treatment) for the elderly.

The Compulsory Character of Social Security

I begin with an issue curiously linked through the concept of multiple selves with the subject of the preceding chapter. That concept illuminates a feature of the social security retirement program—namely, the fact that it is compulsory—that only *seems* remote from euthanasia. If you work for an employer covered by social security (which is now virtually every employer, including the self-employer), you are forced to contribute to the social security program; you cannot make a side deal with your employer whereby in exchange for a higher wage you agree that neither you nor he will make any contribution to the program and in consequence you will have no entitlement to social security benefits when you reach retirement age. Nowadays the main practical reason for the compulsory character of social security is to make sure that there is money in the social security till to honor someone else's social security entitlement. But the original rationale was to force people to save for their old age; and even those critics of the social security system who would prefer to substitute an entirely private system believe (most of them anyway) that people should be compelled to enroll in a private pension system and thus to make provision for their old age. And likewise with the Medicare component of social security: most critics of Medicare would support an alternative system under which people would be forced to buy private medical insurance for their old age.

The reasons most commonly offered for the compulsory character of the social security program are two. The first is paternalism: people are short-sighted and therefore cannot be trusted to make arrangements for the distant future. This would be a good reason if people typically underestimated their life expectancy and therefore the amount of money they should be setting aside for consumption (including consumption of medical services) in old age. But the evidence is to the contrary.[1] The second reason is *Realpolitik:* society won't in fact let people starve to death, or die because they cannot pay for essential medical treatments, so the nonsavers would be free riders.[2] This reason has some support in the fact that persons who have not contributed to social security are entitled to a modest government pension anyway and that the indigent elderly received medical care on a charity basis even before there was a Medicaid or Medicare program.

The concept of multiple selves enables a different approach to be taken. *A* at working age, especially at young working age, is a different person from *A* at retirement age. A_w should not be allowed to condemn A_r to penury by refusing to make any provision for the support of A_r, who will be unable to support himself. A_w on this view is a kind of trustee of *A,* the body that A_w and A_r successively inhabit. A compulsory pension system, like a prohibition against enforceable contracts of assisted suicide, imposes a limited fiduciary duty on the young self. Lawyers will perceive an analogy to the duty that a life tenant owes a remainderman not to waste the assets of the property in which they have their successive interests, as by cutting trees before the trees have reached maturity. The analogy is helpful in showing that the multiple-selves argument for compulsory social security, unlike the paternalistic argument, does not depend on any notion that people are ignorant or that government knows best.

Unfortunately, as we have already seen, there is no good method of determining the relative weight to give the preferences of the different selves. The clearest limit on the claims of the old is the case where the

1. See Daniel S. Hamermesh, "Expectations, Life Expectancy, and Economic Behavior," 100 *Quarterly Journal of Economics* 389 (1985).
2. See, for example, Laurence J. Kotlikoff, Avia Spivak, and Lawrence H. Summers, "The Adequacy of Savings," 72 *American Economic Review* 1056 (1982).

young self wants to sacrifice those claims on behalf of other selves and so is not being selfish. Recalling the trade-off identified by evolutionary biology between the longevity and the reproductive fitness of an organism, we can see that the old self should not be heard to complain if the young self decides to divert resources from the old self to the production of children; that is not a selfish expenditure by the young. But beyond that, perhaps we can do no better than to allow the political process to arbitrate the competing claims of successive selves, as discussed in the last section of this chapter. Contrary to general fears, that process is unlikely to subordinate the interests of the young to the interests of the old completely.

The Allocation of Medical Resources to the Elderly and between Elderly Men and Women

A question even more closely related to that of geronticide is whether society has any obligation to furnish medical care (other than care designed for the alleviation of pain) to the severely demented. This question blends into the broader one of how much and in what form to devote resources to the medical needs of elderly persons—persons who, to put it bluntly, will soon be dead anyway—and into the still broader question, analyzed extensively but inconclusively in the biomedical-ethics literature under the rubric of "triage,"[3] of the allocation of scarce medical resources among competing demanders. I believe that economics can reduce the indeterminacy of that analysis, both generally and with particular reference to the question of medical care for the elderly.

Private expenditures. We should distinguish between allowing an individual or his family to spend his own or its own resources on medical care, a negative liberty, and forcing the taxpayer to pay for it, a positive one. Even the negative liberty is not completely unproblematic. The private health expenditures of the old, that is, expenditures over and above Medi-

---

3. See, for example, Robert T. Francoeur, *Biomedical Ethics: A Guide to Decision Making*, ch. 5 (1983); Robert W. Derlet and Denyse A. Nishio, "Refusing Care to Patients Who Present to an Emergency Department," 19 *Annals of Emergency Medicine* 262 (1990); and, for the fullest discussions, John F. Kilner, *Who Lives? Who Dies? Ethical Criteria in Patient Selection* (1990), and Gerald R. Winslow, *Triage and Justice* (1982). The term "triage" (the French word for "sorting") used to be employed much more narrowly, to denote methods for maximizing the value of emergency medical treatment of battlefield casualties, as by dividing the wounded into those likely to survive without immediate treatment, those likely to die even if they received immediate treatment, and those likely to survive if but only if they received such treatment, and treating only the third group, as distinct from treating everyone on a first-come, first-served basis.

care (which does not reimburse the total expenses of Medicare patients) and other public programs, are large enough to affect the costs of medical care to other people. Persons 65 and older, although less than 13 percent of the American population, account, as noted in chapter 2, for roughly one-third of all expenditures on health. Two-thirds of the elderly's tab is picked up by the government through Medicare and other public programs,[4] but this means that more than 11 percent of the nation's total expenditures on health are private expenditures by the elderly. If a service is provided under conditions of increasing average cost, an increase in demand will raise the market price, and everyone who shops in the market will pay more than he did before. I do not know whether this is true of medical care, especially in the long run, when supply is more elastic. But if it is true, the large private demand by the elderly for health care has probably driven up the prices paid by other consumers of medical services. Such an effect on other consumers, however, would be a purely pecuniary externality; that is, it would be completely offset by the increased revenue of the sellers of medical services. The distribution of income across persons or groups might be affected, but the total wealth of society would be unchanged. Whether economic equality would be promoted is anybody's guess. Not all providers of medical services are wealthy, by any means; indeed most health-care workers are rather poorly paid.

Public expenditures. The analysis would be the same if, instead of paying as they went, the old bought medical insurance policies when young that guaranteed the payment of their medical expenses when they grew old. (This is easier said than done, since future medical costs cannot be forecast reliably decades in advance. But that is a separate problem, though one to which I return.) One might even suppose the analysis unchanged if the expenditures of the old on health care are subsidized, as of course they are, primarily by the federal taxpayer through the Medicare program.[5] It is true once again that to the extent that essential inputs into health-care services are in irremediably short supply, an expansion of the health-care sector will result in higher prices. But we have just seen that the same thing would happen, under the identical assumption of a long-run rising average cost of health care, if the old decided to spend more of their own money on health

---

4. U.S. Senate Special Committee on Aging et al., *Aging America: Trends and Projections* 133 (1991 ed.).

5. To the tune of $102 billion in 1991; $126 billion if other federal programs that provide subsidized medical care to elderly persons are included, primarily the portion of Medicaid that goes to pay the medical expenses of the elderly poor. Id. at 239 (tab. 8-1).

care. The difference between the two cases is that a public subsidy of medical care reduces the total *value* of the economy's output of goods and services, by inducing the old to substitute medical care for things they would value more highly if medical services were priced to them at their market value. If the total annual expenditures on Medicare were simply given to the Medicare-eligible population in cash,[6] the old would be unlikely to spend all their new wealth on medical care. An elderly person who now receives $20,000 in social security retirement benefits a year would not, in all likelihood, if given another $10,000 a year to spend as he wants, use it all to buy health insurance, even if he could not count on public or charitable assistance if he got ill and his insurance benefits ran out. Elderly people sometimes elect, or are nudged by their physicians or by hospitals to elect, marginal medical procedures because the private cost (what they pay) is so much lower than the social cost (what society pays). Medicare has thus brought about a misallocation of resources from the standpoint of economic efficiency.

Is it a serious misallocation? I am not so sure. Although Medicare is too generous in the economic sense of giving the old more medical care than they would pay for if they had an undistorted choice among competing goods and services, no one seems to know how serious the distortion is.[7] And Medicare is not too generous—Ronald Dworkin to the contrary notwithstanding[8]—merely because old people receive more medical care than they would when young sign a contract to receive in a lifetime health-insurance policy. Dworkin is no doubt correct that most young people would not buy a policy that required heavy premiums to defray the expected cost of dramatic though usually futile medical interventions in the last few weeks or months of life. But his argument is nevertheless vulnerable not only to the obvious objections that implementation would require far more information than the government could plausibly be expected to obtain and that no one knows how to price lifetime medical insurance, but also to the subtler objection that to allow the young to make life and death

6. Implying a roughly 50 percent increase in the size of social security pensions. See id. at 239 (tab. 8-1).

7. See generally Jerry L. Mashaw and Theodore R. Marmor, "Conceptualizing, Estimating, and Reforming Fraud, Waste, and Abuse in Healthcare Spending," 11 *Yale Journal on Regulation* 455 (1994).

8. Dworkin, "Will Clinton's Plan Be Fair?" *New York Review of Books,* Jan. 13, 1994, p. 20. For a similar argument, see Dan W. Brock, *Life and Death: Philosophical Essays in Biomedical Ethics* 358–360 (1993) ("prudential allocator" approach). Survey evidence, reviewed in James Lindgren, "Death by Default," *Law and Contemporary Problems,* Summer 1993, p. 185, supports Dworkin's premise that people in some sense don't "want" expensive end-of-life treatments.

decisions for the old is to give one person, the younger self, undue control over a resource (a body) shared with another, the same individual's older self.[9]

This is a common oversight in the philosophical analysis of aging—surprisingly so, since "deconstructing" the self is the sort of thing philosophers like to do. Norman Daniels, discussing the issue of justice between generations, argues that because youth and age are merely different stages of a single life, treating them differently "generates no inequality at all . . . From the perspective of stable institutions operating over time, unequal treatment of people by age is a kind of budgeting within a life." [10] Yet we saw in earlier chapters that it is entirely rational for old people to spend heavily on medical care to extend their lives; they do not have good alternative uses of their resources. The young self may scant his future self's interest in extending life not because the young self is short-sighted or lacks self-control but simply because it has different preferences.

The point is also overlooked by even the best health economists. Sherwin Rosen points out that "focus group explorations of hypothetical life-path experiences showed graphically that people in their twenties have little or no interest in their health prospects for their seventies or even their fifties. A different picture emerges from the responses of people in their fifties or sixties." [11] But Rosen does not think that this presents any normative problem concerning the behavior of the young, provided they have accurate information.[12]

Dworkin proposes to limit the amount of medical care available to the elderly to what the young self would, under conditions of complete information and a just distribution of wealth, be willing to pay for. Not only is the proposal rendered problematic by multiple-selves analysis and the other objections I mentioned; but it is morally unacceptable for much the same reason as Brock's somewhat similar proposal for dealing with the

9. He alludes to this problem in his book *Life's Dominion: An Argument about Abortion, Euthanasia, and Individual Freedom* 257 n. 12 (1993), which refers the reader to a longer, unpublished study. But both the note and the study are confined to the special issue (which I discussed in the preceding chapter) whether we should be able to make decisions binding our future senile self.

10. Norman Daniels, "Justice and Transfer between Generations," in *Workers versus Pensioners: Intergenerational Justice in an Ageing World* 57, 61, 63 (Paul Johnson, Christoph Conrad, and David Thompson, eds., 1989). See also Margaret P. Battin, "Age Rationing and the Just Distribution of Health Care: Is There a Duty to Die?" 97 *Ethics* 317 (1987).

11. Sherwin Rosen, "The Quantity and Quality of Life: A Conceptual Framework," in *Valuing Health for Policy: An Economic Approach* 221, 247 (George Tolley, Donald Kenkel, and Robert Fabian, eds., 1994).

12. Id. at 244, 246.

severely demented, which I discussed in the preceding chapter. Let me turn personal again. In 1987, at the age of 87, my mother broke her hip. When this happened she was already a frail and shrunken old lady with the characteristic symptoms of senile dementia of moderate severity: she suffered from occasional disorientation and confusion, and her short-term memory was gone, causing her conversation to be extremely repetitive. But her essential rationality was intact, and she was living at home with my father. Before the medical advances of recent decades, death would have been the sequel to my mother's breaking her hip, and she would have been thought someone who had reached the natural terminus of a long life. Instead the hip was skilfully repaired, and she lived on. She never walked again, however, and had to be placed in a nursing home. Her mental condition continued to deteriorate. Eventually she lost the use of her hands and her power of speech, and ceased to recognize anyone. She was finally carried away by pneumonia at the age of 90, a shadow, totally bereft of reason ("Without the which we are pictures, or mere beasts").[13]

In 1992, my father-in-law, aged 75 and in ostensibly good health, was diagnosed by doctors at a distinguished medical center as having an untreatable cancer and given three months to live. He accepted the diagnosis and went home. Three months later he began to develop some respiratory distress. A radiologist told him that unless he underwent chemotherapy he would be dead in two weeks. The radiologist did not tell him what would happen if he did undergo chemotherapy. My father-in-law decided in favor of the chemotherapy and was dead after three ghastly weeks. His medical expenses (all picked up by Medicare) for those last three weeks came to $30,000.

The expenditures incurred in prolonging my mother's life by three years and my father-in-law's by one week were, in my opinion, wasted. My mother's and my father-in-law's younger selves would surely have agreed with me on this point, and might even have been willing to sign a contract to that effect. But I cannot think of any feasible method of enforcing such a contract except by concealing treatment options from elderly people, which I do not think Dworkin would approve of doing. You just do not tell people in our society that, although the technology exists to prolong their lives, a judgment has been made that the costs exceed the benefits and therefore the technology will be withheld from them. You do not tell them this, *pace* Dworkin, even if you are in a position to remind them that they agreed when young not to insist on expensive end-of-life treatments. My

13. *Hamlet,* act IV, sc. v, l. 86.

father-in-law's radiologist can be faulted for not having advised my father-in-law of the likely futility and ugly side-effects of the course of chemotherapy being offered, but I do not think the advice would have changed my father-in-law's decision. Americans are fighters, not fatalists.

Of course there is a point beyond which a society will refuse to keep old people alive. That point can be reached quite early in a very poor society, as we saw in chapter 9. But in a society as wealthy as ours, the elderly would have to be consuming a far larger share of the medical budget than they are doing even today for society to decide to close the spigot. My father-in-law was well to do and could have paid for the chemotherapy out of his own assets; and in the case of my mother, the major expense of her protracted old age was the expense of the nursing home, which Medicare did not reimburse. It is right to force elderly people to "spend down" before they qualify for public assistance. But it would not be consistent with contemporary morality to take the next step, as Dworkin would do, and deny all public assistance (and private as well?) that goes beyond what a representative younger self would have agreed to set aside for the medical expenses of his elderly self.

The young self will not be permitted fully to control the old one. And because there is no satisfactory or acceptable analytical procedure for balancing the claims of the young and of the old self, the current old, in effect as proxies for the future old selves of the current young, struggle with the current young in the political marketplace for the allocation of consumption over the life cycle. The increasing productivity of medical expenditures in extending life and in improving the health of the old is increasing the intergenerational tension. The Medicare hospital trust fund is expected to be depleted by the year 2001,[14] at which point the social security tax will have to be raised, benefits cut, or other steps to restore balance taken. The old self has an argument (if only it could make it!) that the ever-increasing productivity of expenditures on medical care warrants a reallocation of resources from the young self; that the marginal dollar will purchase more utility for the old self than it would for the young. The young self, however, may disagree.

Research priorities. The issue of subsidizing health care for the elderly population arises in still another form, that of federal support of medical research on diseases such as heart disease and cancer that afflict old people disproportionately. Not all serious diseases do. Asthma and mi-

---

14. Robert Pear, "Benefit Funds May Run Out of Cash Soon, Reports Warn," *New York Times* (national ed.), April 12, 1994, p. A12.

graine, for example, as well as certain cancers—and of course AIDS—are more common among young than among old people, whereas heart conditions are 10 times more frequent among men 65–74 years old than among *all* men under 45 and 15 times more frequent among men 75 and older than among the under-45 set.[15] The U.S. Public Health Service spends much of its annual research budget on diseases that afflict old people disproportionately (with most of the rest going to AIDS).[16] The marginal benefit of these expenditures may be small, quite apart from "value-of-life" considerations. Old people are highly vulnerable to a large number of lethal or incapacitating diseases. In effect these diseases compete to kill or grievously impair the old. Curing one or two such diseases will eliminate competition for the other diseases, enabling the latter to do more harm than would have been the case had the competitors remained in the field. Curing heart disease saves the patient for cancer, and curing both would save him for nephritis, blindness, or Alzheimer's. The "benefit" that these diseases derive from medical research that cures their rivals is enhanced by the fact that improvements in medical technology benefit persons of weak constitution disproportionately, thus providing easier targets for the lying-in-wait diseases.[17]

This point undermines the kind of naive cost-benefit analysis in which, for example, the benefits of measures to reduce the number of accidental injuries to elderly people are assumed to equal the medical costs of treating those injuries.[18] The assumption disregards the fact that avoiding such an injury sets up the elderly person for another problem that will require medical treatment that could cost as much or even more. The cost of that treatment should be added to the cost of treating the accidental injury in deciding whether the latter treatment is cost-justified.

This is not to suggest that the benefits of measures to improve the health of elderly people are zero. Although longevity is positively related to income and the income of the old has soared in recent times, the increase in longevity (and the reduction in the fraction of the aged that is disabled)

15. See U.S. Bureau of the Census, *Statistical Abstract of the United States 1993* 135 (113th ed.) (ser. 206).

16. William Winkenwerder, Austin R. Kessler, and Rhonda M. Stolec, "Federal Spending for Illness Caused by the Human Immunodeficiency Virus," 320 *New England Journal of Medicine* 1598, 1602 (1989) (tab. 4).

17. See Donald S. Shepard and Richard J. Zeckhauser, "The Choice of Health Policies with Heterogeneous Populations," in *Economic Aspects of Health* 255, 268 (Victor R. Fuchs, ed., 1992). The age-race "crossover" in longevity, discussed in chapter 9, illustrates this point.

18. As in Amy B. Bernstein and Claudia L. Schur, "Expenditures for Unintentional Injuries among the Elderly," 2 *Journal of Aging and Health* 157 (1990).

has far exceeded what is plausible to assign to the increase in income.[19] "Saving" an old person with heart disease for cancer will still give him additional years of life, in all likelihood; and we know that increases in longevity confer substantial private benefits on the elderly, especially if I am correct that the length of remaining life is not an important variable in the demand for life. We also know that concerns that an increase even in healthy longevity will have disastrous social consequences by raising the dependency ratio probably are exaggerated.

Yet it does not follow that just because a young person and an old person may feel an equal dread at the prospect of imminent death, a cure that saves many years of life confers no greater utility than one that saves only a few. This is a case in which both ex ante utility and ex post utility are relevant to the choice of policy. Where the former seems clearly preferable is in cases in which choices sensible when made turn out badly: one takes a fair gamble, but loses and now wants one's stake returned. To use assessments of ex post utility to invalidate ex ante choices would greatly reduce the scope of free choice. In the long run, ex post as well as ex ante utility—utility, period—would be diminished. But if young and old dread death equally, the only basis for choosing between them, if a choice must be made, may be the difference in ex post utility—that the young person will live longer if he is saved.

Even so, it is merely likely, not certain, that medical research that primarily benefits the old is a poorer investment from the social standpoint than medical research that primarily benefits the middle-aged.[20] Consider two alternative medical investments, costing the same and having the same probability of success. (These qualifications are vital and should be borne in mind throughout the discussion. The net benefits of a research program depend not only on the benefits if the program is successful, including spillovers to research on other diseases, but also on the cost of the program and the probability of success.) One investment will extend the life of an 80-year-old to 85 and the other the life of a 60-year-old to 80. In strictly financial terms, the former is quite likely to be the better (which is not to say a good) investment. For it will add "only" 5 years of old age, while the latter

19. For evidence that improved treatment of the characteristic diseases of elderly people is responsible for much of the increase in longevity in recent decades, see George C. Myers and Kenneth G. Manton, "The Rate of Population Aging: New Views of Epidemiologic Transitions," in *Aging: The Universal Human Experience* 263 (George L. Maddox and E. W. Busse, eds., 1987).

20. Cf. Tomas J. Philipson and Richard A. Posner, *Private Choices and Public Health: An Economic Perspective on the AIDS Epidemic* 120–125 (1993), and references cited there, discussing the possible fiscal savings from a disease that kills young people.

investment will add 5 years of productive life and (assuming retirement at age 65) 15 years of old age during which the individual will be receiving social security retirement benefits and incurring heavy, and heavily subsidized, health costs.[21] Those costs may be especially heavy because the individual is constitutionally weak, which is why he would have died at the age of 60 had it not been for the new medical technology.

But costs to the public fisc do not exhaust the considerations relevant to evaluating a public investment. Success in fighting the disease that kills the younger individual is, as we just saw, likely to create greater nonfinancial utility than a similar success with a disease of the old. This is not only because more years of life will be saved and most people derive utility from living, and not only because healthy younger years may confer more utility than sickly older ones. It is also because the older a person is, the fewer surviving family members he is likely to have and the less they are likely to grieve at his death.[22] (The costs of death are not borne by the dying person alone.) I conclude that failing to give priority to life-threatening diseases of the young would signify an inefficient allocation of resources to medical research unless the old were being short-changed in other government services that their taxes support, which is unlikely, or unless medical research on the diseases of the elderly would produce much greater savings of life relative to expenditures.

These are important qualifications and another is that efforts to cure diseases that are greatly feared because they cause premature death will willy-nilly prolong the lives of old people. Heart disease and cancer are principal examples, except to the extent that research can fruitfully be separated between forms of these diseases that affect the young more and those that affect the old more. The incidence of a number of cancers differs dramatically by age group. For example, the incidence of Hodgkin's disease persons is higher in the 20 to 24 age group than in the 85 and over group (4.8 versus 3.8 per 100,000), while conversely the incidence of prostate

21. Thomas Schelling, "Value of Life," in *The New Palgrave Social Economics* 269, 270 (John Eatwel, Murray Milgate, and Peter Newman, eds., 1989). In this vein, it has been argued that "smokers 'save' the Social Security system hundreds of billions of dollars." John B. Shoven, Jeffrey O. Sundberg, and John P. Bunker, "The Social Security Cost of Smoking," in *The Economics of Aging* 231, 244 (David A. Wise, ed., 1989); see also W. G. Manning et al., "The Taxes of Sin: Do Smokers and Drinkers Pay Their Way," 261 *JAMA (Journal of the American Medical Association)* 1604 (1989).

22. Weighting number of family members by closeness of kinship. The longer a person lives, the more likely he is to have surviving grandchildren and other remote descendants, but they are much less likely to grieve deeply for him than a spouse, a parent, or a young child. Another factor in the comparison, to which I return shortly, is the *quality* of additional years of life to young and to old people respectively.

cancer is 0.0 per 100,000 in the younger age group and 328.8 per 100,000 in the older.[23]

Still another complication is that young people are better able than old ones to avoid disease by making changes in their style of living, as by giving up cigarettes, losing weight, reducing the amount of fat in their diet, or moderating their intake of alcohol; most elderly people have already made these changes. The effect of better treatment for diseases of the young may be to induce the young to relapse into unhealthful habits, since those habits cost less the lower the expected disease costs to which the habits give rise. Such relapses, possibly illustrated by the recent increase in obesity in the American population,[24] reduce the effectiveness of medical research on diseases of the young, although they confer net utility on the young.

Another implication of the analysis in this section is that, other things being equal, from a strictly financial standpoint more resources should be devoted to the prevention and treatment of mental illnesses than of physical illnesses. The former are more likely to increase disability without shortening life, so curing them is more likely to remove a disability than to lengthen life. Enabling a person to become a productive worker, without lengthening his life, lowers the ratio of dependent to productive persons. It might therefore be in the interest of the old as a group to support some reallocation of research and treatment funds to mental illnesses.

The question of gender. A neglected and sensitive issue—neglected perhaps because it is sensitive—is the allocation of public funds between research on diseases of old men and research on diseases of old women. We saw in chapter 2 that the life expectancy of women in the United States greatly exceeds that of men and that the difference translates into a decided preponderance of women in the older age groups. Justice between the sexes might seem to require, therefore, that medical research on the diseases of the old be tilted in favor of diseases, such as prostate cancer and coronary artery disease, that kill old men but not (or, as in the case of coronary artery disease, not as soon) old women.[25] Feminists might object that women

23. U.S. Dept. of Health and Human Services, National Cancer Institute, "Annual Cancer Statistics Review, Including Cancer Trends: 1950–1985" III.B.30 (Jan. 1988).

24. Marian Burros, "Despite Awareness of Risks, More in U.S. Are Getting Fat," *New York Times* (national ed.), July 17, 1994, p. 1.

25. In 1990, cancers of the genital organs, which include the prostate, killed 358.5 out of 100,000 men in the 75–84 age group but only 95.3 out of 100,000 women, a difference of almost 4 to 1. U.S. Bureau of the Census, note 15 above, at 97 (ser. 133). Heart disease of all types killed, in this age group, 2,968.2 men out of every 100,000 but only 1,893.8 women. Id. at 96 (ser. 132).

should not be penalized for their "natural" advantage in longevity over men. But such an objection would rest on a biological essentialism rejected by feminists in most other policy settings, such as maternity leave, pregnancy benefits, and abortion rights. Nor is it much of an argument that the greater longevity of women merely compensates them for the higher death rates of women before medicine eliminated most of the risk of dying in childbirth. Women who died long ago are not compensated by the longer life expectancy of modern women.

Here are better, though not necessarily decisive, arguments against trying to equalize the life expectancies of men and women. First, government should not buy into the feminist rejection of biological essentialism and try to offset natural differences between the sexes—especially since government has not as yet done much to offset the natural disadvantages of women. (The abolition of the military draft *eliminated* a traditional advantage of women.) Second, women can take steps to reduce their own life expectancy and increase that of their husbands. Third, women's natural advantage in longevity may be, in part anyway, illusory; as the occupational profiles of men and women converge, so may their mortality statistics. Robert Arking reports an estimate "that about 18% of the sex differential in total mortality may be due to . . . sex-specific hormonal effects on the cardiovascular system, and thus may well represent an intrinsic and perhaps unchangeable risk to males," while "at least 55% . . . can be attributed to destructive behaviors,"[26] such as smoking, which are influenced by occupation and other social factors. Even if women do not become as self-destructive as men as the occupational profiles of the two sexes converge, so that a "voluntary" difference in longevity persists, to pour research funds into diseases avoidable by behavioral changes will reduce the incentive to make those changes and so may have only a minimal effect on the difference.

Fourth, to the extent that men are inherently more vulnerable than women, expenditures on fighting the diseases of men may have a lower payoff in years of life saved because "competition" between diseases to kill men is more intense. A hundred million dollars spent to develop a cure for some disease of women might add a month to female longevity, yet the same expenditure to develop a cure for a disease of men that had the same prevalence might add only three weeks to male longevity.

26. Robert Arking, *Biology of Aging: Observations and Principles* 223 (1991); see also William R. Hazzard, "Why Do Women Live Longer Than Men? Biologic Differences That Influence Longevity," 85 *Postgraduate Medicine* 271 (1989).

Table 11.1 Government Expenditures per Death for Various
Diseases

Disease	Expenditures per Death
AIDS	$79,000
Cervical cancer	7,300
Diabetes	6,300
Kidney disease	5,100
Breast cancer	2,800
Heart disease	1,100
Prostate cancer	800
Lung cancer	600
Stroke	600

So there may be substantial unexploited gains from expenditures on research into the diseases of women. This would be especially likely if at present the research budget were heavily tilted in favor of men, but table 11.1 suggests that it is not.[27] Notice the much higher ratio of expenditures to deaths for breast and cervical cancer (female) compared to heart disease, lung cancer, and prostate cancer (primarily or exclusively male). It is true that AIDS, a disease predominantly of men, swamps all the other diseases, so far as generosity of government spending is concerned. But AIDS is not a disease of *elderly* men. Of all AIDS cases reported in the United States through June 1994, only 2 percent were of men aged 60–64 at age of diagnosis and only 1 percent were of men 65 or older at age of diagnosis.[28]

Yet even if old men are not being favored by the research establishment, the fact remains that a dollar spent on fighting women's diseases is likely to buy more longevity than a dollar spent on fighting men's diseases. This may seem a conclusive economic argument against reallocating medical expenditures from old women to old men, by establishing that the marginal benefit of curing women's disease must exceed that of curing men's diseases. It establishes no such thing. Utility and longevity are related, but they are not interchangeable. A simple form of the relation is given by

27. The source for the data in table 11.1 is "Sickness and Politics: The Influence of Disease Advocates: Cancer vs. AIDS," *Cancer Weekly,* June 8, 1992.

28. U.S. Dept. of Health and Human Services, Centers for Disease Control and Prevention, *HIV/AIDS Surveillance Report,* Mid-Year Edition, 1994, p. 13 (tab. 8). The corresponding percentages for women are 1 (60–64) and 2 (65 and over), but fewer than 20 percent of all cases in the 60-and-over age group are women. Id. at 13 (tab. 8).

$$U = N \cdot Y \cdot V(R). \qquad (11.1)$$

U is the utility of spending one more dollar for medical research on a disease that is likely to shorten the life of either men or women. N is the number of either elderly men or elderly women and Y is the average number of years of life, per individual of the given sex, that the additional dollar spent on medical research saves. V is the value to the average individual of each unit of Y and is a function of R $(= N_m/N_w)$, the ratio of elderly men to elderly women.

In this equation, a shorter extension of life (Y) for men, and even a smaller number of men (N), can be offset by a higher value per unit of additional life (V). Given the imbalance between the number of elderly men and the number of elderly women, an extra month of life for an elderly woman is not necessarily worth as much (in a utilitarian, not a financial, sense) as an extra month of life for an elderly man. That is, V_w may be lower than V_m, offsetting the effect of Y_w's being higher than Y_m. Notice the dual significance of N, the number of men (or women). The more women there are, the more, other things being equal, research expenditures that extend the lives of women will increase total utility. But the more women there are *relative to men* (in other words, the smaller R is), the likelier is the value of extending the life of an elderly man by a given amount to exceed the value of extending the life of an elderly woman by the same amount (that is, $dV_w(R)/dR > 0$, $dV_m(R)/dR < 0$), since a scarcity of elderly men increases women's demand for longer male life.

The trade-off can be made more transparent by breaking equation 11.1 into two equations, one for men and one for women, as in

$$U_m = N_m \cdot Y_m \cdot V_m(R), \qquad (11.2)$$

$$U_w = N_w \cdot Y_w \cdot V_w(R), \qquad (11.3)$$

and then substituting N_m/N_w for R. It is easily shown that U_m will exceed U_w—the expenditure on the men's disease will create the greater utility—if

$$Y_m/Y_w \cdot V_m(N_m/N_w)/V_w(N_m/N_w) \cdot N_m/N_w > 1. \qquad (11.4)$$

I have assumed that the first term is smaller than 1—that a dollar expended on fighting women's diseases will extend life by more than a dollar expended on fighting men's diseases. And the third term also—there are more old women than old men. But what about the second term? The lower the ratio of old men to old women, the likelier is the second term, which measures the relative value of extending elderly male versus elderly female life by a given amount, to exceed 1. It may do so by enough to make the inequality hold. Of course, to the extent that men benefit from a surplus of women, an increase in the ratio of men to women reduces the value of increased male longevity to men; but I assume that this offset is slight.

The argument that I have sketched may sound, if not sexist, at least adverse to women's interests. Not so. Women as a group might benefit from policies that promoted greater equality in the number of elderly men and women—for example policies that added a year to female longevity but two years to male longevity—because it would give elderly women a greater prospect of male companionship, something many of them greatly value,[29] though radical feminists believe them mistaken to do so. We know from chapter 6 that the continuation of sexual activity on the part of elderly women is heavily dependent on marital status.[30] And—though this will change as women work more and accrue greater pension rights—elderly women who are married are far better off financially than ones who live alone.[31] A much higher fraction of men than of women aged 65 and over are married, and the disparity grows with age. Male-female differences in widowhood are particularly striking. In the 65–69 age group, only 7.3 percent of men, but 33.8 percent of women, are widowed; in the 80–84 age group, the figures are 27.3 and 72.3 percent.[32] These disparities would be smaller if men lived as long as women.

In the language of economics, male longevity is *complementary* to female. Hence an increase in male longevity will benefit women, who may therefore be willing to pay ex ante by a reallocation of medical resources from the prevention and cure of women's diseases to the prevention and cure of men's diseases.

This suggestion will seem less outré if one understands its relation to the question whether to shift some medical resources from the diseases of older people to the diseases of younger people. If adding a year of life to a 65-year-old would confer greater utility than adding a year of life to a 75-year-old, then adding a year of life to an old man is likely to confer greater utility than adding a year of life to an old woman, quite apart from the imbalance in numbers, simply because the average old man is younger than

29. For evidence, see Jane Traupmann, Elaine Eckels, and Elaine Hatfield, "Intimacy in Older Women's Lives," 22 *Gerontologist* 493 (1982).

30. For other evidence of the importance of marriage to many older women, see id.; and Timothy H. Brubaker, "Families in Later Life: A Burgeoning Research Area," 52 *Journal of Marriage and the Family* 959, 965–966 (1990).

31. F. N. Schwenk, "Women 65 Years or Older: A Comparison of Economic Well-Being by Living Arrangement," 4 *Family Economics Review*, no. 3, 1991, p. 2.

32. Jacob S. Siegel, *A Generation of Change: A Profile of America's Older Population* 364–365 (1993) (tab. 6A.1).

the average old woman. Notice that this analysis also implies that it might be a good idea to shift medical resources from diseases that particularly endanger whites to those that particularly endanger blacks, given the substantially shorter life expectancy of blacks than of whites. Yet the case for shifting medical resources from women to men is actually stronger than that for shifting such resources either from whites to blacks or from older to younger persons regardless of sex. Once again, the reason is selection bias. A 75-year-old with one year to live may be no more unhealthy than a 65-year-old with one year to live, since the older person, simply by virtue of having survived longer, is likely to have aged more slowly. But in the case of reallocation between the sexes, keeping the (weaker) male alive another year benefits not only him but also his spouse, by postponing her widowhood; and the only cost is that her life as a widow will end (in her death) slightly sooner than if the resources devoted to keeping her husband alive another year were devoted to her instead.

I hope it is clear that I am not *advocating* a reallocation of medical resources from women's to men's diseases. Whether that would be a good thing to do from an economic standpoint requires, at a minimum, plugging numbers into the variables in my equations, something I have not attempted to do. I merely suggest that it is a matter that deserves to be studied. It should not be dismissed out of hand, as one might be tempted to do.

Quality and quantity of life. Age is an issue not only in fiscal decisions concerning health care and medical research, but also in decisions regarding medical treatment. When medical resources are short, as in the classic triage situation, and price is not used to clear the market, should age be a criterion of the decision whom to treat? It frequently is used as a criterion, to the disadvantage of the elderly. English doctors will not provide dialysis to "elderly" sufferers (>55) from kidney disease, and American doctors use age as a criterion for determining admission to the last open bed in intensive-care units and for eligibility for a heart transplant.[33] The use of this criterion is often defensible on strictly "medical" grounds—the elderly patient may be much less likely to survive or otherwise benefit from the procedure than the younger competitor. But not always. What to do?

If it is a true triage situation, so that the question is not how many resources shall go to this group or to that group but who shall die, the use of an age criterion should be relatively uncontroversial. Giving the treat-

33. Kilner, note 3 above, at 77–78. For criticism, see Nancy S. Jecker and Lawrence J. Schneiderman, "Is Dying Young Worse Than Dying Old?" 70 *Gerontologist* 66, 70 (1994).

ment preference to the young will maximize the quantity of life saved, and even more the quality-weighted quantity, since the utility of life tends to decrease with age. Dread of death is on both sides of the balance, so drops out, making a comparison of utilities appropriate.

But we must be careful not to endorse, uncritically, resource decisions that *create* triage situations and by doing so make the use of an age criterion deceptively reasonable. If the number of intensive-care beds is chosen so that managers of intensive-care units are often forced to choose between giving the last empty bed to a young person or to an old person, we should consider whether the nation has sufficient intensive-care capacity. Reducing capacity in order to force the "easy" choice between saving a young life and an old life is akin to not informing elderly persons about treatment options.

So the use of age criteria to allocate medical resources is tricky. But some of the arguments against it are poor. An example is the argument that it is inconsistent with punishing murderers of elderly people as heavily as murderers of young people. No social purpose would be served by encouraging the murder of elderly people by punishing such murder more lightly. The objective of most criminal statutes is to punish the criminal as heavily as is consistent with maintaining marginal deterrence and economizing on expenditures on the criminal-justice system.[34] Neither of these constraints points to a punishment "discount" for murdering the elderly. It is true that "mercy killing," mainly of elderly people, is usually punished more lightly than other murders. Many mercy killings are akin or even equivalent to assisted suicide, which ought probably to carry a different moral charge from murder, although the discussion in the preceding chapter cannot be considered decisive on the question; the discussion was confined to *physician*-assisted suicide. But even people adamantly opposed to legalizing any form of mercy killing do not usually favor punishing the mercy killer as severely as other deliberate killers. No more should they insist that age be ignored when a choice has to be made between saving the life of a young person and saving the life of an old one.

I have touched on the distinction between longevity and quality of life, or between quantity and quality of life, and I want to examine it a little more closely. We have seen that the expected-utility perspective has limitations when the issue is understanding the behavior of old people or evalu-

---

34. Richard A. Posner, "An Economic Theory of the Criminal Law," 85 *Columbia Law Review* 1193 (1985).

ating normative questions concerning them. But it is very helpful in framing the issue of quality versus quantity of life.[35] In a rough but serviceable way (ignoring complications like discounting) we can say that people want to maximize the product of quantity times quality of life. So 10 years of life each of which would confer 100 utiles would yield a lower expected utility than 8 years of life each of which would confer 150 utiles, and therefore the shorter life expectancy will be preferred. I argued that women might actually prefer a slightly shorter life expectancy if the consequence were to increase the utility of their lives when old by making it more likely that they would have male companionship. Their expected utility might be greater. This is not the only thing that society should consider in making decisions on the allocation of medical resources, but it is one thing.

And it has implications for the allocation of medical resources between research on lethal and on nonlethal diseases, say between research on heart disease and research on deafness. One thing or rather pair of things that greatly reduces the utility of elderly life is failing eyesight and hearing, which particularly in tandem make a person feel cut off from life and greatly curtail the range of his or her activities. Yet blindness and deafness have only a slight effect on life expectancy. They reduce the quality rather than the quantity of life. But once it is recognized that expected utility is a product of both quality and quantity, it is no longer obvious that the balance of research on the diseases of the elderly should be heavily skewed, or skewed at all, in favor of the life-threatening diseases. A 2 percent reduction in the prevalence of blindness among elderly people might contribute more to the expected utility of elderly life than a 2 percent increase in elderly life expectancy. Advances in cataract surgery must have contributed greatly to the quality of life of the elderly.

Unfortunately, nothing in the analysis so far supplies a formula for determining how much of society's wealth to devote to the health of elderly people. To the extent that people finance their own consumption in old age, including consumption of medical resources, out of their own pocket (and without the help of any tax subsidies—that is, without dipping into the taxpayer's pocket indirectly as well as directly), by accepting a lower standard of living in their youth and middle age, there is, as I hope I have shown, very little basis for begrudging them a medically affluent old age. The difficult question is how large a claim on public resources they should

35. The expected-utility approach to normative issues in health economics is illustrated by George Tolley et al., "The Use of Health Values in Policy," in *Valuing Health for Policy: An Economic Approach*, note 11 above, at 345. This essay includes an interesting discussion of the benefits of curing senile dementia. Id. at 368–375.

have. Multiple-selves analysis—that normative mischief maker—merely helps to show how difficult the question is. It does not point to a solution. But we may be able to get some help in answering the question by inquiring how much the elderly are taking (through tax and expenditure policies, and in other ways) from the other age groups today and what political checks exist on their taking more tomorrow. These issues will preoccupy us in the remainder of the chapter.

Social Security and Redistribution

If for some purposes an individual is a different person when young and when old, for other purposes he is the same person. Most of us do not want to kill our future old self or even take steps that will impair its longevity, not because we have a sense of responsibility to our body's cotenant but because we consider that future old person to be ourself. The issue of multiple selves arises only in those exceptional cases in which the younger self decides as it were to abandon the older one. It appears to be largely myth that before social security "the vast majority of Americans lived only for the economic moment." [36] David Fischer, whose assessment I have just quoted, supports it with the statement that "in 1910, when the first serious attempt was made to determine the economic status of elderly people in Massachusetts, the findings were grim. Nearly one out of four [of persons 65 or older] were on the dole." [37] Yet his own figures show that the vast majority of these "dole" people were receiving Civil War pensions, and the ratio of the size of those pensions to average wage rates was only slightly lower than the ratio of social security retirement benefits to average wage rates today.[38] Only 7.6 percent of the people in the survey on which Fischer relied were receiving charity or poor relief.[39] All the others (apart from a tiny number in prison) either were classified as "not dependent" or were receiving federal pensions.[40]

36. David Hackett Fischer, *Growing Old in America* 164 (1977).

37. Id. at 161.

38. Judith Treas, "The Historical Decline in Late-Life Labor Force Participation in the United States," in *Age, Health, and Employment* 158, 164–165 (James E. Birren, Pauline K. Robinson, and Judy E. Livingston, eds., 1986).

39. Computed from Fischer, note 36 above, at 161 n. 5.

40. For other evidence that long before social security most elderly Americans were adequately even if not generously provided for, see Carole Haber and Brian Gratton, *Old Age and the Search for Security: An American Social History* (1994), esp. ch. 2; Carolyn L. Weaver, "On the Lack of a Political Market for Compulsory Old-Age Insurance prior to the Great Depression: Insights from Economic Theories of Government," 20 *Explorations in Economic History* 294, 302–316 (1983).

In the normal case, which is that of people sufficiently regardful of their future selves to make at least minimally adequate provision for their old age, it is problematic to speak of a redistribution of wealth from young to old or the subsidizing of the old by the young. Even so, it might seem that laws compelling pension contributions and otherwise granting entitlements to the old might interfere with the preferred pattern of consumption over the life course, even for people who want to have a long and healthy old age. For they may not want to allocate as large a share of their lifetime consumption to their old age as the laws try to make them do. If forced by law to do so, once they get old they will (unless they have a strong bequest motive) live high on the hog, as they cannot redistribute wealth to their younger selves. Yet even when old they may regret that they could not have consumed a larger fraction of their lifetime income when they were young.

This scenario is implausible, it is true, so long as the compulsory benefits and the taxes required to defray them are modest in relation to the covered individual's income. For then he can achieve his desired allocation of consumption over the life course by altering the time profile of his earnings stream, taking less in the form of retirement benefits and more in current income, or by borrowing more when he is young, enabling him to consume more now and less later (when he has to repay his loans). These possibilities may seem to confine the effects of social security to those young selves who care nothing about their old selves—who would like to let them starve. Not so. The program has potentially significant redistributive effects unrelated to the issue of multiple selves; it redistributes wealth among different individuals. Two types of redistributive effect should be distinguished: intragenerational, which is to say the effect on the relative incomes of persons born at the same time, and intergenerational—the effect on the relative incomes of persons born in different generations.[41] Because social security benefits do not rise with income as fast as the social security tax does, the social security program redistributes income from more to less affluent participants of the same age cohort. This effect is reduced but not eliminated by the fact that income and longevity are positively correlated, so that the more affluent tend to collect social security benefits for a longer period.[42]

The more dramatic redistributive effect, however, is intergenerational. The creation of the social security program in 1935 conferred a windfall on

41. For a careful analysis and a review of the literature, see Nancy Wolff, *Income Redistribution and the Social Security Program* (1987).

42. Id. at 124–125.

those persons who were eligible for immediate retirement benefits under it, since they had paid no social security tax. (A similar windfall was conferred on the elderly thirty years later by the creation of the Medicare program.) Their social security benefits were a straight transfer from persons of working age who were paying the tax, though of course some of these taxpayers were sufficiently near retirement age to be able to anticipate a net benefit from social security, paid for by still younger taxpayers. As time passed, lengthening the period during which social security recipients had been employed and paid taxes, the intergenerational transfer diminished, and it has been estimated that persons born in 1960 or later have (unless they are very poor) negative expected benefits from social security.[43]

The redistributive effects of social security are the consequence of its "pay as you go" character, and so would be eliminated if, as in a defined-contribution plan, a person was entitled to social security benefits equal to the annuity that he could purchase with his social security tax payments, no more, no less. A system in which the taxpayer supports the retiree rather than the retiree supporting himself out of his own deferral of consumption invites each generation of old people to use their concentrated political might to plunder the young. Such a system is also highly sensitive to shifts in the ratio of the nonworking to the working population and therefore to birth and immigration rates, retirement ages, the female labor-force participation rate, the unemployment rate, and the longevity of old people—all factors that are both difficult to predict and difficult to influence by changes in social security policy. The rise in the dependency ratio expected early in the twenty-first century (see chapter 2) may require a steep increase in social security taxes in order to maintain the value of social security benefits. Consider a simple model of a pay-as-you-go system in which social security retirement income (r) is generated by a tax at a constant rate t on the wages (w) of workers, where W is the number of workers and R the number of retired persons. Then

$$rR = twW, \tag{11.5}$$

or equivalently,

$$t = (R/W)(r/w). \tag{11.6}$$

43. Michael J. Boskin et al., "Social Security: A Financial Appraisal across and within Generations," 40 *National Tax Journal* 19, 23 (1987). On "generational accounting" generally, see Alan J. Auerbach, Jagadeesh Gokhale, and Laurence J. Kotlikoff, "Generational Accounting: A Meaningful Way to Evaluate Fiscal Policy," *Journal of Economic Perspectives,* Winter 1994, p. 73; and for criticism, see Robert Haveman, "Should Generational Accounts Replace Public Budgets and Deficits?" in id. at 95.

If *R/W,* the dependency ratio, rises by 20 percent, the social security tax rate would have to rise by 20 percent too in order to maintain the existing ratio of retirement to working income.

The effect of an increase in the dependency ratio on the total cost of a retirement system that, like ours, has a medical-care component (Medicare) is magnified by the increased medical expense associated with increased longevity. Annual days of hospital care per person rise from 2.1 for persons aged 65 to 74 to 4.0 for those 75 and above.[44] An increase in longevity thus increases not only the number of years in which a retired person receives benefits but also the annual level of those benefits, when health benefits are included in the retirement package along with a pension. It is no surprise that several foreign countries, including Chile and Singapore, are moving toward a system in which each age cohort finances its own retirement.[45]

Yet in tension with his recent criticism of the pay-as-you-go system,[46] Gary Becker has argued that the system can be viewed as a fair contract between young and old. Adults of working age pay taxes to support the public school system, in effect lending the young money with which to purchase human capital. The young repay the loan when they become adults of working age and the generation that paid for their public school education reaches retirement age, by defraying, through social security taxes, some of the living expenses and medical expenses of that genera-tion.[47] This is an aspect of the earlier point that since our old selves have no vote until we become old, the current old act as their proxies. The point is overlooked in the standard analyses of the redistributive effects of social security because those analyses consider only social security taxes, not school taxes, in figuring the extent to which recipients of social security benefits paid for them when employed.

Another argument for pay as you go is that, contrary to appearances,

44. U.S. Bureau of the Census, note 15 above, at 125 (ser. 185). The figures are for 1991.

45. Gary S. Becker and Isaac Ehrlich, "Social Security: Foreign Lessons," *Wall Street Jour-nal* (midwest ed.), March 30, 1994, p. A18.

46. See id.

47. Gary S. Becker, *A Treatise on the Family* 369–374 (enlarged ed. 1991). The principle of our pay-as-you-go public pension scheme must be distinguished from its actual design, in which practical and political considerations have combined to produce many anomalies. See, for ex-ample, Jonathan Barry Forman, "Promoting Fairness in the Social Security Retirement Program: Partial Integration and a Credit for Dual-Earner Couples," 45 *Tax Lawyer* 915, 926–948 (1992). And Becker does not explain the political mechanism by which a fair contract is struck between different generations; school taxes, on the one hand, and social security taxes and benefits, on the other, are set by different branches of government—by state and local legislatures, and by Con-gress, respectively. It is therefore unclear how a fair contract of the sort suggested by Becker might have emerged from the political process.

the social security system is conferring benefits on the current generation of working age, as well as on the recipients of social security. In the absence of social security, the burden of maintaining the old would fall to a great extent on the younger members of their families. Much of the political momentum for social security came from the added burden on the young and middle-aged when the Depression threw a number of elderly people out of work and many others lost their savings.[48] The problem would be less acute today because private pensions are a larger source of wealth. Yet millions of elderly people still depend on their social security retirement benefits for a decent standard of living, and many of them could not or would not save enough for their old age in the absence of social security.

Even with social security, a considerable burden of elder care falls on adult children (especially women).[49] This may be due in part to the fact that Medicare does not defray the cost of the nonmedical assistance required by many elderly people, and in part to the failure of the private insurance market to offer nursing-home insurance or other long-term elder-care insurance on attractive terms.[50] That failure may be due to radical uncertainty about the future costs of elder care, which are a function of longevity as well as of changes in the price of such care. But a more interesting suggestion is that the demand for such insurance is weak because it primarily protects bequests, since elderly people can, by spending down their assets, qualify for free nursing-home care from the state.[51] A related possibility, suggested by multiple-selves analysis, is that people may decline to buy such insurance because they do not want to transfer income to their future old, sick, quite possibly demented self. This would be consistent with wanting to protect one's consumption in one's *healthy* old age, since long-term care is for the unhealthy. It is not a complete answer. People who are not particu-

48. Brian Gratton, "The Creation of Retirement: Families, Individuals, and the Social Security Movement," in *Societal Impact on Aging: Historical Perspectives* 45, 61–68 (K. Warner Schaie and W. Andrew Achenbaum, eds., 1993).

49. Roxanne Jamshidi et al., "Aging in America: Limits to Life Span and Elderly Care Options," 2 *Population Research and Policy Review* 169, 174–176 (1992); Barbara Adolf, "How to Minimize Disruption Caused by Employees Taking Care of Elderly Relative," 3 *Journal of Compensation and Benefits* 291 (1988).

50. See Jane G. Gavelle and Jack Taylor, "Financing Long-Term Care for the Elderly," 42 *National Tax Journal* 219 (1989); Joseph P. Newhouse, "Comment on Predicting Nursing Home Utilization among the High-Risk Elderly," in *Issues in the Economics of Aging* 200, 202–203 (David A. Wise, ed., 1990).

51. Mark V. Pauly, "The Rational Nonpurchase of Long-Term-Care Insurance," 98 *Journal of Political Economy* 153 (1990).

larly altruistic toward their old selves may be altruistic toward their children and may fear that the latter will incur expenses to care for them. These people may not be worried about protecting bequests—they may not anticipate having any money to leave their children—yet may not wish to impose a kind of "negative bequest" in the form of a burden of support on their children.

Of course to speak of the "burden" of obligations assumed voluntarily, however reluctantly, is to depart from the usual conventions of economic analysis. The vestigial laws mentioned in chapter 9 requiring people to support their destitute parents are not a significant factor compelling Americans to take care of their helpless or impoverished parents, so if they do so they must "want" to. But while many adult children are sufficiently altruistic toward their aged parents to be willing to incur substantial costs in money, time, irritation, distress, and even revulsion rather than neglect or abandon them, they would greatly prefer to shift the burden of caring for their parents, or at least a part of the burden, onto other shoulders. Elder care thus differs from types of consumption from which people derive pleasure. There is plenty of evidence that a sense of filial obligation, like other moral sentiments, can be a source of cost to the person feeling it.[52] From the standpoint of distributive equity, therefore, social security can be defended (how strongly I shall not consider) as spreading at least the monetary component of the burden of elder care among the entire current generation. The greatest benefit is to people in small families; an only child faces a greater burden of supporting his parents in their old age than a child who has many siblings with whom to share it. But as it is large families that derive the greater benefit from school taxes because they have more children to educate and school taxes do not vary with the number of the taxpayer's children,[53] it is at least rough justice that small families should derive the greater benefit from social security.

If we think of the "voluntary" care of the elderly by their families as a

52. See, for example, Nancy J. Finley, M. Diane Roberts, and Benjamin F. Banahan, III, "Motivators and Inhibitors of Attitudes of Filial Obligation toward Aging Parents," 28 *Gerontologist* 73 (1988). Even in Japan, famous for filial piety (see chapter 9), the fall in the size of families, which increases the burden on the younger members of caring for the elderly members, has contributed to a large expansion in public provision of services to elderly persons. Daisaku Maeda, "Family Care of Impaired Elderly in Japan," in *Aging: The Universal Human Experience* 493, 497 (George L. Maddox and E. W. Busse, eds., 1987).

53. At least if we ignore the taxes those children will pay when they grow up and go to work. David Friedman, "Laissez-Faire in Population: The Least Bad Solution" 13 (Population Council 1972).

form of "tax" that transfers wealth from young to old, it becomes relevant to note that the tax is growing. It is growing both because the ratio of elderly people who require care to the number of young and middle-aged people is growing and because the market opportunity costs of women's time are growing.

Even if the intergenerational-contract aspect of social security is set to one side, the size of the transfer from young to old that is brought about by government programs such as social security is difficult to estimate. Federal expenditures benefiting the elderly amounted to $387 billion in 1991,[54] but this is not a net figure. Some fraction of the social security benefits received by the elderly merely offset the contributions they made when they were working and paying social security tax, and can thus be viewed as an annuity for which they paid, rather than a transfer to them. The net transfer varies enormously across persons, depending on income, family situation, the length of time that the person worked, and (since both social security taxes and social security retirement benefits are constantly changing) the person's age cohort.[55] In addition, the elderly pay many billions of dollars in income and other taxes.[56] Although they also receive the benefit of the governmental services that those taxes defray, if they receive fewer such services than other age groups (as is plainly the case with school taxes) their taxes would be offsetting some of the social security benefits that they receive. A further complication is that by encouraging people to retire earlier than they otherwise would, social security reduces the amount of income tax paid by elderly people. There is also the complication introduced by the growing burden of the family elder-care "tax."

The unknown adjustment required by the intergenerational-contract aspect of social security and the adjustment required by its annuity aspect are not additive. If the intergenerational-contract approach is sound, the

54. U.S. Senate Special Committee on Aging et al., note 4 above, at 239 (tab. 8-1).

55. It is estimated that for the cohort that retired in the early 1970s the transfer component in their social security retirement benefits ranged from about 77 to 89 percent. Wolff, note 41 above, at 43; Richard V. Burkhauser and Jennifer L. Warlock, "Disentangling the Annuity from the Redistribution Aspects of Social Security in the United States," 27 *Review of Income and Wealth* 401, 407 (1981). For the cohort retiring in the middle 1980s it has been estimated that the transfer component fell to about 67 percent. Michael J. Boskin et al., note 43 above, at 20.

56. Barry Windheim and Charles Crossed, "Salaries and Wages Reported on Income Tax Returns, by Marital Status and Age, 1983," *Statistics of Income Bulletin,* Winter 1987–1988, pp. 65, 73–75 (tabs. 6–9); Sheldon Danziger et al., "Income Transfers and the Economic Status of the Elderly," in *Economic Transfers in the United States* 239, 256 (Marilyn Moon, ed., 1984). I have not found more recent data.

social security taxes paid by workers are not contributions to their own pensions but reimbursements of the cost borne by their parents' generation in educating them.

Old Age and Democratic Theory

So we do not know how large the net transfer from young to old is, but it probably is positive rather than negative and it may be very large.[57] There would be little reason for concern if it reflected merely a spontaneous outpouring of altruism or affection by the working part of the population for the old. But this is implausible, for reasons explored in chapter 9. There is altruism toward people afflicted by conditions such as poverty and ill health which may be correlated (nowadays mostly the latter) with old age, but the natural response would be to try to alleviate those conditions rather than to scatter bounty over the old as a class. The present scale of transfers to elderly, whether just or unjust as a matter of moral or economic theory,[58] would be incomprehensible were it not for their political power. That power is an accident of the fact that, as explained in chapter 6, the low cost of time of the elderly, the homogeneity of their interests, and the disfranchisement of children makes the elderly a highly effective political pressure group on behalf of policies that favor them.

Nothing in political or moral theory implies that a group which votes more heavily than its percentage of the population because it has low costs of time, and votes disproportionately effectively because of the focus and homogeneity of its interests, is *morally* entitled to the political power that these attributes confer. To the extent that the old can be trusted to vote disinterestedly, their disproportionate power would not be very troubling. But they cannot be trusted so, because they have a strong interest in policies that redistribute wealth toward them. This interest is not much mitigated by the altruistic feelings of old people toward their children and grandchildren. The altruistic elderly can offset public transfers to them by making gifts or bequests if they want, and this course is preferable to them to losing the transfers, because it maximizes the power of the old. Although elderly people may be more disinterested voters than younger ones because the expected gains and losses to them from particular policies are truncated by

---

57. See Danziger et al., note 56 above, at 264.

58. Becker, note 47 above, at 370–373, presents some evidence that the elderly are not being over-repaid for the "loan" they made to the young to finance the latter's education. Nor is it certain that the elderly are receiving more than our future elderly selves would legitimately demand if they had a voice in current policy deliberations.

the prospect of death, this is probably not a very important factor either. Most elderly people have a significant remaining life expectancy, and those near death are unlikely to vote.

I do not mean to suggest that age is the only factor that influences a vote by an older person; for example, educated old people may vote for public school bond issues because they value education, even though they do not have children of school age.[59] There are nevertheless grounds for concern that the elderly have disproportionate voting power, especially in contrast to the disenfranchised at the other end of the age continuum—children. A Utopian solution would be to give each child a vote, half of which would be cast by each parent. It would not be an unworkable or even a particularly cumbersome solution. The danger of fraud would presumably be no greater than in the case of the dependent deduction from income tax, and it would probably be less since the gains from fraud would be smaller. This child-weighted voting scheme would go some way toward redressing a political balance that appears to be skewed in favor of the interests of those who are nearing the end of their life and against the interests of those who have the greatest life expectancy.

I said "appears" to be skewed; for the danger of excessive redistribution to the old as a consequence of their disproportionate voting power may be overstated, quite apart from the fact that some elderly people "undo" public wealth transfers to them by gifts and bequests to their children. The pressure for redistributing wealth from young (or middle-aged) to old is self-limiting. As the percentage of old people increases, causing the dependency ratio to rise, the burden on each young earner of redistribution to the old rises even if the average benefits received by the old do not. The increased individual burden should stiffen the young's opposition to any further increases in benefits to the old. Even if the old are a better organized and more effective political pressure group than persons of working age, at some point the cost to the latter of redistributing wealth to the former will reach a level at which organization for effective political resistance becomes feasible. That level will be reached sooner, the faster the dependency ratio rises. There is thus a natural, though not necessarily an optimal, political equilibrium in the struggle between young and old selves.

This point is somewhat blunted, however, by the phenomenon of "sunk" social security taxes.[60] Even if a person has not yet retired, and

59. For evidence, see James W. Button and Walter A. Rosenbaum, "Seeing Gray: School Bond Issues and the Aging in Florida," 11 *Research on Aging* 158 (1989).

60. Boskin et al., note 43 above, at 30–31.

considers the social security program excessively favorable to the elderly, in evaluating the expected benefits to himself from the program he will ignore the social security taxes that he has already paid; they are sunk costs, unrecoverable. If he is nearing retirement, most of the expense of social security to him will lie in the past and all the benefits in the future, so it may well be in his interest to resist any curtailment of benefits rather than to support such curtailment coupled with lower taxes. There is a natural alliance between the elderly and the almost-elderly, magnifying the political power of the former beyond even what is implied by their formidable numbers and voter turnout.

The effect of the self-interest of the young in checking the size of governmental wealth transfers to the old might be expected to be especially great in a society such as ours in which old people are not revered. Yet this point seems hard to square with the fact that Japan, in which old people are still revered (if less so than formerly), has a much higher savings rate than the United States. One might expect Japanese to save less, confident that in their old age they could "free ride" on their children.[61] But maybe I have the causation backwards. Maybe the high social status of elderly Japanese results from their having saved heavily during their working years, thus increasing their wealth in old age and becoming respected because of that wealth, not because of their age.

A second reason not to fear excessive redistribution to the old too much is that it can be checked at less political cost than many other redistributions extracted by interest groups. Because the approximate number of old people can be predicted some years in advance (although the rapidity of medical progress is making such predictions increasingly uncertain) and because relatively few old people will be around for more than another decade or two,[62] it is possible to exploit the discounting of future costs to present value by passing laws now that will limit transfers to the old in the future. It is also possible to exploit the inertia of the political process (laws are difficult to repeal even if the political balance has shifted against them) in order to provide some security against the repeal of such laws when the future becomes the present. Consider the law enacted in 1983 raising the

61. Edward P. Lazear, "Some Thoughts on Savings," in *Studies in the Economics of Aging* 143, 162 (David A. Wise, ed., 1994).

62. In a sense they are "transients," whom we expect to have less political weight than "permanent" members of the polity. But of course the contrast is exaggerated. No one lives forever; and the nearly old will tend to identify with the old, thus increasing the number of (functionally) old and their staying power.

age of entitlement for full social security retirement benefits from 65 to 67 in the year 2023[63] (and also increasing the discount for claiming social security benefits at age 62 from 20 percent to 30 percent). The law cannot hurt *any* current recipients of social security retirement benefits, because all these people have qualified already. The people hurt are those who are now working who will have to work longer before they receive benefits. They incur a loss measured by the present value of the future lost benefits—a modest amount because of discounting to present value.[64] And this small loss is offset by the gain from not having to pay the higher social security taxes that would be necessary to fund larger benefits in the future, or more precisely from the part of the gain that will be received by the children and other family members of the current old people. Not too much should be made of *that* gain, however. There is always the possibility that in the future as in the present the elderly will have sufficient political power to make the young pay for higher social security retirement benefits, and the further possibility that raising the retirement age will result in more applications for social security *disability* benefits,[65] a program that in effect accelerates the payment of social security retirement benefits to any worker who can establish that he is totally disabled.

When the gains and losses that a proposed policy will visit on politically powerful groups are small (here because of discounting to present value), considerations of the public interest, which is to say of the costs and benefits of policies to diffuse groups such as consumers or taxpayers, are apt to play a larger, and often a decisive, role in the shaping of policy. It would be difficult otherwise to understand how laws punishing crime get passed and enforced, since the beneficiaries (besides lawyers and law enforcers) are a diffuse group—the entire law-abiding public.

If increases in longevity are accompanied by improvements in the health of the aged, as they appear to be, one might think that raising the age of retirement would be an automatic and costless response to the fact that

63. Actually the age is to be increased by a month every year beginning in 2000.

64. At a discount rate of 3 percent, the present value of $1 to be received in 40 years (2023 − 1983) is 31 cents. It is not clear that the benefits to future generations from more efficient policies should be discounted similarly—or at all. The social discount rate may be zero, although I doubt it (see next chapter). But if people's political behavior is assumed to be guided mainly by private rather than social benefits and costs, the question of the correct social discount rate is distinct from the political feasibility of legislation that reduces the entitlements of future generations.

65. Thomas N. Chirikos and Gilbert Nestel, "Occupational Differences in the Ability of Men to Delay Retirement," 26 *Journal of Human Resources* 1 (1991).

the age of onset of old age was rising. I think this is largely true (see chapter 2), although it may seem to overlook the factor of boredom, emphasized in previous chapters. If after some point the disutility of work increases as a function of time worked rather than of age, lengthening people's working life will impose disutility on them even if, because of better health, their capabilities for work and their wages do not decline before the new, higher age of retirement. But this assumes that the only effect of increased healthy longevity would be to lengthen people's careers. There would be other effects. Graduate education might become more attractive, because it postpones entry into the workforce. Careers such as the military that are geared to facilitating the worker's taking up a second career at the end of his period of service would also become more attractive. Most important, career-switching would be facilitated because the increased length of one's remaining working life would increase the return to mid-life investments in acquiring new human capital.

As is well known, social security benefits are overindexed for inflation. If this feature were corrected, benefits would (without new legislation) grow more slowly than average wages, because the benefits are not indexed for real (that is, inflation-adjusted) wage increases.

Still another consideration that argues against becoming too worried about the voting power of the elderly is the contribution which that power makes to political stability. Recall the point from chapter 8 that elderly voters tend to be conservative in the sense of resistant to new fashions in public policy. Resistance to new ideas, a characteristic by-product of the age-related decline in fluid intelligence, is no virtue in scientific fields, where objective procedures exist for winnowing good ideas from bad. There are no such procedures in politics (or at least they operate very slowly), and as a result bad new ideas—as fascism and communism once were—can quickly become deeply entrenched. A large elderly voting population, by retarding the adoption of new political ideas, can reduce the inherent riskiness of a political system. Another and in politics an apt term for being receptive to new ideas is "impressionable." We might not want the electorate to be dominated by impressionable voters, and we might consider the transfers that the elderly receive from the young as, in part, compensation for the contribution that elderly voters make to political stability, from which the young benefit as well.

An offsetting consideration, however, is that elderly voters may be particularly susceptible to radical ideas when packaged as revivals of old ideas—which they may be. Elderly voters, it appears, disproportionately supported Hitler in the elections that paved the way for his ascension to power.[66]

A final argument against the idea that the elderly have a dangerous excess of voting power brings us back once again to the concept of multiple selves. Every young and middle-aged person has a future self of which he may not be—probably is not—a completely trustworthy fiduciary, just as parents are not entirely trustworthy fiduciaries of their children because their interests are not identical. As a practical matter, the current elderly represent not only their own interests but also those of the future elderly selves of people who are still young. The argument that I made earlier for giving parents extra votes in order to increase the weight of children's interests in the political process can be made for tolerating the "excess" voting power of the elderly as well, in order to assure that the process will give adequate weight to the interests of future elderly selves.

Balancing all the comforting facts marshaled in this section, however, are two counterweights. One has to do with truncated horizons; the other with free riding. I said that the current old can be thought of as proxies for the future old (the future selves of the current young and middle-aged). But this is not likely to work for projects whose payoffs are long deferred, for example research on a cure for cancer not expected to be found until the year 2020. For by then the current old will be dead. The persons who are most interested in such a project are the future old people—who are the current young.

Second, while it appears to be politically feasible both to curtail Medicare and social security *in futuro,* and (so far) to refuse public subsidization of home care for elderly people who need assistance to cope with the challenges of daily living but not medical assistance, it is not politically feasible either to deny the elderly medical care (as we saw in discussing Dworkin's proposal) or to abandon them should they need home care. The burden of the former will fall on Medicaid when Medicare and private insurance runs out and the burden of the latter on family, friends, and social workers.[67] These will be costly burdens for which society (viewed as the aggregate of its members) will pay in one way or another unless people are forced to save more for their old age. The burdens will grow in real terms as the fraction of elderly people grows and as more and more elderly people live

---

66. See Richard F. Hamilton, *Who Voted for Hitler?* 61–62, 512 n. 46 (1982).

67. I emphasize home care rather than institutional care because the former is greatly preferred by elderly persons for reasons explained in chapter 6.

to the really advanced ages at which heavy medical and home-care costs are unavoidable, even if—what at the moment seems unlikely—the relative cost of medical and home care does not continue to grow. It is not yet apparent what public or private means exist for preventing the elderly from shifting these burdens to taxpayers and family members. They cannot be counted on to make adequate provision through private savings, because of the conflict between young and old selves that I have stressed throughout the book.

On this view—which incidentally provides another reason for reallocating expenditures on medical research from fatal to merely disabling physical and mental conditions of the elderly—curtailing social security, Medicare, Medicaid, or other public benefits is not much more than changing the bookkeeping, or more precisely changing the identity and relative shares of taxpayers and other bearers of the costs of the elderly. This is an exaggeration, of course. As I pointed out in discussing Medicare, a change in the structure of public programs can create incentives to economize. The elderly would, I argued, be better off if they could commute the expected value of their Medicare entitlement to cash to spend on anything they liked; and the result would be a reduction in the nation's overall bill for health. And private medical charity would no doubt be more skimpy than public. Yet even the abolition of all public programs for the support of the elderly might not result in a dramatic reduction in the medical and other consumption costs of the growing phalanx of elderly Americans.

But as always we must be careful to maintain perspective, or, stated differently, to reckon in all benefits as well as all costs. Middle-aged people who incur heavy expenses for the home care of their aged parents will (they or their future selves!) some day be old themselves and want such care. And those heavy expenses are in part the unavoidable by-product of advances in medical and scientific knowledge that are extending healthy middle age, postponing old age, and by this combination generating enormous utility to which the burden of elder care is probably a relatively minor offset. A greater one may be the emotional toll that unhealthy old age takes of the elderly and their families.

The focus of this chapter has been on intergenerational wealth transfers, nonpecuniary as well as pecuniary—and conjectured as well as proven. The social security retirement program, Medicare, other special public programs for the aged that I have not even discussed, publicly financed medical research on diseases that disproportionately afflict elderly people, and treatment decisions that avoid the use of age as a criterion for allocating scarce medical resources bring about in the aggregate a large gross redistribution of wealth from young to old; but the net redistribution is another matter. The net intergenerational redistributive component of the largest program of public transfers to the old—the social security retirement program—may be small, or conceivably if improbably even negative, when the annuity value of the social security taxes paid by the recipients of social security retirement benefits during their working lives is subtracted from the benefits; when due regard is given to the fact that the generation that is receiving these benefits paid in the form of school taxes for a large part of the taxpaying generation's human capital that in turn generates the tax revenues that defray the cost of social security retirement benefits; and when the effect of social security in reducing the caretaking burden on the children of elderly parents and grandparents is taken into account as well.

Some of the arbitrary-seeming features of our public old-age programs, moreover, appear to somewhat better advantage in a careful analysis. The compulsory feature of the social security program, for example, can be defended by reference to the concept of multiple selves. Not through shortsightedness, but through sheer indifference, the young self may abandon his future old self. Compelled savings for retirement, like refusals to enforce suicide pacts and efforts to discourage harmful addictions, may reflect society's unwillingness to treat the current self as the "owner," for all purposes, of the body of which he is the temporary tenant. Multiple-selves analysis also undermines the suggestion that Medicare is overly generous because most young people would if given a choice be unwilling to make "lavish" provision for their medical needs in old age. This is just another example of the propensity of the young self to weight his own utility much more heavily than that of his future old self. On strictly fiscal grounds, it is even possible to defend the heavy allocation of medical resources to the diseases of the old, because saving young people for old age may well add more to net expected lifetime costs of health care than moderately prolonging the lives of people who are already old would do. On broader grounds of utility, however, it would undoubtedly be better to concentrate resources more heavily on the diseases of the young.

I argued that the allocation of public resources in the medical sphere should probably be shifted somewhat in favor of mental illnesses, because here a cure or substantial improvement is less likely merely to "save" the patient for another disease. Most controversially, I stressed the possible benefits of a shift in the allocation of public resources for medical research in favor of men's diseases over women's. The enormous and growing imbalance between the number of elderly men and the number of elderly women—"in favor of" the women—so reduces the marital and sexual opportunities of elderly women that it is plausible (though no stronger term can be used, in light of the qualifications that I suggested) that, ex ante, women would be made better off by a reallocation of expenditures to medical research designed to increase the longevity of men faster than that of women, at least for a time. The general point which this suggestion illustrates is that quality as well as quantity of life must be taken into account in determining what allocation of medical resources will maximize expected utility.

There are plenty of objections to details, some of them very big details, of the nation's current old-age programs;[68] and it would be reckless to suggest that the programs approach optimality or to deny the possibility that they involve a large and perhaps unconscionable transfer of wealth from young to old. The dramatic imbalance in voting power between young and old—with children having no votes at all, and the elderly voting disproportionately even to their share of the adult population—fuels such a concern. But subtle factors that limit the dangers created by elderly voting power are easily overlooked. Among other things: The "conservatism" in the sense not of a political slant but of resistance to novelty that is characteristic of the elderly voter is a force ordinarily though not invariably for healthy political stability. The larger the transfer of wealth from young to old, the easier it is to organize the young in effective political opposition to further such transfers. The ability to forecast (more or less)[69] the number of elderly at specific periods in the future, in conjunction with legislative inertia, which makes it difficult to repeal legislation once it is adopted, facilitates legislative curtailment of future benefits for the elderly; the costs of such legislation will be borne by a future generation of elderly, while the benefits in lower taxes will begin to accrue immediately. Even the "excessive" voting power of the old may be justified, by the role of the current old as proxies for our otherwise unrepresented future elderly selves.

I admitted that the analysis might be too static. The burdens of medical care and nonmedical home care will grow as the population of elderly grows, and quite possibly faster.[70] Someone will have to pay, since it is

68. Raymond G. Batina, "On the Time Consistency of the Government's Social Security Benefit Policy," 29 *Journal of Monetary Economics* 475 (1992).

69. The less is emphasized in Kenneth G. Manton, Eric Stallard, and Burton H. Singer, "Methods for Projecting the Future Size and Health Status of the U.S. Elderly Population," in *Studies in the Economics of Aging,* note 61 above, at 41.

70. Recall, however, the caveat in chapter 2 against exaggerating the impact of rising costs of health care on the aggregate social costs of the elderly population.

highly unlikely that the elderly will actually be denied the care they need. That "someone" may not be the elderly themselves when they are young, given the conflict between young and old selves. There is a real policy dilemma here, and no feasible solution handy, although a greater emphasis on quality-improving as distinct from longevity-enhancing medical research offers the possibility of at least a partial solution. Even disregarding that possibility, I suggested that the heavy costs of elder care are offset by the benefits, to those who bear those costs, of modern medicine and science in postponing (while elongating) old age. Healthy middle age has been extended; one cost is the burden that the middle aged must shoulder for the expenses of the old, for old age has inevitably been extended as well.

12

Legal Issues of Aging and Old Age: A Sampler

Although the Social Security Act is the most important law relating to old age, the actual administration of the Act has generated relatively few issues of application and interpretation whose intelligent resolution requires the sort of understanding of aging and old age that I have tried to develop in this book. Yet there are many such issues under other laws. The most interesting concern the law's effort to eliminate discrimination on grounds of age in employment. To that subject I devote the next chapter, while in this one I discuss several other subjects involving legal regulation that bears on the elderly: the federal law governing pensions (other than those provided through the social security system); the tort rules applicable to elderly injurers and victims; the punishment of elderly offenders and the continued imprisonment of elderly people who were convicted when young of crimes for which thesentence was life in prison without possibility of parole; and the bearing of senile dementia on legal capacity and responsibility. The laws relating to assisted suicide, and to living wills and related methods of regulating MDELs (medical decisions at end of life), were discussed in chapter 10.

The sample of legal issues relating to the elderly that I discuss in this chapter is a small one. Other interesting issues include the shielding of the assets of elderly people in bankruptcy, the legal rights of grandparents, the obtaining of informed consent to medical experimentation on demented patients, and the rights of persons confined to nursing homes against their will yet without either a formal commitment order or the employment of physical force to confine them.[1]

Pension Law

In 1974 Congress passed the Employees Retirement Income Security Act (ERISA).[2] This complex statute is a major source of litigation in the federal courts, although much of that litigation concerns issues unrelated to the subject of this book. For, despite its title, the statute regulates employer health and welfare benefits as well as pensions and provides a federal forum for litigating contractual disputes over the terms of particular pension or other covered plans. The statute's principal significance in relation to age is its impact on the employer's choice between a defined-benefit and a defined-contribution pension plan and its regulation of the former type.[3]

A defined-benefit plan promises to pay the employee a fixed annual pension based on the employee's wage in his last year or last few years of work and on his years of service. The higher his terminal salary and the longer he has worked for this employer, the larger his pension entitlement will be. For example, the plan might entitle him to an annuity income equal to 1 percent of his terminal salary times his number of years of service, so that if he retired after 30 years with the company he would be entitled to

---

1. See, regarding these issues, Daniel L. Skoler, "The Elderly and Bankruptcy Relief: Problems, Protections, and Realities," 6 *Bankruptcy Developments Journal* 121 (1989); Madeline Marzano-Lesnevich, "Grandparents' Rights," *New Jersey Lawyer,* Jan./Feb. 1991, p. 46; Robert L. Schwartz, "Informed Consent to Participation in Medical Research Employing Elderly Human Subjects," 1 *Journal of Contemporary Health Law and Policy* 115 (1985); Carthrael Razin, Comment, " 'Nowhere to Go and Chose to Stay': Using the Tort of False Imprisonment to Redress Involuntary Confinement of the Elderly in Nursing Homes and Hospitals," 137 *University of Pennsylvania Law Review* 903 (1989). On the legal problems of elderly people generally, see Peter J. Strauss, Robert Wolf, and Dana Shilling, *Aging and the Law* (1990); Joan M. Krauskopf et al., *Elderlaw: Advocacy for the Aging* (2d ed. 1993) (2 vols.).

2. 29 U.S.C. §§ 1001 *et seq.* For helpful economic analyses of the pension aspects of ERISA, see Jeremy I. Bulow, Myron S. Scholes, and Peter Menell, "Economic Implications of ERISA," in *Financial Aspects of the United States Pension System* 37 (Zvi Bodie and John B. Shoven, eds., 1983); Laurence J. Kotlikoff and David A. Wise, "Pension Backloading, Wage Taxes, and Work Disincentives," in *Tax Policy and the Economy,* vol. 2, p. 161 (Lawrence H. Summers, ed., 1988).

3. On the difference between the two types of plan, see Zvi Bodie, Alan J. Marcus, and Robert C. Merton, "Defined Benefit versus Defined Contribution Plans: What Are the Real Trade-Offs?" in *Pensions in the U.S. Economy* 139 (Zvi Bodie, John B. Shoven, and David A. Wise, eds., 1988). Although defined-contribution plans are much more numerous, defined-benefit plans hold in the aggregate more assets. Pension and Welfare Benefits Administration, "Abstract of 1990 Form 5500 Annual Reports," *Private Pension Plan Bulletin,* Summer 1993. But see note 10 below and the text accompanying it.

receive an annual pension equal to 30 percent of his final year's wage. Thus, in a defined-benefit plan the employee's entitlement is independent of the amount of the employer's contributions to the plan or of the plan's investment performance.

In a typical defined-contribution plan, contributions are made by both employer and employee to a separate account for each covered employee.[4] When the employee retires, the amount of money in his account, which will be the sum of his and his employer's contributions plus any interest or other return earned on those contributions from investing them, is used to buy an annuity that will give him and his spouse an assured income for the rest of their lives. (In some plans, the employee gets a lump sum rather than an annuity.) So while in a defined-benefit plan the investment risk is borne by the employer or by the plan (or the plan's insurer), in a defined-contribution plan it is borne by the employee, though he should be able to reduce that risk by investing the contributions in a diversified portfolio of securities.

The allocation of the risk of inflation in the years after retirement is reversed in the two types of plan. Benefits in a defined-pension plan are stated in nominal terms (so many dollars a year until the employee dies), whereas benefits under a defined-contribution plan are paid to the employee upon retirement and can then be invested in vehicles that will give him at least some protection against inflation. I have not seen an explanation of why the benefits in defined-benefit plans are not indexed against inflation.

A defined-benefit plan has the greater effect on the age profile of the employer's workforce. Within limits fixed by the federal pension and age-discrimination laws, employers can adopt benefit formulas that make it highly disadvantageous for employees to quit before—or fail to quit at—a particular age, such as 55, 60, or 65. A defined-contribution plan is not as well adapted to manipulating the term of employment, since the amount of the employee's retirement benefits is not within the control of the employer, although it is influenced of course by the amounts contributed.

Because benefits under a defined-benefit plan are tied to the employee's final salary, such a plan provides greater although not complete assurance of stable (though not necessarily full) replacement of wage

---

4. In some defined-contribution plans, only the employee contributes. But this is a detail without economic significance, since, as we shall see in the next chapter, workers pay for benefits by accepting lower wages, even if the employer is the nominal payor.

income; the employee's accustomed standard of living will be more or less preserved in retirement. Benefits under a defined-contribution plan depend strictly on the amount contributed and on the investment performance of the contributions.

If the employer is the better risk-bearer, the defined-benefit form will generally be more attractive to employees than the defined-contribution form, although differences in vesting rules and the omnipresent risk of inflation complicate the trade-offs. The defined-benefit form also facilitates optimal investments in human capital, as we shall see, and confers tax advantages on the employer when the plan is overfunded, that is, when its assets exceed its pension liabilities. The income on those assets will inure in part to the employer because it will not all be needed to defray the employer's pension liabilities, and that income will accumulate tax free because the plan is a tax-exempt entity. So there is actually a tax incentive to overfund.

What about an incentive to underfund? Before the enactment of ERISA, pension liabilities in a defined-benefit plan could be and often were liabilities of the pension plan alone rather than of the employer as well. If the plan was underfunded because contributions had been inadequate, investment performance disappointing, or actuarial projections inaccurate, the loss fell on the employees; in this way some of the investment risk was shifted back to them. If the plan was overfunded, the employer's shareholders, being the residual claimants to the plan's funds after all entitlements of employees were honored, reaped the gain.

Depending on the rules of vesting and of crediting years of service adopted by the particular plan, a worker who left before retirement age might find himself with a pension benefit worth much less than his contributions and perhaps worth nothing at all. So he had a strong incentive to remain with the same company until he reached retirement age. This incentive both reduced the mobility of labor and increased the employer's power to expropriate employees' firm-specific human capital by implicitly threatening to fire them before their pension rights vested if they insisted on a salary commensurate with their value to the company. Indeed, quite apart from human-capital considerations, one could imagine an employer reducing the employee's wage to a point at which the wage and the pension benefit together would just exceed the employee's wage in his next best job. The year before the employee retired and became eligible for the pension, the wage could be zero—or even negative; the employee would pay to be allowed to work long enough to become entitled to his pension.

Before concluding that pension practices were exploitative before

ERISA, we must remind ourselves that the terms of retirement, including pension rights, are a matter of negotiation between employer and prospective employee, not a unilateral imposition. Even if, as was and is common, the employer refused to negotiate separately with each employee but offered terms of employment on a take it or leave it basis, and even if the employees were not represented by a union (with which the employer could not lawfully refuse to negotiate), competition among employers would give prospective employees a choice between different wage-benefit packages. The packages offered by some employers would emphasize good retirement or other benefits at the cost of lower wages, while those offered by other employers would emphasize high wages at the expense of less generous or secure retirement or other benefits. Employees would tend to be sorted to employers according to the individual employee's preferences regarding risk and the allocation of consumption over the life cycle.

Even incomplete vesting was not a scam, or an impediment to optimal mobility of labor. By making pension benefits contingent on the employee's remaining with the firm and performing satisfactorily, incomplete vesting facilitated the recovery by employers of their investment in their employees' firm-specific human capital. It also solved the last-period problem: not only with the stick (the threat of discharge before pension rights vested) but also with the carrot, since pension benefits in a defined-benefit plan are heavily influenced by the employee's wage in his last years of employment. The incentive of employers to abuse the power that incomplete vesting conferred on them to renege on their unwritten contract to deal fairly with their employees could be expected to be held in check by the employer's concern with preserving a reputation for fair dealing (if he lost that, he would have to pay new employees higher wages) and by the bargaining power that the possession of firm-specific human capital confers on a worker. If the worker quits in anger or disgust, or is fired to eliminate his pension benefits, the firm must invest in training a green employee to replace him.[5]

These market checks on the exploitation of employees by employers did not work perfectly; very little does. In particular they could not be ex-

---

5. Cf. Donald P. Schwab and Herbert H. Heneman III, "Effects of Age and Experience on Productivity," 4 *Industrial Gerontology* 113 (1977). For an excellent review of the modern economic theory of the pension contract, see Richard A. Ippolito, "The Implicit Pension Contract: Developments and New Directions," 22 *Journal of Human Resources* 441 (1987); for fuller treatment, illustrating what has become a vast literature, see the essays in *Pensions, Labor, and Individual Choice* (David A. Wise, ed., 1985). The modern theory views the pension contract as a device for imparting proper incentives to workers; the older theory saw it merely as a form of savings stimulated by favorable tax treatment.

pected to work well when an employer was in its last period.[6] But there is no persuasive evidence that pension abuses were so widespread as to justify the imposition of a complex scheme of federal regulation. On the contrary, careful empirical research has shown that before ERISA opportunistic discharges of workers covered by a pension plan were rare and that ERISA has had no detectable impact on discharges of covered workers.[7]

ERISA's principal thrust, so far as pertains to retirement (recall that ERISA also regulates medical and other employee-benefit plans), is to require that defined-benefit plans vest the employee's pension rights after he has been a participant in the plan for five years and to back up this requirement by limiting pension "backloading." The term refers to the practice of making pension benefits, even if vested, so age-dependent that, until retirement age is reached, the value of the employee's pension right is very small. Other pension-related objects of the law were to create a federal judicial remedy for breach of the fiduciary obligations of pension plans to the participants in and beneficiaries of the plans, to reduce underfunding of pension plans, and, through the Pension Benefit Guaranty Corporation, an agency created by the Act, to guarantee pension entitlements against the consequences of underfunding. These last two objects work at cross-purposes, since the existence of guaranteed pension benefits undermines the market checks on underfunding. Workers and their unions will press less hard for adequate funding of their pension benefits if they know there is a government backstop. The analogy to federal deposit insurance, which increases the incentive of financial institutions to make risky loans, is plain. Apparently the checking provisions of ERISA are inadequate. There are fears of an eventual pension crisis to rival the savings and loan debacle of the 1980s.[8]

ERISA's effect on pension backloading has been small; defined-benefit plans remain heavily backloaded.[9] The Act has, however, made defined-

6. See, for example, Daniel Fischel and John H. Langbein, "ERISA's Fundamental Contradiction: The Exclusive Benefit Rule," 55 *University of Chicago Law Review* 1105, 1132 (1988).

7. Christopher Cornwell, Stuart Dorsey, and Nasser Mehrzad, "Opportunistic Behavior by Firms in Implicit Pension Contracts," 26 *Journal of Human Resources* 704 (1991); Richard Ippolito, "A Study of the Regulatory Impact of ERISA," 31 *Journal of Law and Economics* 85, 91–102 (1988).

8. See Carolyn L. Weaver, "Government Guarantees of Private Pension Benefits: Current Problems and Market-Based Solutions" (unpublished, American Enterprise Institute, Aug. 1994, forthcoming in *Public Policy toward Pensions* [John B. Shoven and Sylvester J. Schieber, eds.], Twentieth Century Fund).

9. Laurence J. Kotlikoff and David A. Wise, *The Wage Carrot and the Pension Stick: Retirement Benefits and Labor Force Participation* (1989); cf. Bodie, Marcus, and Merton, note 3 above, at 143.

benefit plans more costly for employers (per dollar of benefits) and more secure for employees. But with costs and benefits both greater, it is difficult to assess the Act's net effect on the system of private pensions. It may have been small. Interest rates have generally been higher since 1974 than before then, so that (depending on corporate tax rates) the tax benefits of over-funding have increased. The Act does not forbid overfunding, although it makes it slightly more difficult for the employer to recapture the over-funded portion of the pension plan's assets for its shareholders. The effect of interest rates in magnifying the tax benefits of overfunding have tended to offset the Act's effect in making defined-benefit plans less attractive to employers. It is true that since the late 1970s the tide has been running in favor of defined-contribution plans (especially 401(k) plans, which allow employees to make tax-deferred contributions to retirement accounts).[10] But whether ERISA has been a factor in this trend is unclear.

By limiting incomplete vesting, the Act has tended to reduce the con-trol of employers over their older employees, since the pension benefits of such employees are securely vested. Such a loss of control would be ex-pected to lead employers to invest less in the firm-specific human capital of their employees, and—because employers would have a smaller invest-ment in them to protect and the employees would have less incentive to perform well (not being faced with a substantial loss of pension benefits if they were fired)—to resort more frequently to an explicit or implicit threat of discharge in order to maintain discipline. The extent of these effects is not known.

The biggest objection to ERISA is the absence of persuasive theoreti-cal or empirical grounds for thinking that the market in private pension entitlements was not working adequately before 1974. Most of the abuses discussed in the legislative history concerned multiemployer pension plans administered by unions—hardly a representative case of the operation of unregulated labor markets. Yet if there were no social security law, so that all pensions were private, but it was desired on multiple-selves or other grounds to compel young people to put aside something for their old age, it would be necessary to set minimum pension levels, limit under-funding, forbid assigning or borrowing against pension entitlements, and perhaps adopt other regulations as well in order to prevent employers and employees from striking side deals that would trade meaningful pension

10. John R. Woods, "Pension Coverage among Private Wage and Salary Workers: Prelimi-nary Findings from the 1988 Survey of Employee Benefits," *Social Security Bulletin,* Oct. 1989, p. 2.

rights for higher wages and thereby empower the young employee to condemn his future old self to starvation, private charity, or the dole. If social security benefits are considered adequate provision for our future selves, it is unclear why we need ERISA. But if social security were replaced by a law that "simply" required people to save for their old age, something like ERISA would be necessary to make the law more than an empty gesture.

Unless the law did no more than require employees to make a specified level of contributions to defined-contribution plans. But that is a big "unless," as it would greatly curtail the use of defined-benefit plans by making defined-contribution plans compulsory. If defined-benefit plans have any efficiency justifications (and we have suggested several), this governmentally compelled substitution would be a source of social costs.

Elderly Tortfeasors and Tort Victims

The cluster of issues to which I turn now, while somewhat esoteric, provides good illustrations of the value of economic analysis for the understanding and appraisal of legal rules and practices. The first issue is whether tort law ought to hold old people (whether as injurers or as victims) to a lower standard of care than young people, on the theory that the old are incapable of coming up to the same standard. Tort law does this with regard to children and the blind. Holding children and blind people liable for injuries that the adult and sighted could have avoided at reasonable cost but that children and the blind could not avoid because they have a much higher cost of care would not reduce the number of accidents caused by these classes; it would merely shift the cost of those accidents from victim to injurer.[11] I exaggerate slightly. As we saw in chapter 6 in connection with the driving behavior of old people, accidents can be avoided not only by greater care but also by avoidance or curtailment of the activity that generates accidents as an unintended by-product. The old can drive less, and will do so if the expected cost of driving includes an expected cost of liability to pay damages to accident victims. In just the same way, the blind can go out less and parents can keep their children under greater restraint.

The difference between old people on the one hand and blind people and children on the other, and the reason I conjecture why the law has not

11. William M. Landes and Richard A. Posner, *The Economic Structure of Tort Law* 123–131 (1987).

fixed a more "realistic" standard of care for the former group as it has for
the latter ones, is that the cost to the old of avoiding inflicting accidental
injuries is lower than that of the child or the blind person. The old driver
can substitute time for the sharper vision and quicker reflexes of a younger
driver. And because most old people are retired and therefore are not commuters, the value of driving to them is diminished, which reduces the cost
to them of avoiding accidents by reducing the amount of driving they do
and so making up for any irremediable deficit in care by a change in activity level. If the standard of tort liability for the old were fixed with reference to the average physical capabilities of old people, the incentive of
the old to take feasible steps along both the care and the activity dimensions to avoid causing accidents would be reduced with no corresponding
social gain.

That the value of driving to the average elderly person is less than that
to the average young person is a good argument for holding the elderly to
the same standard of care as the young, but is not a good argument for
holding them to a higher standard. As I emphasized in chapter 6, tort liability as well as concern with self-protection has, together with the low
average value to the elderly of driving, already curtailed the amount of
driving by the elderly; the amount that remains is likely to confer substantial benefits on them.

Old people are frequent victims of accidents, including fatal accidents.
In 1990, 26,213 Americans 65 years old and older were killed in accidents,
of which almost 30 percent were automobile accidents.[12] Some of these
accidents were tortious, which raises the question how to estimate the value
of an elderly life for purposes of tort compensation. Estimation of the
purely financial loss is no more difficult than in the case of the death of a
young person—in fact easier, when a forecast of earnings is required, because the period for which the forecast must be made will be shorter. But
what about the nonpecuniary value of life to a person who does not have
many years to live in any event, and those years perhaps of limited utility
to him because of anticipated poor health? It might seem intuitively obvious that the value of life would be much less for the average old person
than for the average young one, but the discussion in chapter 5 of elderly
persons' "dread of death" should make us skeptical.

William Landes and I have suggested that the proper way to value life
for purposes of assessing tort damages is to determine from studies of seat-

---

12. U.S. Bureau of the Census, *Statistical Abstract of the United States 1993* 93 (113th ed.)
(ser. 128); National Safety Council, *Accident Facts* 12 (1993 ed.).

belt use and other measures that people take to protect themselves from injury how much people are willing to pay to avoid the risk of accident that the defendant created by his tortious conduct, and to divide that amount by the risk.[13] So if the defendant had created a .000001 risk of death and the victim would have demanded $1 for bearing such a risk, the amount of damages that should be awarded if, the risk having materialized, the victim was killed would be $1 million. This is the correct measure of damages because it confronts potential injurers with the expected cost of their dangerous conduct ($1). If they spend less than this on accident avoidance, they are negligent in both the economic and the closely related legal sense.

Although many studies seek to infer the "value of life" (perhaps misnamed) by the method that Landes and I believe could be used to compute tort damages in death cases,[14] I am not aware of any that investigates the effect of age on the amount of care demanded of potential injurers. But if the analysis in chapter 5 is correct, old people should be expected to demand as much or almost as much care as young ones, despite their truncated life expectancy, and possibly more; and this implies, by the method proposed by Landes and me, that they should be entitled to damages for loss of the nonpecuniary value of life at least as great as young victims of wrongful death are entitled to. Corroboration for the suggestion that the old demand as much care from potential injurers as the young do—or even more—is provided by evidence that persons aged 65 and over are more likely to be regular seatbelt users than younger people.[15] Admittedly, this does not *prove* that the old will pay as much as, let alone more than, the young for the same reduction in the risk of injury and death. Their cost of time is lower, though this is a trivial consideration when one is speaking of fastening a seatbelt; more important, their risk of being injured or killed in an automobile accident is much greater. If the risk were twice as great, we would expect them to demand the same level of care as young people even if the utility to them of their remaining life were only half as great as that of the young.

Nevertheless it is apparent that elderly people do not consider their

13. Landes and Posner, note 11 above, at 187–189; see also Erin Ann O'Hara, "Hedonic Damages for Wrongful Death: Are Tortfeasors Getting Away with Murder?" 78 *Georgetown Law Journal* 1687, 1697–1700 (1990).

14. See references in Marvin Frankel and Charles M. Linke, "The Value of Life and Hedonic Damages: Some Unresolved Issues," 5 *Journal of Forensic Economics* 233, 237–243 (1992), and the very interesting discussion in Sherwin Rosen, "The Value of Changes in Life Expectancy," 1 *Journal of Risk and Uncertainty* 285 (1988).

15. Isaac Ehrlich and Hiroyuki Chuma, "A Model of the Demand for Longevity and the Value of Life Extension," 98 *Journal of Political Economy* 761, 781 (1990) (tab. 5).

lives to be of negligible value merely because just a few years remain to them. So we would expect the tort damages awarded in cases in which elderly persons had been killed to be substantial, at least in those jurisdictions that do not confine recovery in wrongful death cases to purely pecuniary losses sustained by survivors. The qualification is important. Originally those were the only losses recoverable in a wrongful-death suit. The common law did not award damages in death cases; and the earliest wrongful-death statutes, which altered the common law rule, merely provided a remedy for the decedent's dependents, who had been deprived of his support. This is still the regime in some states. Strictly interpreted, it limits damages to the pecuniary loss suffered by the survivors, and this will ordinarily be slight when the decedent is retired. (It may even be negative: death accelerates bequests.) Damages for nonpecuniary losses are, however, increasingly allowed in suits for wrongful death, under one rubric or another, such as loss of companionship.[16] And a number of states now try to compensate the loss to the decedent himself, rather than just the loss to survivors. For example, a Missouri statute allows the estate of the resident of a nursing home to maintain a wrongful death suit against the home, and the reason behind the statute is, precisely, the unlikelihood that a resident of a nursing home would be providing support or other services to anyone.[17] Yet only one state, Connecticut, plus the federal courts in civil rights tort suits, goes all the way and allows damages for loss of the enjoyment (utility) of life[18]—what are called "hedonic" damages—although juries often award damages for this loss sub rosa, as by exaggerating the decedent's lost earnings or his conscious pain and suffering before death.

Jurisdictions that do allow the recovery of damages for nonpecuniary losses in death cases also allow the recovery of damages for pecuniary losses in such cases, so we would expect total damages in wrongful-death cases involving old victims to be on average lower than in cases involving young ones. More precisely, we would expect that the ratio of damages in wrongful-death cases involving younger victims to damages in wrongful-

16. See Dan B. Dobbs, *Law of Remedies: Damages—Equity—Restitution,* vol. 2, § 8.3(5) (2d ed. 1993). The point was made with express reference to elderly plaintiffs in Borer v. American Airlines, Inc., 563 P.2d 858 (Cal. 1977).

17. See Stiffelman v. Abrams, 655 S.W.2d 522 (Mo. 1983).

18. O'Hara, note 13 above, at 1692 n. 26; see also Dobbs, note 16 above, § 8.3(5), p. 443; Andrew Jay McClurg, "It's a Wonderful Life: The Case for Hedonic Damages in Wrongful Death Cases," 66 *Notre Dame Law Review* 57, 62–66, 90–97 (1990), esp. 65 n. 33; cf. Annotation, "Excessiveness or Adequacy of Damages Awarded for Personal Injuries Resulting in Death of Retired Persons," 48 A.L.R.4th 229 (1986).

death cases involving older victims will be greater than 1 but smaller than the ratio of the purely financial losses of the two groups.

Consistent with this expectation, in a sample of verdicts in wrongful death cases rendered in 1992 and 1993 the average verdict in 73 cases in which the victim was between 65 and 85 years old was $1.2 million, which was 73 percent of the $1.7 million average for victims aged 25 to 45.[19] And in a study of tort compensation in fatal airplane accidents, the ratio of compensation received when the victim was in the 40 through 49 age group (the peak age group for receipt of compensation) to the compensation received when the victim was 70 or older was 7.17, whereas the ratio of the purely financial loss (present value of anticipated future earnings and retirement income) of the victims in the two age groups was 8.49.[20] The difference in result between the two samples is striking. The airplane-accident sample is older, and the much higher ratio of young decedents' to old decedents' damages than in the more recent (1992–1993) sample may indicate that the severe limitations that most jurisdictions traditionally placed on damages for nonpecuniary losses in wrongful death cases are waning.

The largest fatal-accident sample I have found comprises 224 verdicts in wrongful death cases, rendered by juries in the courts of Cook County, Illinois, between 1959 and 1979.[21] The peak age is 46 through 50; the 17 plaintiffs in that group obtained an average verdict of $294,682. The 24 plaintiffs in the highest age group (61 through 70) obtained an average verdict of $145,861, which was 49.5 percent of the average verdict for members of the younger group. Despite the age of the sample, the results are much closer to those of the most recent sample. Within the 61–70 group, however, the average verdict falls rapidly with age, being only $40,498 for decedents aged 66 through 70; but the size of this subsample is very small (10).

One would expect the ratio of verdicts for elderly tort victims relative to the verdicts for nonelderly victims to be higher in nondeath cases, since the same accident is expected to inflict a more severe injury on the victim the older he is. This is confirmed by Cook County data. For verdicts in all

19. The sample was obtained from the LRP-JV computerized database of jury verdicts, which is available on West Publishing Company's "Westlaw" system.

20. Computed from Elizabeth M. King and James P. Smith, *Economic Loss and Compensation in Aviation Accidents* 35, 48 (RAND Institute for Civil Justice R-3551-ICJ 1988) (tabs. 4.4, 5.7).

21. The sample was obtained by Professor George L. Priest of the Yale Law School in connection with his ongoing study of tort litigation in Cook County.

such cases brought by victims of automobile accidents (including accidents to pedestrians), the peak age was again 46 through 50 (n = 349), and the average verdict was $43,034, compared to $28,159 for the 61 through 90 age group (n = 383). The average verdict of the elderly victims in the nondeath cases was thus 65.4 percent of that of the nonelderly victims, compared to only 49.5 percent in the death cases. It may seem odd that the average verdict of the elderly victims does not *exceed* that of the non-elderly, if the average injury is more severe. But, precisely because the *expected* injury is more severe to the elderly, we can expect them to take more efforts to reduce that severity, as by fastening their seatbelts more—which we know they do. And damages in nondeath as in death cases include lost earnings, and these are higher for people who are working than for retired people—indeed, retirement income is not diminished at all by a disabling accident. The younger the comparison group, the more likely are the damages of elderly victims of nonfatal accidents to equal or even exceed those of young victims, since younger victims are likely both to have lower earnings and to be injured less severely. Consistent with this suggestion, the average damages of the 61-to-90 group ($28,159) were 136.8 percent of the average damages of the 26-to-40 group ($20,590; n = 1150).

Studies of the value of life bear on age in the following respect: they show that in deciding what premium to demand for dangerous work, young workers discount the cost of future injury or death at a high rate.[22] It could be argued that they should be held to this decision if they are later killed or injured. But this would ignore the multiple-selves problem. The fact that the young self has relatively little consideration for the old should not automatically determine the rights of the old. The behavior of elderly people with regard to matters of personal safety suggests that they do not value their lives at the discounted value set on those lives by their young selves. For similar reasons explained in chapter 4, the fact that young persons might be unwilling to buy insurance that would provide for their medical and other needs should they be disabled by an accident in their old age is not a persuasive argument against awarding full tort damages in cases of such disability.

Elderly Offenders and Prisoners

Chapter 6 identified as a potential problem of deterrence the truncation of punishment for the old offender when punishment takes the form of im-

22. W. Kip Viscusi, "The Value of Risks to Life and Health," 31 *Journal of Economic Literature* 1912, 1921 (1993).

prisonment. This problem can be alleviated although not solved by placing greater emphasis on fines as a method of punishment of the old. This is not done at present. The federal sentencing guidelines do state that "age may be a reason to impose a sentence below the applicable guideline range when the defendant is elderly and infirm and where a form of punishment such as home confinement might be equally efficient as and less costly than incarceration."[23] But there is no reference to fines. The only point that seems to have occurred to the authors of the guidelines with respect to elderly offenders is that their feebleness makes them less of an escape risk, so a laxer form of incarceration than confinement to a prison may be effective (and will cost less). It is not a good point. To the extent that their physical or mental infirmities "imprison" elderly offenders in their home anyway, home confinement will have little or no effect as punishment; the increment of confinement will be too small, and possibly nil. To solve this problem by imposing harsher conditions of confinement on the elderly and infirm offender would be barbarous. Imprisonment seems not to be the answer for elderly offenders; more consideration should be given to the use of fines.

The obvious objection is that many offenders, old as well as young, are insolvent. Yet this may not be quite so serious an obstacle to the greater use of fines as a method of deterring elderly offenders as it would be to deterring young ones. The old offender is likely to have some social security or other retirement income, so that a fine payable in installments, for the rest of his life if necessary, can bring about a dramatic reduction in his standard of living. Should he have a big lump of property (and this is more likely in the case of an old offender than in the case of a young one), chances are that he ascribes great utility to that lump—maybe he has a strong bequest motive—so again he can be hurt badly by a heavy fine. Indeed, he can be hurt more in this case than in the first, since, in the case of elderly persons, installment fines suffer from the same defect as imprisonment: truncation due to the abbreviated life expectancy of the elderly. But unless truncation is a more serious problem with fines (and why should it be?), they are superior to imprisonment because cheaper to administer.

23. United States Sentencing Commission, *Guidelines Manual* § 5H1.1, p. 303 (Nov. 1994). The Violent Crime Control and Law Enforcement Act of 1994, § 70002, 18 U.S.C. § 3582(c)(1)(A), authorizes the release at age 70 of a prisoner who has served at least 30 years in prison pursuant to a federal sentence of mandatory life imprisonment for having committed three or more violent felonies, provided the defendant is not a present danger to the safety of any other person or the community. This is a step in the right direction, but applies to only a tiny subset of criminal defendants.

The most serious problem of criminal punishment of the old comes from the increasing frequency of life sentences, mainly of young offenders, who are numerous, without possibility of parole. The statute that ordained the federal sentencing guidelines also abolished parole for offenders sentenced under the guidelines. The states are moving in the same direction. There is a danger, though it seems not yet to have materialized, at least in the federal prison system, that the abolition of parole will result in a substantial increase in the number and percentage of elderly prisoners. According to statistics furnished me by the U.S. Bureau of Prisons, as of March 17, 1994, 5 percent of federal prison inmates were aged 51–55, 3 percent were 56–60, 2 percent were 61–65, and only 1 percent (compared to almost 13 percent of the U.S. population as a whole) were over 65. Even though it is widely believed—plausibly, in view of the trend to longer sentences and to abolishing parole—that the number of elderly prisoners is soaring,[24] the total percentage of federal prisoners over 50 years old in 1994— 11 percent—was essentially unchanged from five years earlier, when 12 percent of prisoners had been 50 years old or older.[25] But it is too soon to measure the impact of recent changes in punishment practices. Young offenders harshly sentenced within the last decade and ineligible for parole will not be elderly for several more decades.

We have time to consider carefully, therefore, whether we want to have substantial numbers of geriatric prisoners. I believe we should not want that. Since old people, even if they committed serious crimes in their youth, generally are harmless now that they are old, the incapacitative function of criminal punishment is not served by retaining them in prison. Since most violent crimes are committed by relatively young people, by the time the prisoner reaches old age the chances are that his crimes have been largely forgotten, reducing retributive pressures for continued punishment, unless his crimes were of a particularly heinous character—and, fortunately, such crimes are still relatively rare. And the deterrent effect of such punishment is apt to be negligible, because of the discounting of future costs to present value, or more dramatically the tendency of one's young self to write off one's old self. Consider a 20-year-old murderer sentenced to life imprisonment without possibility of parole. Suppose his life expectancy at age 20 is 55 years. Consider the incremental deterrence from imprisoning him af-

24. Gary Marx, "Some Would Free Inmates Held in Chains of Age," *Chicago Tribune,* June 13, 1994, p. 1.
25. Peter C. Kratcoski and George A. Pownall, "Federal Bureau of Prisons Programming for Older Inmates," *Federal Probation: A Journal of Correctional Philosophy and Practice,* June 1989, pp. 28, 30.

ter he reaches the age of 70. At a discount rate of 10 percent, a cost of $1 to be paid 50 years hence is equal to only $0.0085 today, which is to say less than 1¢; for the entire period between ages 50 and 55 it is much less than a nickel. This is monetary discounting, but (as multiple-selves analysis implies) nonmonetary cost and benefits are also discounted by most people. Criminals probably have on average very high discount rates. One reason people become criminals is that their opportunities for lawful earnings are meager, in part presumably because they have not invested heavily in their human capital; and we know that the higher one's discount rate is, the less one is likely to invest in one's human capital, since the costs are incurred in the present but the benefits are obtained in the future. Not too much weight should be placed on this consideration, however. An alternative reason for not investing heavily in one's human capital is that the expected return may be small, perhaps because one is not sufficiently intelligent to benefit significantly from education or on-the-job training or, as a consequence of poverty, discrimination, or other factors, one does not have access to education or training. But if, despite this qualification, criminals do tend to have high discount rates, the prospect of having to spend additional years in prison when old is unlikely to have a significant deterrent effect on the young criminal.

So the social benefits, in terms of any of the influential theories of the purpose of criminal punishment, of keeping young offenders in prison when they become elderly probably are slight, except in the case of particularly atrocious offenses; and here capital punishment is a possibly attractive alternative, as I shall note. The discounted present cost of imprisoning the youthful offender when, many years later, he is elderly may also seem small. But it may not be. The discount rate applicable to public expenditures (here, expenditures on building and operating prisons) is lower than the private discount rate of the average criminal. Indeed, it may be zero.[26] The argument that it is low or even zero draws support from the idea of multiple selves. Discounting the costs to be borne by future generations in effect treats the members of those generations as future stages in the life of the present generation rather than as different persons. If we are wrong to discriminate against our future selves, even more clearly are we wrong to discriminate against future persons whom we have no arguable right to control.

---

26. See, for example, Derek Parfit, *Reasons and Persons* 480–486 (1984); Tyler Cowan and Derek Parfit, "Against the Social Discount Rate," in *Justice between Age Groups and Generations* 144 (Peter Laslett and James S. Fishkin, eds., 1992).

Granted, this analysis has more force with regard to discounting utility than with regard to discounting wealth. If real (inflation-adjusted) incomes are rising over time in dollar terms and the marginal utility of income diminishes as income rises, a dollar of future income will confer less utility on the future recipient of that dollar than a dollar today would confer on a present recipient, assuming the two individuals have similar values and preferences.[27] But I do not require a social discount rate of zero to make my point, which is simply that the costs of re⁺
prison when he is old are likely to swamp the benefits.

The higher medical expenses of elderly persons, however, do not figure in my analysis. Not only are there potentially offsetting cost savings because an old prisoner creates a less acute problem of security than a young one, but if the old prisoner is released he will incur the same medical expenses and they will be paid for by the government too, through the Medicaid or Medicare programs. True, he may be healthier in prison than out, and so incur lower medical costs if he is not released, but by the same token he is likely to live longer in prison, and therefore incur greater lifetime medical expenses.

The older the prisoner was when he committed the crime, the less weight discounting will have in determining the optimal length of imprisonment. So it would not be wise to have a rule automatically releasing all offenders when they reach retirement age, as it were, even if it is certain that they will commit no further crimes. Otherwise there would be no effective punishment for crimes committed by persons on the verge of retirement. It does seem to me, however, that all prison sentences should be capped at 40 or 50 years, or at least that parole should be retained for prisoners of advanced age.[28] For crimes so heinous that such sentences seem too short, capital punishment may be preferable to adding on meaningless but not costless increments of imprisonment.

Comparison between this section of the chapter and the previous one indicates that the tort system has a better (though not perfect) grip on the special problems presented by old age than the system of criminal justice does. This is not surprising. Other studies have found evidence, and offered theoretical reasons, for the proposition that common law (that is, judge-made) systems of regulation are more responsive to economic considera-

27. Gordon Tullock, "The Social Rate of Discount and the Optimal Rate of Investment: Comment," 78 *Quarterly Journal of Economics* 331 (1964); William J. Baumol, "On the Social Rate of Discount," 58 *American Economic Review* 788, 800–801 (1968).

28. Even without parole, the governor, or in the case of federal crimes the President, can use the power of clemency to commute the elderly prisoner's sentence.

tions than legislative systems are;[29] and legislation looms larger in the modern criminal law than it does in tort law. In the next section, we consider some additional evidence concerning the common law's grasp of the problems of old age.

Dementia and Capacity

The bearing of senile dementia on legal capacity—such as the capacity to make a will or a contract, or to testify as a witness—and legal responsibility, for example for criminal acts, presents fascinating issues of both an analytical and a practical character. We know that senile dementia, as distinct from the mild cognitive impairment that is an especially common but relatively minor affliction of old age,[30] is progressive. So it would be absurd to declare a person incompetent to change his will, sign a lease, testify in court, or be prosecuted for a criminal act, merely upon proof that he had displayed the earliest symptoms of senile dementia, such as occasional disorientation and loss of short-term memory. It would be equally absurd to ascribe legal capacity or responsibility to a person so demented that he did not recognize the members of his immediate family. But where in the continuum between these extremes should the line be drawn? The increasing prevalence of senile dementia makes this an urgent question.[31]

Paradoxically, the progressive character of the disease enables the question to be avoided in some cases. For it implies that an individual who has been determined to be mentally competent (despite his dementia) at time t must have been competent at all earlier times.[32] So if a criminal defendant is determined to be competent to stand trial, this implies that he was competent at $t - n$ to commit the crime for which he is to be tried, assuming that commission of the particular crime did not require greater mental capacity than is required to follow events at trial and confer with counsel.[33]

The last qualification invites attention to a critical point: the type and amount of mentation required for an act vary significantly among the many

29. See Richard A. Posner, *Economic Analysis of Law* (4th ed. 1992), esp. pt. 2.

30. See chapter 1. The distinction has long been recognized by the law. See, for example, In re Will of Wicker, 112 N.W.2d 137, 140–141 (Wis. 1961).

31. See Edward Felsenthal, "Judges Find Themselves Acting as Doctors in Alzheimer's Cases," *Wall Street Journal* (midwest ed.), May 20, 1994, p. B1.

32. Senile people often flicker in and out from day to day, so it is important that t be a sufficiently extended period to enable a reliable determination of the individual's average mental capacity.

33. See, for example, United States v. Rainone, 32 F.3d 1203, 1208 (7th Cir. 1994).

different acts to which the law attaches legal significance. This is a general point about challenges to mental competence. It is clearest when the issue is responsibility rather than capacity. The law attaches sanctions, criminal or otherwise, to conduct in the hope of discouraging it; that at least is a major goal of sanctioning. From the standpoint of deterrence the issue is not the defendant's sanity or intelligence, but his deterrability. One observes that many people who are retarded or psychotic nevertheless respond to incentives—for example, buy less of a good when the price rises, and avoid obvious dangers—sufficiently to be able to live on their own, rather than having to be institutionalized. Why should they not also be influenced by threat of punishment or (less probably) civil liability for transgressions known by them to be such? There rightly is no generalized defense of insanity or mental defect to legal responsibility. To avoid legal responsibility a defendant must show that his mental condition made it impossible for him to understand or respond to the law's "signals" concerning the consequences of particular conduct.

The same thing is true with respect to senile dementia. I think the court was right, therefore, in *In re Estate of Peterson*[34] to hold that the fact that a man whose will was challenged was 83 years old, blind and (at least to some degree) senile, was unable to feed or clothe himself, and had "hallucinations of little horses flying around the room and wrinkling their noses at him, and his chasing them away by spitting at them," did not necessarily show that he was incompetent to destroy his old will and make a new one.[35] There was testimony that he had had lucid conversations with others concerning the will. For example, he had told one person that the beneficiary under the old will had received enough from him in gifts—a perfectly sound reason for making a new will with a new beneficiary. It would be different if he had thought that the beneficiary of his old will was one of the little horses or was responsible for their harassment of him.

Another way to understand the law's refusal to attach controlling significance to an individual's being afflicted with senile dementia is by noting that the effect of dementia on an individual's capacity to make a rational judgment is a function not only of the stage of the disease but of his mental

34. 360 P.2d 259, 267 (Nev. 1961). For similar cases, see In re Will of Wicker, note 30 above; Wright v. Kenney, 746 S.W.2d 626 (Mo. Ct. App. 1988). For a case finding that the testator's senility had progressed to a point at which he was incompetent to make a will, see Creason v. Creason, 392 S.W.2d 69 (Ky. 1965).

35. Similar cases with a similar result, although involving deeds rather than a will, are O'Brien v. Belsma, 816 P.2d 665 (Ore. Ct. App. 1991); Feiden v. Feiden, 542 N.Y.S.2d 860 (App. Div. 1989), and Weir v. Ciao, 528 A.2d 616 (Pa. Super. Ct. 1987). All three cases note the "lucid interval" phenomenon. See note 32 above.

capacity when the disease began. If *A* had an IQ of 100 on the eve of exhibiting the earliest symptoms of senile dementia, and by the time he made his new will his IQ had declined to 80, he would be at the same mental level as *B,* a young person, mildly retarded, who has an IQ of 80 (90 percent of the population has a higher IQ). So the question would be: are persons having IQs of 80 competent to make wills? (Yes.)

This approach is a little simplistic, I admit, because the mental consequences of senile dementia are not identical to those of all other forms of mental impairment, even if a "bottom line" IQ assessment would score them the same. In particular settings the loss of short-term memory that is a conspicuous symptom of senile dementia may bear more heavily on *A*'s mental capacity than on, say, *B*'s inability to read complex documents. Or more lightly. The court in *State v. Manocchio*[36] was wrong to think that cross-examination designed to bring out a witness's loss of short-term memory would tend to show that his memory of events fifteen years earlier must be equally or more impaired. But the principle is sound: it is the individual's mental capacity, rather than whether the limitations of that capacity are due to something classified as a disease, in which the law takes an interest.[37]

I am led by this analysis to question the reasoning of *Davis v. Cox.*[38] A woman sued her adult daughter for the wrongful death of the woman's husband (the daughter's father). The father was senile; "his condition vacillated between irrational behavior and drug induced quietude and his memory was almost entirely gone."[39] He moved in with his daughter and her husband, who gave him their bedroom. The bedroom contained a chest of drawers, in one of which there was a loaded pistol that the daughter had forgotten to remove when her father moved in. One morning the father opened the drawer, took out the pistol, and shot himself. The court held that it was foreseeable to the daughter "that an ambulatory senile patient subject to spells of 'wildness' " might come upon the loaded pistol and, having found it, would "mindlessly use it to work injury on himself or another."[40] But why assume that the father had acted "mindlessly?" Senile people often are aware that they are senile—or in any event that something is terribly wrong with them—and, depending on the individual's values and

36. 523 A.2d 872 (R.I. 1987).

37. This point is clearly recognized in the cases. See, for example, Dulnikowski v. Stanziano, 172 A.2d 182, 183–184 (Pa. Super. Ct. 1961).

38. 206 S.E.2d 655 (Ga. Ct. App. 1974).

39. Id. at 656.

40. Id. at 657.

circumstances, this may provide an entirely rational motive for suicide. It is unclear whether that is what happened in *Davis*. It is not even certain that the father intended to shoot himself. But it was a mistake to assume, as the court appears to have done, that everything a demented person does is irrational. In a will contest, courts examine what might be termed loosely the "objective" rationality of the testator for corroboration or refutation of an inference of competence. Recall that in the *Peterson* case the beneficiary of the revoked will had been provided for, and this provided a rational motive for the revocation of the old will and the making of the new one. The same approach could have been used, or at least considered, in the *Davis* case. But the continued stigmatization of suicide makes judges reluctant to acknowledge that it can be a rational act.

13

Age Discrimination by Employers and the Issue of Mandatory Retirement

Even before the enactment of ERISA made it more likely that an employer would resort to the threat of discharge (a threat that to be credible would have to be carried out from time to time) in order to discipline its employees, Congress had made it more difficult to fire older employees by enacting the Age Employment in Discrimination Act in 1967.[1] The Act, as subsequently amended, forbids employers to discriminate on grounds of age against any employee aged 40 or over. Originally the protected class was 40 to 65, so mandatory retirement at age 65 was permitted. The lid was raised to 70 in 1978 and removed altogether in 1986. Mandatory retirement at any age, along with any other measures retail or wholesale by which an employer treats an employee worse because of age, is, with a few exceptions, now forbidden. I argue that the age discrimination law is largely ineffectual but that to the extent it is effective it has a perverse impact both on the welfare of the elderly and on the equality of income and wealth across the entire population. The age discrimination law is at once inefficient, regressive, and harmful to the elderly.

---

1. 29 U.S.C. §§ 623 *et seq.* For contrasting evaluations, both emphasizing the economics of the statute, see Richard A. Epstein, *Forbidden Grounds: The Case against Employment Discrimination Laws,* ch. 21 (1992), and Stewart J. Schwab, "Life-Cycle Justice: Accommodating Just Cause and Employment at Will," 92 *Michigan Law Review* 8 (1993). Many states have their own laws forbidding age discrimination in employment, and there are other federal statutes forbidding age discrimination, such as the Age Discrimination Act, 42 U.S.C. §§ 6101 *et seq.,* but I shall ignore these other laws.

The Nature and Consequences
of Age Discrimination in Employment

Animus discrimination. The justification offered for the law was that people over 40 are subject to a form of prejudice, "ageism," that is analogous to racism and sexism. After putting to one side the use of the word as a synonym for anything that disadvantages an older worker[2] (so presbyopia would be "ageist"), we can posit two kinds of ageism, only one plausible. The implausible is a systematic undervaluation, motivated by ignorance, viciousness, or irrationality, of the value of older people in the work place. This is sometimes referred to as "animus discrimination." I do not deny that there is resentment and disdain of older people in our society (see chapter 9), or widespread misunderstandings, some disadvantageous to the old. I have given a number of examples; recall from chapter 7, for example, that elderly people may seem old-fashioned because they "cling" to "outmoded" methods, yet the outmoded methods may be "clung to" only because the *incremental* benefit of the latest method is slight.

But the present chapter is about the work place. Even apart from competitive pressures for rational behavior, which are considerable in private markets, the people who make employment policies for corporate and other employers and most of those who carry out those policies by making decisions about hiring or firing specific workers are at least 40 years old and often much older. It is as if the vast majority of persons who established employment policies and who made employment decisions were black, federal legislation mandated huge transfer payments from whites to blacks, and blacks occupied most high political offices in the nation. It would be mad in those circumstances to think the nation needed a law that would protect blacks from discrimination in employment. Employers—who have a direct financial stake in correctly evaluating the abilities of their employees and who for the most part are not young themselves—are unlikely to harbor either serious misconceptions about the vocational capacities of the old (so it is odd that employment should be the main area in which age discrimination is forbidden) or a generalized antipathy toward old people.

To put the point differently, the kind of "we-they" thinking that fosters racial, ethnic, and sexual discrimination is unlikely to play a large role in the treatment of the elderly worker.[3] Not because a young person will (in

2. The sense in which it is used in William Graebner, *A History of Retirement: The Meaning and Function of an American Institution, 1885–1978,* ch. 2 (1980).

3. Cf. John Hart Ely, *Democracy and Distrust: A Theory of Judicial Review* (1980).

all likelihood) someday be old; to put too much weight on the continuity of personal identity would slight the multiple-selves issue. But because the people who do the hiring and firing are generally as old as the people they hire and fire and are therefore unlikely to mistake those people's vocational abilities. One should not be surprised at how slight and equivocal the evidence that employers misconceive the ability of older workers is. Such workers do have trouble finding new jobs at high wages. But this is because the wages in their old jobs will have reflected firm-specific human capital that disappeared when they left and that they cannot readily replace because of the cost of learning new skills, and also because the proximity of these workers to (voluntary) retirement reduces the expected return from investing in learning new skills.[4]

One study found that "nearly 90 percent of [elderly] job losers' wage reductions are explained by the nontransferability of the workers' firm-specific skills and knowledge or seniority."[5] The authors ascribed the remaining 10 percent to age discrimination, but they had no basis for this ascription. The 10 percent, as they acknowledged, was merely "a residual remaining after accounting for other factors"[6]—and among the factors not accounted for was a possible age-related decline in capability. As the study was of the wages in new jobs of elderly workers who had lost their previous jobs, the possibility that the workers sampled were underperformers was indeed a significant one. The very next essay in the collection, a study of young and old workers employed by the same firm, finds that the *entire* difference in wages between the two groups is due to differences in investment in human capital.[7] And as I pointed out in chapter 4, empirical findings that workers 65 or older perform their jobs as well as younger workers in the same enterprise are vitiated by selection bias: demonstrably unsatisfactory older workers will have been fired or nudged into retirement. The fact that *some* elderly people are able to perform to an employer's satisfaction is consistent with many not being able, in which event we would expect the average wages of elderly workers to be lower for reasons unrelated to discrimination.

4. Dian E. Herz and Philip L. Rones, "Institutional Barriers to Employment of Older Workers," 112 *Monthly Labor Review,* April 1989, pp. 14, 20.

5. David Shapiro and Steven H. Sandell, "The Reduced Pay of Older Job Losers: Age Discrimination and Other Explanations," in *The Problem Isn't Age: Work and Older Americans* 37, 47 (Steven H. Sandell, ed., 1987).

6. Id. at 48.

7. Paul Andrisani and Thomas Daymont, "Age Changes in Productivity and Earnings among Managers and Professionals," in *The Problem Isn't Age: Work and Older Americans,* note 5 above, at 52.

One might think that if substandard elderly workers are weeded out, the average wages of the elderly employed would be no lower than those of the nonelderly employed, unless there were discrimination. But some of those weeded out of their current employment because they no longer perform to their employers' satisfaction will not leave the labor force; instead they will find lower-paying jobs, commensurate with their diminished capabilities, and their wages will depress the average.

The very idea of "animus" age discrimination rests on its own misconceptions—for example that employers insisted on mandatory retirement at fixed ages because they underestimated the capabilities of older people.[8] As we shall see, that was not the reason.

Statistical discrimination. The form of ageism (if it should be called that) that is more plausible and better substantiated than animus discrimination against the old consists of attributing to all people of a particular age the characteristics of the average person of that age. It is an example of what economists call statistical discrimination and noneconomists "stereotyping": the failure or refusal, normally motivated by the costs of information, to distinguish a particular member of a group from the average member. Age, like sex, is one of the first facts that we notice about a person and use to "place" him or her. We do this because we operate with a strong, though often an unconscious, presumption, echoing the rigid age grading that structures activities and occupations in many primitive societies, that particular attitudes, behaviors, and positions in life go with particular ages. "We judge one another with a notion of what status goes with what age: he's old to be a student, young to be a professor, old to marry, young to retire. Some people sometimes are 'off time' but most people most of the time 'act their age.' "[9]

The presumption that age matters in these ways is rational. Otherwise this book would have no subject; any talk of "65-year-olds" or "octogenarians" would be as irrelevant to public policy as talk about the attitudes and behaviors of people with green eyes or chestnut hair. But there is a great deal of variance in the capacities, behaviors, and attitudes of persons

8. Erdman B. Palmore, *Ageism: Negative and Positive* 5 (1990).

9. Arlie Russell Hochschild, *The Unexpected Community* 21 (1973). On the salience of perceived age in making judgments about a person's traits, see Robert Bornstein, "The Number, Identity, Meaning and Salience of Ascriptive Attributes in Adult Person Perception," 23 *International Journal of Aging and Human Development* 127 (1986). And for a brief but serviceable summary of theories of statistical discrimination, see Paula England, "Neoclassical Economists' Theories of Discrimination," in *Equal Employment Opportunity: Labor Market Discrimination and Public Policy* 59, 60–63 (Paul Burstein, ed., 1994).

in particular age groups and, partly as a result, great overlap between the capacities of persons in different age groups. People age at different rates and from different levels of capacity. So if age is used as a proxy for attributes desired or disliked by an employer, some people who are entirely competent to perform to the employer's specifications will not be hired, or will be fired or forced to retire to make away for young people who actually are less able.

This phenomenon does not, however, make age discrimination in employment inefficient any more than the substitution in some other field of activity of a rule (for example, do not drive faster than 65 miles per hour) for a standard (do not drive too fast for conditions) need be inefficient. A rule is simpler to administer than a standard and therefore cheaper, and the cost savings may exceed the loss from disregarding circumstances that may make the rule disserve the purposes behind it in a particular case. Rules have higher error costs but lower administrative costs, standards lower error costs but higher administrative costs, and the relative size of the two types of cost will determine the efficient choice between the alternative methods of regulation in particular settings. Statistical discrimination is an example of rule-based behavior, and since it is a method of economizing on information costs we can expect it to be more common in settings where those costs are high. One is not surprised therefore that age grading (like literalism, another example of rule-based behavior designed to economize on information costs) is more common in primitive than in advanced societies.[10] Yet even in advanced societies rules are frequently more efficient than standards; so mandatory retirement, and other employment classifications based on age, cannot be condemned out of hand as archaic. Few of us would be comfortable if airline pilots or military officers could not be forced to retire at any age without proof of individual unfitness.[11]

Age grading illustrates how statistical discrimination can sometimes operate in favor of, rather than against, a particular group, here by ascription of the maturity, wisdom, and disinterest possessed by some old people to all or most of them. Another circumstance that has favored the old is that few people understand selection bias. People generalize from the impressive performance of octogenarian judges that octogenarians have unsuspected capabilities; but the advanced age at which most judges are ap-

---

10. Richard A. Posner, *The Economics of Justice* 169–170 (1981).

11. The age discrimination law permits mandatory retirement of airline pilots at age 60, and the pilots' union objects. For evidence of relevant age-related decline, see Joy L. Taylor et al., "The Effects of Information Load and Speech Rate on Younger and Older Aircraft Pilots' Ability to Execute Simulated Air-Traffic Controller Instructions," 49 *Journal of Gerontology* P191 (1994).

pointed operates to draw judges from an unrepresentative segment of the aging population. If the elderly benefit from statistical discrimination as well as being hurt by it, maybe they would enjoy an undue advantage over other groups if the law succeeded in eradicating statistical discrimination against, as distinct from statistical discrimination in favor of, the elderly. I would not put too much weight on this factor, however. For reasons stated earlier, I would expect *employers* to have a generally clear-headed notion of the characteristics of the average worker in the different age groups and not be fooled by selection bias.

Mandatory retirement—a blanket rule against retaining a worker who has reached a specified age, regardless of the particular worker's actual productivity—has three supports besides the general benefits of a rule. First, knowing far in advance the age at which one will retire facilitates an individual's financial and retirement planning. A person could always *decide* he was going to retire at some particular age, yet he might fear that he might change his mind—the multiple-selves problem, once again.

Second, because full social security benefits are available at age 65 and are sharply reduced until 70 if the recipient continues working after reaching 65, there are powerful financial advantages to retiring at 65. If, therefore, few workers would want to continue working after that point, the benefits from individualized assessment of their fitness to do so will be small, yet there are apt to be significant fixed costs of establishing and operating the requisite machinery of assessment. This point suggests that the abolition of mandatory retirement is unlikely to have a big effect on the labor-force participation of the elderly, and we shall encounter evidence of this later.

Third, if, as is plausible, a significant decline in a worker's performance is probable within a few years after he reaches 65, the benefits from individualized assessment will be reduced further because they will be realized for only a short period. The costs of such assessment will rise, moreover, because the employer will have to monitor the performance of workers who have reached the stage of life at which a decline in job performance is highly probable more carefully than the performance of younger workers.

Conceivably the reaction against mandatory retirement, and the concern with age discrimination generally, may reflect the fact that statistical discrimination, being a function of information costs, probably is negatively correlated with education and IQ, since educated and intelligent people can absorb and use information more easily than other people. The "rigid" or "authoritarian" personality that psychologists associate with discriminatory attitudes[12] can be given an economic meaning: people of lower intelligence or less education employ cruder screening devices, such as stereotyping. As information costs fall on average in a society, statistical discrimination increasingly becomes the domain of the uneducated and the unintelligent, so class prejudice may incline the society's elite to disparage or even forbid the practice.

I wonder how apt this point is to age discrimination in employment, though. The difference between an employee and an independent contractor has a bearing on this question. The difference is this: the employee does not sell his output to his principal, as the independent contractor does, but instead is paid for his time. Usually this is because the worker's output is difficult to value precisely, which may be because it is team output rather than individual output. The difficulty of valuation implies that assessment of the employee's contribution to the firm will be probabilistic rather than certain. The employer will be trying to infer that contribution from characteristics of the worker and of his performance. One characteristic is the worker's age. We know that age is often correlated with performance; and with age being directly observable and performance not, it may be entirely rational for even the most intelligent employer to use the former as a proxy for the latter.

Whether this procedure should be viewed as a form of "discrimination" in an invidious sense may be doubted, unless it is somehow unfair to judge a person as a member of a group rather than as an individual. Is it unfair? We do it all the time, and could hardly act otherwise. Lacking unmediated access to the "inner man" or complete knowledge of his life history, we relentlessly "type" people and base our judgments on this typing. If, as in the example of team output in a business enterprise, individual evaluation would cost a lot, one needs an argument for forcing other people to shoulder the cost. If employers are forbidden to use efficient methods of evaluation, their labor costs will rise, and it is now generally accepted that increases in payroll taxes or other labor costs are borne largely by the workers themselves, in the form of reduced wages or benefits.[13] The increase in cost operates as a tax, and the incidence of a tax does not depend on which side of the market (here, employer or employee) the tax is assessed on.[14] If

---

12. See, with specific reference to "ageism," Palmore, note 8 above, at 53–54.

13. See Jonathan Gruber and Alan B. Krueger, "The Incidence of Mandated Employer-Provided Insurance: Lessons from Workers' Compensation Insurance," 5 *Tax Policy and the Economy* 111 (1991), and studies cited in id. at 117–118.

14. See, for example, Joseph A. Pechman, *Federal Tax Policy* 223–224 (5th ed. 1987); Laurence Kotlikoff and Lawrence Summers, "Tax Incidence," in *Handbook of Public Economics* 1043, 1047 (Alan Auerbach and Martin Feldstein, eds., 1987).

employers are forced by law to keep on inefficient elderly workers, workers as a whole, few of whom either are wealthy or are guilty of "ageism," will in effect be taxed for the benefit of these elderly workers—yet the elderly, prosperous recipients of substantial public largesse, are implausible candidates for the status of an oppressed class (see chapter 2).

Anyway the law cannot, merely by outlawing a particular form (or many particular forms) of discrimination, force employers to judge every worker as an individual. The costs of information are too high. They may be particularly high in the case of elderly workers. As we saw in the first chapter, variability in performance in an age cohort tends to grow as the cohort ages. The greater the variability in a population of workers, the longer the employer will have to search in order to find workers suitable to his needs, unless he relies on some simple proxy or rule of thumb. The costs of individualized assessment will be high. Increased variability may also make the value of such assessments greater; but remember that the expected return from selecting the very best worker (if he is old) will be truncated, because an older worker is unlikely to continue working for long.

Deprived of the age proxy, some employers will use other proxies for ability or performance, such as test results, thus "discriminating" against workers whose performance those proxies underpredict. Airlines, for example, if forbidden to impose mandatory retirement on their pilots, might raise their standards of physical fitness, with the result that some perfectly competent young pilots might be forced out. Some employers denied the use of the age proxy will throw up their hands and, unable to distinguish between good and bad workers of the same age, treat both groups indiscriminately, with the result that bad workers will benefit at the expense of good ones. This is just another form of statistical discrimination. The victims of the two different forms of statistical discrimination—the victims of lumping together people of disparate abilities though the same age (the form of statistical discrimination that the law encourages), or of treating separately people who have the same abilities but are of different age (the form of statistical discrimination that the law forbids)—will be different. But there will still be victims. And the victims of the age discrimination law, as distinct from the victims of what the law calls age discrimination, may be people more marginal, more necessitous, than the average elderly worker. Some evidence for this conjecture is that, as we shall see, most plaintiffs in age discrimination cases are not "workers" at all, but managers, professionals, and executives.

This discussion does not settle the question whether age discrimination is efficient, but it bears on it. As with other forms of discrimination, statistical discrimination against the aged worker may impose an external cost—that is, a cost to nonparties to the transaction between a given employer and a given worker or applicant for work. If the exceptional aged—those young in mind, body, and spirit—cannot cash in their exceptionality in the employment market because very few employers will look behind chronological age in making employment decisions, they will have a suboptimal incentive to invest in their human capital because the payback period will be artificially truncated. A middle-aged professional who rationally believes that he has and will retain youthful energy and intellectual flexibility will nevertheless forgo making an investment in human capital that would not be completely amortized until he was 70 years old, if he thinks that he will be forced to retire at age 65 or denied a promotion merely because of the average characteristics of his age cohort. The resulting underinvestment in human capital is the joint product of individual decisions by a multitude of employers no one of whom would be better off incurring substantial costs to identify the handful of exceptional elderly workers. It is not a complete answer that an individual worker might, by accepting a lower wage, induce the skeptical employer to make an exception in his favor. The prospect of having to accept such a wage cut would reduce the expected return to the exceptional employee's investment in his human capital and thus the amount that he would be willing to invest. Also, as I shall point out, the age discrimination law may as a practical matter rule out such transactions.

The argument that statistical discrimination is inefficient in the case of age is unpersuasive. When the costs of making individualized assessments of employees' performance are prohibitive, as they often are, prohibiting the use of the age proxy will lead to the substitution of other proxies. The problem of underinvestment will be shifted, not solved. Whoever is "unfairly" disadvantaged by the new proxy, in the sense that it does not measure *his* abilities accurately (perhaps he does not do well on pen-and-pencil tests because of deficiencies in his formal education, but is an excellent worker nevertheless), will lack the incentive to make the optimal investment in his human capital. And if the new proxies are less efficient than age—as they probably will be, because otherwise they would in all likelihood have been adopted without government prodding—wages will fall because employers' labor costs will be higher, and with lower wages there will be less incentive for workers to invest in their human capital.

Only if other proxies—other handles for statistical discrimination—are, unlike age, more costly to the employer than individualized assessment will forbidding the use of the age proxy respond to the problem of underinvestment in human capital by the exceptional elderly worker, by inducing individualized assessment. This is unlikely, though no stronger statement is possible on the basis of existing knowledge. And one does wonder how serious the problem of underinvestment in human capital by the exceptional aged ever was. Regardless of federal regulation, employers would be unlikely to have the identical policies about retirement. There never was a time when all employers had a policy of mandatory retirement at fixed ages. Competent workers wanting to retire late or not at all—always a minority of all workers—would tend either to be sorted to employers having compatible retirement policies or to become self-employed.

The Effects of the Age Discrimination in Employment Act

The previous section questioned the need for a law against discrimination on grounds of age. But we have the law, and we must now consider more carefully its probable effects both on elderly workers and on the rest of society. The first thing to note is the misfit between the scope of the Act and the concerns of the elderly. The prohibition against mandatory retirement is clearly related to those concerns, since mandatory retirement before 65 was rare. But the Act's general prohibition against age discrimination kicks in when a worker turns 40. I have done a study of court cases under the Act (see discussion below), and only 10 percent of the plaintiffs in my sample of cases, including those plaintiffs who challenged mandatory retirement, are 65 or older—a smaller percentage than the percentage of elderly people in the U.S. population as a whole. The main reason is plain enough; most people who are 65 or older are voluntarily retired, so are not protected by the Age Discrimination in *Employment* Act. Yet the Act was "sold" by means of emotional rhetoric concerning the plight of the elderly, in 1967 still viewed as a disadvantaged segment of American society, even though the Act seems to have been designed and to be administered in the interest primarily of nonelderly workers. It is unlikely that an age discrimination statute so configured would benefit the elderly much, and we are about to see that it may harm them.

Of course, since an elderly person's income is apt to depend significantly on his income when he was in his prime working years, a statute that increased the incomes of workers in those years could be thought to be benefiting the elderly. But even if we disregard the multiple-selves problem (the benefited elderly self may not be the same person as the younger self who receives benefits under the age discrimination law), we shall see that, ex ante, the beneficiaries of the law probably bear the costs of it as well, and therefore do not, on average anyway, obtain a net benefit from it.

Hiring cases. We know that, wholly apart from any laws, employers are reluctant to hire older workers. The cost of training an older worker is higher than that of training a younger one because of the age-related decline of fluid intelligence, while the expected return to the investment in training is lower because the older worker has a shorter working life expectancy.[15] The age discrimination law adds to the costs of employing older workers, and hence to the reluctance of employers to employ them, by giving them more legal rights against their employer than younger workers have. By thus reducing the hiring prospects of older people, the Act perversely impairs the incentive of the exceptional old to invest in their human capital, by reducing the expected return to such an investment.

The Act does forbid age discrimination in hiring as well as in firing, demotions, wages, and so forth. But it is largely ineffective against hiring discrimination because of the extreme difficulty of proving substantial damages in such cases. Damages are not the only relief available in a suit under the Act; injunctive relief is also possible. But the disappointed applicant is unlikely to be satisfied with an order requiring the employer to hire him; he would be entering upon the employment under most inauspicious circumstances.

The reason that substantial damages are difficult to prove in hiring cases is that ordinarily the plaintiff-applicant, if hired, would have received a wage only slightly higher than his reservation wage; for if the job that he applied for pays much more than his present job, he will have great difficulty persuading a jury that he was the best-qualified applicant. (If his next best wage was $20,000, it is hardly likely that, if only he had been younger, the defendant would have offered him $100,000.) The monetary stakes in a discharge case will often be much greater. If the discharged employee's wage contained a return for firm-specific human capital, that wage will be higher, maybe much higher, than he could get elsewhere—especially if he is too close to retirement age, or too inflexible with regard to learning new skills, for a new employer to think it worthwhile to invest in new specific

15. For empirical evidence of employers' reluctance to hire older workers, see Robert M. Hutchens, "Do Job Opportunities Decline with Age?" 42 *Industrial and Labor Relations Review* 89 (1988). Although health costs are also higher for older workers, it is not a violation of the age discrimination law for the employer to take these costs into account in designing a wage-benefits package for his employees.

capital for him. The difference between what the old worker was paid before he was fired and the much lower wage that is the best he can hope for in a new job provides the measure of his compensatory damages.

So it is no surprise that a large sample of litigated age discrimination cases contained *no* hiring cases; more than two-thirds of the cases involved termination (discharge or involuntary retirement), with most of the others involving promotion or demotion.[16] A more recent study, of age discrimination complaints lodged with the Equal Employment Opportunity Commission, finds that 87.9 percent of the complaints in which no other form of discrimination was alleged besides age discrimination involved termination, only 8.6 percent hiring.[17]

My own study is of all court cases under the Age Discrimination in Employment Act in which a final decision was rendered between January 1, 1993, and June 30, 1994, on other than procedural grounds and was reported in Westlaw, the West Publishing Company's computerized database of judicial decisions. Table 13.1 summarizes the results, broken down by form of age discrimination alleged and also by the outcome of the litigation.

Limited as it is to reported court cases, the sample is not random and cannot be assumed to be representative. In just the single year ending September 30, 1993, the EEOC received 19,884 complaints of age discrimination.[18] Only a small and nonrandom fraction of the complaints filed with the EEOC end up in court,[19] and only a fraction of that fraction is decided on the merits rather than being settled or being disposed of on a procedural ground, and is reported in Westlaw. There are no data on the outcomes of the other proceedings.

16. Michael Schuster and Christopher S. Miller, "An Empirical Assessment of the Age Discrimination in Employment Act," 38 *Industrial and Labor Relations Review* 64, 71 (1984) (tab. 3); see also Michael Schuster, Joan A. Kaspin, and Christopher S. Miller, "The Age Discrimination in Employment Act: An Evaluation of Federal and State Enforcement, Employer Compliance and Employee Characteristics: A Final Report to the NRTA-AARP Andrus Foundation" iv (unpublished, School of Management, Syracuse University, June 30, 1987).

17. George Rutherglen, "From Race to Age: The Expanding Scope of Employment Discrimination Law," tab. 5 (University of Virginia Law School, May 1994; forthcoming in *Journal of Legal Studies,* June 1995). A person who believes that he has a claim under the Age Discrimination in Employment Act may complain to the EEOC, which is empowered to sue on the person's behalf. If, as is usually the case, the EEOC decides not to sue, the person may then sue on his own. Or he may bypass the EEOC and sue without having filed a complaint with the agency, provided only that he notifies it of his intent to sue.

18. EEOC News Release, Jan. 12, 1994, p. 4 (tab. 3).

19. But remember that some court cases do not originate in complaints to the EEOC; filing a complaint with the EEOC is not a prerequisite to suit.

Table 13.1 Reported ADEA Decisions by Outcome and by Type of Discrimination, 1993

Type	Plaintiff Won	Defendant Won	% Plaintiff Won	% Type
Discharge	27	127	17.5	35.8
Constructive discharge[1]	2	26	7.1	6.5
RIF[2]	4	122	3.2	29.3
Mandatory retirement	6	4	60.0	2.3
Promoted/Demoted[3]	1	27	3.6	6.5
Hiring	2	43	4.4	10.5
Other/Mixed	7	32	17.9	9.1
Total	*49*	*381*	*11.4*	*100.0*

[1] Employee quit because employer made the working conditions unbearable for him.

[2] Reduction in force, discussed later in this chapter.

[3] Employee complains about failure to be promoted, or about being demoted.

My study is consistent with the earlier studies in finding that hiring cases are relatively rare—only 10.5 percent of the total cases in the sample. The vast majority involved a termination of one kind or another. Furthermore, the plaintiff won only two of the hiring cases—a winning percentage of only 4.4 percent. In general, plaintiffs did very poorly, winning only 11.4 percent of the cases they brought. Such success as they did have (outside of the other or mixed category) was, with the exception of the two hiring cases, confined to cases that involved a termination. No plaintiff complaining about a promotion or a demotion obtained a money judgment.

A low winning percentage for plaintiffs in a class of cases is not (provided it exceeds zero!) conclusive evidence that these cases are "losers" for plaintiffs to bring. Two points are important. The first is that a low winning percentage could be an effect of high damages awards. The higher the award if the plaintiff wins, the likelier he is to sue even if the probability of winning is small. It is just like a lottery: the bigger the pot, the longer the odds that the organizers of the lottery can set and still sell tickets. The second point is that a winning plaintiff in an age discrimination suit is entitled to reimbursement of his attorney's fees by the defendant on top of any damages awarded, while a losing plaintiff can be ordered to pay the defendant's attorney's fees only if the suit was frivolous.

Neither point is compelling in light of the results of my study. In the 29 cases in which the plaintiff obtained damages in lieu of or in addition to equitable relief, the average damages award was $257,546. This is an unimpressive figure when one considers not only that the risk of winning nothing is very great—so that when averaged together with the cases in my sample in which the defendant won, the total damages awarded come to only $29,360 per case, a modest expected gain for a federal case litigated all the way to final judgment—but also that cases involving large stakes are likely to be overrepresented in a sample of cases litigated to judgment. For, in general, the greater the stakes in a case, the more likely the case is to be litigated rather than to settle.[20]

If courts awarded a winning plaintiff attorney's fees large enough to compensate the plaintiff's lawyer, ex ante, no matter how small the probability of his winning, then, unless lawyers were risk averse and could not assemble a large enough pool of cases to eliminate the risk of losing a particular case in the pool, every case in which the probability of the plaintiff's winning exceeded zero would be brought. But usually the courts award the winning plaintiff the attorney's fee he actually incurred, with no multiplier to reflect the risk of loss. I do not have complete figures for the attorney's fees awarded in the cases in my sample, but in the 10 cases in which the award of attorney's fees was disclosed, the average award ($97,449) was 37.8 percent of the damages award. Projected to the entire sample, this would raise the expected judgment (damages plus attorney's fees) from $27,466 to $40,469, which is still a modest amount for a federal case litigated to judgment. When one considers that more than 100 million people are employed in this country, a large percentage of them over 40, the total number of suits that left a trace in Westlaw, and even the 20,000 complaints lodged with the EEOC in a somewhat shorter period, are meager. The outcomes of the cases in my sample suggest why.

Damages in a hiring case are expected to be even lower on average than in a termination case. The award in the sole hiring case in my sample in which damages were awarded was $63,000, far below the average of cases in which damages were awarded, though the case was remanded for a determination whether the age discrimination had been willful, in which event the plaintiff would be entitled to a doubling of his damages. Suppose he gets his double damages, for a total of $126,000; and suppose that the same amount is awarded in the other hiring case the plaintiff won, in which the damages award is undisclosed. When these amounts are averaged over the 45 hiring cases in the sample, 43 of which the defendant won, the expected damages (ex attorneys' fees) in this class of case is only $5,689. So it is no surprise that so few hiring cases are brought. My guess is that they

---

20. Richard A. Posner, *Economic Analysis of Law* 556 (4th ed. 1992).

are brought mainly by inexperienced lawyers. Experienced lawyers rarely litigate federal cases in which both the probability of winning *and* the judgment if the case is won are low; the expected cost of the suit is likely to swamp the expected benefit. The causality could run in the opposite direction; hiring plaintiffs lose *because* they are represented by inexperienced lawyers. But this is unlikely. If experienced lawyers can win a particular type of case, they will be drawn to it.

The high ratio of termination to hiring cases is not a peculiarity of *age* discrimination cases.[21] The essential feature that distinguishes the damages potential of a hiring case from that of a firing case—absence versus presence of significant firm-specific human capital—is unrelated to the nature of the discrimination charged, except that the older the plaintiff is, the more such capital he will have accrued, which will magnify his claim for damages in a firing case. A point made even by scholars who support the laws against employment discrimination is that the more likely a member of a protected group is to bring a termination suit and the less likely he or she is to bring a hiring suit, the greater will be the disincentive of employers to hire the members of such groups.[22]

Firing (and other discharge) cases. I have said that only if the employee is let go is an age discrimination case likely to get as far as an award of damages or any other remedy. And yet the merits of awarding substantial damages even in such cases could be questioned, on the following ground which has not, however, so far as I am aware, ever been advanced by an employer, although it is firmly rooted in the basic human-capital model. We recall from chapter 3 that part of a wage that reflects the greater value to the firm of an employee who has firm-specific human capital may be generated by the *employer's* contribution to that capital. The employee himself pays for the employer's investment in the employee's *general* human capital—skills that he can employ elsewhere in the economy—by accepting a lower wage. The employer would have no protection against the employee's using that capital to obtain a higher wage from another employer, and he therefore will not pay for it. But the employer will pay for a share, possibly a very large share, of the employee's firm-specific capital, because the employee by definition cannot obtain a return on that capital from another employer. The greater the share of this capital that the employer pays for, the lower will be the turnover of employees (for they will

21. John J. Donohue III and Peter Siegelman, "The Changing Nature of Employment Discrimination Litigation," 43 *Stanford Law Review* 983, 1015 (1991).

22. Id. at 1024.

have a higher salary) and hence the likelier will the employer be to reap the benefit of its investment.[23]

This analysis argues for allowing the employer to deduct from damages in an age discrimination firing case that portion of the difference between the wage he paid the employee, and the lower wage that the employee would command in his best alternative employment, that represents a return on specific human capital for which the employer paid. The employer loses this investment in the employee's human capital by losing the employee, and should not have to pay twice—first by swallowing the loss of the investment, and then by in effect "buying" the investment back by having to pay damages measured by its value.

The argument is sound, but it is too exotic, and the computations required by it are too difficult, to be likely to commend itself to the courts. Its real significance to an evaluation of the effects of the Age Discrimination in Employment Act lies in directing attention to the fact that employers have their own incentives, unrelated to law, to avoid firing competent employees of any age, even if replacements are available. The employer has invested in the employee, and if the employee is still productive the employer is continuing to earn a return on the investment.

The analysis to this point suggests that insofar as the age discrimination law forbids discrimination against individual employees, as distinct from discrimination against age-defined classes of employees (mainly through mandatory retirement at fixed ages, about which more later), it may, like ERISA, have little effect. The abuse against which it is directed, the arbitrary treatment of older workers, would be rare, at least in private markets, even without the law. It would be rare because, as with ERISA, employers have market incentives to avoid the abuse. But the qualification "at least in private markets" is significant. The age discrimination law also applies to public employment and to employment by colleges, universities, foundations, and other not-for-profit employers. Public and not-for-profit employers can be expected to discriminate more than private for-profit employers, for two reasons. They face fewer market pressures to minimize their labor costs; and the constraint on their obtaining profits gives them an incentive to substitute nonpecuniary for pecuniary income, and one form of nonpecuniary income is avoiding undesired personal associations.[24] Of

23. Gary S. Becker, *Human Capital: A Theoretical and Empirical Analysis, with Specific Reference to Education* 33–49 (3d ed. 1993).

24. See Armen A. Alchian and Reuben A. Kessel, "Competition, Monopoly, and the Pursuit of Money," in *Aspects of Labor Economics* 157 (National Bureau of Economic Research 1962); Posner, note 20 above, at 350, 652–653.

the 256 cases in my sample for which the necessary information is available, 23 percent were brought against government employers and 7.8 percent against nonprofit employers; these percentages greatly exceed the percentages of the labor force for which these two classes of employer account.

So: age discrimination against individual workers in whom the employer has invested significant firm-specific human capital is unlikely, at least by private employers, while age discrimination against other workers, and against older persons seeking jobs, is unlikely to be rectified by the age discrimination law because plaintiffs drawn from these categories are unlikely to have a substantial financial stake in suing.

Further evidence of the likely inefficacy of the law is the very poor win rate of plaintiffs in age discrimination cases, as shown in table 13.1. It is a surprising statistic because, unlike the situation in other employment discrimination cases until the 1991 amendments to the civil rights laws, plaintiffs in age discrimination cases are entitled to a jury if their case gets as far as trial. But few cases do. In my sample, while plaintiffs won 47.7 percent of the 20 percent of the cases that went to verdict, 74.7 percent of the cases were disposed of by summary judgment, meaning that there was no triable issue; and plaintiffs won only 1.6 percent of those cases.[25]

Why do most age discrimination plaintiffs do so poorly? When the Age Employment in Discrimination Act was enacted back in 1967, many employers were practicing age discrimination (primarily of the statistical sort), and doing so openly. It took some time for the message that age discrimination was now an unlawful practice which if continued must be concealed to filter down to the corporate personnel who make the actual employment decisions. They continued for some years blithely to generate "smoking gun" evidence of age discrimination. By now, however, employers have largely succeeded in purging such slogans as "you can't teach an old dog new tricks"[26] from the vocabulary of their supervisory and personnel staffs.[27] Some evidence that age discrimination cases are indeed increasingly difficult for plaintiffs to win comes from comparing the winning

25. The sum of 20 percent and 74.7 percent is only 94.7 percent; the remaining cases were disposed of by other forms of judgment.

26. Or "old dogs won't hunt," held evidence of age discrimination in Siegel v. Alpha Wire Corp., 894 F.2d 50, 55 (3d Cir. 1990).

27. "It is important to *sensitize all managers to the fact that any type of age reference, even in informal conversations, may have a negative impact on the organization's position* [in an age discrimination suit]." Robert A. Snyder and Billie Brandon, "Riding the Third Wave: Staying on Top of ADEA Complaints," *Personnel Administrator,* Feb. 1983, pp. 41, 45 (emphasis in original).

percentage of plaintiffs in my sample (11.4 percent) with the much higher percentage in the Schuster sample (32 percent), which was drawn from cases decided between 1968 (the first year after the enactment of the age discrimination law) and 1986.[28] But the difference may reflect, in part anyway, differences in the design of the studies.

In the absence of smoking-gun evidence of age discrimination, now difficult to come by, a plaintiff must as a practical matter show that an equally competent but younger employee was treated better. Such proof is difficult because of the intangible elements in evaluating a worker's performance other than in the simplest jobs—and the simplest jobs do not generate the plausibly high damages claims that repay the costs and uncertainties of litigation. The simplest jobs require little human capital, whether general or specific, and (partly for that reason) pay low wages.

Moreover, a firm that wants to get rid of an older employee can often do so with near impunity by cashiering a younger employee at the same time. One hears rumors that this is a common practice. It may be feasible because there is high turnover among young employees anyway and the firm may not yet have invested much in the young employee's firm-specific human capital (a principal reason *why* turnover of young employees is high) and so has little to lose from firing him, though concern with reputation must inhibit this Machiavellian strategy to some and perhaps to a great extent. The "RIF" (reduction in force) is a related strategy; victims of RIFs who complain on age discrimination grounds do very poorly—in table 13.1, even more poorly than victims of alleged age discrimination in hiring. (More on RIFs shortly.)

Another thing that makes it hard for the employee to win an age discrimination case is that older employees tend to be more costly to a firm than younger ones, by virtue of receiving a larger package of wages and benefits. The more costly they are, the more difficult it is to ascribe their discharge to their age, as distinct from their expense. The older employee may be more productive by reason of his greater experience, or he may be

---

28. See references in note 16 above. It is interesting to note that the winning rate of the plaintiffs in my sample is only about half that of plaintiffs in all employment discrimination cases (that is, including racial, ethnic, and sexual discrimination cases along with age discrimination cases). See John J. Donohue III and Peter Siegelman, "Law and Macroeconomics: Employment Discrimination Litigation over the Business Cycle," 66 *Southern California Law Review* 709, 756 (1993) (fig. 4); Theodore Eisenberg, "Litigation Models and Trial Outcomes in Civil Rights and Prisoner Cases," 77 *Georgetown Law Journal* 1567, 1578 (1989). But these studies, like the Schuster studies of age discrimination, deal with an earlier period (1977 to 1988) than my study, so are not strictly comparable.

paid a higher wage either to discourage shirking in his last period of employment or as a reward (akin to a pension in the contract theory of pensions, examined in chapter 12) for not having shirked previously. If he is more productive, then he is not in fact more costly to the firm than a younger, less well paid, but also less productive worker. And if he is being paid a so-called "efficiency" wage either to discourage shirking or to repay the "bond" that he posted as a young employee by accepting a lower salary in exchange for an implicit promise of compensation later if he behaved, he is merely receiving the benefit of his bargain. But a court is not apt to tumble to the reason why the older employee is not *really* being "overpaid" and to see therefore that the employer is reneging on an implicit contract. All the court can see is that the employer had a reason unrelated to age for firing the older worker—he was more expensive.

Courts could try to deal with this problem by treating "discrimination" based on salary as a form of age discrimination, since age and salary tend to be positively correlated. But maybe because this would make it difficult for firms to take rational steps to reduce their costs when they find, for whatever reason, that they are paying wages in excess of the market, the Supreme Court has rejected this approach.[29]

My analysis suggests that age as such is unlikely to be a good predictor of the likelihood of the plaintiff's winning an age discrimination suit. The older the employee, the easier it will be for the employer to make a plausible case that the employee was fired because he was failing or too expensive, and not because of his age as such. The length of time the plaintiff was employed by the defendant is likely to be a better predictor of the likelihood of the plaintiff's winning. It is a proxy for the amount of specific human capital invested in him, hence the amount of his damages, hence the likelihood of his having sufficiently large expected damages to be able to attract a competent lawyer to represent him. It is true that the larger the expected gain from suit to the plaintiff, the larger the expected loss to the defendant, who therefore can be expected to defend more vigorously the higher the stakes. But there is a double asymmetry. First, there is some threshold of expected gains from suit below which a potential plaintiff cannot make a credible threat to sue. Second and more interesting, the defendant normally has more to lose in an age discrimination case than the plain-

---

29. Hazen Paper Co. v. Biggins, 113 S. Ct. 1701 (1993). That is the interpretation placed on *Hazen* by such cases as Anderson v. Baxter Healthcare Corp., 13 F.3d 1120, 1125–26 (7th Cir. 1994) (see also Hamilton v. Grocers Supply Co., 986 F.2d 97 [5th Cir. 1993]), although Schwab, note 1 above, at 45 and n. 148, is not sure it is the correct interpretation.

tiff has to win, because a victory for the plaintiff will encourage other suits against the defendant.[30] This asymmetry is greater, the smaller the monetary stakes, since those stakes are symmetrical. So it will be harder for plaintiffs to win small cases than big ones. In a small case the plaintiff will find it impossible to hire an excellent lawyer because the expected gains from suit are so slight, while the defendant will be willing to pay to hire such a lawyer because it will fear the effect of losing the suit on the number of future claims against it.

The asymmetrical relation of employee and employer in the small case may justify the "one-way" attorney's fee shifting that is the norm in age discrimination as in other discrimination cases. (That is, the winning plaintiff normally obtains an award of attorney's fees, while the winning defendant normally does not.) But in view of judicial reluctance to award fee multipliers, it is unlikely that one-way attorney's fee shifting eliminates the asymmetry.

Mention of age-related decline makes it timely to note that the interaction between the Age Discrimination in Employment Act and the Americans with Disabilities Act (ADA)[31] has yet to be explored by the courts, so recent is the latter Act; it was enacted in 1990, and the employment provisions did not become fully effective until July 1994. The legislative history is pretty emphatic that old age is not in itself to be deemed a disability.[32] Yet the characteristic age-related ailments and deficits, such as frailty, mild cognitive impairment, lack of energy and strength, and failing hearing and vision may be.[33] In that event employers may be forced to adjust the demands they make on older workers in order to make it easier for the older worker to remain employed, just as employers are required to do for workers suffering from more conventional disabilities such as paralysis or blindness. For the Americans with Disabilities Act does not merely forbid discrimination against disabled workers who can perform to the employer's normal expectations (hence who are not really, or at least relevantly, disabled). It also requires the employer to make "reasonable accommodations" to the worker's disability.[34] In the case of a worker hobbled by age this conceivably might require the employer to offer him lighter work,

---

30. As noted in Rutherglen, note 17 above, at 27–28.

31. 42 U.S.C. §§ 12101 *et seq.*

32. S. Rep. No. 116, 101st Cong., 1st Sess. 22 (1989).

33. "Disability" is broadly defined to include "a physical or mental impairment that substantially limits one or more of the major life activities of [the disabled] individual." 42 U.S.C. § 12102(2)(A).

34. 42 U.S.C. § 12112(b)(5)(A).

shorter hours, or lower output quotas, since the Act provides that " 'reasonable accommodation' may include . . . job restructuring." [35] The ADA may succeed in helping older workers where the ADEA has been ineffective. But it is too early to tell.

Early-retirement offers. At least one important aspect of the Age Discrimination in Employment Act has, it might seem, surely been effective without much litigation: the prohibition of mandatory retirement at fixed ages. The existence of a policy of mandatory retirement is not concealable, so it is doubtful that much litigation has been required to extirpate the practice. It is noteworthy that there were only 10 mandatory-retirement cases in my sample and that plaintiffs won 6—a much higher win rate than in any other category of case. Here, surely, the Act has been efficacious.

Not necessarily. Employers can, without violating the law and often without incurring heavy other costs, manipulate the age distribution of their employees through offers of early-retirement benefits.[36] The reasons these offers are not very expensive are twofold. First, the right to take early retirement on terms sufficiently advantageous to make the exercise of the right attractive is a form of employee compensation no different from any other fringe benefit. Its value is uncertain but so is that of health or life insurance, the value of which to an individual worker depends on his individual health and longevity, which cannot be known with anything approaching certainty in advance. The more munificent the early-retirement offer, therefore, the less the employer need pay in wages and other benefits.

The creation of a generous early-retirement program funded (in equilibrium) by a reduction in the wage level would, it is true, make the em-

---

35. 42 U.S.C. § 12111(9)(B). See generally Daniel B. Frier, Comment, "Age Discrimination and the ADA: How the ADA May Be Used to Arm Older Americans against Age Discrimination by Employers Who Would Otherwise Escape Liability under the ADEA," 66 *Temple Law Review* 173 (1993).

36. Michael C. Harper, "Age-Based Exit Incentives, Coercion, and the Prospective Waiver of ADEA Rights: The Failure of the Older Workers Benefit Protection Act," 79 *Virginia Law Review* 1271, 1278–1279 (1993). For evidence that such offers are effective in bringing down the average age of the work force, see Laurence J. Kotlikoff and David A. Wise, *The Wage Carrot and the Pension Stick: Retirement Benefits and Labor Force Participation* (1989); James H. Stock and David A. Wise, "Pensions, the Option Value of Work, and Retirement," 58 *Econometrica* 1151 (1990); Rebecca A. Luzadis and Olivia S. Mitchell, "Explaining Pension Dynamics," 26 *Journal of Human Resources* 679 (1991); Robert M. Lumsdaine, James H. Stock, and David A. Wise, "Pension Plan Provisions and Retirement: Men and Women, Medicare, and Models," in *Studies in the Economics of Aging* 183 (David A. Wise, ed., 1994). And for specific evidence that employers use early-retirement offers to "get around" legal restrictions on mandatory retirement, see Edward P. Lazear, "Pensions as Severance Pay," in *Financial Aspects of the United States Pension System* 57, 82–84 (Zvi Bodie and John B. Shoven, eds., 1983).

ployer more attractive to workers who set a high value on leisure relative to pecuniary income,[37] whereas the employer might prefer workers with a stronger work ethic. The more employers who adopt such programs, however, the less will be the effect on the composition of any given employer's work force.

The second factor holding down the net cost to the employer of offering early retirement is that the risk to an employee of turning down even a rather chintzy such offer may be so great that offers of early retirement need not be princely to induce widespread acceptance. Unless the employee can prove that the employer's package of retirement and other benefits is not a bona fide benefits plan, but is instead designed to evade the statute's prohibition against age discrimination—and that is not an easy thing to prove—the employer can penalize the employee for refusing an offer of early retirement by offering lower benefits to employees who retire later.[38] The making of an offer of early retirement, moreover, does not commit the employer to retaining until normal retirement age an employee who turns down the offer. Herein lies the greatest risk to the employee of turning the offer down. An offer of early retirement usually reflects a desire by the employer to reduce the number or average age of its employees, and if not many employees take up the offer, and even if many do, the employer may resort to other measures for achieving the desired size and composition of his work force. The employee knows this, and knows therefore that if he turns down an offer of early retirement today, he may be fired or laid off tomorrow. And he knows that this may happen in circumstances in which it will be impossible for him either to prove age discrimination and thus obtain compensation, because the employer can demonstrate the business necessity for his reduction in force, or to find alternative employment at an equivalent wage, especially if his current wage includes a return to firm-specific human capital. I have mentioned the plight of the elderly job-seeker before and now I add that there is empirical evidence that older workers remain unemployed longer than younger ones in the wake of a plant closing or move, even after correction for the fact that they have a

37. For empirical evidence, see Olivia S. Mitchell and Gary S. Fields, "The Economics of Retirement Behavior," 2 *Journal of Labor Economics* 84, 103 (1984).

38. Public Employees Retirement System v. Betts, 492 U.S. 158 (1989). The provision of the age discrimination law on which *Betts* was based, which exempted bona fide benefits plans, was modified by the Older Workers Benefit Protection Act, Pub. L. No. 101–433, 104 Stat. 978 (1990) (codified at 29 U.S.C. § 621). But employers retain considerable latitude in withholding benefits to workers who turn down offers of early retirement. Harper, note 36 above, at 1309–1321.

higher reservation wage as a result of having pension income to fall back on.[39]

Of course the early retiree may also confront an inhospitable job market. Early "retirement" is a bit of a misnomer. The early-retirement benefits may be too meager to finance a comfortable retirement. But the employee who declines the offer and is then discharged not only lacks the cushion of early-retirement benefits, which might at the least have financed a more leisurely and productive job search; he also bears the stigma of involuntary termination.

The risk to employees of turning down an offer of early retirement is brought out in the following bit of lawyers' advice to employers:

> Most companies conduct RIFs [reductions in force] in two phases. The first phase is generally a voluntary program in which the company offers incentives to induce early retirement or other voluntary separation by those employees who are not yet eligible for normal retirement. The second phase is the involuntary termination plan, focusing upon position elimination, job performance, or some mix of the two. Management should form oversight committees to ensure that each phase will comply with company policy and applicable law.[40]

So anyone who doesn't take the hint and retire early becomes a candidate for phase 2—involuntary termination. And, should this happen, he cannot count on having a good claim of age discrimination, let alone getting a good job with another employer. Recall from table 13.1 that only 2 out of the 84 RIF plaintiffs in the sample won.[41] If the possibility of such an outcome is set to one aside, as being negligible, then, in the notation of inequality 4.2, an employee who declines the offer of early retirement may have to discount I_p, the annual pecuniary income from continuing to work rather than taking early retirement, by a probability substantially less than 1 that he will actually receive that income, either from his present employer or from some future employer, in any years between now and the normal

39. Douglas A. Love and William D. Torrence, "The Impact of Worker Age on Unemployment and Earnings after Plant Closings," 44 *Journal of Gerontology* S190 (1989).

40. Michael R. Zeller and Michael F. Mooney, "Legally Reducing Work Forces in a Recessionary Economy," *Human Resources Professional,* Spring 1992, pp. 14, 15.

41. For other evidence that victims of RIFs are rarely successful in age discrimination suits, see Christopher S. Miller, Joan A. Kaspin, and Michael H. Schuster, "The Impact of Performance Appraisal Methods on Discrimination in Employment Act Cases," 43 *Personnel Psychology* 555, 568 (1990).

retirement age. And we know that the lower I_p is (or more realistically kI_p, where k is the probability of remaining employed and $0 < k < 1$), the greater the incentive to take early retirement.

The analysis suggests that it might actually pay an employer to engage in outright age discrimination from time to time in order to increase the incentive of older employees to elect early retirement. The demonstrated likelihood of such discrimination would increase the number of employees who accepted the offer of early retirement, or would enable the employer to achieve his target number of acceptances with a less attractive early-retirement offer, or would do both. The rationally calculating employer would trade off this benefit of discrimination against the cost in damages and other expenses of violating the Age Discrimination in Employment Act. We have seen that these apparently are small. But of course they may be small because employers do not follow this strategy, and they may not because of the costs in the form of a bad reputation that an employer who treats his workers with such calculated ruthlessness would incur. He might have to pay for ruthlessness with higher wages.

Even if the employer is law-abiding, and even if he does not announce a "phase 2" (involuntary termination), the employee who turns down an offer of early retirement takes a considerable risk. For if not enough employees accept the offer, the employer may decide to institute a reduction in force, though it was not his original intention to do so. And even if the RIF hits older and younger employees indiscriminately, some of the employees who refused offers of early retirement will be among those riffed, and they will be worse off than they would have been had they accepted the offer and worse off than younger workers, who will, on average, have better employment opportunities elsewhere. Knowing this, each older offeree has an increased incentive to accept the offer. The strategy of making an early retirement offer followed by a RIF resembles two-tiered tender offers in the corporate merger market, where shareholders of the target firm compete for the generous front-end offer so as not to be stuck with the less generous back-end offer.

Offers of early retirement are not a panacea from the standpoint of the employer concerned about the age distribution of his employees. To the extent that the statutory abolition of mandatory retirement was not anticipated, employers were unable to "charge" workers (in the form of lower wages or other benefits) for the value of the option of taking early retirement. Also, the employer cannot be certain how many or which workers will accept the offer of early retirement. If he underestimates the acceptance rate, or if key workers elect early retirement, he may find himself having to incur the costs of rehiring workers to whom he has just paid early-retirement benefits.[42] The "which" problem should be separated from the "how many" problem. Bountiful offers of early retirement might lead to an undesired reduction in the quality of the employer's work force. But this is improbable. It is true that one group of workers likely to jump at such offers consists of those who have excellent alternative job prospects; any income from a new job would be in addition to their retirement benefits from the old one. These will tend to be the best workers—the most adaptable and energetic. The employer can try to hire them back—but his effort to do so will signal to them their value to him, and they will demand a high wage. However, this group of workers will be balanced by three other groups. The first consists of those who are particularly afraid that if they refuse the offer of early-retirement benefits they will be terminated shortly anyway, without the benefits; and they will tend to be the poorer workers. The second group consists of those who attach a high value to leisure; they will tend to be the less committed and enthusiastic workers. The third group consists of those elderly workers who for reasons that may be unrelated to any particular fears of being fired or any unusual demand for leisure find early retirement a preferable alternative to continuing to work. While these workers may be competent, we must remember that, by hypothesis, the employer instituted the early-retirement program in an effort to reduce the average age of his work force, so he derives a benefit from inducing a more or less random selection of aging workers (random with regard to their competence) to leave. In the employer's eyes, at least—and I have suggested that there is no reason to suppose them misperceiving—the result is to increase the average cost-adjusted quality of his work force.

Early-retirement offers appear to be common in many situations in which the employer is not interested in reducing the average age of his work force. If it is often efficient wholly apart from any desire to get around the age discrimination law, this is some indication that the costs of adapting it for that purpose are not likely to be terribly high.

The alternative to offering early retirement as a method of dealing with the problem of a superannuated work force is to identify underperforming

---

42. Frank E. Kuzmits and Lyle Sussman, "Early Retirement or Forced Resignation: Policy Issues for Downsizing Human Resources," *S.A.M. Advanced Management Journal,* Winter 1988, pp. 28, 31; Mark S. Dichter and Mark A. Trank, "Learning to Manage Reductions-in-Force," *Management Review,* March 1991, pp. 40, 41; William H. Honan, "New Law against Age Bias on Campus Clogs Academic Pipeline, Critics Say," *New York Times,* June 15, 1994, p. B6; see also Joseph W. Ambash and Thomas Z. Reicher, "Proper Planning Key to Avoiding Discrimination Suits," *Pension World,* May 1991, pp. 14, 15.

workers of any age and fire them. The drawback to this alternative is not only the risk of an age discrimination suit, but also the cost of making individual performance evaluations. All the employer may know is that his work force is "too old"; he may not be able, at tolerable cost, to determine (at least in advance) which of the older workers is not carrying his load. This, along with the maintenance of harmonious labor relations, may be a more important consideration in the substitution of the carrot of early-retirement offers for the stick of termination than the risk of an age discrimination suit, since the expected cost of such a suit to the employer may well be small.

What kind of worker brings an age discrimination suit? As a judge I have been struck by the number of cases in which a salesman contends that he was fired because of his age. This impression is confirmed by my study. Of 388 cases for which the information is available, 38 (9.8 percent) were brought by salesmen, excluding retail sales clerks.[43] At first glance the large number of such cases is surprising. Salesmen are paid largely on a piece-rate basis, so that if their productivity diminishes, whether because of age or for any other reason, their compensation and hence cost to the employer automatically falls.[44] But, to recur to an earlier point, if there are fixed costs of employment, as there are, a reduction in wages will not necessarily compensate the employer for the reduction in the worker's output, just as in the parallel case of part-time work; so also if the salesman has an exclusive territory, so that if he falls down on the job his employer's sales will diminish.

The frequency of cases involving salesmen may be due to two factors. First, selling is more strenuous than most other white-collar work,[45] and while this will induce earlier retirement, it will also induce more discharges of workers who have not yet reached retirement age. Second, salesmen often have a large amount of firm-specific human capital (much of it *relational* human capital, as discussed in chapter 3—specifically, a network of valuable customer contacts). This makes it less likely that they will be fired

43. Graebner, note 2 above, at 44–49, has a fascinating discussion of a wave of hostility to old salesmen in the period 1900 to 1924, when youthful physical energy was believed to be the key to successful salesmanship.

44. Laurence J. Kotlikoff and Jagadeesh Gokhale, "Estimating a Firm's Age-Productivity Profile Using the Present Value of Workers' Earnings," 107 *Quarterly Journal of Economics* 1215, 1236 (1992).

45. For evidence, see Pauline K. Robinson, "Age, Health, and Job Performance," in *Age, Health, and Employment* 63, 69 (James E. Birren, Pauline K. Robinson, and Judy E. Livingston, eds., 1986).

Table 13.2 Distribution of ADEA Plaintiffs, Compared with Work Force as a Whole

	% of Sample	% of Work Force
Clerical	22.6	21.7
Manual	16.7	48.6
Professional/Managerial	50.9	23.4
Sales	9.8	6.3

but if they are fired it creates the prospect of very sizable damages, since their alternative wage is likely to be far below what they were receiving when they were fired. The second-largest award of damages in the sample was in fact obtained by a salesman.[46] In contrast, employees whose principal human capital is general rather than specific, so that their alternative wage is close to the wage they were receiving when fired, or whose wages are in any event too small for the prospect of an award of lost wages to warrant the bother and expense of a lawsuit, will rarely show up as plaintiffs.

Consistent with this conjecture, most age discrimination suits are brought by professional or managerial employees, who have high salaries; and most plaintiffs are in their fifties, and so have accumulated a lot of specific capital and therefore have a substantial damages claim.[47] In my study, 234 of 388 cases were brought by professional, managerial, or sales employees—more than 60 percent. This figure is greatly disproportionate to the share of these classes of workers in the working population as a whole, as shown in table 13.2.[48]

46. By a curious coincidence, this case came up to my court on appeal, and it fell to me to write the opinion affirming the judgment in the salesman's favor. EEOC v. G-K-G, Inc., 39 F.3d 740 (7th Cir. 1994). I was not aware at the time that the case was in my sample. I should point out that many salesmen have, by virtue of their network of customer contacts, *market*-specific capital, that is, capital they can carry with them to competitors of their present employer, who will often try to prevent this by requiring his salesmen to sign covenants not to compete, as in the *Suess* case cited in chapter 3. See Paul H. Rubin and Peter Shedd, "Human Capital and Covenants Not to Compete," 10 *Journal of Legal Studies* 93 (1981).

47. On both points, see Schuster and Miller, note 16 above, at 68 (tab. 1); Schuster, Kaspin, and Miller, note 16 above, at iii (59.3 percent of cases filed by managerial and professional employees). "The ADEA has become a grievance mechanism primarily utilized by white males and white-collar workers." Christopher S. Miller et al., "State Enforcement of Age Discrimination in Employment Legislation" 18 (unpublished, Syracuse University, School of Management, n.d.).

48. The differences in percentages between the case sample and the population as a whole are statistically significant at the conventional 5 percent level except with respect to the clerical workers.

The largest number of plaintiffs in the sample were in the 55 to 59 age group and the second largest in the 50 to 54 and 60 to 64 groups; only 24.3 percent were younger than 50. Young people would not have accumulated as much firm-specific human capital and therefore would have lower damages. Elderly people (only 8.6 percent of the plaintiffs were 65 or older) would be either retired, and therefore no longer protected by a statute protecting employees (unless they had been involuntarily retired), or close to retirement, in which event their expected damages would be low, just as in the case of young workers.

As other studies have shown, blacks and women are underrepresented as plaintiffs in age discrimination cases.[49] One explanation is that blacks and women don't "need" to file an age discrimination suit as much as white males, because they have other civil rights statutes to base a suit on. This is not a plausible explanation, as it is normally advantageous to sue on as many tenable claims as one has. A more likely explanation is that blacks and women tend to have smaller investments in human capital, including firm-specific human capital, than white males.[50] The smaller that investment, the less the expected gain from bringing an age discrimination suit.

Given who the plaintiffs are, the Age Employment in Discrimination Act cannot realistically be characterized as progressive legislation. To the extent that the employer must factor into his labor costs the expected costs of damages judgments or settlements along with all the other costs of complying with (or violating) the Act, he will pay lower wages. He will try to lower the wages of those classes of workers most likely to bring and win age discrimination suits, but a perfect match-up cannot be expected, and this means that the costs of the Act will be borne in part at least by average workers. The Act's effect is thus to redistribute wealth from younger to older workers, or, after it has been in effect for many years, from the same workers' youth to their middle age; and, to a lesser extent, from average workers to members of the professional and managerial class (including commissioned salesmen), who account for most age discrimination cases.

These wealth effects are a clue to how statutes like the Age Discrimination in Employment Act and ERISA get passed in the first place even

49. See, for example, note 47 above; Rutherglen, note 17 above, at 21–22. I do not have the racial identity of the plaintiffs in my sample, but I do have their sex: 24.9 percent were women, which is only slightly more than half their percentage of the total U.S. work force.

50. For evidence regarding women, see Elizabeth Becker and Cotton M. Lindsay, "Sex Differences in Tenure Profiles: Effects of Shared Firm-Specific Investment," 12 *Journal of Labor Economics* 98, 107–108 (1994); Elisabeth M. Landes, "Sex-Differences in Wages and Employment: A Test of the Specific Capital Hypothesis," 15 *Economic Inquiry* 523 (1977). I do not have evidence regarding firm-specific human capital of blacks.

though they are likely to have few effects in the long run other than to raise labor costs somewhat. They have substantial *one-time* effects, on the current generation of employers and employees. ERISA transferred substantial expected wealth from the federal taxpayer to the participants in underfunded pension plans, and the Age Discrimination in Employment Act increased the job security of a number of workers (notably professors, as we shall see), subject to the qualifications discussed earlier. After employers have had time to adjust to the new regime and the current generation of employees has given way to the next, most of the costs imposed by the laws will be shifted back to employees, so that workers as a whole, including the members of the current generation as they age, will on average derive no benefit from the laws.

Of course to the extent that multiple-selves analysis is valid, a redistribution of wealth from one's young self to one's old self is not the same thing as moving wealth from one's left trouser pocket to one's right pocket. Nevertheless the welfare of the two selves is closely linked, in much the same way that the welfare of a man and of a woman is closely linked, through joint consumption, in marriage. As a result, efforts to prefer old over young, like efforts through sex discrimination law to prefer female over male, are unlikely to have substantial net redistributive effects. If sex-discrimination law increases employers' labor costs, resulting in lower wages to male employees, the wives of those male employees will suffer.[51] Similarly, laws that redistribute wealth from young to old harm the old to the extent that the old self internalizes the welfare of the young self. Also, the redistribution in question here is from young to middle aged rather than young to old, and the multiple-selves perspective is less consequential in the former case.

The effects on the economy summarized. I have emphasized the extent to which the goals, at least the ostensible goals, of the Age Discrimination in Employment Act appear to have been subverted as a result of rational profit-maximizing conduct by employers. But it would be a mistake to conclude that the Act's effect on the economy has been negligible (although probably it has been small), even if costs of litigation and of legal counseling are ignored. The transition costs, both the costs of gearing up for compliance with the new law and the costs of revising the terms of

---

51. Richard A. Posner, "An Economic Analysis of Sex Discrimination Laws," 56 *University of Chicago Law Review* 1311 (1989). There is an offset: husbands of wives who are benefited by laws against sex discrimination benefit also. But the offset is only partial, because fewer women than men work and working women are less likely to be married than working men.

employment in order to reestablish the employer's desired age profile, should not be ignored just because they are transitional.[52] They can, however, be minimized by advance notice of the law. Congress wisely gave universities eight years' notice of the abolition of mandatory retirement at fixed ages, though the universities were, as we shall see, insufficiently wise to take advantage of this breathing space.

It is possible that the Act, rather than raising the average retirement age—a stated objective, motivated by the hope of reducing the cost of the social security program—has, by encouraging offers of early retirement some of which are accepted by employees whom the employer does not want to lose, reduced the average retirement age, inducing an inefficient substitution of leisure for work. Although evidence presented in the next section of this chapter casts doubt on that particular suggestion, the Act has undoubtedly caused other labor-market distortions, as we have seen, including discouraging the hiring of elderly workers. Another way in which the Act may have hurt elderly workers is by discouraging contracts in which a worker agrees to work for a reduced wage, because of his diminished capacity, in lieu of being discharged. Such contracts would not be common even if there were no law against age discrimination, because of the fixed costs of employment and other considerations that we encountered in the discussion of retirement in chapters 3 and 6. Still, there might be some. The age discrimination law does not forbid such contracts, but it makes them unattractive to employers. It is much easier to escape liability by discharging a worker whose productivity has diminished because of his age than by attempting to justify paying a lower wage to the elder of two workers who have the same job.

The law causes another distortion. In chapter 9, I pointed out that new firms are likely to have a younger age distribution than old ones, because they do more hiring and most hires are of young workers; older workers tend to be locked into their existing employments by their firm-specific human capital and also to be less adaptable to new situations. This suggests that the age discrimination law discriminates in favor of new firms because a smaller proportion of their employees are in the protected class (which, remember, begins at age 40) and because, as I have pointed out, the law is far more effective against discrimination in firing than in hiring. A possibly offsetting factor, however, is economies of scale in

52. Louis Kaplow, though highly critical of transitional relief (including delayed implementation), acknowledges that it may be efficient when adjustment costs are high. Kaplow, "An Economic Analysis of Legal Transitions," 99 *Harvard Law Review* 509, 591 n. 251, 592 n. 254 (1986).

compliance with complex laws. These economies would tend to disfavor new firms relative to old ones because the former would be on average smaller.

The Economics of Mandatory Retirement

I want to examine more closely the effects of the 1986 amendment to the Age Discrimination in Employment Act that abolished mandatory retirement at any age in most occupations. A mundane but important point is that most workers *want* to retire when they reach what has been the normal retirement age. A few must want to stay on; otherwise firms would never have imposed mandatory retirement. But many who do want to stay on can negotiate mutually satisfactory terms with employers for doing so.[53] And if not, they can, as we have seen, be gently pried out, even after mandatory retirement has been abolished, by means of offers of early retirement on advantageous terms. It has been estimated that prior to the 1978 amendment to the Age Discrimination in Employment Act that raised the minimum mandatory retirement age from 65 to 70, only 5 to 10 percent of retired workers had been retired involuntarily.[54] This may be an overestimate. For the year following the passage of the amendment saw no interruption in the steady downward trend in the percentage of persons 65 and older employed.[55] In addition to offering the carrot of early retirement, employers can wield a stick: they can require their workers to work harder, in the expectation that the disutility of working harder will fall disproportionately on the older workers and induce them to retire "voluntarily."[56] It would be very difficult as a practical matter for a worker to challenge such a tactic successfully under the age discrimination law.

So it would not be surprising if the 1986 amendment had had no effect except to confer windfalls on the relative handful of workers sufficiently likely to hang on to induce a sweetening of early-retirement offers. But of

53. See generally Robert L. Kaufman and Seymour Spilerman, "The Age Structures of Occupations and Jobs," 87 *American Journal of Sociology* 827 (1982).

54. Philip L. Rones, "The Retirement Decision: A Question of Opportunity?" *Monthly Labor Review,* Nov. 1980, pp. 14, 15; see also Joseph F. Quinn, Richard V. Burkhauser, and Daniel A. Myers, *Passing the Torch: The Influence of Economic Incentives on Work and Retirement* 85–87, 199 (1990).

55. Rones, note 54 above, at 15–16. A subsequent study confirms that the 1978 amendment, which raised the minimum mandatory retirement age to 70, had no significant effect on the rate of participation in the labor force of persons 65 and over. Edward F. Lawlor, "The Impact of Age Discrimination Legislation on the Labor Force Participation of Aged Men: A Time-Series Analysis," 10 *Evaluation Review* 794 (1986).

56. Rones, note 54 above, at 15.

this we cannot be certain. The downward trend in the labor-force participation rate of elderly men did finally bottom out, in 1985, and it has risen
moderately since (see figure 2.7). The rise has been greater for women, but
this means little; one would expect the labor-force participation rate of elderly women to be growing without regard to any legal changes, simply
as a function of the greatly increased participation of women in the labor
force in recent decades. But it is conceivable that the rise in the labor-
participation rate of elderly men has been due, at least in part, to the abolition of mandatory retirement, although further study would be necessary in
order to separate out other possible causal factors.

The 1986 amendment may have had a perverse effect on economic
equality. We know from chapter 3 that education steepens the age-income
profile—lower wages during the schooling period being made up by higher
wages later—so earnings peak later for the educated worker and he is
therefore more likely to want to work to an advanced age than a less educated worker. This implies that the abolition of mandatory retirement is
likely to benefit mainly the better-educated, who are also likely to be the
abler workers and therefore have higher incomes beyond what is necessary
merely to compensate them for their greater investment in human capital.
This is further evidence that the Age Discrimination in Employment Act is
regressive.[57] But it is regressive only in the short run, neutral in the long,
since in the long run the highly educated will pay for the opportunity of
working longer than their employer would like by accepting lower wages
in their earlier years.

Let us take a closer look at the history and rationale of mandatory
retirement. It did not become common until after World War II.[58] Its advent
coincided with the provision of pension benefits on a systematic basis by
large firms to all their long-time employees. The combination of a pension
plan with mandatory retirement protects the worker against a penurious old
age and the employer against having to pay a wage to a worker who is no
longer productive yet may actually be receiving a wage premium in order
to counteract his incentive to slack off in his last period. Even if the worker
is not receiving an incentive wage premium, and even if there is no contractual impediment to a reduction in his wage,[59] age-related decline in capa-

57. See Edward P. Lazear, "Why Is There Mandatory Retirement?" 87 *Journal of Political
Economy* 1261, 1281–1283 (1979).

58. James H. Schulz, *The Economics of Aging,* ch. 3 (5th ed. 1992).

59. And there may be, especially if the worker is covered by a collective bargaining agreement. Unions want employers to have as little discretion as possible to discharge workers. So it is
no surprise that before mandatory retirement was abolished, unionization and mandatory retire-

bility may have reduced his productivity to the point where the employer would be better off replacing him. The employer could discharge the worker or force him to retire. But in the absence of mandatory retirement at a fixed age the employer would have to make a costly and (to the worker) humiliating determination that the worker had ceased to be sufficiently productive to justify retention. Because of its relation to incentive wage premia, union protections, and concern with avoiding stigma, mandatory retirement at fixed ages, rather than being a symptom of the exploitation of older workers or the operation of a mindless ageism, is correlated with employment terms and practices that favor older workers.[60]

Mandatory retirement may also reduce an employer's agency costs (the costs of aligning employees' incentives with those of the employer). When involuntary retirement is at the discretion of the employer, employees who want to work past the normal retirement age will have an incentive to forge alliances with their supervisors that may undermine the loyalty of both sets of employees, the supervised and the supervisory, to the employer. This concern may help explain why the federal civil service was one of the earliest institutions to adopt mandatory retirement. The goal was to sever the "personal ties and informal bonds" that continued to characterize relationships within the civil service long after the formal abolition of the spoils system.[61]

Mandatory Retirement of Judges and Professors

As a former professor and present federal judge, I should perhaps apologize for devoting a separate section of this chapter to the issue of mandatory retirement for members of these two famously tenured professions. But I do not think that it is self-interest alone that makes me think the issue a fascinating one.

Consider to begin with the highly unusual retirement system for federal judges, a system that has never included mandatory retirement. Judging is light work that confers substantial nonpecuniary income; this makes I_0 in inequality 4.2 strongly positive for most judges, discouraging retirement. And because the removal of a federal judge is a cumbersome under-

---

ment were strongly positively correlated. Duane E. Leigh, "Why Is There Mandatory Retirement? An Empirical Reexamination," 19 *Journal of Human Resources* 512, 525 (1984).

60. As not only economists realize. See Carole Haber and Brian Gratton, *Old Age and the Search for Security: An American Social History* 108–109 (1994). But see Martin Lyon Levine, *Age Discrimination and the Mandatory Retirement Controversy* (1988), a powerfully argued lawyer's brief against mandatory retirement, questioning the economic rationale for the practice.

61. Graebner, note 2 above, at 87.

taking,[62] it might seem all but impossible to get rid of a federal judge incapacitated by old age. In a sense it is. And yet the problem of age-induced incapacity in the federal judiciary has not been a serious one. To begin with, because judging is light work, senility is virtually the only condition short of death that disables a judge from performing at a satisfactory although not necessarily distinguished level. Stated otherwise, the curve of age-related judicial decline is relatively flat, reducing the social gains from involuntary retirement. Second, through the institution of senior status explained in chapter 8, federal judges can retain full salary (and actually increase their net after-tax income) while carrying a lighter caseload. It is a deal that few federal judges can resist. And here is the kicker: once a judge takes senior status, he serves at the pleasure of the judicial council of his circuit, which can reduce or eliminate the senior judge's caseload (of course without affecting his salary) if it decides that he is incapable of performing at a minimum level of competence. This is one reason why not all judges take senior status as soon as they can. But most do sooner or later. As a result the absence of mandatory retirement has not reduced the quality of federal adjudication substantially and conceivably may even have increased it, both by making employment as a federal judge a more attractive career for lawyers who anticipate a vigorous and productive old age and by eliminating the last-period problem that would arise if judges looked forward to postjudicial employment. Although like other part-time work senior status makes it more difficult for the employer to recover fixed labor costs such as office rent (senior judges do not give up or share offices), those costs are relatively low; most judges do not yet work with expensive machinery. A final consideration is that judges who have served for ten years but have not yet reached the minimum retirement age of 65 are nevertheless entitled to retire at full pay if they become totally disabled. This

---

62. Article III of the Constitution entitles judges to remain in office "during good behavior." If this means as long as they don't commit high crimes or misdemeanors, which are the stated grounds for impeachment, then it is not clear that failing powers alone, not being an ethical flaw, are a valid ground for removal even by impeachment, let alone by any means short of (and hence cheaper than) impeachment. See Melissa H. Maxman, "In Defense of the Constitution's Judicial Impeachment Standard," 86 *Michigan Law Review* 420 (1987). Congress has sought to skirt the problem by enacting legislation which empowers the judicial council of each of the federal circuits (the governing committee of judges of the circuit) to certify a judge as disabled and terminate the assignment of any further cases to him. 28 U.S.C. § 372(c). Since the judge would not be removed from office, this procedure may not violate Article III, although the issue has never been definitively resolved. Informal pressures have usually sufficed to bring about the retirement of a judge physically or mentally disabled because of extreme old age or otherwise. Charles Gardner Geyh, "Informal Methods of Judicial Discipline," 142 *University of Pennsylvania Law Review* 243, 284–285 (1993).

fat carrot has made it largely unnecessary to wield the stick of compelled retirement for disability.[63]

I am not prepared to argue that the senior-judge system is *in fact* superior to mandatory judicial retirement at a fixed age. We know from chapter 8 that senior judges have a lower output than the regular judges. Since they are paid the same, it follows that they are less productive unless the average quality of their opinions is higher, which it is not. But the diminution in productivity has to be compared with the costs, in a reduction in the quality of judicial candidates and in last-period problems, of imposing mandatory retirement on judges. Such a comparison (using citation counts to proxy quality of judicial output) should be possible, since the state judiciaries have different tenure provisions, but has not to my knowledge been undertaken.

Federal judges generally do not view the institution of senior status as I am doing, that is, as an alternative to mandatory retirement. The prevailing view in the federal judiciary is that senior judges are working for "free" (apart from staff and other office costs) since they could retire at full pay. But nothing in the Constitution requires that judges be allowed to retire at full pay. The generous retirement provision, like a generous early-retirement offer, is a method of inducing retirement in a system in which mandatory retirement is unavailable.[64] Its generosity cannot be taken as given when the issue (however academic, given Article III of the Constitution) is whether it would be better to institute mandatory retirement.

The problem discussed earlier of the possible effects of generous retirement offers on the quality of a work force might seem especially acute with respect to judges. The ablest might be expected to retire as soon as possible in order to pursue lucrative opportunities in the private practice of law, while the worst would have no incentive to retire because they would not have those opportunities, and they could not as a practical matter be forced to retire. The critical difference is that federal judicial retirement is not *early* retirement. The earliest possible age of retirement is 65, and at

63. See preceding footnote.

64. The fact that the generosity of the judicial retirement system is functional does not mean that it is generous *because* it is functional. Judges are a type of civil servant, and federal civil servants have proved to be an effective interest group, among other things in extracting unusually generous retirement benefits. Ronald N. Johnson and Gary D. Libecap, *The Federal Civil Service System and the Problem of Bureaucracy: The Economics and Politics of Institutional Change* 89–91, 112, ch. 6 (1994). An additional point is that because public discontent with the remuneration of public employees focuses on salaries—the costs of information make it difficult for the voting public to cost out an entire compensation package—legislatures tend to bias the compensation of these employees toward nonsalary benefits and perquisites, including pensions.

that age few judges have a stomach for the pressures and risks of practice when they can retain and exercise their judicial office at full pay yet with a substantially reduced workload. The qualification ("when they can retain . . .") is important. Even though few judges will take up the practice of law at age 65 *if they can continue judging on a part-time basis with no reduction of salary,* remove that condition and the number would be greater, and perhaps large.

Analysis of mandatory retirement for academics is broadly similar to that of judges, though there are some important differences.[65] Academic work is light and confers nonpecuniary benefits which normally exceed any nonpecuniary costs of the work. The combination implies that many academics, like many judges, would prefer not to retire at the usual retirement age. This is especially likely at the elite research universities, where teaching loads are light. A multivariate study of the age at which academics retire found that "tenured faculty members in the arts and sciences retire later when their jobs consist in large part of research, when their teaching loads are lighter, and when they teach good students"[66]—in other words, when the nonpecuniary benefits of work are large and the nonpecuniary costs small. The better the university, the more likely these conditions are to be satisfied. So it is generally agreed that the abolition of mandatory retirement will prove to be significant mainly for the relative handful of elite research universities.[67]

The authors of the study were surprised to find that the average age of retirement was unrelated to whether the college or university had a mandatory retirement age.[68] They should not have been surprised. The leitmotif of this chapter is that an employer can use offers of early retirement to bring about its desired age distribution of employees. Mandatory retirement is merely one instrument. Yet every private university (as distinct from public university or public or private college) in the authors' sample had mandatory retirement. This is not surprising either. Since the net nonpecuniary benefits of working past the "normal" retirement age tend to be greater in those institutions (most elite research universities are private, and none,

---

65. See Epstein, note 1 above, at 459–473, for a highly critical analysis of the abolition of mandatory retirement for academics; also Honan, note 42 above. For a more favorable view, see National Research Council, *Ending Mandatory Retirement for Tenured Faculty: The Consequences for Higher Education* (1991).

66. Albert Rees and Sharon P. Smith, *Faculty Retirement in the Arts and Sciences* 23 (1991).

67. See, for example, National Research Council, note 65 above, at 38.

68. See Reese and Smith, note 66 above, at 22–23.

obviously, are colleges), the cost of offers sufficiently lavish to induce most older faculty to retire early would be greater too.

Of course there would be no *reason* to try to induce older faculty to retire unless academic performance tends to decline with age. Nor would either mandatory retirement or early-retirement incentives be important if it were feasible to fire declining faculty members for cause. These points turn out to be related.

Although tenured academics can be removed for cause more easily than federal judges can be, this is an empty observation. Elite universities are not much worried about downright incompetents. Distinguished academics are not immune from aging; their capabilities, like those of other people, tend to decline with age. But since distinguished academics are declining from a high level, they will ordinarily retain enough ability into their seventies and even eighties to perform passably. In the notation of earlier chapters, the higher m, the performance peak, is, the longer it will take, other things being equal, for performance to intersect r, the minimum capability for the job in question. The university wants its older faculty members to retire only so that it can hire younger persons who would be even better because they would be at or approaching their peak years, rather than past their peak. Not being as good an employee as a potential replacement would be is not the usual understanding of "cause" for involuntary termination; to demonstrate "cause" the university must demonstrate incompetence, immorality, or insubordination.[69] Tenure protection is rarely (though not never) necessary to prevent the replacement of a better by a worse employee. Apart from its rare invocation by the politically unpopular, tenure protection for academics serves primarily as protection precisely against being fired when their value in the academic market falls below that of the young academics clamoring to take their place.

So the power reserved in every tenure contract to fire for cause is not likely to be of much more help in removing older faculty than impeachment is in removing older judges. And because fluid intelligence is a larger component of research capability than of adjudicative capability, the age-related curve of decline of academics is steeper than that of judges, at least at the elite universities, where research is emphasized more than teaching. Also (and again especially at research universities) the relation between older and younger academics is more competitive than that between older

69. See, for example, Drans v. Providence College, 383 A.2d 1033, 1039 (R.I. 1978); Robert Charles Ludolph, "Termination of Faculty Tenure Rights Due to Financial Exigency and Program Discontinuance," 63 *University of Detroit Law Review* 609 (1986).

and younger judges; older academics may hang on in order to block the appointment or advancement of youthful challengers. This is an argument against delegating the power of faculty appointments to faculty. We can expect a reduction in that delegation as one response to the abolition of mandatory retirement.

We need to know *how* steep the age-related decline of faculty performance is, for that is the key to how costly the abolition of mandatory academic retirement is likely to prove. The profile of course differs by field, paralleling the differences in age profiles of creativity that I discussed in chapter 7. The multivariate study mentioned earlier confirmed that there is an age-related decline in academic research,[70] but noted that since the decline begins at age 35 and is gradual, the decline between ages 65 and 70 is slight. The authors found this reassuring. They should not have. A slight decline in performance between 65 and 70 is consistent with a steep decline between 71 and 75, or 71 and 80. The study sample did not include enough professors over 70 to venture estimates of the performance of this group. It would be question-begging to extrapolate from the performance of younger faculty to that of older faculty.

Like other employers, universities can obtain or at least approximate their preferred age profile of employees by offering early retirement on attractive terms. The judiciary lacks this flexibility under existing law. Senior status and the rules governing social security taxes and entitlements provide some inducement to judicial retirement; universities could offer their faculty members more. The long-run cost to universities, as to other employers, need not be high, since the prospect of early retirement on generous terms will reduce the wage demands of young faculty. The universities had eight years in which to prepare for the abolition of mandatory retirement and could during that time have reduced wages or benefits (or, for tenured faculty, the rate of increase in wages or benefits) to fund the option of continued employment that the law would require them to offer their faculty members beginning in 1994. I am not aware that any universities did this, even though young faculty members are (and presumably were then) well aware that the law gave them a valuable option,[71] and might be expected to realize they might have to pay for it.

---

70. Reese and Smith, note 66 above, at 70 (fig. 4–3). To similar effect, see Alan E. Bayer and Jeffrey E. Dutton, "Career Age and Research-Professional Activities of Academic Scientists: Tests of Alternative Nonlinear Models and Some Implications for Higher Education Faculty Policies," 49 *Journal of Higher Education* 259 (1977).

71. Honan, note 42 above, quotes a 33-year-old assistant professor of history as saying "I'm glad about the change in the law, because I myself may not wish to retire when I'm 70."

Because of lack of preparation, universities may, like other employers forced by the Age Discrimination in Employment Act to abandon mandatory retirement at fixed ages, experience a one-time loss measured by the early-retirement benefits that they are paying to faculty members whose wage-and-benefit package did not, when negotiated, reflect the expected value of such benefits. This loss may be greater than that incurred by most other employers affected by the Act's successive waves of lifting (and finally removing altogether) the minimum mandatory retirement age, since tenure makes it difficult for a university to hold an implied threat of termination over the heads of its faculty employees. One effect of the abolition of mandatory retirement for professors may be, therefore, a movement to abolish academic tenure in order to reduce the cost of early-retirement offers—and also to counteract the potentially serious effect of the abolition of mandatory retirement on the quality of faculty at elite universities. Recall that early-retirement offers are likely to be snapped up by both the best and the worst workers—but by the latter only because there is an implied threat of termination if they refuse the offer, and that threat is weak in the case of tenured professors. Only the best professors have strong incentives to take early retirement. The best older professors tend to be those who remain active in research and may therefore welcome retirement as an opportunity to allocate even more time to research; who are not jealous of the young and therefore do not fear displacement by them; who are more likely to be scrupulous and self-aware and therefore to worry about overstaying their welcome; and who have attractive opportunities for employment elsewhere. The worst older professors do not engage in research any more; they may not enjoy teaching, but they are not likely to have heavy teaching responsibilities, because students will avoid their classes; and they may enjoy faculty intrigue. They may be jealous and fearful of the competition of the young and insensitive to their own decline. And they will have no good opportunities for employment elsewhere. Hence the abolition of mandatory retirement for academics may, though probably only at elite universities, reduce the average quality of the faculty unless tenure is abolished.

The prohibition against mandatory retirement of federal judges poses a less serious social problem. This is not only because most judges who decide not to retire are capable of creditable performance of their duties at what in other occupations would be considered bizarrely advanced ages, and not only because mandatory retirement would have adverse effects on the selection and incentives of judges, but also because there is no danger of old judges' blocking the advancement of the young. Judges do not appoint, and rarely even influence significantly the appointment of, their successors.

It is time to wind up. There are polar positions on the situation of elderly people in the United States of today. One is that they are—or would be, were it not for extensive government transfer and regulatory programs—an oppressed class no different from blacks or women or homosexuals; are or would be, that is, victims of a pervasive "ageism" just as vicious and irrational as racism, sexism, or homophobia are thought to be; victims of false stereotypes concerning the mental and physical capacities of elderly people that make them despised by the young and by themselves and that exclude them from the workplace. The opposite position is that the elderly are pampered parasites, denying the reality of aging, selfishly employing their disproportionate political power to siphon the wealth of the country into the support of their ever more clamorous demands for generous pensions and extravagant medical care, dooming the country to gerontocratic stagnation and mediocrity.[72] The discussion in the chapters in the closing part of this book, and in the earlier parts as well, suggests that neither extreme position is tenable. The evidence that there really is a process called aging that takes its toll of everyone, albeit at different rates, generating palpable and often occupationally relevant physical and mental differences between older and younger persons, is more compelling than any evidence thus far advanced to demonstrate occupationally relevant differences in the fundamental capacities of men and women, whites and blacks, or persons who differ in their sexual orientation. And while, as I have continually emphasized, the young self and the old self may for some purposes be different persons, they are connected by bonds of altruism and personal identity far closer than those that link the dominant and subordinate participants in other relations argued to be discriminatory. So it is implausible (and for the further reason that there appears to be a genetic basis for the respect and affection that most people accord to the elderly members of their families) either to cast young and old in an "us-them" opposition that might explain discrimination against elderly people, or to infer discrimination from policies such as mandatory retirement that treat elderly people differently and superficially—but only superficially—less favorably than

---

72. For responsible statements of the respective polar positions, compare Howard Eglit, "Health Care Allocation for the Elderly: Age Discrimination by Another Name?" 26 *Houston Law Review* 813 (1989), with Jan Ellen Rein, "Preserving Dignity and Self-Determination of the Elderly in the Face of Competing Interests and Grim Alternatives: A Proposal for Statutory Refocus and Reform," 60 *George Washington Law Review* 1818 (1992).

young people. In many fields of endeavor, especially highly creative fields, where fluid intelligence is more important to success than crystallized intelligence, the declension of ability with age is very steep. It is sentimental to pretend otherwise, or to treat rare exceptions as stating the rule.

Many of the prevalent misunderstandings about aging and old age result from simple methodological errors, above all a failure to correct for selection or retention bias. Studies that show that elderly workers are as good as younger ones, thus making the frequent preference of employers for young over old workers seem irrational—"ageist"—overlook the fact that the employer will have gotten rid of those elderly employees who could not perform up to snuff. The ones whom the employer retains will therefore not be representative of the average abilities of their age cohort. The broader point is that failure to correct for selection bias can cause observers to exaggerate the capabilities of the old, and thus see discrimination where there is none, by mistaking the exceptional members of an age cohort for its average members.

So they are not a victim class, our old people; and we saw that they were not victims even before the modern era of age-friendly social welfare legislation that began with the enactment of the Social Security Act in 1935. Practices that appear to discriminate against the elderly, such as mandatory retirement at fixed ages or late vesting of pensions—practices that the law has taken upon itself to change, though apparently with little effect—have strong efficiency justifications and little or no tincture of injustice. Today at any rate, in this country at any rate, the elderly are on average highly prosperous. Which is not to deny the existence of false, denigrating stereotypes about the elderly, such as that they are sexless, or that they are a terror on the roads. I have been at pains throughout this book to dispel such stereotypes. Yet the more myths I puncture, the more I may seem to lend credence to the claim that the elderly are indeed victims if not of discriminatory practices then at least of discriminatory attitudes, much like Jews or Asians in this country. But misunderstandings about groups to which one does not belong and with which one may not have much face-to-face contact are pervasive, and are an unmysterious product of the fact that the costs of information are positive and often high. It is difficult to see how or where current misunderstandings about old people are hurting them. Employers have a real stake in understanding the capabilities of employees and potential employees, and there is no convincing evidence that before the flood of protective legislation employers *systematically* undervalued older workers or exploited or otherwise mistreated them, for example with regard to the late vesting of pension rights; I do not of course deny the existence of isolated errors and abuses. A neglected point is that costs of information about people may lead to over- as well as under-estimation of qualities. It is possible, for genetic reasons discussed in chapter 9, that people exaggerate the wisdom and other good qualities conventionally associated with elderly people, and that they ascribe the characteristic good qualities of the elderly—in a reversal of statistical discrimination and through a neglect of selection bias—to elderly people who do not possess them.[73]

Yet it is probably true that old people in the United States of the present day do not command the respect and affection they once did. The fact that they are materially and in point of health better off on average than they ever were has its underside: they are less appealing objects of charity and solicitude. Stated otherwise and more positively, loss of popularity is the price that elderly Americans pay, probably willingly in most cases, for the dramatic increase in their prosperity and political influence. Demographic changes—a falling birth rate and a falling death rate, the latter due to the higher incomes of the old but above all to the advance of medical technology—have greatly increased both the relative and the absolute size of the elderly population. They are less scarce, so less valued. Most important perhaps are social changes, including mass education and the increasing rapidity of social, economic, and technological change—the increasing dynamism of American society—that have reduced the social value of the memories, wisdom, and experience of the elderly.

But we must bear steadily in mind that if not as valued as they once were, the elderly in America are a lot wealthier. When they were less wealthy, they had more respect; as they became wealthier, respect for them declined. The keel remains even. The elderly in America are not and never were a vulnerable, pariah class; but neither were or are they a class of parasites. They do vote more and thus have more political power than other age groups, yet it has proved feasible to curtail transfers to the elderly, provided that a long transition period is allowed. There is a natural though not necessarily an optimal equilibrium between the demands of the old for support and the willingness of the young to supply that demand. The hundreds of billions of dollars in transfers to the old that are carried on the books of the federal government are an imposing but misleading emblem of generational redistribution; they are not net figures. In part they replace

---

73. For evidence of favorable stereotypes of old people in our society, see Mary Lee Hummert et al., "Stereotypes of the Elderly Held by Young, Middle-Aged, and Elderly Adults," 49 *Journal of Gerontology* P240 (1994).

transfers that young people would make voluntarily to their old selves through greater savings for retirement. In part they compensate the old for the expense of educating their children's generation and commute into cash what would otherwise be a heavy burden borne by adult children of tending their aged parents. In part they reflect an irresolvable tension between the claims of the young self and the old self within each of us. In part they simply reflect a falling birth rate and a falling death rate, the combined effect of which has been to shift the center of gravity of the dependent population from the dependent young to the dependent old without actually increasing net dependency, though the maintenance of an even keel is due in part to the increased labor-force participation rate of women, which has both increased the number of job holders and, indirectly, reduced the number of children.

The huge expenditures on medical care for elderly people, and for medical research that is increasing the longevity of the elderly, are not wasted merely because the elderly have, at best, relatively few years of remaining life. They dread death as much as the young. The subsidization of those expenditures through the Medicare program can be criticized, however, as giving the elderly more medical care than they "really" want; a subsidy earmarked for a particular service, as distinct from a cash subsidy, which the recipient can use for anything he wants, is a recipe for overuse. As this example shows, even if the direst predictions about the effects of our old-age laws on the economy are unfounded, as I believe they are, all is not right with our policies toward the aged. Among many examples, the federal pension law (ERISA) appears to have been a response to largely nonexistent problems and its costs of administration, though modest in the overall scheme of things, appear to buy no benefits. The Age Discrimination in Employment Act is a particularly misbegotten venture in tilting at the windmills of ageism, and not only because most elderly people are retired and therefore are outside the scope of the Act. The Act may have few long-term effects of any sort. Its commands are readily avoidable, probably at modest long-run cost, by offers of early retirement (which are self-financing in the sense that, like other fringe benefits, they are ultimately paid for by the workers themselves in the form of lower wages); by avoidance, at what appears to be only a slight legal risk, of hiring elderly workers; and by matching (as through a carefully designed reduction in force) the termination of unwanted older workers with the termination of some young ones in whose firm-specific human capital the employer has not yet invested heavily. This means that the Act does little good for the aged (and some harm to them) and little harm to the rest of the population, except that its abolition of mandatory retirement probably has hurt the elite universities. Yet this particular wound is in part a self-inflicted one because the universities failed to take advantage of the opportunity that a generous transition period gave them to shift the costs back to the faculty. The beauty of early-retirement offers, from the employer's standpoint, as a method of circumventing the age discrimination law is that, in the long run, he can probably make the offerees pay for their own early-retirement benefits, when they are young.

I have said that to describe the elderly of our society either as victims or as exploiters is inaccurate. The multiple-selves perspective that I have so stressed invites consideration of a third possibility: that the prolongation of life has placed the unity of the self under increasing pressure. The years that are added at the end of life are years of diminished capability, and generally of impaired health and diminished utility as well. Young people know this, and may not want to make generous provision for those future years, just as they may not want to make generous provision for the contingency of becoming severely disabled, an analogous case. But when they become old, their point of view changes. They want to live (not all of them, but most). Not only or even mainly because of their political power, society will not abandon them, even if the costs of caring for them and attending to their medical needs are very high. The financing of those costs presents a policy dilemma, since the young will resist being forced to pay either in taxes or in compelled savings for the level of care that their old selves will demand or that the current old are demanding. Multiple-selves analysis does not point the way to a solution to this dilemma; on the contrary, it shows why a solution will be difficult to devise.

The diminished utility of an ever more protracted old age is a concern in its own right. All the hard knocks that utilitarianism has taken from philosophers have not much diminished the importance that the average person, and indeed the above-average and even the philosophical person, attaches to happiness. If old age were happier, the tension between the young self and the old self would be less, so it would be easier to finance old age. It is possible, though not certain, that we can make old age happier, by some reallocation of medical resources from the diseases of old women to the diseases of old men, and from lethal to nonlethal diseases of the elderly.

We are in danger of losing sight of the fact that the costs associated with adding years to the end of life—"low-value" and high-medical-cost years for most people—are a by-product of improvements in income, preventive medicine, and medical treatments that have shifted the boundary between middle age and old age, in effect extending the former. Old age begins later and lasts longer; the "begins later" means that low-value, high-medical-cost years are being transformed into high-value, low-medical-cost years at the same time that years of the first sort are being tacked on at the end of life. When all costs and benefits are reckoned in, there is no solid basis for concluding that the aging of the population has been or in the foreseeable future will be a source of *net* diminution in the overall welfare of the American people.

So I end on an optimistic note. But social prophecy has not been the principal goal of the book. I have mainly tried to formulate an economic theory of human aging and old age, building upon the seminal contributions of the human-capital economists but drawing on other fields both inside and outside of economics, ranging from imaginative literature and philosophy both ancient and modern to cognitive psychology, medicine, and evolutionary biology. This theory employs a broader conception of aging than the one that human-capital economists employ. It is a conception that emphasizes the process of aging, that provides a simple but realistic framework for understanding a variety of age-related attitudes and behaviors, and that enlarges the domain of rational choice to include the choices that we make for and in old age, including, for some of us, the choice of when to die. Such at least has been my ambition. I acknowledge the possibility that the vastness of the subject, the rapidity with which the relevant social, economic, and medical context is changing, and my own limitations of knowledge, technique, and time have caused my reach to exceed my grasp. If so, take this book not as arrival but as embarkation, or as a glimpse of the promise of multidisciplinary inquiry guided by economics, or even merely as an invitation to meet the challenges of modernity—of which our rapidly aging population is one—with better social science.

Index

Accidents and accident avoidance, 111n,
115–116, 127; accident rate of elderly drivers, 122–127; care versus
activity-level responses, 123–124,
126, 306; seatbelt use by elderly,
307. *See also* Driving, Tort law
Addiction, 116. *See also* Habit
Adjudication. *See* Judges
Adoption, adult, 209
Age discrimination, 7, 319–357; "animus," 320–322; statistical, 322–
328, 359–360. *See also* Age Discrimination in Employment Act,
Social status of elderly
Age Discrimination in Employment Act,
319–357, 361; abolition of mandatory retirement by, 319, 349–357;
age versus salary discrimination,
336–337; aggregate economic effects of, 347–349; and Americans
with Disabilities Act, 338–339;
asymmetric stakes of parties, 337–
338; awards of attorneys' fees under, 331–332, 338; damages in
cases under, 329–335; effects of,
328–357; differential effects of on
large versus small firms, 348–349;
discrimination by public versus pri-

vate employers, 334–335, 351; hiring cases, 329–333; incidence of
costs of compliance with, 346–347;
percentage of elderly plaintiffs, 328;
politics of, 346–347; redistributive
effects of, 346–347, 350; reduction
in force (RIF) cases, 331, 336, 341–
342; "smoking-gun" evidence,
335–336; who sues, by age and occupation, 345–346
Age grading, 7, 62n; as method of sorting workers to jobs, 208; in modern
society, 219, 322–324
Age-cohort effects, 136n, 151
Age-earnings profile, 52–55
Ageism, 20, 204, 320, 351, 359. *See also*
Age discrimination, Social status of
elderly
Agency costs, 351. *See also* Efficiency
wage
Aging, of animals, 26; defined, 18; evolutionary theories of, 25–30, 74–
75, 202–203; male versus female,
274; normal, 8, 17–24; of organizations, 227–229. *See also* Psychology of aging
Agricultural societies, status of elderly
in, 210–218

365